Rethinking the Green State

This innovative book is one of the first to conduct a systematic, comprehensive analysis of the ideals and practices of the evolving green state. It draws on elements of political theory, feminist theory, post-structuralism, governance and institutional theory to conceptualize the green state and advances thinking on how to understand its emergence in the context of climate and sustainability transitions. Focusing on the state as an actor in environmental, climate and sustainability politics, the book explores different principles guiding the emergence of the green state and examines the performance of states and institutional responses to the sustainable and climate transitions in the European and Nordic context in particular. The book's unique focus on the Nordic countries underlines the importance of learning from the Nordics, which are perceived to be at the forefront of climate and sustainability governance as well as historically strong welfare states.

With chapter contributions from leading international scholars in political science, sociology, economics, energy and environmental systems and climate policy studies, this book will be of great value to postgraduate students and researchers working on sustainability transitions, environmental politics and governance, and those with an area studies focus on the Nordic countries.

Karin Bäckstrand is Professor in Environmental Social Science at the Department of Political Science at Stockholm University, Sweden.

Annica Kronsell is Professor at the Department of Political Science at Lund University, Sweden.

Routledge Studies in Sustainability

Critiquing Sustainability, Changing Philosophy
Jenneth Parker

Transdisciplinary Sustainability Studies
A heuristic approach
Katri Huutoniemi and Petri Tapio

Challenging Consumption
Pathways to a more sustainable future
Edited by Anna R. Davies, Frances Fahy and Henrike Rau

Democratic Sustainability in a New Era of Localism
John Stanton

Social Practices, Interventions and Sustainability
Beyond behaviour change
Edited by Yolande Strengers and Cecily Maller

The Politics of Sustainability
Philosophical perspectives
Edited by Dieter Birnbacher and May Thorseth

Promoting Sustainable Living
Sustainability as an object of desire
Justyna Karakiewicz, with contributions from Audrey Yue and Angela Paladino

Rethinking the Green State
Environmental governance towards climate and sustainability transitions
Edited by Karin Bäckstrand and Annica Kronsell

Rethinking the Green State

Environmental governance towards
climate and sustainability transitions

Edited by Karin Bäckstrand
and Annica Kronsell

Routledge
Taylor & Francis Group

LONDON AND NEW YORK   from Routledge

First published 2015
by Routledge

2 Park Square, Milton Park, Abingdon, Oxon OX14 4RN
711 Third Avenue, New York, NY 10017, USA

Routledge is an imprint of the Taylor & Francis Group, an informa business

First issued in paperback 2017

British Library Cataloguing-in-Publication Data
A catalogue record for this book is available from the British Library

Library of Congress Cataloging-in-Publication Data
Rethinking the green state : environmental governance towards climate and
sustainability transitions / edited by Karin Bäckstrand and Annica Kronsell.
    pages cm
  1. Green movement. 2. Environmental policy. 3. Sustainability –
Government policy. I. Backstrand, Karin. II. Kronsell, Annica.
JA75.8.R48 2015
320.58–dc23   2014047325

ISBN: 978-1-138-79251-7 (hbk)
ISBN: 978-1-138-74371-7 (pbk)

Typeset in Goudy
by HWA Text and Data Management, London

To our families

'*Rethinking the Green State* provides a fresh stocktaking of theoretical and empirical research on the green state while also introducing some new ideas, such as transition theory. This is a very engaging and welcome intervention that will revitalise the debate about the role of the state in the quest for a sustainable world.'

– *Professor Robyn Eckersley, University of Melbourne, Australia*

'Bäckstrand and Kronsell are to be commended for an excellent volume that explores the state's role in environmental governance. The book pays particular attention to the emerging global challenge of climate change, offers interesting typologies of state responses to environmental issues, and suggests a more developed theorization of the Green state.'

– *James Meadowcroft, Professor and Canada Research Chair,*
School of Public Policy, Carleton University, Canada

Contents

Figures

Tables

Contributors

Rickard Andersson is a PhD candidate in Political Science at Lund University, Sweden. His research is focused on green political thought, political philosophy and conceptual analysis.

Karin Bäckstrand is Professor in Environmental Social Science at the Department of Political Science at Stockholm University. Her research and teaching revolves around global environmental politics, the role of science in environmental policy, the politics of climate change in the UN and EU and the democratic legitimacy of global governance.

Elizabeth Bomberg is Senior Lecturer and Deputy Head of Politics at the University of Edinburgh. Her area of expertise is comparative environmental politics and policy, with a substantive focus on movements, climate change, energy and sustainable development, and a geographic emphasis on the Europe and the US.

Matthew Cashmore is Associate Professor at the Department of Development and Planning, Aalborg University Copenhagen, Denmark. He is an environmental social scientist who works principally with qualitative research methods in studying environmental governance. Matthew focuses on the use of environmental policy instruments and critically explores issues that cluster around the topics of knowledges, participation, power, values and justice.

Martin Fritz is a researcher at the EUROLAB, Data Archive for the Social Sciences at GESIS – Leibniz Institute for the Social Sciences in Cologne, Germany. His research interests include the environmental social sciences and the sociology of work as well as the analysis of social structures and quantitative empirical research methods. He is also a lecturer at the University of Bonn where he teaches courses on statistics and social theory.

Roger Hildingsson is a PhD candidate in Political Science at Lund University. His research concentrates on environmental politics, sustainability and climate governance, the environmental state and energy policy. In his PhD thesis *Governing Decarbonisation: The State and the New Politics of Climate Change* he studies how the state can engage in governing low-carbon transitions towards decarbonization.

Erik Hysing is Associate Professor in Political Science at Örebro University and Dalarna University, Sweden. His academic work has mainly focused on policy change, governance, and public administration within the field of sustainable development and environmental politics. His most recent work, conducted at the University of Gothenburg, Sweden, focused on how environmental and democratic aspects were handled in the process of introducing a congestion tax in Gothenburg.

Jamil Khan is Associate Professor. He teaches and conducts research on energy and climate politics at the Department of Environmental and Energy Systems Studies at Lund University, Sweden. His research interests cover urban climate governance, low carbon transitions, deliberative democracy and the intersection between welfare and green politics.

Åsa Knaggård is Senior Lecturer at the Department of Political Science at Lund University. She studies the interrelation between science and politics in multiple contexts and is presently involved in a project on scientific outreach. She teaches Swedish and Comparative Politics as well as Environmental Politics.

Max Koch has completed both his PhD and *Habilitation* in Sociology at the Freie Universität Berlin and is currently a Professor at the Department of Social Work and Social Welfare, Lund University. His research focuses on political economy and ecology, social theory and the analysis of social structures, labor markets and welfare regulation, particularly in comparative perspective.

Annica Kronsell is Professor at the Department of Political Science at Lund University, Sweden. Annica teaches and conducts research in International Relations and Gender, Feminist theory and Environmental and Climate Politics. She has extensive experience in interdisciplinary research collaboration regarding climate, sustainability and environmental issues.

Björn-Ola Linnér is Professor in Environmental Change at the Department Thematic Studies and the Centre for Climate Science and Policy Research, Linköping University, Sweden. His research focuses on international cooperation on climate change and linkages to food and energy security as well as sustainable development goals.

Eva Lövbrand is Associate Professor at the Department of Thematic Studies at Linköping University, Sweden. Her work revolves around the role of ideas, knowledge and expertise in environmental politics and governance. Eva's work has been extensively published in journals such as Global Environmental Politics, Science, Technology and Human Values, and Critical Policy Studies.

Håkan Pihl is Associate Professor and teaches organization, strategy and environmental economics at the School of Economics and Management,

Lund University, Sweden. His research interest is in international business and environmental policy, especially related to new institutional economics and adjacent theoretical traditions.

Marina Povitkina is a PhD candidate in Political Science at the University of Gothenburg. In her dissertation she compares performance of democratic and autocratic regimes in provision of public goods and environmental protection. Other research interests include quality of government, natural resource management, governance of marine resources and fisheries, political and social organization of small island states.

Jaap G. Rozema is a PhD candidate at the School of Environmental Sciences, University of East Anglia in Norwich, United Kingdom. He focuses on the mutual influence of institutional design and political culture on civic engagement with environmental policy in the context of political and scientific authority.

Helena Olofsdotter Stensöta is Associate Professor in Political Science at the University of Gothenburg. She specializes in gender, ethics, public policy and administration. She has explored the conditions and impacts of an empathetic state, and discussed how it relates to gender equality and how the ideas of care can inform public administration.

Tuula Teräväinen-Litardo is Doctor of Social Sciences at the University of Helsinki, Finland. Her research interests focus on political promises of clean technologies and societal expectations and implications of innovation-driven policies. Currently Teräväinen-Litardo studies the governance of green growth and sustainability particularly in Northern Europe and the global South.

Paul Tobin is a Post-Doctoral Researcher in the Environment Department at the University of York, UK. His PhD explained climate policy variation in developed states, focusing particularly on Austria, Finland, Germany and Sweden. His current research post examines the impact of austerity on European environmental policy.

Acknowledgements

The idea for this book was initiated when we were asked to convene a working group on the theme of The Green State, at the biannual Nordic Environmental Science Conference (NESS) hosted in June 2013 by the University of Copenhagen, Denmark. Draft versions of most of the chapters were presented and discussed during the two-day intense working group sessions where many of the topics covered in the book were raised in lively and inspiring discussions. The NESS conference proved to be an excellent venue for gathering researchers around a common theme and provide space for the kind of intellectual exchanges to become the foundation for a book project such as this one. The workshop deliberation convinced us that there was a need to revisit the scholarly debate around the prospects for the green state. In the fall of 2013, more concrete ideas of a book structure, theme and chapters took form in a fruitful and intense conversation.

We want to express our gratitude to all the authors of this book, who have deepened our understanding of ideas and practices of the green state and for their tremendous effort and patience in revising their chapter drafts. The work with this book would not have been possible without the support of generous funding from the Lund University Center of Excellent for Integration of Social and Natural Dimensions of Sustainability, a Linnaeus program sponsored by the Swedish Research Council Formas 2008–2018. Editorial assistance is a central component in editing a book. We are indebted to our research assistant Fanny Johansson who had made our lives easier through her effective and hard work, as well as cheerful spirit and wonderful help in pulling together the manuscript. We are also very grateful to Bethany Wright at Routledge/ Earthscan for recognizing the importance of the theme for environment and sustainability scholarship and for the speedy, professional and patient response. We want to thank several anonymous reviewers who challenged us to push the boundaries of the book to achieve theoretical and empirical synthesis and to make a distinct contribution to the green state scholarship. We are particularly grateful for continued intellectual deliberations in the interdisciplinary community of climate and environmental scholars at Lund University and in the Environmental Politics Research Group at the Department of Political Science. We are also thankful for the support, joyful interventions and help from colleagues and friends. Finally, this book would not have been made without the tremendous support from our families. We take full responsibility for any errors and omissions remaining in the book.

Karin Bäckstrand and Annica Kronsell
Lund, Sweden, November 2014

1 The green state revisited

Karin Bäckstrand and Annica Kronsell

Introduction

How can democratic and advanced industrialized states respond to multiple problems relating to current environmental, climate and sustainability crises? Skeptics say that the state lacks the capacity to handle problems of the complexity and magnitude that humankind is witnessing, with extreme weather, rising temperatures, floods and droughts (IPCC 2014), the continuous over-use of natural resources like water, land and forests and the depletion of biodiversity (UNEP 2012). Political ecologists question that the state, through its institutions and policies, can mobilize resources and people to take on the challenge of such a daunting task, particularly as the state is deeply entrenched in an economic system and production processes that have caused the problem in the first place. The centrality of the economic imperative of industrialized states in the global north has arguably led to an unsustainable economic system (Barry 2012) that has created affluence through globalization, exploitation of resources and wage differences (Harvey 2010). The economic imperative is problematic, as Robyn Eckersley wrote in 2004, and remains tenacious for the green state.

A review of the literature reveals little faith in the capacity of the state to deal with climate problems; instead, hope is often found elsewhere. Peter Newell and Matthew Paterson (2010) put their faith in the possible transformations of the economy, others to businesses and finance that will rejuvenate itself to become green (cf. Lovins and Cohen 2011). The expanding scholarship on non-state actors and transnational governance arrangements argue that these surpass both states and international organizations (Bulkeley *et al.* 2014; Hoffman 2011; Stripple and Bulkeley 2013). New forms of environmental governance arrangements and non-state actors with "agency beyond the state" take on important governance functions, and compensate for implementation and legitimacy deficits as the states fail (Biermann and Pattberg 2012; Bäckstrand *et al.* 2010). Other focus on levels or sites of governance beyond the sovereign state where transformation to climate protection and sustainability is enhanced: a reformed United Nations in terms of a World Environment Organization (Biermann 2014), or a strong EU polity and leadership (Biedenkopf and Dupont 2013; Gupta and Grubb 2000; Wurzel and Connelly 2011). Finally, other scholars highlight the importance of cities and municipalities to advance climate transitions in urban areas (Bulkeley *et al.* 2010). Despite its many merits, these various literatures sidestep the state, neglect its potential, and lack conceptualization of the role of the state polity in dealing with environmental challenges.

The lack of attention to the role of the state permeates the environmental governance scholarship, which largely focused on non-state actors (Andonova *et al.* 2009). Nevertheless, this literature often implicitly assumes a functioning state or alternatively, a state entrenched in capitalism. It seldom argues explicitly what the role of the state is, or is expected to be, to mobilize environmental governance arrangements towards climate and sustainability objectives. More optimistic accounts point to the genesis of an environmental or green state and refer to the mounting empirical evidence that environmental policy, since the 1960s, has become a core component and regulatory domain of state activity (Meadowcroft 2005). The state has gradually taken on larger responsibilities such as limiting pollution of water and air, adopting goals of overarching sustainable development and, more recently, steered the society through transformation of the fossil fuel-based energy system and economy (Meadowcroft 2012). There is a renewed focus on the state not least in the area of climate change in the light of the current deadlock in multilateral climate negotiations on the road to Paris 2015, and the collapse of carbon markets. Neither international negotiations nor market governance have delivered the aggregative climate policy mechanism needed to keep within the 2 degree target. It appears as if it is only the state that has the kind of power and authority needed, to orchestrate collective responses to current environmental problems. Thus, the ambition of this book is in line with what Barry and Eckersley (2005: x) argue as a need to "reinstate the state as a facilitator for progressive environmental change rather than environmental destruction."

Aim, research questions and methodology

The aim of this book is to take stock of the state as an actor in environmental, climate and sustainability politics, approached from different theoretical, empirical and methodological vantage points. It represents an intervention to renew the focus on the role of the state in climate and sustainability governance by revisiting the literature on the green state and bring new empirical insights of the role of the state in propelling governance toward sustainability and climate transitions. The book revisits the green literature that emerged some ten years ago (Barry and Eckersley 2005; Christoff 2005; Eckersley 2004; Meadowcroft 2005) to enrich the contemporary conceptual and empirical debates of what is meant by a green state. We combine two scholarly literatures – state theory and transition theory – that are central building blocks that are arguably essential for understanding the contemporary greening of the state. They serve as a foundation for understanding the green state for this book and to bring the state back into environmental politics (Duit 2014). The core research questions of the book are:

- How has the green state been theorized from different perspectives such as political theory, governance and institutional theory?
- Which states perform well and merit the label green?
- Are certain types of states, such as welfare states, better equipped to make the transition to a low-carbon society?
- What are some institutional responses among the green state to the transition to climate objectives?
- How can current institutions and governance forms be reformed toward societal goals of low-carbon and sustainability transitions?

We revisit the green state scholarship and further refine green state theories in the light of empirical studies of environmental, sustainability and climate governance in Europe, the Nordic countries and the US. The book combines theoretical conceptualization of the green state with systematic empirical analysis of the implications of environmental and climate governance, linking measurable effects on environmental, climate and welfare issues to state practices. The contributors advance multiple understandings of the state from critical to constructivist understanding across fields of comparative politics, environmental policy, international relations, political theory and feminist theory. Our focus on the state implies a focus on the polity. Polity can be conceived as the collective of state institutions, administrations and principles for decision-making. We do this by revisiting the scholarship on the green state and by examining empirically through various case studies how the polity is implicated in climate and sustainability governance.

Eckersley's *The Green State* (2004) was pioneering in advancing thinking on what the green state may look like. Although many have followed up her work, the field remains under-theorized and lacks systematic empirical evidence particularly in the area of climate governance. There is ample room for theoretical development and empirical analysis on the prospect for the state to emerge as an important vehicle for the transition toward a decarbonized and sustainable future. During the last decade scholarly work on environmental governance has advanced by exploring institutions and different modes of governance, comparing policies, including the diffusion of new policy instruments in Europe and beyond (Wurzel, Zito and Jordan 2013). Less attention has been devoted to investigate how state action or the state polity matters in this respect. Lately, we note a renewed interest in the field with Andreas Duit's most recent work on the state and the environment as an example. We agree with Duit that core questions in the field lend themselves to comparative analysis, such as in asking why certain states perform better than others in terms of regulatory output (Duit 2014: 8), however, we propose there is a need for the role of the state polity to be more deeply theorized. Moreover, Andrew Jordan and colleagues have in recent work brought attention to the role of the state in polycentric climate governance through the analytical prism of policy innovation (Jordan and Huitema 2014).

The neglect of the role of state action in collective environmental problem solving in the green politics scholarship stems from a deep-seated skepticism toward the institutions of the state and market economy, which are viewed as the very cause of the environmental crisis. The eco-anarchist strain in green political theory, represented by the work of Bookchin (1974, 1990), argues for a radical decentralization to meet the ecological challenge (de Geus 1996). This is also a reaction to the eco-authoritarian thought by Ophuls (1973) who proposes that a centralist state with absolute power – an ecological leviathan – is necessary to collectively respond the environmental threats and ecological scarcities. The overlapping literatures on the green state, and the role of state and state polity in environmental, climate and sustainability transitions, have emerged in the impasse between the eco-authoritarian centralization and eco-anarchist accounts of decentralization and radical participation.

Before elaborating on the theoretical building blocks of the book, a note on the research methodologies and the case selection is warranted. While guided by our common research questions, this book rests on pluralism of theoretical perspectives and methodologies. The various chapters illustrate that the green state can be fruitfully studied by employing a range of different methodological approaches (large-*n* studies, case studies, discourse and normative analysis). The purpose is neither to integrate nor to evaluate the usefulness of the various methods, but to, first, clarify how different methodologies are instrumental in answering the research questions and, second, to demonstrate how a pluralism of methodologies enables broader understandings of the role of the state.

Some contributions start in political theory and normative approaches, while others are empirically oriented toward hypothesis testing and large-*n* comparisons or single-case studies. Different ontologies and epistemologies are associated with these various methodologies. Quantitative and comparative studies are illustrated by Koch and Fritz's Chapter 5, examining whether there is a synergy between the green state and welfare state by using data on European states' welfare and environmental performance indicators. Constructivist approaches, such as Chapter 11 by Cashmore and Rozema, use governmentality as an analytical perspective to examine the institutional response to climate change mitigation, and to what extent these approximate green statehood. Knaggård and Pihl (Chapter 12) show how the green state polity can be studied through a thought experiment by comparing and contrasting climate and monetary policies.

The states that are investigated empirically in this study are predominantly advanced industrialized democracies and welfare states. This remains a limitation in the green state scholarship in general and this book also reflect this shortcoming as it only includes developing states in a sample of island states comparing environmental policy outputs (see Chapter 6 of this volume by Povitkina). Eckersley (2004) has argued that the Scandinavian states most closely resemble the ideal of a green state and echoes research that has championed Nordic countries as environmental pioneers and leaders (Andersen and Liefferink 1997). This book critically re-examines to what extent these findings are still valid a decade after the literature emerged. The Nordic welfare countries are not typical, but their experiences with environmental governance are highly relevant and provide an important test bed and laboratory for examining processes of green statehood. We also argue that the green state scholarship has not sufficiently examined the implication of the climate change threat for the prospect of green transformation of the state. We revisit the experience of the Nordic countries through the climate challenge lens, however, we compare with the North American experience in two chapters on prospects for green statehood on the federal level and in the state of California. All chapters in this volume revolve around the role of state institutions in climate and sustainability governance. We argue that this focus on *polity* is an important contribution as much governance scholarship has focused on *policy* and, more specifically, on environmental policy. All chapters revisit the green state literature in specific dimensions and relate their empirical and theoretical findings to the prospects of transformation toward the green state. They provide an opportunity for deepening the theoretical knowledge of key aspects of the green state.

The remainder of this chapter contextualizes the green state in relationship to a general and broader critique of the state as a vehicle for ecological modernization, discusses it in relation to state theories and through the different typologies found in the scholarship on the green state, and arrives at a broad conceptualization that is employed in the chapters. After a review of the green state literature, one building block in our theorization of the green state, the chapter surveys the literature on transition theory, which is a relatively novel field that expanded the last years as an alternative approach to study how the state can be transformed to accommodate climate and sustainability objectives. The emphasis on change and transformation is arguably lacking in the theories of the green state. Accordingly, transition theory, which provides the other building block, can contribute with an understanding of the conditions for transition toward green statehood. Finally, the four different sections of the book are introduced with a presentation of the individual chapter contributions. The conclusion presented in the final chapter of the book pulls together the theoretical, empirical and normative contributions in the book by revisiting the research questions and systematically relating them to the key findings of the chapters.

Theorizing the green state

In this section we theorize the green state by building on literatures found in green political theory including state theories as well as typologies of the green state – environmental policy, comparative politics, international relations and transition theory which specifically addresses the conditions for change and transformation towards green statehood. By revisiting and synthesizing the green state scholarship with various academic literatures, we will provide the theoretical building blocks that guide the different contributions in the book as they more deeply explore and develop specific dimensions of the green statehood.

Theories and typologies of the green state

In this section we conceptualize and outline several typologies and definitions of the green state. We have not settled for a single overarching definition of the green state guiding all the chapters in the book, but allow the authors to rely on a useful definition of the green state in the context of their particular case study. A note on terminology, while we use the concept of green state for the purpose of this book, the "environmental state" (Meadowcroft 2012), "ecostate" (Duit 2011, 2012) and the "ecological state" (Meadowcroft 2005; Lundquist 2001) are frequently used as interchangeable terms. Our definition is more general than Christoff's (2005) terminology as he refers to the green state as an ideal type while the notion environmental state frequently captures real-world existing states.

There is a divide between definitions and categories in the field of comparative environmental politics based on empirical assessments of the environmental performance of states on one hand, and the ideal types advanced in normative theories of the green state in political theory and critical political ecology on the other hand. In the words of Hildingsson and Khan (Chapter 9 of this volume):

> the green state is a generic concept that could mean many things. Depending on one's approach, the green state could be seen as either a normative or an analytical construct, as a counterfactual ideal of ecological responsiveness to strive for – or an evolving institutionalization of ecological responsibilities that can be empirically assessed.

Thus, the green state literature emanates from two traditions.

One tradition emerges from normative and green political theory which stipulate the normative features of a green state, including typologies, ranging from a green state committed to biocentric and eco-citizenship values to a neoliberal environmental state that is market-oriented and relies on weak ecological modernization (Christoff 2005: 42–3; Hysing, Chapter 2, this volume). The green state is, in this vein, a normative or even utopian ideal, founded upon ecological sustainability and biocentric values, which should be the overarching social, economic and political goals of the state. The other tradition is empirical-oriented and found, for example, in the field of comparative environmental politics on single, small-*n* or large-*n* studies analyzing how states have responded to ecological pressures in terms of regulation and institutional output (Dryzek *et al.* 2003; Duit 2014). In this context, the green state is an empirical phenomenon and in comparative studies often relative to how other states have performed. It is sometimes measured in terms of certain institutions of the state (e.g. environmental ministry) or policies (e.g. CO_2 taxes) or as environmental performance (e.g. ecological footprint;[1] see Koch and Fritz in Chapter 5 and Povitkina in Chapter 6 of this volume).

This book aligns itself with a definition of the green state that allows for an empirical analysis of existing states in Europe, the Nordic countries and the

United States, recognizing the problem of using too minimal a definition. For example, Elizabeth Bomberg (in Chapter 7 of this volume) defines the green state as "one capable of developing policies and practices designed to limit harmful emissions and achieve a sustainable future for its citizens. Such a state would assume responsibility for environmental harm domestically but also seek to develop ecologically responsible statehood globally." Duit (2012) follows the empirical tradition as he defines the ecostate based on what states have actually accomplished. The problem with using a definition that is all-encompassing is that most states in the industrialized world (and many developing states) that have developed environmental legislation and administrations, would qualify as green states. The growth of environmental regulation and institutions has not been matched by strong environmental performance, reduction of ecological footprints and reaching sustainability or climate objectives.

The normative contributions of the green scholarship thus become highly useful to critically examine green states. One such ideal construct based in critical political ecology and normative theory is found in Eckersley (2004: 2), who says:

> By 'green state' I simply do not mean a liberal democratic state that is managed by green party governments with a set of programmes … Rather I mean a democratic state whose regulatory ideals and democratic procedures are informed by *ecological* democracy rather than *liberal* democracy. Such a state may be understood as a postliberal state insofar it emerges from an immanent (ecological) critique.

In this vein, only typically environmentally pioneering states like Sweden can be considered as green states or at least close to the ideal (see Paul Tobin in Chapter 8 of this volume).

In a similar fashion, Peter Christoff outlines green states as ideal types in continuum from strong to weak green states: "*Green states*, were they to exist, would be characterized by the predominance of types of state activity aimed at strong ecological modernization" (Christoff 2005: 41). Further, he argues that green states also demonstrate high levels of state capacity and intervention, eco-citizenship, strong commitment to biocentric values, human welfare and ecological protection. *Environmental welfare states*, where Sweden and the Netherlands serve as prime examples, have, according to him, a weaker institutionalization of ecological values, moderate values of eco-citizenship and environmental capacity for state intervention. *Environmental neoliberal states*, such as the US and Australia, are defined by strong market orientation, weak ecological modernization and low budgetary commitment to social and environmental welfare protection. Christoff also outlines an ideal type of *eco-fascist state* along the lines of Ophuls (1973) with authoritarian features but with a high commitment to biocentric values. However, this state based on neo-Malthusian values has no real-world approximation.

Typologies in empirical analysis of green states are often influenced by green political theory as are the typologies employed in this book. This may pose a challenge since green political theorists have often embraced anti-statist positions whereby the state is considered a problem rather than a solution (Bookchin 1990). On the one hand this is because green political theory tends to emphasize that the potential for change lies in social movements and in deliberations in civil society and the green public sphere, not with the state (Dryzek *et al.* 2003). On the other hand, this is due to states' historic trajectories as institutions co-evolving with the quest for material consumption, ever-expanding growth and economic development, embedded in a competitive and conflict-prone international state system (Hurrell 2006: 170; Paterson 2007).

Dryzek *et al.*'s (2003) and Hunold and Dryzek's (2005) work provides insights in what they consider a crucial aspect for the green state, namely the relationship between the state and civil society. They do this in a set of studies that exemplify how assessments of green states can combine political theory with comparative history. Dryzek *et al.* (2003) conclude that a polity that is inclusive but dictates participation of civil society in formalized ways is less conducive to environmental policy making than a model that allows for pluralistic environmental deliberations in the public sphere and outside formalized and organized channels. The latter is also a more vital space. In their analysis, it is Germany that is the most likely candidate for a state that can enact a green transformation in terms of strong ecological modernization. The relationship between the green public sphere and the state is an important dimension of the green state and seen as crucial in the case of the US (Bomberg, Chapter 7, this volume) and relevant for the green growth debate in the Finnish context (Teräväinen-Litardo, Chapter 10, this volume).

The green state and the economic imperative

The relationship between economic development and the state is central in the debates on green statehood. Many argue that a major obstacle to the development of the green state is that the core imperative of the state is economic growth and capital accumulation (Barry and Eckersley 2005: 260–63). Marxist perspectives are skeptical to the prospect for the state to reconcile economic growth (and the production and consumption patterns that seem essential to economic growth) with protection of the climate and the environment (Koch 2006). In Marxist-inspired state theory, social and environmental policies are considered responses to long-term societal trends that are closely related to the development of the capitalist economy. Marxist influenced state theory predicts conflict between winners and losers of states' increasing regulation and intervention in area of climate and environment. Indeed, green state theories have been accused of taking this problem of capitalism too lightly (Paterson 2007: 549). Debates on *decoupling* economic growth from material and ecological impacts and calls for zero growth by the anti-growth segments of the environmental movements reflect the conflict between growth and sustainability.

Contrary to this, theories of ecological modernization (EM) are optimistic about the possibility of the market to solve environmental problems through state intervention (Hajer 1995; Mol and Spaargaren 2000; Young 2000) by arguing that economic growth can go hand in hand with environmental protection, less pollution and lower emission levels. Ecological modernization is grounded in a view that the economy evolves over time, to become increasingly efficient and less resource intense, eventually leading to decoupling, i.e. that the economy can grow without environmental damage. Proponents of ecological modernization conceive of technological innovation as a solution to environmental degradation, rather than its cause. Through innovation, environmental concerns can be integrated in production and result in energy efficiency. Transition theories, which are discussed further below, fit this logic of ecological modernization, as they view innovation as the key in the transformation to a green state. Ecological modernization depends on the neoliberal, capitalist market. This is a mutual dependency because the current economic system is dependent on the efficiency garnered by ecological modernization for it to become sustainable (Weale 1993: 207).

Green state scholars are critical to the values of efficiency and profit that steer capitalist markets, and are more agnostic about the role of technical innovation for the green state while still recognizing the need for market mechanisms. This is evident in the distinction that Peter Christoff (2005) makes (see also Spaargaren and Mol 2010) between different types of ecological modernization – from weak to strong – in terms of the relationship or balance between the role the market is allowed to play and the existence and importance of biocentric values in the state (see Chapter 8 of this volume). The win-win discourse of ecological modernization re-aligning environmental protection goals with market economy can be seen as a response to restructure and reform the state toward larger ecological values (Hajer 1995). Concepts such as green economy and green growth represent more recent attempts to reconcile economic growth and environmental protection (UNEP 2011).

Greening welfare states

Many environmental scholars have argued that the welfare state has the greatest potential to accommodate environmental, sustainability and climate goals. Meadowcroft (2005: 10) draws parallels between the genesis of the welfare state and the environmental state, which both have in common the extension of state authority in new social and political domains as a response to market failure and lack of voluntary action. The welfare state has historically been set up to deal with the negative externalities of the market and the social and human costs arising from it and, hence, the welfare state has the institutions, processes and policies in place that make it possible to secure the provision of environmental public goods (Duit 2011). It is likely, and in line with welfare state theories (Esping-Andersen 1990) that green welfare states also come in varieties, due to different regime types, which in Duit's (2011) interpretation includes the whole set of institutions and policies of the state. Green welfare states can be differentiated along two dimensions: how long and how extensively the state has provided institutions that deal with environmental public goods and, second, the amount of resources allocated to rectify the problems of externalizing environmental costs. Gough and Meadowcroft (2011) argue that thinking through different welfare regime types is highly relevant in analyzing how the state is dealing with climate change. Climate change poses both direct and indirect risks, as it accentuates the need for adaptation with indirect threats to welfare due to adaptation costs, which may cause distributional conflicts. Carbon taxes, for example, affect poor communities disproportionally.

In 'A green fist in a velvet glove' Lennart Lundqvist (2001) also sees this potential in the welfare state. His normative criteria for what he calls the ecological state is a state with a fairly strong degree of authority in decision making at multiple levels – the green fist – employing resource management and comprehensive ecological planning, but that this necessarily has to be coupled with a strong democratic state – the velvet glove – where there is broad deliberation on scientific expertise and knowledge on ecological issues in various democratic settings from the local to the global. For Lundqvist economic growth and ecological concerns are not mutually exclusive or conflicting; in contrast, greening is successful when ecological evaluations have become as important as economic ones (*ibid.*: 469). While Gough and Meadowcroft (2011) consider the welfare state the best equipped actor to take on these challenges, they suggest that in order to decarbonize the welfare state, there is a need to foreground wellbeing toward a decommodified production where work hours and commodity consumption are decreased. Thus, welfare states and green states have similarities but also differ on important accounts (Meadowcroft 2005, 2012).

For example, the welfare state is seen as a complement to a growing economy while in the green state continuous economic growth is not possible as consumption and production patterns must be kept within ecological limits or "planetary boundaries" (Meadowcroft 2012). Private property rights tend to trump collective solutions (Eckersley 2004: 85–104). Also the constituencies who can be mobilized for the welfare state and the green state differ: the working class and trade unions for the welfare state and the green parties and environmental movements for the green state. Furthermore, much decision making takes place through strategic bargaining which tends to be reactive or preventive at best (*ibid.*) and the policy process is guided by administrative rationality which does not deal with ecological risk (Kronsell and Bäckstrand 2010). Environmental interests and long-term interest are only weakly represented. Moreover, in contrast with the welfare state that primarily is nationally oriented, the green state acts collectively with other states in a global and multilateral setting as environmental problems have transboundary and international dimensions (Meadowcroft 2005: 12).

The discussion on the greening of the welfare state centers on the process and the possibility of transformation. According to Meadowcroft it is empirically verified, as he argues that the environmental state, while far from perfect, has taken on and expanded its regulatory functions not only by responding to and preventing environmental problems, but also by promoting values of sustainable development and engaging in the transformation of dominant societal and economic practices (*ibid.*: 76). The contribution to this volume by Hildingsson and Khan (Chapter 9) also highlights transformation; their conception of a decarbonized state is "a state engaged in promoting transformative social change." Eckersley (2005: 80) takes a normative perspective and argues that the transformation toward the green state should take place at various levels: in policy instruments, in policy goals and through changes in the policy paradigm or hierarchy of goals as well as the overall understanding of the role of the state in climate, sustainability and environmental issues. While she says that transformation should take place through learning, green change and reflexivity, in line with other green state scholars, she has less to say about the processes of transformation. To this end, we turn to sustainable transition theory.

Sustainable transition theory

Transition theory is a multidisciplinary scholarly field that studies the conditions for innovation and system change in socio-technical systems (for an overview see Markard *et al.* 2012). This literature is about the conditions for change and systemic transformations over time and is concerned with governance for transformation toward sustainability and climate objectives. It proposes that transformation happens in relation to multiple levels between niches and regimes, and in landscapes where the other two are embedded (Grin *et al.* 2011).

The landscape provides the context for transformation (Kemp *et al.* 2007a; Smith *et al.* 2005; Smith and Kern 2009) as transitions always occur in an environment of a broader context of norms, which are institutionalized over time (De Haan 2010: 27). The landscape consists of dominant discourses that order society and culture, give significance and legitimation to, as well as frame issues and discourses of, regime actors (Geels 2010, 2011a; Smith *et al.* 2010). The landscape is the slowest to change of the three levels. To relate landscape to state theory, we are aided by Smith and Kern (2009), who suggest that structural factors affect the polity, as path-dependencies of institutions set the conditions for transitions.

A regime is "the (network of) actors that exercise constitutive power" (Avelino and Rotmans 2009: 560) – that is, the power to establish or enact a social order tied to a certain distribution of resources. A regime consists of resources and institutions, and the power of regimes is exercised through practices that distribute privilege and resources, but also in more subtle ways by adhering to and applying the normative power of the social order of the landscape. The relevant regimes are found by asking which actors benefit from production, innovation and market solutions. They are empowered by the current regime and also capture the agenda (Meadowcroft 2009; Smith and Kern 2009; Smith and Stirling 2010; Voss and Bornemann 2011). Transition researchers have their focus on socio-technical regimes related to innovation, for example in transport and energy systems. 'Old' technologies, which are related investments and institutions, are incumbent regimes representing an obstacle for transformation. Transition theory is interested in how this regime can be circumvented and changed. The role of politics and of institutions is more recent in transition theory (Meadowcroft 2011; Stirling 2014). Geels (2014) argues that incumbent regimes consist of policy makers and business actors who are interdependent and form alliances which make the regimes resistant to change since regime actors can mobilize various power strategies to resist change.

Change does occur and transformation happens when the incumbent regime is weakened by the influence of niches. Niche is the third concept used in transition theory and they exist outside and independent of the regimes. In niches new ideas that encourage transition can flourish (Schot and Geels 2008). According to transition management studies, new niches can be encouraged by creating participatory arenas where a diverse set of relevant actors can meet, deliberate and generate innovation – new niches – leading to transitions (Kemp *et al.* 2007a, 2007b; Loorbach and Rotmans 2006; Loorbach 2010). Transition theorists argue that, to bring about change, the participants should represent different interests and agendas but must be willing to debate and discuss as well as have a desire to transform the current regime and to challenge vested interests.

The political science scholarship on sustainability and environmental governance has emphasized the need for inclusive policy processes that allow a broad range of societal actors to be engaged in processes of communication, democratization and deliberation (Baber and Bartlett 2005; Dryzek 2005). The broad inclusion of various stakeholders, citizens together with experts and government representatives, can be a way to safeguard legitimacy for the kind of transitions required to reach climate objectives and to secure compliance and implementation of decisions taken (Bäckstrand *et al.* 2010; Dobson and Bell 2006; Eckersley 2004). Research by transitions scholars, like Foxon *et al.* (2009), demonstrates that broad participation is essential to the success of a transition strategy. At the same time, evaluations of different 'experiments' aiming to stimulate niche development speak of the tendency that open deliberations in these arenas often turn into more pragmatic, short-term solutions in the end (Smith and Stirling 2008).

An important dilemma in transition studies is how to have open broadly participative deliberative processes without running the risk of the agenda being captured by the most powerful actors representing the incumbent regime. That is why transition management scholars in particular stress the importance of having a selective and exclusive approach to participation, and only support and include actors who are 'niche players.' Niche actors have a strong desire for change and transformation of the current system, and also have the expertise, knowledge, and motivation to work for this change and there is an emphasis on actors who are forward thinking: "Frontrunners are key to transition processes… in particular real go-getters with an overly amount of energy and enthusiasm" and they should be given organizational, mental, as well as juridical and financial space to act (Loorbach and Rotmans 2010: 243). The justification for this is based on research where it has been noted that powerful regime actors easily capture the agenda, and actors who may represent new thinking and innovation easily become hostages to the process (Smith and Kern 2009; Smith and Sterling 2008, 2010).

The most important lessons from the multi-level perspective provided by transition studies for green state theory, are that transformation takes place in the dynamic relation between niches, regimes and landscapes, and that change emerges from niches. Consequently, it is essential to advance, support and nourish niches, so that they can challenge and transform existing regimes. With the development of transition theory in a multidisciplinary direction the concept niche has been used generously, to include for example social and local movements (Seyfang and Haxeltine 2012; Seyfang and Longhurst 2013) and cities (Geels 2011b; Hodson and Marvin 2010). The implications for green state theory is that we need to think seriously about the relationship between the polity and various niche actors and networks that can enhance the transformation toward the green state. For example, what are the optimal relations between the polity and potential niches? How can the development of niches take place in the green state without niches becoming hostages to the process?

The regime concept is helpful as we can think about the polity as a diversified entity, perhaps with different regimes (i.e. alliances between policy makers and industrial or business actors in different sectors, such as energy, transport, housing, conservation, etc.). In line with this, Frank Geels (2014) demonstrates how regimes as part of the polity resist change through varied use of power. Accordingly, the important questions for green state theory are: which incumbent regimes are resisting change in the green state? What alliances of actors are involved and what are their means of power for resisting change?

It should be noted that transition theory emerged from technical innovation studies and consequently has some limitations. First, the field of transition studies analyze governance from a rather simplistic view and a managerial perspective, although studies are becoming increasingly sophisticated (cf. Frantzeskaki *et al.* 2012). Second, the role of governments and state institutions has remained largely unexplored in transition theory until very recently (Meadowcroft 2011) and the empirical focus has been overwhelmingly on the energy sector. Third, for the most part transition studies work with market mechanisms for innovation and a belief that decoupling is possible (i.e. that economic growth is possible in the green state). Concepts such as green growth and a green economy suggest that with increased efficiency and new technology there can be increased growth, welfare, environmental protection and CO_2 reductions without increasing ecological footprints or exhausting resources.

Outline of the book

Part I: Theorizing the green state

The three chapters in the first section develop the conceptualization of the green state in this introduction by theorizing the green state from governance theory, state theory and political theory. Different conceptualizations of green state are related to the governance of sustainable development, the notion of sovereignty and conception of non-state actors. Erik Hysing (Chapter 1) does this in relation to challenges posed in the scholarship on governance of sustainable development (GSD). His aim is to establish a more nuanced understanding of the potentials of the green state by reinstating the state in the scholarly field of governance for sustainable development. He highlights the key challenges the state faces in governance for sustainable development with regard to policy, polity and political dimensions, and elucidates the functions and responsibilities the green state brings to address these challenges. His starting point is that the state is uniquely placed in the transition towards a more sustainable society, however this cannot be limited to a traditional state that functions with top-down, pre-planned and hierarchical steering. The challenges of sustainable development relate to the complex character and the uncertainty of the problems to be dealt with. To handle this in an adequate way, the green state should be a reflexive, listening and learning organization that can use the state policy toolbox wisely by combining hard steering and voluntary instruments. An obstacle for the green polity is the integration of cross-sectoral sustainability objectives in a context where sectorization is the common principle for decision-making. Furthermore, there is a need to coordinate between levels, from local to the international. Networks are suggested as possible forms to manage this, and can work more effectively under the authority of the state polity because it is more likely to assure accountability and transparency. Governance for sustainable development needs the state because it requires not only flexibility and adaptability but, more so, political institutions that are stable to assure democracy and the existence of a green public sphere. The green state possesses a unique capacity and legitimacy to foster and lead the transition toward a more sustainable society. Rather than being neglected or lost within the scholarly field of GSD, the state should be brought forward as an important actor in governance for sustainable development.

Eva Lövbrand and Björn-Ola Linnér (Chapter 2) are interested in what the role of the state is in climate politics and governance. Their chapter analyzes how the scholarship on non-state climate politics and governance represents the state. Inspired by a process-oriented ontology of the state, they interpret how properties of statehood are imagined, construed and 'performed' in a review based on 40 journal articles identified through an open search in the database SCOPUS. Three types of climate statehood – the responsive pluralist state, the decentered partnering state, and the limited post-colonial state – are identified across the journal articles in terms of how they construe the role of the state versus non-state actors in climate governance. Based on general state theory, they discuss how these state types resonate with the typology of green forms of statehood. Since non-state actors are involved in many governance functions in the climate domain this might imply that the locus for authority and governance has changed, which they explore by studying how the role of the state is constructed in the boundary between state and non-state actors in the climate governance literature. The focus of the analysis is on the process of setting boundaries, which is where, they argue, implicit assumptions about statehood are also reproduced.

They locate one dimension for understanding the capacity for the state to take on the challenges that climate governance demands in the scholarly literature, and argue that such scholarly interventions create regimes of truth that define what is possible for the state, in the context of climate politics.

Is the state capable of systematically prioritizing the achievement of sustainability, or in other words, is sovereignty compatible with sustainability and ecological protection? This question is the point of departure in Rickard Andersson's Chapter 4, which critically examines the prospect for greening sovereignty from key writings in political theory by Kant. He argues that the theory of the green state is conditioned by a concept of sovereignty and needs to be rethought since it is incapable of systematically prioritizing sustainability. The chapter proposes that Kant's method of philosophizing can serve as an historical precedent for how the green state and sovereignty can be rethought in order to transcend its present shortcomings. Thus, the chapter is intended to advance current understandings of the green state from political theory.

Part II: Performance of the green state in a comparative perspective

The chapters in the second section examine the performance of green state through quantitative methods among European and island states, and through a single case study of the US. Max Koch and Martin Fritz (Chapter 5) take a starting point in a research field that studies welfare states in relation to environmental performance and green transformation. Koch and Fritz start in the argument posed in that literature, namely that the specific characteristics of welfare states also make them better equipped to deal with distributive, social and environmental effects. The welfare state can craft environmental and climate responsibility onto its existing institutions and decision-making logic, thereby creating a synergy effect between social, economic and environmental ambitions. This synergy hypothesis is tested in Koch and Fritz's empirical analysis of 28 European countries at two points in time, in 2005 and 2010. In order to explore the synergy between welfare states and environmental performance the authors use two indicators for welfare: the Gini index for income equality and social stratification and the state's social expenditure as a percentage of gross domestic product. The indicators for ecological performance are electricity generated from renewables, carbon dioxide emissions per capita and the ecological footprint measurement. Koch and Fritz differentiate between welfare, social democratic, conservative and liberal regimes. The hypothesis is that the synergy between climate and environmental performance would be highest in social democratic states and lowest in liberal states. The analysis shows that welfare states tend to foster high levels of regulation in climate and environmental policies but this did not lead to better environmental performance when measured through the three indicators. States with high levels of welfare and environmental regulation also have large ecological footprints as they use natural resources extensively. The hypothesis that social democratic welfare states perform the best holds only for two countries: Sweden and Austria. The most sustainable countries of those studied were those with lower socio-economic development but also with the lowest level of environmental policy.

Marina Povitkina's 'The "green" potential of small island states' (Chapter 6) also focuses on how factors such as state characteristics and geography affect the prospect for the green state. Povitkina begins by a systematic survey of the geographical conditions of small states and what implications these conditions have for their political institutions and for environmental vulnerability. The characteristics of small island states, such as their geographical features – smallness, remoteness – facilitate responsive democracies, good institutions and collaborative environmental and natural resource management which, according to the green state scholarship, constitute factors that are also conducive to greening. At the same time, small island states are also more vulnerable to ecological risk. The theoretical arguments are used to find the relevant mechanisms and motivation behind small islands' potential of developing into green states.

Elizabeth Bomberg (Chapter 7) investigates the prospects for the United States to emerge as a green state, and asks what such a transformation would require. While US is currently perceived as laggard when it comes to environmental and climate policy, it was pioneering in environmental policy in the 1970s (Lundquist 1980). The framework used in the chapter identifies the institutional and ideological barriers that have stymied progress towards green statehood and then explores how such barriers might be overcome and allow a transformation of the state. It highlights how institutional features of the polity, such as veto points, become entrenched and create path dependencies and sunk costs that make transformation difficult. Neoliberalism is an ideological barrier making it difficult for the US to move toward a green statehood. The US resembles the ideal of an "environmental neoliberal state" by promoting economic growth and technological innovation. As individualism means freedom from the state, a strongly anti-state ideology permeates the public discourse in the US. For example, climate denialism reflects semtiments turning the call for climate action into something negative and un-patriotic, undesirable for US central state action. This doubt framing of the climate issue completely dominates the US public discourse and media narratives together with the powerful frame of the anti-statism. The transformation to the green state, Bomberg argues, is only possible if it also involves a transformation of this public discourse and a green public sphere

Part III: Transforming the state toward climate objectives: Nordic experiences

The set of chapters in the third section addresses how the state can be transformed to reach climate objectives in the Nordic context. Expressed differently, this section provides an analysis of how modern governments are tackling the green and climate transition in a range of fields such as economics, social innovation, welfare, technology, regulation, consumption and behavior. This section critically scrutinizes arguments by green state scholars that the Nordic countries are forerunners in environmental policy making. The focus is on the ambitions of policy makers and on institutional changes and political activities of Sweden and Finland to transform toward climate objectives. It focuses on the ideas and practices, and less on the material conditions of climate and sustainability transitions. As noted in the study by Koch and Fritz (Chapter 5), Sweden is the only country among the Nordics for which the synergy hypothesis was confirmed: Sweden scored high on all dimensions – welfare, ecological performance and climate friendliness – while the other Nordic countries did not perform as well.

In the 'Blue and yellow makes green?' (Chapter 8), Paul Tobin examines climate change policy in Sweden, which is acknowledged widely as a global pioneer in the field. He seeks to determine whether Sweden's climate change policies during the first term of the new Conservative/Liberal government 2006 to 2010 were ambitious enough to live up to ideals of a green state. Tobin relies on typologies by green state scholars arguing that a green state must exhibit *strong* ecological modernization, expressed in biocentric values and market-oriented policies. In order to become a green state, it is argued that a state must exhibit strong ecological modernization, marrying pro-capitalist and technologically-led policies with biocentric values. Sweden has been widely acknowledged as a global pioneer in the field of climate policy. It is argued that although Sweden was a climate policy pioneer, it is not a green state.

Hildingsson and Khan's 'Towards a decarbonized green state?' (Chapter 9) focuses particularly on how decarbonization can propel transformative change toward the green state. They define the decarbonized state as an emerging green state that through commitments to prevent climate change and governance strategies strives for considerable reductions of emissions through the decarbonization of societal structures. Key sectors in the carbon economy – electricity, transport and industry – are analyzed to assess the degree of carbonization. The authors argue that low carbon-emission goals have spurred not only emission reductions but also technical and policy innovation, exemplified with developments in the Swedish heating and electricity sectors. In studying how transitions toward a low-carbon economy and sustainable societal development can be achieved, the chapter combines innovation studies and policy studies with important insights on how sustainability transitions and transformative policy pathways can be instigated and governed.

Teräväinen-Litardo's contribution 'Negotiating green growth' (Chapter 10) provides a detailed empirical analysis of Finland's green growth debate and asks what kind of policy structures regarding state and society relations are important for the green state in dealing with sustainability and climate objectives. It also raises questions about the economic imperative of the state: how it is negotiated, transformed and articulated through different discourses. Finally, it points to the need to ask not only what kind of economic development is relevant for the green state but also what is the role of innovation in sustainability transitions and ultimately for the green state. She elaborates on how Finnish policy makers negotiate around the notion of green growth as a way to accomplish sustainability transitions. The state has an important role because it can define the kinds of economic measures and technological development that are essential for a carbon transition process. The policy structure is essential to this because it regulates and determines the relations between the state and societal actors. Finland works with a consensus and cooperation model. Following Dryzek *et al.* (2003) and reading Teräväinen-Litardo, Finland's active inclusive model of decision making would lead to a state that is less engaged with civil society and more with established interests, which is reflected in the discourses and policies on green growth.

Part IV: Transforming the polity toward climate and sustainability objectives

The final section of the book presents three chapters that are concerned with the green polity. They analyze the institutions and the policy processes of the green state and ask whether and how they can be transformed toward long-term climate and sustainability objectives.

Matthew Cashmore and Jaap G. Rozema (Chapter 11) apply the analytical perspective of governmentality, which they suggest is a highly useful way for enriching the understanding of the practices of the green state. They critically approach the green state in order to reveal the power dynamics in emerging practices on climate change in state institutions. Through a careful empirical analysis of the case of California policy makers' adaptation planning they convey a rich account of state conduct in struggling to deal with climate adaptation issues in processes toward greening of the state. Planning documents are viewed as guidance documents that purposefully try to shape actors' ways of being, knowing and acting. The issue of climate adaptation is framed as urgent, with a need to act because the imminent threat, in case of inaction, will amount to higher costs. The conduct of adaptation planning in California reveals recognition of the inevitability of change in response to climate change. The call for long-term perspectives and holistic thinking does not question the status quo or the prevailing economic, political or sociocultural patterns. The measures suggested in adaptation planning, are to be systematically achieved in a stepwise and technocratic manner. Climate change can be managed and contained within existing economic and societal practices.

In 'The green state and the design of self-binding' (Chapter 12), Åsa Knaggård and Håkan Pihl compare the Swedish climate and monetary policy to analyse what we can learn from the self-binding features in monetary policy. The green state literature identifies the state as a central actor for creating sustainable development, and argues for changes of policy as well as the polity. Constitutional design, as a form of self-binding instrument, represents a mean for achieving such changes. They ask if long-term environmental policies expressed in short-term targets and delegated to independent authorities with effective instruments is a way forward for the green polity. The conclusion is that the self-binding instruments found in monetary policy has important advantages and can, with modifications, provide valuable experiences for developing a green state.

Through the comparison between monetary and climate policy, the dilemma between effective policy-making and democracy is highlighted.

Annica Kronsell and Helena Stensöta's 'The green state and empathic rationality' (Chapter 13) starts in feminist theory to argue that empathic rationality is a useful normative foundation and a steering principle for governance in the green state. They argue that the challenges confronting a green state are similar to the problems recognized by feminist ethics of care theory. In the chapter the core notions in the ethics of care are outlined. Interdependence, contextuality and responsiveness are relevant for advancing the green state in thinking on the relationship between human and natural ecosystems, and between current future generations. Kronsell and Stensöta propose that empathic rationality can serve as an ethical foundation for the green state and exemplify how.

Note

1 Ecological footprint is a general indicator that assesses the overall environmental impact of countries, individuals (or other entities) by looking at resource use, consumption patterns and land use (Wackernagel and Rees 1998).

References

Andersen, M. and Liefferink, D. 1997 *European Environmental Policy: The Pioneers*. Manchester University Press, Manchester.

Andonova, L., Betsill, M. and Bulkeley, B. 2009 Transnational climate governance. *Global Environmental Politics* 9(2): 52–73.

Avelino, F. and Rotmans, J. 2009 Power in transition: an interdisciplinary framework to study power in relation to structural change. *European Journal of Social Theory* 12(4): 543–69.

Baber, W. and Bartlett, R. 2005 *Deliberative Environmental Politics*. MIT Press, Cambridge, MA.

Bäckstrand, K., Khan, J., Kronsell, A. and Lövbrand, E. (eds) 2010 *Environmental Politics and Deliberative Democracy: Examining the Promise of New Modes of Governance* 129–42. Edward Elgar, Cheltenham.

Barry, J. 2012 Climate change, the cancer stage of capitalism and the return of limits to growth. In Pelling, M., Manuel-Navarrete, D. and Redclift, M. (eds) *Climate Change and the Crisis of Capitalism* 129–42. Routledge, Abingdon.

Barry, J. and Eckersley, R. (eds) 2005 *The State and the Global Ecological Crisis*. MIT Press, Cambridge, MA.

Biedenkopf, K. and Dupont, C.A. 2013 Toolbox approach to the EU's external climate governance. In Boening, A., Kremer, J-F and van Loon, A. (eds) *Global Power Europe*, vol 1. Springer Verlag, Berlin.

Biermann, F. 2014 *Earth System Governance: World Politics in the Anthropocene*. MIT Press, Cambridge, MA.

Biermann, F. and Pattberg, P. (eds) 2012 *Global Environmental Governance Reconsidered*. MIT Press, Cambridge, MA.

Bookchin, M. 1974 *Post-scarcity Anarchism*. Wildwood House, London.

Bookchin, M. 1990 *Remaking Society: Pathways to a Green Future*. South End Press, Boston, MA.

Bulkeley, H., Vanesa Casán, B., Hodson, M. and Marvin, S. 2010 *Cities and Low Carbon Transitions*. Routledge, Abingdon.

Bulkeley, H., Andonova, L., Betsill, M., Compagnon, D., Hale, T., Hoffmann, M., Newell, P., Paterson, M., Roger, C. and Vandeveer, S. 2014 *Transnational Climate Change Governance*. Cambridge University Press, New York.

Christoff, P. 2005 Out of chaos, a shining star? Toward a typology of green states. In Barry, J. and Eckersley, R. (eds) *The State and the Global Ecological Crisis* 25–52. MIT Press, Cambridge, MA.

De Geus, M. 1996 The ecological restructuring of the state. In Doherty, B. and de Geus, M. (eds) *Democracy and Green Political Thought* 188–211. Routledge, London.

De Haan, J. 2010 *Towards Transition Theory*. PhD dissertation, Erasmus University, Rotterdam.

Dobson, A. and Bell, D. (eds) 2006 *Environmental Citizenship*. MIT Press, Cambridge, MA.

Dryzek, J. 2005 *The Politics of the Earth: Environmental Discourses*, 2nd edn. Oxford University Press, Oxford.

Dryzek, J., Downies, D., Hunold, C., Schlosberg, D. and Hernes, H. 2003 *Green States and Social Movements: Environmentalism in the United States, United Kingdom, Germany and Norway*. Oxford University Press, Oxford.

Duit, A. 2011 The ecological state: cross-national patterns of environmental governance regimes. Retrieved November 20, 2014 from www.southampton.ac.uk/C2G2/media/Stockholm-Soton/Duit%20(2011).pdf.

Duit, A. 2012 Adaptive capacity and the ecostate. In Boyd, E. and Folke, F. (eds) *Adapting Institutions, Governance, Complexity and Social-Ecological Resilience* 127–47. Cambridge University Press, Cambridge.

Duit, A. (ed) 2014 *The State and the Environment: A Comparative Study of Environmental Governance*. MIT Press, Cambridge, MA.

Eckersley, R. 2004 *The Green State: Rethinking Democracy and Sovereignty*. MIT Press, Cambridge, MA.

Esping-Andersen, G. 1990 *The Three Worlds of Welfare Capitalism*. Polity, Cambridge.

Foxon, T.J., Reed, M.S. and Stringer, L.C. 2009 Governing long-term social-ecological change: what can the adaptive management and transition management approaches learn from each other? *Environmental Policy and Governance* 19: 3–20.

Frantzeskaki, N., Loorback, D. and Meadowcroft, J. 2012 Governing societal transitions to sustainability. *International Journal of Sustainable Development* 15(1–2): 19–36.

Geels, F. 2010 Ontologies, socio-technical transitions (to sustainability), and the multi-level perspective. *Research Policy* 39: 495–510.

Geels, F. 2011a The multi-level perspective on sustainability transitions: responses to seven criticisms. *Environmental Innovation and Societal Transitions* 1: 24–40.

Geels, F. 2011b The role of cities in technological transitions: analytical clarifications and historical examples. In Bulkeley, H., Castán Broto, V., Hodson, M. and Marvin, S. (eds) *Cities and Low Carbon Transitions* 13–28. Routledge, Abingdon.

Geels, F. 2014 Regime resistance against low-carbon transitions: introducing politics and power into the multi-level perspective. *Theory, Culture and Society* 31(5): 21–40.

Gough, I. and Meadowcroft, J. 2011 Decarbonizing the welfare state. In Dryzek, J., Norgaard, R. and Schlosberg, D. (eds) *The Oxford Handbook on Climate Change and Society* 490–503. Oxford University Press, Oxford.

Grin, J., Rotmans, J. and Schot, J. 2011 *Transitions to Sustainable Development: New Directions in the Study of Long Term Transformative Change*. Routledge, Abingdon.

Gupta, J. and Grubb, M. (eds) 2000 *Climate Change and European Leadership. A Sustainable Role for Europe?* Kluwer Academic Publishers, Dordrecht.

Hajer, M. 1995 *The Politics of Environmental Discourse: Ecological Modernization and the Policy Process*. Oxford University Press, Oxford.

Harvey, D. 2010 *The Enigma of Capital: And the Crises of Capitalism*. Profile Books, London.

Hodson, M. and Marvin, S. 2010 Can cities shape socio-technical transitions and how would we know if they were? *Research Policy* 39(4): 477–85.

Hoffman, M. 2011 *Climate Governance at the Crossroads: Experimenting with a Global Response after Kyoto*. Oxford University Press, Oxford.

Hunold, C. and Dryzek, J. 2005 Green political strategy and the state: combined political theory and comparative history. In Barry, J. and Eckersley, R. (eds) *The State and the Global Ecological Crisis* 75–95. MIT Press, Cambridge, MA.

Hurrell, A. 2006 The state. In Dobson, A. and Eckersley, R. (eds) *Political Theory and the Ecological Challenge* 165–82. Cambridge University Press, Cambridge.

IPCC 2014 *Fifth Assessment Report*. Intergovernmental Panel on Climate Change, Geneva.

Jordan, A. and Huitema, D. 2014 Policy innovation in a changing climate: sources, patterns and effects. *Global Environmental Change* 29: 387–94.

Kemp, R., Rotmans, J. and Loorbach, D. 2007a Assessing the Dutch energy transition policy: how does it deal with dilemmas of managing transitions? *Journal of Environmental Policy & Planning* 9(3–4): 315–31.

Kemp, R., Loorbach, D. and Rotmans, J. 2007b Transition management as a model for managing processes of co-evolution towards sustainable development. *International Journal of Sustainable Development and World Ecology* 14(1): 78–91.

Loorbach, D. 2010 Transition management for sustainable development: a prescriptive, complexity-based governance framework. *Governance* 23(1): 161–83.

Loorbach, D. and Rotmans, J. 2006 Managing transitions for sustainable development. *Environment and Policy* 44: 187–206.

Loorbach, D. and Rotmans, J. 2010 The practice of transition management: examples and lessons from four distinct cases. *Futures* 42: 247–46.

Lovins, L.H. and Cohen, B. 2011 *Climate Capitalism: Capitalism in the Age of Climate Change*. Hill & Wang, New York.

Lundquist, L. 1980 *The Hare and the Tortoise: Clean Air Policies in the US and Sweden*. University of Michigan Press, New York.

Lundqvist, L. 2001 A green fist in a velvet glove: the ecological state and sustainable development. *Environmental Values* 10: 455–72.

Markard, J., Raven, R. and Truffer, B. 2012 Sustainability transitions: an emerging field of research and its prospects. *Research Policy* 41(6): 955–67.

Meadowcroft, J. 2005 From welfare state to ecostate. In Barry, J. and Eckersley, R. (eds) *The State and the Global Ecological Crisis* 3–23. MIT Press, Cambridge, MA.

Meadowcroft, J. 2009 What about the politics? Sustainable development, transition management, and long term energy transitions. *Policy Sciences* 42: 323–40.

Meadowcroft, J. 2011 Engaging with the *politics* of sustainability transitions. *Environmental Innovation and Societal Transitions* 1(1): 70–75.

Meadowcroft, J. 2012 Greening the state. In Steinberg, P. and VanDeveer, S. (eds) *Comparative Environmental Politics: Theory, Practice and Prospects* 63–87. MIT Press, Cambridge, MA.

Mol, A.P.J. and Spaargaren, G. (eds) 2000 *Ecological Modernisation Around the World: Perspectives and Critical Debates*. Frank Cass, London.

Newell, P. and Paterson, M. 2010 *Climate Capitalism: Global Warming and the Transformation of the Global Economy*. Cambridge University Press, Cambridge.

Ophuls, W. 1973 Leviathan or Oblivion? In Daly, H. (ed) *Toward a Steady State Economy*. Freeman, San Francisco, CA.

Paterson, M. 2007 Environmental politics: sustainability and the politics of transformation. *International Political Science Review* 28(5): 545–56.

Schot, J. and Geels, F. 2008 Strategic niche management and sustainable innovation journeys: theory, findings, research agenda, and policy. *Technology Analysis and Strategic Management* 20(5): 537–54.

Seyfang, G. and Haxeltine, A. 2012 Growing grassroots innovations: exploring the role of community-based initiatives in governing sustainable energy transitions. *Environment and Planning C: Government and Policy* 30(3): 381–400.

Seyfang, G. and Longhurst, N. 2013 Desperately seeking niches: grassroots innovations and niche development in the community currency field. *Global Environmental Change* 23(5): 881–91.

Smith, A. and Kern, F. 2009 The transitions storyline in Dutch environmental policy. *Environmental Politics* 18(1): 78–98.

Smith, A. and Stirling, A. 2008 *Social–Ecological Resilience and Sociotechnical Transitions: Critical Issues for Sustainability Governance*. Working paper. STEPS Centre, University of Sussex, Brighton.

Smith, A. and Stirling, A. 2010 The politics of social–ecological resilience and sustainable socio-technical transitions. *Ecology and Society* 15(1): art. 11.

Smith, A., Stirling, A. and Berkhout, F. 2005 The governance of sustainable socio-technical transitions. *Research Policy* 34: 1491–1510.

Smith, A., Voss, J.-P. and Grin, J. 2010 Innovation studies and sustainability transitions: the allure of the multi-level perspective and its challenges. *Research Policy* 39: 435–48.

Spaargaren, G. and Mol, A.P.J. 2010 Sociology, environment, and modernity: ecological modernization as a theory of social change. In Mol, A.P.J., Sonnenfeld, D.A. and Spaargaren, G. *The Ecological Modernisation Reader*. Routledge, Abingdon.

Stirling, A. 2014 Transforming power: social science and the politics of energy choices. *Energy Research and Social Science* 1: 83–95.

Stripple, J. and Bulkeley, H. 2013 *Governing the Climate: New Approaches to Rationality, Power and Politics*. Cambridge, Cambridge University Press.

Swyngedouw, E. 2010 Apocalypse forever? Post-political populism and the spectre of climate change. *Theory, Culture, Society* 27: 213–32.

Swyngedouw, E. 2011 Depoliticized environments: the end of nature, climate change and the post-political condition. *Royal Institute of Philosophy Supplement* 69: 253–74.

UNEP 2011 *Towards a Green Economy*. United Nations Environment Programme, Nairobi.

UNEP 2012 Taking the pulse of the planet connecting science with policy. UNEP Global Environmental Alert Service. Retrieved July 30, 2014 from http://na.unep.net/geas/archive/pdfs/GEAS_Jun_12_Carrying_Capacity.pdf.

Voss, J.-P. and Bornemann, B. 2011 The politics of reflexive governance: challenges for designing adaptive management and transition management. *Ecology and Society* 16(2): art. 9.

Wackernagel, M. and Rees, W. 1998 *Our Ecological Footprint*. New Society Publishers, Gabriola Island, BC.

Weale, A. 1992 *The Politics of Pollution*. Manchester University Press, Manchester.

Weale, A. 1993 Ecological modernization and the integration of European environmental policy. In Liefferink, J.D. Lowe P.D. and Mol, A.P.J. (eds) *European Integration and Environmental Policy*. Belhaven Press, London.

Wurzel, R. and Connelly, J. (eds) 2011 *The European Union as a Leader in International Climate Change Politics*. Routledge, Abingdon.

Wurzel, R., Zito, A. and Jordan, A. 2013 *Environmental Governance in Europe. A Comparative Analysis of New Environmental Policy Instruments*. Edward Elgar, Cheltenham.

Young, S. (ed) 2000 *The Emergence of Ecological Modernization. Integrating the Environment and the Economy?* Routledge, New York.

Part I
Theorizing the green state

2 Lost in transition?

The green state in governance for sustainable development

Erik Hysing

Introduction

After twenty years with sustainable development being "the dominant global discourse of ecological concern" (Dryzek 2013: 147) there is deep-felt disappointment with its contribution to tackling key environmental problems (Voss and Kemp 2006). The problems of continued unsustainability are increasingly being depicted as not only a market failure, but also a governance failure. Sustainable development does not simply happen; society needs to be governed into sustainability (Adger and Jordan 2009) by "reforming practices of socio-political governance to encourage shifts toward a more environmentally sustainable and equitable pattern of development" (Meadowcroft 2009: 323).

Although environmental issues – and climate change in particular – have become legitimate and salient concerns of states (Meadowcroft 2012), criticism of limited state capacity, legitimacy, and authority has been both vigorous and diverse, ranging from neoliberal portrayals of an ineffective state that needs to be rolled back in favor of markets, to eco-Marxist perceptions of the state as a defender of a capitalist society that is functionally dependent on economic growth (Eckersley 2004; Meadowcroft 2012). Many of today's environmental problems have been attributed to failures of state governance, which has provoked a massive interest in governance reforms and commitments to new modes of governance (Griffin 2010). As a consequence, it has almost become a truism within policy and academic debate on governance for sustainable development (GSD) that we need to look beyond the state to find effective and legitimate governance arrangements for collective action capable of handling the complex, dynamic, and diverse challenge of sustainable development (Hajer and Wagenaar 2003; Kemp *et al.* 2005; van Zeijl-Rozema *et al.* 2008).

The importance of state action in environmental governance has, however, received increasing recognition and spurred calls for a reinvention and retheorization of the state as an important object of study (Barry and Eckersley 2005; Compagnon *et al.* 2012; Duit 2008; Eckersley 2004; Evans 2012; Hysing 2010; Lundqvist 2001; Meadowcroft 2009; Mol 2007). As highlighted within the scholarly field of GSD, we cannot rely on a 'state fix' for environmental problems. The task of social transformation is simply too great to be handled through steering from the top (Meadowcroft 2007). Neither should the challenges facing the state in GSD be used as an excuse for resigning ourselves to the idea of the powerless state (Barry and Eckersley 2005). Society's transition towards a more sustainable future cannot be achieved in a top-down, pre-planned, hierarchical way; it needs a broader palette of approaches in which the state takes on partially different roles and responsibilities. This, in turn, necessitates reforming – not replacing – the state, both in terms of its ways of interacting with society (governance) and its political orientation (sustainable development) while ensuring that key values (e.g. democracy) and capacities (regulative and redistributive powers) that are upheld by the state remain in place.

As a contribution to the theoretical endeavor of establishing a more nuanced understanding of the potentials of the green state, the aim of this chapter is to reinstate the state in the scholarly field of GSD by highlighting the key challenges the state faces in GSD with regard to policy, polity, and political dimensions, and to elucidate and discuss the functions and responsibilities the green state brings to efforts to address these challenges.

Building on Eckersley (2004) and Meadowcroft (2005), I argue that the green state can be seen as harboring the key political authority and steering capacity to take action against environmental problems in terms of having the requisite financial, administrative, and political resources. This capacity is based on unique features of states, such as their monopoly on the legitimate use of force and the legal right of sovereignty, but also on an extended state authority to regulate and supply a broader range of welfare services. Environmental actions taken by the state are also uniquely legitimated through representative democratic procedures and institutions. Furthermore, the green state adopts a normative orientation towards the creation of a sustainable society (Eckersley 2004). Although such a (re)orientation faces severe constraints imposed by the anarchic international system, global capitalism, and democratic deficits (*ibid.*: chs. 2–4), these challenges do not completely erode the potential for states to place ecological concerns at the core of their activities (Meadowcroft 2005) and thereby take the first step towards transforming themselves into "ecological stewards" (Eckersley 2004: 3). This does not mean that environmental values are established as the overriding political goal. The state discussed here "remains enmeshed with the dominant political and economic institutions we know today" (Meadowcroft 2005: 6), which involves the necessity to balance multiple, competing interests and goals. This is also characteristic of the state itself, which should not be conceived as "one unitary, rational actor but as a complex multitude of public actors … operating within a parliamentary framework, that is, rudimentary guidance and restrictions come from elected politicians" (Hysing 2009: 315; see also Chapter 3, this volume).

In order to adequately capture key challenges for the state in GSD, a multi-dimensional approach was used that gives consideration to political processes (politics), institutional structures (polity), and policy content (policy) (Duit 2008: 11; Lange *et al.* 2013: 403). Following Beck's definition (1994: 22), the policy dimension refers to the substance of political programs and policies, including both the ends – the definitions of problems and solutions and the formulation of objectives and goals – and the means – the choice and design of policy instruments and strategies – of public policy. The polity dimension refers to "the institutional constitution of the political community with which society organizes itself" (*ibid.*: 22) and encompasses the forums and arenas in which politics and policymaking take place (Lange *et al.* 2013). Finally, the political dimension is defined as "the process of political conflict over power-sharing and power positions" (Beck 1994: 22). It includes the relative power of political actors and the forms of interest intermediation in the process of translating societal preferences and interests into policy choices and collective action (Lange *et al.* 2013). These three dimensions will be used to structure the following discussion of the key challenges of GSD and the potential for the green state to respond to them.

Governance for sustainable development – policy

The challenges that GSD poses in relation to the policy dimension range from agenda-setting to implementation. Many of these issues derive from the complexity, contested nature, and genuine uncertainty of sustainable development as a policy goal or vision. What does sustainable development mean? On what grounds should we make policy decisions? And how should we go about implementing them? In the following, the contested nature of sustainable development as a concept, the uncertainty that surrounds GSD, and the development of new environmental policy instruments are discussed.

A contested concept

At the very heart of GSD is the idea of *sustainable development*, famously defined as "development that meets the needs of the present without compromising the ability of future generations to meet their own needs" (WCED 1987: 43). This is a highly ambitious and extremely ambiguous goal of societal change, involving multiple and frequently conflicting values and goals (Voss *et al.* 2007). Sustainable development is an essentially contested concept, beset by fundamental disagreement over its meaning and importance as well as the scale of necessary reforms (Jordan 2008; Hopwood *et al.* 2005). It is argued that the concept is so fuzzy and all-inclusive that anyone can endorse it without committing to anything (Swyngedouw 2007). However, since the 1992 Rio conference a majority of states have subscribed to the concept of sustainable development (at least rhetorically) and many advanced liberal democracies have adopted it as a core policy goal squarely at the center of environmental policy (the US being an exception; see Chapter 7, this volume) (Lafferty and Meadowcroft 2000). Some argue that the all-inclusiveness of the concept will promote debate and deliberation rather than conflict and confrontation, to the benefit of advancing environmental concerns (Hajer 1995), while others argue that it contributes to green-washing business as usual; being "at best an empty phrase and at worst a Trojan horse" (Voss and Kemp 2006: 3).

The concept of sustainable development gives only vague guidance to policymakers on how to actually handle conflicting and contradictory values, or which values should be given priority under what conditions (Voss and Kemp 2006; Voss *et al.* 2007). Regardless of whether it is considered a normative point of reference or an operational strategy, the concept risks losing its action-guiding capacity (Christen and Schmidt 2012). This has led many observers to conclude that goals and visions need to be decided in a more reflexive, deliberative, interactive, and inclusive manner that involves diverse groups of societal actors (Voss *et al.* 2007; Loorbach 2010). As long as GSD is perceived as the search for synergies between various values, this approach seems well founded. However, GSD is also a normative and political undertaking that unavoidably involves trade-offs between societal interests and values (Voss *et al.* 2007) and necessitates the making of tough prioritizations – decisions that are necessary for handling environmental problems but that will not satisfy everyone – as well as providing for closure and authoritative decisions (Meadowcroft 2007). Increased participation and deliberation has many benefits, but this is something that the representative democratic state is better equipped to deal with. Elected politicians are authorized (generally within a constitutional framework that protects basic civil liberties and human rights) to balance different values and interests as well as to act on normative visions for the common good; and they are held accountable for their decisions. Authoritative governing is not exclusive to states; non-state actors can gain authority through expertise, moral suasion, or market mechanisms, but they often lack the key state properties of accountability and transparency (Bulkeley 2012). State power comes with vital (if not perfect) safeguards to ensure that it is exercised according to rule of law, is subject to public scrutiny, is conducted under democratic control, and is properly accountable to citizens (Eckersley 2004). These are vital characteristics when translating sustainable development into political programs and policies.

Uncertainty

Complexity and uncertainty are other key challenges facing the state in GSD. Knowledge about problems and solutions is often limited and value-laden, and is regularly contested. Scientific knowledge is recognized as a necessary but not sufficient ingredient in designing policy options for sustainable development (Lundqvist 2004). One reason for this is that GSD is supposed to handle policy problems in the intersection of society, technology, and nature, a combination that disciplinary science is ill-equipped to handle (Voss *et al.* 2007). To further complicate matters, the public no longer simply accepts the truths of scientific expertise (Bäckstrand 2003).

Acknowledging the limits of science, many argue that the stakes are too high, the knowledge too uncertain and contested, and the urgency too great to let a few 'experts' govern society. Instead of closed interaction between experts and decision-makers, more public and broader involvement and deliberation (Bäckstrand 2003; Eckersley 2004; Lidskog and Sundqvist 2011) as well as new forms of reflexive and adaptive governance (e.g. experimentation and learning-by-doing; see Voss and Kemp 2006; Loorbach 2010; Evans 2012) are needed to cope with uncertainty and complexity. The administrative state is founded on instrumental rationality and accords substantial status to what is viewed as objective and neutral scientific expertise (Dryzek 2013: ch. 4; Paterson *et al.* 2006). In this vein the state handles environmental problems by seeking to eliminate uncertainty and ambiguity, as well as to optimize policy measures by isolating discrete parts of a complex reality. However, because ambiguity is an essential feature of sustainable development, it is impossible to achieve complete scientific certainty about the problems or optimal solutions. For this reason, the state is portrayed as inherently inflexible and un-reflexive (Eckersley 2004; Dryzek 2013; Voss and Kemp 2006). Although this characterization is relevant in relation to some state institutions and practices (Dryzek 2013), it is important to recognize that the administrative state relies on and harbors key competences for environmental governance. State agencies have expertise, practical know-how, and experience regarding a broad range of environmental problems as well as a diversity of governance measures, including procedures for widening the range of voices and increasing reflexivity and learning (e.g. the precautionary principle, public inquiries, impact assessments, and community right-to-know legislation; see Eckersley 2004). Environmental officials, who often have devoted a substantial portion of their professional lives to mastering their specific field, hold much of society's practical environmental knowledge and know-how (Evans 2012; Hysing 2013). Despite claims about the reduced trust in and credibility of science, such expertise remains a powerful source of epistemic authority in directing environmental policymaking. In light of the importance of finding a balance in policymaking between legitimacy and participation on the one hand and professional competence on the other, this state-based expertise is vital for GSD.

New environmental policy instruments

Some would argue that the novelty of GSD concerns not what is done, but how it is done. The effectiveness and legitimacy of command-and-control instruments that largely entrust expert-led state agencies with formulating objectives, assessing effects, and enforcing implementation (Voss *et al.* 2007), has been questioned when faced with ambiguous goals, contestation of scientific expertise, and a more neoliberal ideological agenda. Although "traditional policy tools including regulation, planning, and tax-based instruments remain an essential part of the arsenal of governance for sustainable development" (Meadowcroft 2009: 335), a new set of policy tools has been given preference, either to supplement or supplant command-and-control instruments. On a general level this change is often portrayed as a shift from hard to soft instruments, the latter characterized as non-binding, voluntary, flexible in implementation, lacking sanctions, and focusing on developing procedures rather than requirements (Treib *et al.* 2007). A range of new environmental policy instruments (NEPI) have been promoted, including eco-labeling; flexible market mechanisms and tradable permits; and voluntary agreements, codes of conduct, and best practices. These instruments are often "proposed, designed and implemented by non-state actors, sometimes working alongside state actors, but sometimes also independently" (Jordan *et al.* 2005: 481). However, these new modes of governance are dependent on the overarching regulatory framework provided by the state, without which few (if any) of these novel tools would function (Jordan *et al.* 2013). State actions have also been necessary for the establishment of these instruments. An example of this is the way forest certification – often portrayed as a prime example of NEPI – was implemented in Sweden. Initial deregulations of the national forest policy combined with increased environmental ambitions set the scene for the introduction of certification schemes, a process during which public endorsement as well as threats of re-regulation from the government; expertise and mediation by state agencies; and actual participation by the state-owned forest company all proved vital for its success (Hysing 2009).

The reconfiguration of the state toolbox toward including more cooperative, market-based, and voluntary mechanisms is closely associated with the advent of ecological modernization (EM), which aims to bring about a gradual shift towards sustainability by utilizing market forces to push for environmental reforms (not fargoing structural changes) through technological innovation and green consumerism (see Chapter 1, this volume). EM generally perceives the state as in need of restructuring from being a regulator to a facilitator (Mol and Jänicke 2009), a prime example being how state actors facilitated the Swedish forest certifications described above. The main reason that the state was drawn into environmental governance was to address market failures. By using regulation, subsidies, and information, state actors can pressure business to take environmental considerations into account and internalize hitherto externalized costs (Duit 2008; Meadowcroft 2005). The historical experiences indicate that a greener and more responsible business sector can be expected to emerge in the context of strong state regulations and rules of the game (Compagnon *et al.* 2012; Lundqvist 2001). In a context of intensified pressure from global capitalism, the environmental regulatory role of the state has become more rather than less important, in order to balance corporate power and mitigate the effects of market externalities (Eckersley 2004).

Governance for sustainable development – polity

Scholars of GSD portray a political landscape in which the state is not the unchallenged epicenter of governance, and the power to tackle environmental problems is more dispersed and fragmented. This entails the integration of environmental policy in other policy sectors (e.g. agriculture, energy, and transport); governance across multiple levels, as a way to better address global and local environmental problems; and network governance, involving actors from state, market, and civil society in environmental governance.

Environmental policy integration

A cornerstone in GSD is environmental policy integration (EPI), which recognizes the cross-sectoral character of many environmental problems. EPI involves integrating environmental issues and objectives into non-environmental policy sectors rather than handling them within a distinct environmental policy domain. EPI has been advocated from the normative standpoint that all sectors in society have the responsibility to do their part to protect the environment, but also as an efficient *modus operandi* contributing to more rational and efficient policies (Nilsson and Persson 2003; Lundqvist 2004). Environmental governance has traditionally been characterized by a state institutionalization based on functional differentiation and specialization. Although this approach has been argued to be successful in handling discrete environmental problems, it has been criticized for negative side-effects such as compartmentalization and departmental worldviews leading to broader perspectives being neglected, important issues falling between jurisdictions and responsibilities, and negative spill-over between sectors (Eckersley 2004; Kemp *et al.* 2005). A holistic approach to governing is often perceived as central for successful GSD and it has been strongly argued that responsibility for the environment, rather than being allocated to a specialized state administration, should be shared across sectors, whereby public policies and practices may be reappraised or at least reformulated in terms of sustainable development (Baker and Eckerberg 2008).

Weale (2009) cautions that it might be better to strengthen national environmental administrations than to issue ambitious but unenforceable policies of environmental integration. Empirical assessments indicate that commitments to EPI aiming to give principled priority to environmental protection have in many cases been more symbolic than effective when it comes to changing prioritizations on the ground (Jordan and Lenschow 2010). Even when successfully integrated into sector policymaking, environmental concerns are in constant danger of being overwhelmed by more immediate (and dire) needs and interests (Meadowcroft 2012). The green state that is able to establish a strong national environmental authority will ultimately be necessary in order to provide the political, legal and budgetary framework for effective EPI. Given sufficient authority, power, and resources, such central authority can contribute vital steering capacity at the center, provide clear lines of overall responsibility and co-ordination, mediate inter-departmental conflicts, concentrate resources and functions, and provide comprehensive cross-sectoral planning, in addition to being an environmental champion vis-à-vis other state interests, and monitoring and enforcing EPI in relation to other sectors (Lafferty and Hovden 2003).

Multi-level governance

Perhaps the most fundamental aspect of the shifting polity is the recognition that many environmental problems extend across political boundaries and thus challenge the capacity, autonomy, and reach of even the most powerful nation-state. As a consequence, it is argued that global environmental governance needs to be significantly strengthened (Biermann and Pattberg 2012). It has, however, been widely argued that processes of internationally negotiated coordination and cooperation between sovereign states – resulting in environmental agreements and regimes – are too slow and cumbersome, and thus largely insufficient in themselves for achieving GSD. The state-centric international order has been challenged and complemented by a multi-centric and multi-level system of global governance beyond the state, where power is shared across multiple levels – supranational, national, and subnational – as well as within a diverse set of actors and arrangements that transgress national boundaries and derive authority through market power, epistemic communities, international bureaucracies, civil society involvement, etc. (Biermann and Pattberg 2012; Bulkeley and Jordan 2012; Jagers and Stripple 2003). A key question is the extent to which an overarching architecture of global environmental governance – including the diversity of formal and informal governance efforts – must restrict state sovereignty (Biermann 2007). State sovereignty is frequently argued to hinder global environmental solutions, but it also constitutes the basis for democratically legitimate environmental action. The legitimacy of mechanisms for governance beyond the state is a serious concern (Biermann and Pattberg 2012) and even if new global arrangements for legitimate and effective global governance can emerge over time, in the foreseeable future, states – as bearers of democratic legitimacy as well as exercising considerable power – remain critical for environmental governance, both as individual polities and as critical nodes within regional and international systems (Barry and Eckersley 2005; Bulkeley and Jordan 2012). State-led and treaty-based regimes provide important international norms of environmental rights and responsibilities and represent overlapping governance structures that supplement rather than undermine existing state-based structures. Rather than moving beyond the sovereign state system, these regimes remain the most feasible means to democratize global environmental governance (Eckersley 2004).

It is often observed that states are too small to deal with global environmental problems but too large to deal with local ones (*ibid.*). Since the adoption of Agenda 21, the motto 'think globally, act locally' has increasingly inspired local environmental initiatives and action, making urban and local environmental governance an important part of GSD (e.g. Baker and Eckerberg 2008). Although local communities have been shown to be capable of self-governance to overcome collective action problems (Ostrom 1990), and strong sentiments within the environmental movement favor decentralization to strengthen legitimate and effective action (Carter 2007), local environmental governance has been criticized for not being equipped to handle cross-border environmental problems that require coordinated action, involve free-rider problems, and are opposed by NIMBY political sentiments (Paterson *et al.* 2006). The principle of state sovereignty (see Chapter 4, this volume), though challenged, still grants state actors key functions in coordinating local communities within their territory and speaking for them at the global level (Compagnon *et al.* 2012; Lundqvist 2001).

The European Union (EU) has evolved into an important actor in global environmental governance as well as a key polity in its own right. In this complex system of multi-level governance characterized by overlapping jurisdictions and interdependencies, state authority is argued to be dispersing upwards to more or less autonomously acting supranational institutions (e.g. the European Commission) and downwards to local and regional government, leaving states unable either to control collective decision-making in the EU or to mediate between the domestic and international realms (Bache and Flinders 2004). Although the EU is increasingly integrated into the logic of national environmental politics and policymaking, the states retain the capacity to resist being bypassed and to defend their policy preferences (acting as 'gatekeepers') by largely setting the ground rules for EU institutions and controlling the manner in which EU policies are implemented (Compagnon *et al.* 2012; Fairbrass and Jordan 2004).

Network governance

Scholars portray GSD as being the shared responsibility of public and private actors rather than the sole responsibility of the state (van Zeijl-Rozema *et al.* 2008). The task of social transformation is simply too great to be handled by steering from the top (Meadowcroft 2007). Thus, instead of state-led hierarchical institutions, GSD is to be performed through networks characterized by interdependency, trust, deliberation, and reciprocal influence between public and private actors. This shift towards network governance can be conceived of as a hollowing out of the state (Rhodes 1997) where additional resources and policy support from business and civil society are seen as needed to address complex environmental problems. Hope is also placed in networks to revitalize democracy through further broad participation and deliberation, affording a larger proportion of stakeholders – contextually interpreted in terms of a given policy issue rather than a given territory – a voice in policymaking. This is expected to increase the quality and effectiveness of public policy by incorporating alternative forms of knowledge and interests, forestalling implementation deficits, and producing a more legitimate and responsive government that is better equipped to handle environmental problems (Bäckstrand *et al.* 2010). Networks are, however, portrayed as weak in the areas of representation and accountability (Khan 2013).

The extent to which the support and resources mobilized through networks come at the price of transferring state influence and power to market and civil society actors remains very much an open question. Although state actors rely more on interaction and negotiation than on a conventional, authority-based style of governing (Pierre and Peters 2005), they still often have a privileged position in relation to other network participants because of their access to substantial financial, administrative, and political resources. As such, state actors are well-positioned to manage or meta-govern networks (Sørensen 2006). In addition, traditional environmental regulations and institutions largely remain the bedrock of the environmental policy systems in which new modes of governance function (Jordan 2008). Through the shadow of hierarchy (Scharpf

1994), state actors have key functions and responsibilities in structuring the conditions and ground-rules for networks, not only facilitating, enabling, and coordinating, but also adjusting legal rights and responsibilities, creating new institutional arenas, providing political incentives and visions, encouraging alternative voices, etc. (Meadowcroft 2007; Sørensen 2006). Nesting new modes of governance within the institutional framework of democratic government has also been deemed essential to ensuring effectiveness and legitimacy (Weale 2011) as well as ensuring substantial and procedural environmental rights and responsibilities (Eckersley 2004).

Governance for sustainable development – politics

GSD is often characterized as particularly challenging for democratic politics as it requires a global political reach, intergenerational justice, and political representation for non-humans (Eckersley 2004; Hysing 2013; Lidskog and Elander 2007). Essentially, GSD is about handling conflicting values about what constitutes a good life and the allocation of benefits and burdens – processes that generate winners and losers. As a consequence, "politics and political processes lie at the heart of governance for sustainable development" (Meadowcroft 2009: 335). However, the political nature of GSD remains the subject of debate. In the following, we discuss the political character of GSD and how it shapes the strategies and power of environmental advocates.

Environmental issues were established on the political agenda following vigorous criticism of how society misused natural resources. This process was characterized by visible political conflicts between diverging societal interests, with the environmental movement and green parties being positioned as political advocates for a green ideology largely in conflict with the dominant growth-oriented discourse. Sustainable development differs from traditional environmental politics in that it (1) provides a common umbrella under which political actors all can be 'pro-sustainability' while in reality having highly diverging interests and values, and (2) favors consensus-seeking, deliberation, and compromise over open contestation between political alternatives in solving environmental problems. As such, GSD has been described as restricting politics to "the art of the possible" – promoting policies that work within existing institutional frameworks rather than radically challenging this framework (changing the parameters of what is considered possible; Swyngedouw 2007). Blühdorn (2013) uses the expression "the post-ecological turn" to refer to a fundamental shift in environmental politics whereby the more radical ecological critique of modern society inherent in earlier forms of environmental politics has been exhausted, and governance of (un)sustainability has become more about providing reassurance to citizens that appropriate action is being taken than about actually addressing fundamental problems of an unsustainable society. This is most clearly illustrated by ecological modernizations' exclusive focus on measures that can function within existing institutions of market capitalism and a modern welfare state (Mol and Jänicke 2009).

Such a focus on compromises, consensus-seeking, and managerial solutions risks depoliticizing environmental issues and impoverishing democracy (Swyngedouw 2007). While environmental issues remain political in the sense that there are ongoing debates, contestations, and power struggles over the issues, what is at stake is environmental politics – the procedures, practices, and institutions that in modern society have been centered on the state and that serve the purpose of mediating between conflicting interests in an orderly, democratic, and non-violent fashion (cf. Kenis and Lievens 2014). As argued by Beck (1994), traditional politics is losing its polarizing and utopian quality in environmental issues. Political actors largely fail to produce clear alternatives and visions of how to govern society towards sustainability. For this reason, the traditional polities of national parliaments and state institutions risk losing their political qualities, while sectors of society that in the old order were seen as non-political, such as consumption and transportation, are now being increasingly politicized. In this new rationality, the responsibility, competence, and action capacity for dealing with environmental problems are being redistributed from the regulative state to responsible and rational individuals (Bäckstrand *et al.* 2010).

The post-ecological turn also affects advocates of more radical agendas (Blühdorn and Welsh 2007), changing the environmental movement from a counter-culture into a well-established political actor roaming the halls of power (Evans 2012). State inclusion of environmental interests is often considered a major success, but also carries a risk of co-optation, reducing pressure for radical environmental reforms and negatively impacting the democratic vitality of civil society (Dryzek *et al.* 2003). It is, however, also important to recognize that states also uphold the basic civil and political rights that underpin the critical independence and robustness of a green civil society and, by extension, a functional green public sphere (Eckersley 2004). For radical green theorists the state has always been a lost cause, an immutable facilitator of environmental destruction that needs to be replaced by alternative governance arrangements (Barry and Eckersley 2005), but even moderate environmentalists have increasingly been changing strategy; cooperating and networking with (green) business – previously portrayed as the natural enemy – as well as utilizing market forces to induce changes in individual behavior (e.g. shopping habits) as alternatives to lobbying for state regulation (Mol 2000). As the conflict lines in environmental politics become more diffuse, making it difficult to separate friend from foe, important conditions/drivers for political contestation are lost, and without political struggle, radical reforms of and by the state are unlikely.

Conclusion

GSD aims to address problems of insufficient environmental considerations in existing public policy, polity, and politics. However, this has often also led researchers to overlook the roles and responsibilities of the state. Traditional state-led approaches to environmental governance have been dismissed, marginalized, or discredited, and key functions performed by state actors have been disregarded or are expected to be replaced by new modes of governance. As argued by scholars of GSD, broad participation and deliberation over the goal of sustainable development are necessary, but so is having an accountable body able to make authoritative decisions, mediate between societal interests and find trade-offs, and promote the common good. Furthermore, in dealing with complexity and uncertainty GSD certainly requires reflexivity and the incorporation of alternative perspectives and forms of knowledge, but it also needs the expertise and know-how invested in the administrative state. GSD requires cooperative, voluntary, and market-based instruments, but also a regulative framework within which these instruments can function and which can serve as a bulwark against market imperfections and corporate power. GSD requires a broader societal engagement that extends across policy sectors and levels as well as engages market and civil society actors, but it also needs steering capacity to be maintained at the center, from which environmental actions can be championed, coordinated, and democratically legitimated. GSD requires compromises, consensus-seeking, and managerial solutions, but also (re)politicization, critical debate, and contestation between different political visions of sustainable development. Finally, GSD requires flexibility, adaptability, and resilience, but also stable political institutions that can secure key democratic processes and values. Recognizing not only the weaknesses, but also the strengths of state governance, we gain a more nuanced understanding of the state's potential to redress the ecological crisis as well as its unique capacity and legitimacy to foster and lead a stable and safe transition towards a sustainable society. Thus, rather than being forgotten and lost, the green state should be put forward as a key actor for this transition in the academic field of GSD.

Consequently, we need to engage in a critical discussion of the story of a shift *from government to governance*; viewing this discursive construct of the weak state in its ideological context and recognizing that it serves some societal interests to the disadvantage of others. The arguments against the state in terms of its inherent inadequacy to provide legitimate and effective governance in the face of 'new' challenges of sustainable development might not be the result of any inherent failure of state-based governance per se, but rather be due to green issues not reflecting dominant (neoliberal) values and interests. In other words, when it comes to environmental governance, it is not the state that is the problem but rather the lack of a *green* state. Governance reforms are important, but simply changing modes of governance without making an effort to strengthen popular and political support for the environment will not be enough. It risks contributing to states internalizing the weak state story and using it as an excuse to neglect their role as 'ecological stewards,' thus making the story a self-fulfilling prophecy.

Acknowledgements

Earlier versions of this chapter were presented at the Nordic Environmental Social Science conference in Copenhagen, and the Social and Political Science on Climate Change seminar in Örebro. I thank the participants at these events for their helpful comments. Special thanks go to Karin Bäckstrand and Annica Kronsell, whose very insightful and constructive comments helped to substantially improve the chapter.

References

Adger, W.N., and Jordan, A., 2009 Sustainability: exploring the processes and outcomes of governance. In Adger, W.N., and Jordan, A., (eds) *Governing Sustainability* 3–31. Cambridge University Press, Cambridge.

Bache, I., and Flinders, M., (eds) 2004 *Multi-level Governance.* Oxford University Press, Oxford.

Bäckstrand, K., 2003 Civic science for sustainability: reframing the role of experts, policy-makers and citizens in environmental governance. *Global Environmental Politics* 3(4): 24–41.

Bäckstrand, K., Khan, J., Kronsell, A., and Lövbrand, E., 2010 The promise of new modes of environmental governance. In Bäckstrand, K., Khan, J., Kronsell, A., and Lövbrand, E., (eds) *Environmental Politics and Deliberative Democracy: Examining the Promise of New Modes of Governance* 3–27. Edward Elgar, Cheltenham.

Baker, S., and Eckerberg, K., 2008 Introduction: in pursuit of sustainable development at the sub-national level: the 'new' governance agenda. In Baker, S., and Eckerberg, K., (eds) *In Pursuit of Sustainable Development: New Governance Practices at the Sub-national Level in Europe* 1–25. Routledge, Abingdon.

Barry, J., and Eckersley, R., 2005 An introduction to reinstating the state. In Barry, J., and Eckersley, R., (eds) *The State and the Global Ecological Crisis* ix–xxv. MIT Press, Cambridge, MA.

Beck, U., 1994 The reinvention of politics: towards a theory of reflexive modernization. In Beck, U., Giddens, A., and Lash, S., (eds) *Reflexive Modernization: Politics, Traditions and Aesthetics in the Modern Social Order* 1–55. Polity Press, Cambridge.

Biermann, F., 2007 'Earth system governance' as a crosscutting theme of global change research. *Global Environmental Change* 17: 326–37.

Biermann, F., and Pattberg, P., 2012 Global environmental governance revisited. In Biermann, F., and Pattberg, P., (eds) *Global Environmental Governance Reconsidered* 1–23. MIT Press, Cambridge, MA.

Blühdorn, I., 2013 The governance of unsustainability: ecology and democracy after the post-democratic turn. *Environmental Politics* 22(1): 16–36.

Blühdorn, I., and Welsh, I., 2007 Eco-politics beyond the paradigm of sustainability: a conceptual framework and research agenda. *Environmental Politics* 16(2): 185–205.

Bulkeley, H., 2012 Governance and the geography of authority: modalities of authorization and the transnational governing of climate change. *Environment and Planning A* 44: 2428–44.

Bulkeley, H., and Jordan, A., 2012 Transnational environmental governance: new findings and emerging research agendas. *Environment and Planning C* 30: 556–70.

Carter, N., 2007 *The Politics of the Environment: Ideas, Activism, Policy*, 2nd edn. Cambridge University Press, Cambridge.

Christen, M., and Schmidt, S., 2012 A formal framework for conceptions of sustainability – a theoretical contribution to the discourse in sustainable development. *Sustainable Development* 20: 400–10.

Compagnon, D., Chan, S., and Mert, A., 2012 The changing role of the state. In Biermann, F., and Pattberg, P., (eds) *Global Environmental Governance Reconsidered* 237–63. MIT Press, Cambridge, MA.

Dryzek, J.S., 2013 *The Politics of the Earth: Environmental Discourses*, 3rd edn. Oxford University Press, Oxford.

Dryzek, J.S., Downes, D., Hunold, C., and Schlosberg, D., with Hernes H-K 2003 *Green States and Social Movements: Environmentalism in the United States, United Kingdom, Germany, and Norway*. Oxford University Press, Oxford.

Duit, A., 2008 *The Ecological State: Cross-National Patterns of Environmental Governance Regimes*. EPIGOV paper No. 39. Ecologic Institute for International and European Environmental Policy, Berlin.

Eckersley, R., 2004 *The Green State: Rethinking Democracy and Sovereignty*. MIT Press, Cambridge, MA.

Evans, J.P., 2012 *Environmental Governance*. Routledge, Abingdon.

Fairbrass, J., and Jordan, A., 2004 Multi-level governance and environmental policy. In Bache, I., and Flinders, M., (eds) *Multi-level Governance* 147–64. Oxford University Press, Oxford.

Griffin, L., 2010 Editorial: Governance innovation for sustainability: exploring the tensions and dilemmas. *Environmental Policy and Governance* 20: 365–9.

Hajer, M., 1995 *The Politics of Environmental Discourse: Ecological Modernization and the Policy Process*. Clarendon Press, Oxford.

Hajer, M., and Wagenaar, H., 2003 Introduction. In Hajer, M., and Wagenaar, H., (eds) *Deliberative Policy Analysis: Understanding Governance in the Network Society* 1–30. Cambridge University Press, Cambridge.

Hopwood, B., Mellor, M., and O'Brien, G., 2005 Sustainable development: mapping different approaches. *Sustainable Development* 13: 38–52.

Hysing, E., 2009 Governing without government? The private governance of forest certification in Sweden. *Public Administration* 87(2): 312–26.

Hysing, E., 2010 Governing Towards Sustainability: Environmental Governance and Policy Change in Swedish Forestry and Transport. PhD thesis, Örebro University, Sweden.

Hysing, E., 2013 Representative democracy, empowered experts, and citizen participation: visions of green governing. *Environmental Politics* 22(6): 955–74.

Jagers, S.C., and Stripple, J., 2003 Climate governance beyond the state. *Global Governance* 9(3): 385–99.

Jordan, A., 2008 The governance of sustainable development: taking stock and looking forwards. *Environment and Planning C: Government and Policy* 26(1): 17–33.

Jordan, A., and Lenschow, A., 2010 Environmental policy integration: a state of the art review. *Environmental Policy and Governance* 20: 147–58.

Jordan, A., Wurzel, R.K.W., and Zito, A., 2005 The rise of 'new' policy instruments in comparative perspective: has governance eclipsed government? *Political Studies* 53: 477–96.

Jordan, A., Wurzel, R.K.W., and Zito, A.R., 2013 Still the century of 'new' environmental policy instruments? Exploring patterns of innovation and continuity. *Environmental Politics* 22(1): 155–73.

Kemp, R., Parto, S., and Gibson, R.B., 2005 Governance for sustainable development: moving from theory to practice. *International Journal of Sustainable Development* 8(1–2): 12–30.

Kenis, A., and Lievens, M., 2014 Searching for 'the political' in environmental politics. *Environmental Politics* 23(4): 531–48.

Khan, J., 2013 What role for network governance in urban low carbon transitions? *Journal of Cleaner Production* 50(1): 133–9.

Lafferty, W., and Hovden, E., 2003 Environmental policy integration: towards an analytical framework. *Environmental Politics* 12(3): 1–22.

Lafferty, W., and Meadowcroft, J., 2000 Patterns of governmental engagement. In Lafferty, W., and Meadowcroft, J., (eds) *Implementing Sustainable Development: Strategies and Initiatives in High Consumption Societies* 337–421. Oxford University Press, Oxford.

Lange, P., Driessen, P.P.J., Sauer, A., Bornemann, B., and Burger, P., 2013 Governing towards sustainability – conceptualizing modes of governance. *Journal of Environmental Policy and Planning* 15(3): 403–25.

Lidskog, R., and Elander, I., 2007 Representation, participation or deliberation? Democratic responses to the environmental challenge. *Space and Polity* 11(1): 75–94.

Lidskog, R., and Sundqvist, G., 2011 Science-policy-citizen dynamics in international environmental governance. In Lidskog, R., and Sundqvist, G., (eds) *Governing the Air: The Dynamics of Science, Policy, and Citizen Interaction* 323–59. MIT Press, Cambridge, MA.

Loorbach, D., 2010 Transition management for sustainable development: a prescriptive, complexity-based governance framework. *Governance* 23(1): 161–83.

Lundqvist, L.J., 2001 A green fist in a velvet glove: the ecological state and sustainable development. *Environmental Values* 10: 455–72.

Lundqvist, L.J., 2004 *Sweden and Ecological Governance: Straddling the Fence.* Manchester University Press, Manchester.

Meadowcroft, J., 2005 From welfare state to ecostate. In Barry, J., and Eckersley, R., (eds) *The State and the Global Ecological Crisis* 3–24. MIT Press, Cambridge, MA.

Meadowcroft, J., 2007 Who is in charge here? Governance for sustainable development in a complex world. *Journal of Environmental Policy and Planning* 9(3): 299–314.

Meadowcroft, J., 2009 What about the politics? Sustainable development, transition management, and long term energy transitions. *Policy Sciences* 42(4): 323–40.

Meadowcroft, J., 2012 Greening the state? In Steinberg, P.F., and VanDeveer, S.D., (eds) *Comparative Environmental Politics: Theory, Practice, and Prospects* 63–87. MIT Press, Cambridge, MA.

Mol, A.P.J., 2000 The environmental movement in an era of ecological modernization. *Geoforum* 31: 45–56.

Mol, A.P.J., 2007 Bringing the environmental state back in: partnerships in perspective. In Glasberger, P., Biermann, F., and Mol, A.P.J., (eds) *Partnerships, Governance and Sustainable Development* 214–36. Edward Elgar, Cheltenham.

Mol, A.P.J., and Jänicke, M., 2009 The origins and theoretical foundations of ecological modernisation theory. In Mol, A.P.J., Sonnenfeld, D.A., and Spaargaren, G., (eds) *The Ecological Modernisation Reader: Environmental Reform in Theory and Practice* 17–27. Routledge, Abingdon.

Nilsson, M., and Persson, Å., 2003 Framework for analysing environmental policy integration. *Journal of Environmental Policy and Planning* 5(4): 333–59.

Ostrom, E., 1990 *Governing the Commons: The Evolution of Institutions for Collective Action.* Cambridge University Press, Cambridge.

Paterson, M., Doran, P., and Barry, J., 2006 Green theory. In Hay, C., Lister, M., and Marsh, D., (eds) *The State: Theories and Issues* 135–54. Palgrave Macmillan, Basingstoke.

Pierre, J., and Peters, B.G. 2005 *Governing Complex Societies: Trajectories and Scenarios*. Palgrave Macmillan, Basingstoke.

Rhodes, R.A.W., 1997 *Understanding Governance: Policy Networks, Governance, Reflexivity and Accountability*. Open University Press, Maidenhead.

Scharpf, F.W., 1994 Games real actors could play: positive and negative coordination in embedded negotiations. *Journal of Theoretical Politics* 6(1): 27–53.

Sørensen, E., 2006 Metagovernance: the changing role of politicians in processes of democratic governance. *American Review of Public Administration* 36(1): 98–114.

Swyngedouw, E., 2007 Impossible 'sustainability' and the postpolitical condition. In Krueger, R., and Gibbs, D., (eds) *The Sustainable Development Paradox: Urban Political Economy in the United States and Europe* 13–40. Guilford Press, New York.

Treib, O., Bähr, H., and Falkner, G., 2007 Modes of governance: towards a conceptual clarification. *Journal of European Public Policy* 14(1): 1–20.

van Zeijl-Rozema, A., Cörvers, R., Kemp, R., and Martens, P., 2008 Governance for sustainable development: a framework. *Sustainable Development* 16: 410–21.

Voss, J.-P., and Kemp, R., 2006 Sustainability and reflexive governance: introduction. In Voss, J.-P., Bauknecht, D., and Kemp, R., (eds) *Reflexive Governance for Sustainable Development* 3–28. Edward Elgar, Cheltenham.

Voss, J.-P., Newig, J., Kastens, B., Monstadt, J., and Nölting, B., 2007 Steering for sustainable development: a typology of problems and strategies with respect to ambivalence, uncertainty and distributed power. *Journal of Environmental Policy and Planning* 9(3): 193–212.

Weale, A., 2009 Governance, government and the pursuit of sustainability. In Adger, W.N., and Jordan, A., (eds) *Governing Sustainability* 55–75. Cambridge University Press, Cambridge.

Weale, A., 2011 New modes of governance, political accountability and public reason. *Government and Opposition* 46(1): 58–80.

WCED 1987 *Our Common Future*. The World Commission on Environment and Development ('the Brundtland Report'). Oxford University Press, Oxford.

3 Governing beyond or with the state?

State conceptions in studies of non-state climate action

Eva Lövbrand and Björn-Ola Linnér

Introduction

What role does the state play in contemporary climate politics and governance? This is a question that has been brought to the fore in the wake of the 2009 UN climate conference in Copenhagen, and that also informs many of the chapters in this volume. The demonstrated inability of the state system to offer a long-term response to the rising atmospheric concentrations of greenhouse gases prior to and during the infamous Copenhagen conference did not only bring about a crisis in confidence for UN climate diplomacy (cf. Victor 2011). It also prompted many scholars of international relations to look 'beyond the state' for more effective forms of global climate governance. Today there is an abundant literature that investigates the diverse ways by which non-state or sub-state actors and networks such as environmental NGOs, corporations, and city networks contribute to public rule-setting and steering (Okereke *et al.* 2009). By drawing attention to the rise of hybrid, non-hierarchical and network-like modes of governing across political scales, work in this field has challenged the assumption that the state is the sole, or even principal, agent of climate politics and governance. As non-state actors shoulder an increasing number of governance functions in the climate domain, we have learned that the institutional locus for authority and governance has changed.

In this chapter we ask what this recent interest in non-state climate action tells us about the capacity of the state to respond to the challenges posed by climate change. We contend that scholarly analyses of climate governance 'beyond the state' harbor important assumptions about the properties, limits and performance of the state that can inform the continued study of green statehood. By definition, the very notion of the non-state cannot be separated from the understanding of the state. Nonetheless, this intimate relationship often remains implicit or under-theorized by work in this field. Although important efforts have been made to assess the political effects of an increasingly fragmented and transnational global climate governance order, Bulkeley and Schroeder (2012: 744) note that the scholarship on non-state climate action often reproduces a '"reductive dichotomy of public/private' and state/non-state, which masks both the plurality of actors and practices that might be considered in such terms and also the ways in which they are the product of ongoing political processes." In this chapter we bring this implicit boundary work to the fore. Rather than searching for a definition that will fix the boundary between the state and society, we examine how this uncertain, yet powerful, distinction is conceived and performed by the very theories that we as scholars apply.

Our analysis is based on 40 journal articles derived from an open literature search in the SCOPUS database. SCOPUS was chosen since it is the largest abstract and citation database of peer-reviewed literature in the social sciences, containing around 5,900 journal titles. Our literature search was conducted in three steps. First we performed a scoping study with keyword searches for climate change and different non-state actors and hybrid/private forms of governance (e.g. non-governmental organizations, business, city networks, markets). The searches were made in the title, abstract and keywords of peer-reviewed journal articles published until the end of 2012, and produced approximately 10,600 results. We used the analysis function in SCOPUS to view the popularity of the different terms over time and found that there was a sharp rise in the use of most terms in the mid-2000s. As a second step we restricted our search terms to climate change/ greenhouse gases/global warming and non-state/private/non-governmental. The 480 articles resulting from this search were extracted into Excel and the abstracts were analyzed according to the non-state actors, modes of governance and policy issue in focus. In the third phase of the review, we limited our sample to those articles that explicitly address state/non-state relations in climate politics and governance. By using the search terms non-state, state, and climate change/ global warming/greenhouse gases we arrived at 40 articles that primarily feature in journals of international relations (see Table 3.1 in the Appendix to this chapter). These articles were subject to a thorough content analysis and sorted according to the explicit or implicit assumptions about the nature, boundaries and capacity of the state in the governance of climate change. From here we identified three types of statehood that cut across our sampled journal articles and work as the reference point for the rise of non-state climate action. We call these (1) the responsive pluralist state, (2) the decentered partnering state, and (3) the limited post-colonial state.

We will in the following outline what characterizes these three types of statehood and compare how they construe the role of state vs non-state actors in the governance of climate change. As a second step, we discuss how these state types resonate with the typology of green forms of statehood outlined by Peter Christoff (2005) and further developed by Robyn Eckersley (2004) and James Meadowcroft (2005, 2012). Following the theme of this book, we ask where in the spectrum of green and environmental forms of statehood that we find the literature on non-state climate action. Naturally it is difficult to draw any far-reaching conclusions on the basis of 40 journal articles. Our sample is limited and therefore also the perspectives and views represented. We do therefore not claim to offer a full account of the rich and diverse scholarship on climate governance beyond the state. More modestly, our aim is instead to draw attention to some ontological assumptions that underpin work in this field and to discuss the political imagination they foster for the continued governance of climate change.

Our analysis is informed by an anti-foundational and process-oriented ontology of the state that approaches the state/non-state boundary as the contingent effect of complex social and historical relations (Jessop 2001). This analytical approach owes much to Michel Foucault's rethinking of modern government and statehood in the late 1970s (Foucault 1991). In a famous lecture series at the Collège de France in 1978–9, Foucault questioned the scholarly fascination with the state's genesis, its history, its advance, its powers and abuses. According to Foucault "the state, no more probably today than at any other time in history, does not have this unity, this individuality, this rigorous functionality, no, to speak frankly, this importance" (*ibid.*: 103). In Foucault's analytics of government the state has no essence, nor is it approached as a universal or autonomous source of power. The question to be asked about the state is thus not what it is, but *how* it is exercised and with what effects. The intention of this anti-foundational approach is not to dispute that there are objects to which concepts such as 'the state' refers. The aim is rather, as Walters explains (2012: 18), to shift the study from objects as naturally given to the historically contingent practices that produce those objects as their effects.

In this chapter we argue that scholarly analyses of climate governance 'beyond the state' belong to the manifold cognitive and material practices that make up the mysterious entity that we today call 'the state.' Sociologists of science have for some time pointed at the close interplay between scientific representations of the world and interventions in that world (McKenzie *et al.* 2007; Mol 2002). In contrast to the widespread conception of science as an activity whose sole purpose is to study and know the world, this anti-foundational literature has suggested that science is a performative activity that is involved in the very constitution of the world that it studies. When observing, measuring and theorizing about specific objects, scholarly work also enacts those objects (McKenzie *et al.* 2007). It is of course difficult to say anything general about the performative effects of the vast and diverse literature on non-state climate action. The interweaving of words and actions, representations and interventions, is seldom straightforward and can take many forms. While scientific interventions rarely are directly translated into policy interventions they do, however, produce ideas, concepts and tools that may affect how political life is understood and enacted. Scholarly work is therefore far from innocent. As we argue in this chapter, it forms part of the "regimes of truth, the practices and strategies that ontologise the world in the first place" (Walters 2012: 57) and hereby define realm of the possible for climate politics.

Theorizing the state, the non-state and the green state

Efforts to theorize the modern nation-state have a long history and have taken many turns during the past century. While there are many competing ways of explaining what is meant by the state, Mitchell (1991) notes that most state definitions rest upon a distinction between the state and society. In the postwar era, political research has offered multiple interpretations of this distinction. At one extreme end we find society-oriented or pluralist state theories. Work in this field is often associated with political scientists Easton and Almond who in the 1950s questioned the vagueness of existing state definitions and the narrow focus of political research they offered. In contrast to the science of the state developed by old institutionalism in the first half of the 20th century (Bevir and Rhodes 2010), these pluralist scholars wanted to expand the analytical scope of comparative politics beyond the political machinery of the modern nation-state. In a time when the Cold War was unfolding and the USA and Europe witnessed domestic struggles against subversion, the discipline of political science required a new research agenda broad enough to include extra-governmental phenomena and institutions such as political parties, interest groups and mass media, "located on the uncertain boundary between society and the state and thus not clearly covered by conventional state theory" (Mitchell 1991: 79). In order to account for and explain the basic problems of civic loyalty and political cohesion across national jurisdictions, Easton claimed that political research had to abandon the empirically mysterious entity called the state and instead develop a macro-societal analysis of political systems (Easton 1957).

At the other end of the analytical spectrum we find neo-statist efforts to bring the state back in This return of the state in political research emerged in the 1970s as a reaction to the rise of society-oriented state theories, and represents a mode of analysis that aims to take seriously the role of states as actors (Bevir and Rhodes 2010: 29). Reaching out to Weber's definition of the state as an entity, which upholds the claim to the monopoly of the legitimate use of physical force in the enforcement of its order, state-centric theorists such as Skocpol, Krasner and Nordlinger opted for a strong actor-model of relative state autonomy (Passoth and Rowland 2010). Rather than assessing the form, function and impact of the state in terms of factors rooted in the organization, needs and interests of society, Jessop (2001: 153) notes that the neo-statist literature assumes that state's activities and impacts are better explained in terms of its own distinct properties as an administrative or repressive organ. In this account, the state – embodied in the political institutions and apparatuses of the modern nation-state – can be understood as a unitary actor or a restricted system of decision-making:

> [T]here are distinctive political pressures and processes that shape the state's form and functions; that give it a real and important autonomy when faced with pressures and forces emerging from the wider society; and that thereby give it a unique and irreplaceable centrality both in national life and the international order.
>
> (Jessop 2001: 153)

Green conceptions of the state are diverse and therefore difficult to firmly locate in this analytical spectrum. As noted by Barry (1999) green political theory has traditionally represented an inherently anti-statist position. For greens the modern nation-state embodies many of the ecological, political, social and ethical problems that they are concerned with solving, such as materialism, instrumentalist valuation of nature, administrative rationality, institutionalized violence and hierarchy (*ibid.*: 80). By approaching the state as a destructive and self-serving actor, with its own interests and agenda, early work in this field suggested that the state cannot be entrusted to secure the public goods of social order and environmental protection. This pessimism was particularly strong in the eco-anarchist and bioregional literatures and resulted in calls for the decentralization of state power in favor of small-scale, post-sovereign communities (Bookchin 1982). However, the green critique of the state has also produced eco-authoritarian arguments and calls for supra-national forms of rule that reinstate ecological limits in a time of scarcity and crisis (Ophuls 1977).

More recent green political theorizing has taken a different route and begun to explore how the environmentally destructive potential of the modern nation-state can be tamed and transformed in greener directions (see Chapter 1, this volume). Rather than rejecting or circumventing the state, several green political theorists have sought to make use of the state as a vehicle for environmental protection and justice. Peter Christoff (2005) offers a useful typology of different state types or ideals found in this literature. Most of these green or environmental statehoods are located in the pluralist end of the state-theoretical spectrum, but offer different conceptions of how the state interplays with civil society. *The green state* is grounded deliberative ideals of democracy and is characterized by its commitment to strong or reflexive ecological modernization. Robyn Eckersley (2004) describes the green state as a public ecological trustee that fosters reflexive citizens ready to transcend their private interests in favor of the greater ecological good. By giving all those potentially affected by environmental risks a meaningful opportunity to participate or be represented in decisions that generate those risks, the state is here reinvented as a moral agent with the capacity to re-direct social and economic activity towards ecologically sustainable and just outcomes. To Eckersley this moral purpose and character of the green state does not originate with the state. Instead it is the effect of a vibrant public sphere and active ecological citizens "that take responsibility for the state as their creation" (*ibid.*: 245).

The environmental welfare state represents a less radical rethinking of the purpose and activities of state. As explained by Meadowcroft (2005) this latter state type has taken on environmental protection as an essential responsibility of public power and hereby come to extend state authority into new domains of social life. It is a state that has capacity to monitor environmental risks, to reconcile environmental objectives with other societal goals, to deploy effective policy instruments and to finance and legitimize its activities. The environment is thus more central to the activities and structures of the state itself (Meadowcroft 2012: 66). However, in contrast to the green state, the environmental welfare state does not presuppose any deeper structural transformations in the economic system or state institutions. Neither does it presuppose active or reflexive environmental citizenship. This is a trait that the environmental welfare state shares with *the environmental neo-liberal state.* Christoff (2005) describes this latter state type as one with moderate to strong environmental welfare capacity and a strong bias towards market-oriented solutions. It is a state that embraces the idiom of weak ecological modernization and hereby sets out to decouple economic activity from environmental degradation through technology innovation and the creation of environmental markets. In this process of environmental management, the environmental neo-liberal state collaborates closely with a range of societal actors. However, it does so without challenging what Eckersley (2004: 108) calls the dogmas of liberalism, including "muscular individualism," "the sanctity of private property" and "material plenitude."

In the following section of this chapter we use the state-theoretical traditions outlined above as a backdrop to our review of the journal literature on non-state climate action. Interestingly, none of the 40 articles included in our review relate to debates on greener forms of statehood. Instead, they belong to a set of analytical traditions that explicitly have challenged the state-centric horizon of political research. By drawing attention to the manifold non-state activities taking place in the name of climate protection, work in this field has sought to open up a broader conception of politics that makes it possible to approach non-state actors as governors in their own right. However, by doing so, we argue, work in this field indirectly displays ontological assumptions about the nature, limits and capacity of the state in a time of environmental concern. As such it also offers an interesting inroad for analyses of state greening. In the following we outline and compare three types of statehood found in the sample of 40 journal articles.

The responsive pluralist state

Nine of the journal articles included in our review are grounded in a liberal institutionalist tradition of international relations research (for a full list, see Table 3.1 in the Appendix to this chapter). This is a tradition that has made major contributions to our understanding of international environmental cooperation and regime formation. Following Krasner's (1989) original definition, the term regime refers to the rules, organizations, basic norms and principles involved in the global governance of particular issue areas such as climate change. Liberal institutionalist theory is state-centric in the sense that it sees states as the main regime members and thus the primary mechanisms for addressing collective action problems such as climate change. States negotiate international treaties, set up organizations to govern those treaties and agree upon the decision-making procedures that govern future negotiations within that issue area. Within this context states are typically posited as rational self-interested actors, engaged in instrumental calculations over the costs and benefits of international cooperation relative to non-cooperation.

The presence of and advocacy by 'non-sovereign actors' in environmental affairs has, however, begun to challenge this state-centric ontology. The capacity of non-state actors to influence states' preferences and behavior, and hereby indirectly affect international cooperation on climate change, is a central theme that runs across the nine articles that we sort into this category. Schroeder (2010), for instance, studies how indigenous communities participate in and seek to influence the interstate crafting of the REDD+ mechanism by building coalitions and constituencies, disseminating their positions, lobbying or advising national governments in the creation and implementation of rules. Because indigenous peoples often are marginalized domestically, she finds that many tropical forest communities have cultivated practices in bypassing their governments by building advocacy in the international climate negotiations (Schroeder 2010: 329). Downie (2012), in turn, examines the strategies employed by environmental NGOs such as the Environmental Defense Fund in order to influence the US position on emissions trading in the negotiations prior to the adoption of the Kyoto Protocol in 1997. He finds that there are strategic opportunities for non-state actors to influence state behavior in the course of a protracted negotiation and hereby steer negotiations toward their preferred outcomes (*ibid.*: 317). This conclusion is supported by Skjærseth's and Wettestad's (2010) study of the EU Emissions Trading System (EU ETS). They find that the entrepreneurial leadership exercised by members of the European Commission during the set up and evolution of the EU ETS made it possible to alter the EU member states' previously hostile approach to emissions trading and hereby mobilize support for a European emissions market.

In all these accounts the state emerges as a responsive social actor that takes the presence, arguments and ideas advocated by non-state actors seriously. Rather than being an instrumental affair among self-interested states, international climate politics is here portrayed as a vibrant social arena where non-state actors and advocacy groups are invited to express their views and lobby government delegates. As noted by Schroeder (2010: 328), the climate convention process is shifting towards greater stakeholder participation at the conferences of the parties, not through their participation in the formal negotiations, but through increased engagement of constituencies, informal interaction among observer and party delegates, dissemination of information in exhibits and trade fairs and exchange of ideas and experiences in side events and parallel events. When prolonged over time, Downie (2012: 317) finds that interactions of this kind may allow the ideas and norms of non-state advocacy groups to filter through to policy elites and hereby give traditionally weak actors considerable agency to influence state behavior.

Such non-state advocacy does, however, not challenge the proposition that states are the principal international environmental rule-makers, neither does it mark a decisive break with underlying assumptions about international cooperation. As noted by Betsill and Bulkeley (2006: 146), the significance of non-state participation is in the regime literature primarily measured in terms of the extent to which environmental NGOs and business groups shape, facilitate and change the behavior of nation-states and hereby create conditions in the international system that enhance or diminish the prospects for international climate cooperation. While the nation-state remains at center stage, the nine articles that we sort into this category do, however, move beyond the traditional understandings of the state as a closed, unitary and rational actor with exogenously given interests and intentions. The state may be defined in terms of national government, but its interests appear less straightforward than in traditional regime theory and more open to persuasion from domestic and internationally coordinated non-state groups and policy entrepreneurs. By highlighting the many interactions and interrelations between state officials and members of intergovernmental and non-governmental organizations and groups in the international governance of climate change, the nine articles included in this category give rise to a pluralist conception of the state as a responsive actor whose activities are shaped and reformed in relation to societal actors, in particular, pressure groups.

The decentered partnering state

The second and largest bulk of articles included in this review also conveys a pluralist account of statehood, but departs from the state-centrism of regime theory (for a full list, see Table 3.1 in the Appendix to this chapter). Wedded in the language of global governance, the 19 articles that we sort into this category examine the changing role of the state in an increasingly complex, interdependent and transnational world order. Central to this analytical tradition is the observation that the world is in a process of a fundamental transformation from a system of highly autonomous states to one where states are increasingly enmeshed in a complex web of political, social and economic relationships. After the collapse of the Cold War, the globalization of economies, the advent of social movements, and the growth of intergovernmental and non-governmental organizations, global governance scholars have suggested that the locus of power and politics has changed in favor of supranational and subnational actors.

Okereke *et al.* (2009) suggest that the language of global governance provides the conceptual space to interrogate how actors such as international organizations, global social movements, nongovernmental organizations (NGOs), transnational scientific networks, business organizations and multinational corporations are involved in the governance of climate change 'beyond' the international climate regime and the formal structures of government. From this analytical horizon the state-centrism of regime theory appears incomplete as it takes into account only the international arena of interstate negotiations, public policies and those non-state actors that try to influence international agreements. As observed by Pattberg and Stripple (2008), global climate governance is marked by a much broader mosaic of actors and sites. Current developments in global climate governance are, they claim:

> signs of the gradual institutionalization of a transnational public sphere in world politics, where the establishment of norms and rules and their subsequent implementation are only to a limited extent the result of public

agency in the formal sense, but often the outcome of agency beyond the state.

(Pattberg and Stripple 2008: 369)

The rise of carbon markets, corporate codes of conduct, public–private partnerships and transnational city networks are in several articles highlighted as illustrative examples of this more complex and transnational climate governance order.

Streck (2004), for instance, studies the central role of private market actors in the set-up of a functioning carbon market around the Clean Development Mechanism (CDM) of the Kyoto Protocol. She contends that market mechanisms, such as the CDM, epitomize the rise of new collaborative network structures that grant non-state actors a variety of voluntary, semi-formal and formal roles in formulating policy responses and implementing international treaties (*ibid.*: 297). Bäckstrand (2008) analyzes the rise of transnational climate partnership networks, ranging from UN registered public–private partnerships to voluntary technology partnerships between states, in a similar light. She defines climate partnerships as multi-sectorial public policy networks that bring together public sector, business and civil society in the governance of climate change (*ibid.*: 77). Betsill and Bulkeley (2006), in turn, draw our attention to the growing transnational climate activity of cities. Sub-state initiatives such as the Cities for Climate Protection program are here not primarily interpreted as a response to pre-defined policy goals set by national governments or international treaties such as the Kyoto Protocol. City networks on climate change instead emerge as important sites of climate governance in their own right that complicate conventional distinctions between global and local processes, state and non-state actors (*ibid.*).

It is important to note that none of the articles included in this category bear witness of a state in retreat. The demonstrated growth in climate governance arrangements beyond the state is not interpreted as a sign that states and their agencies are marginalized within the realm of climate governance. On the contrary, it is ironically the persistence of the state, claims Pattberg (2012), that has triggered many transnational alternatives to public governance of climate change. He views the rise of voluntary corporate carbon standards such as the Carbon Disclosure Project or the Global Reporting Initiative as a direct response to governmental climate policies and the broader international legal context offered by the UN Framework Convention on Climate Change and the Kyoto Protocol (*ibid.*). Also Bäckstrand (2008) cautions observers to interpret the rise of a partnership discourse in climate governance as a sign that the sovereign state is outdated and replaced by networked governance. Although many transnational climate partnerships have emerged in response to the regulatory deficit permeating the international climate regime, they operate in the shadow of hierarchy as states and international organizations are delegating rule setting or implementation functions to non-state actors (*ibid.*: 75). In other words, governing beyond the state does not necessarily entail governing without the state (Okereke *et al.* 2009).

What we are witnessing, claim Betsill and Bulkeley (2006), is instead a redefinition of the scope and scale of state activity. In contemporary climate governance the state does not govern in isolation but works in close interplay with actors purporting to represent affected communities and interests. Non-state actors operating across different political scales and traditionally discrete policy sectors share responsibility with the state for defining problems and implementing legitimate solutions to climate change. These transnational spheres of authority "are not separate from, or alternative to, state-based power but are inextricably bound up with it" (*ibid.*: 152). This decentered conception of the state departs from the hierarchical outlook of regime theory. While it gives support to the notion of the state as a social actor whose interests and activities are constituted in close interplay with the non-state actors and groups, the boundaries of the decentered partnering state appear much more "dynamic, porous, fragile and malleable" (Bulkeley and Schroeder 2012: 744).

The limited post-colonial state

Eight journal articles reviewed in this chapter break significantly with the pluralist conceptions of statehood outlined above (for an overview, see Table 3.1 in the Appendix to this chapter). In contrast to the global climate governance literature that draws conclusions about the changing role of the state based on empirical examples from advanced industrial societies, this category of articles primarily speaks about the state's limited capacity to govern climate risks in the developing world. As such it resonates with the literature on weak, fragile, or even failed, post-colonial states (for a recent overview, see Compagnon *et al.* 2012). This is a field of political research that explores how the states that emerged from decolonialization have managed to meet the major criteria of effective statehood (e.g. control of the legitimate means of force, capacity to implement political decisions and to enforce the law). The limited or failed post-colonial state is characterized by a combination of centralization, bureaucratic authoritarianism and lack of policy effectiveness. It is a state run by corrupt political entrepreneurs and bureaucrats that see non-state involvement in government affairs as an undue interference that may erode government control over society (*ibid.*).

Two of the journal articles included in this category reproduce this state conception and points to the limited capacity of the post-colonial state to meet the civil unrest and transnational security threats resulting from observed and projected changes in the climate. Butler and Gates (2012) study how the environmental security of pastoralist groups operating in the rangelands of East Africa can be ensured also under the imperfect gaze of the state. Since these communities are highly vulnerable to drought and stock disease, the authors find that social conflicts are likely to arise if states fail to recognize and safeguard the property rights of different pastoral groups (*ibid.*). Jasparro and Taylor (2008), in turn, examine how the projected impacts of climate change in South East Asia may produce failed states and environments conducive to non-state threats and social conflict. They find that climate change is likely to intensify the existing socioeconomic and ecological pressures that are feeding regional mobility, piracy and human trafficking in the area, while at the same time undermining the legitimacy of political leaders and institutions in already weak states (*ibid.*). None of these accounts resemble the responsive pluralist state or the decentered partnering state outlined above. Instead the state here emerges as a weak agent that lacks the institutional capacity to reduce climate vulnerabilities of societal actors and groups, or as a repressive authoritarian force that may use coercive measures to re-establish social order in face of climate-induced security threats.

Dodds (1998: 727) notes that recent claims concerning the ending of state sovereignty and the declining importance of territorially based politics seem quite literally out of place when one considers the experiences of many developing states. In many regions beyond the global North, transnational issues such as climate change have not led to the demise of the nation-state but instead given rise to new geopolitical strategies and alliances to enhance the territorial power of states. Fisher's (2012) study of non-state involvement in Indian climate politics bears evidence of this claim. She finds that the Indian federal state has enrolled several municipal and civic climate networks in a supportive coalition to gain leverage for Indian climate nationalism and Southern solidarity in the UN climate negotiations. Domestically, however, the primacy of the state remains. In contrast to the decentered liberal democratic state, which governs in partnership with non-state actors, Fisher's study suggests that the Indian federal state reaches out to non-state actors only to the extent that they help to implement and extend the reach and efficacy of centralized state policies (*ibid.*: 125).

This latter example from Indian climate policy-making and implementation challenges the notion that all post-colonial states are failed or unable to respond to climate-induced risks. It does, however, reproduce an authoritarian understanding of the state and the processes by which state interests on climate change are legitimated in interplay with societal groups. Among the reviewed articles we only find one study from the developing world that deviates from conceptions of the limited post-colonial state. This study addresses adaptation challenges in South Africa and suggests that efforts to reduce climate vulnerabilities has brought about less hierarchical and more pluralist forms of governing (Koch *et al.* 2007). Informed by the language of global governance, the authors suggest that the state must form alliances with various non-state organizations in order to effectively respond to climate-induced risks.

Linking the non-state to the green state

To what extent do the state conceptions emerging from the literature reviewed in this chapter resonate with the typology of green states outlined above? We find many parallels between the pluralist forms of statehood identified in our review and Meadowcroft's environmental welfare state. The lion share of the sampled journal articles bear evidence of a state that takes the climate challenge seriously and collaborates with non-state actors to devise and implement effective and legitimate solutions. Despite the apparent governance deficit in the lingering interstate negotiations (Bäckstrand 2008), the responsive pluralist state is attentive to the environmental concerns and interests of non-state actors and groups in the crafting and implementation of international policy responses to climate change. By consulting environmental NGOs, business groups, scientific experts and city networks prior to and during the UN climate conferences, the state emerges as a democratically responsive actor open to moral arguments that extend beyond their immediate material and economic interests.

A majority of the articles reviewed here also speaks of a state that is deeply involved in the development of more decentralized forms of climate governance beyond the international regime (Okereke *et al.* 2009). In the quest for ecological modernization, the decentered partnering state collaborates with a host of non-state actors across multiple political scales to bring about international carbon markets, corporate carbon standards, and public–private partnerships. These initiatives resonate with Christoff's description of the environmental neo-liberal state, but seem to lack the reflexive ambitions of Eckersley's green state. On the one hand, networked forms of climate governance challenge the administrative imperatives and centralized structures of governance to which the green state is a critical response. On the other hand, the economic logic underpinning market-based and corporate climate governance arrangements has been charged with hollowing out the state, reinforcing neoliberalism and accelerating the privatization of climate governance (Bäckstrand 2008). As suggested by Forsyth (2010: 693), there is no harm in referring to climate policy networks as partnerships since they involve forms of shared discussion and capacity building. But evidence has suggested that climate partnerships might be motivated more out of public relations, brand management, or general advocacy rather than create the circumstances where citizens and civil society organizations can participate and deliberate with investors about the scope of effective and legitimate climate action (*ibid.*).

This critique suggests that the eco-modernizing strategies of the decentered partnering state may not be reflexive enough to bring about the green state. The reflexive ecological modernization envisioned by Eckersley (2004: 74) entails calling "into question the very processes of technological innovation and capitalist economic modernization, along with the interests and ends it serves." Such reflexivity requires inclusive forms of deliberation that make it possible to challenge the preferences of political and economic actors when those can be shown to exacerbate climate risks and hereby undermine generalized interests such as climate stability (*ibid.*: 96). None of the reviewed journal articles tell us if or how the new forms of state/non-state collaboration fostered by the decentered partnering state live up to these high communicative standards. Schroeder's (2010) study of indigenous group representation in the interstate climate negotiations does, however, bear evidence of the limitations of interest group advocacy and participation in the global governance of climate change. While indigenous peoples have been active in international diplomatic venues for some time, Schroeder finds their participation constrained by a weaker legal standing than other non-state constituencies, lack of support from their national governments, and lack of resources and capacity of engagement.

A radical green transformation of the responsive pluralist state and the decentered partnering state would entail the introduction of new forms of political representation, participation and dialogue that give equal voice to all those potentially affected by environmental risks, "regardless of social class, geographical location, nationality, gender, or species" (Eckersley 2004: 112). Bargaining among organized interests, claims Eckersley, gives those actors who are better resourced, better informed and strategically located vis-à-vis the centers of power, distinct advantage over socially and economically marginalized groups. The green state is indeed pluralist and democratically responsive in the sense that it is made up in close interplay with a transnational citizenry. However, it is also post-liberal and radically plural in its defense for the long-term generalizable interest over short-term private interests (*ibid.*: 98). While the two pluralist forms of statehood emerging from our literature review seem to fall short of these high communicative standards, they suggest a gradual rethinking of how the liberal democratic state engages with and defines its citizenry. Many of the articles reviewed in this chapter point to the emergence of a political infrastructure that is linking up transnational communities at risk, and, through widespread non-state involvement in climate governance arrangements, is building popular support for stronger environmental regulation across political scales. As such the pluralist and decentered forms of climate statehood outlined above may indeed represent a step towards a greener democratic state.

The extent to which such greening can transpire to the developing world remains to be seen. Scholarly representations of the limited post-colonial state do indeed seem distant from the reflexive, pluralist ideals advanced in green political theory. But then again, Meadowcroft (2012: 80) reminds us that we cannot expect the greening of all states to resemble that of industrialized democracies with their decades of institutional stability and high regulatory capacity. After all, the very project of state greening, grounded in the historical trajectory of the modern welfare state and in communicative standards inherited from the Frankfurt School, is in itself a particular historical phenomenon that may not fit all societies at all times. A central question for continued analysis is thus how the broad and heterogeneous category of developing states that, at times, "struggle for legitimacy amid contentious state-society relations stemming from legacies of colonialism and authoritarian rule" (*ibid.*: 81), can and should respond to the challenges posed by climate change. To date, green state theory has given us few answers to this question.

Conclusions

In this chapter we have assessed how the recent scholarship on non-state climate action imagines, construes and represents the state in a time of climate concern. Rather than approaching the state as a historical constant, with a single origin and fixed identity, we have drawn upon a process-oriented ontology of the state to understand how the mysterious entity that we call the state is made up or performed by the very theories that we as scholars apply. Following

Mitchell (1991) we contend that detailed analyses of the processes by which the uncertain, yet powerful, distinction between the state and society is produced offer important inroads to such anti-foundational analyses of state making. This distinction must not be taken as the boundary between two discrete entities, but is here approached as the contingent *effect* of an ongoing boundary-work in which political research is deeply engaged.

The multitude of statehoods emerging from our literature review suggests that the conception and meaning of the state is far from settled in studies of climate politics and governance. The state's boundaries with society remain "elusive, porous and mobile" (*ibid.*: 77). Hence, rather than re-producing the "reductive dichotomy" of public/private and state/non-state referred to above (Bulkeley and Schroeder 2012: 744), we find that many of the articles included in our literature review are complicating these divides by illustrating how the state is negotiated, contested and remade in close interplay with society. Three conclusions can be drawn from our analysis. First, the state remains central in the governance of climate change. Although our literature review focused on scholarly analyses of climate action 'beyond the state,' none of the 40 articles included in our study bear evidence of a state in retreat. Rather than being undermined or circumvented by the rise of non-state climate action, the state still seems indispensable for effective climate action. A second, and closely related, finding from our study is that the state takes many forms in the governance of climate change. Whereas the lion share of our sample of articles speaks of a decentered pluralist state that governs in close partnership with non-state actors, several articles maintain a strong actor model of relative state autonomy. In the developing world post-colonial states, sometimes weak or failed but most of the time authoritarian, are responding to the risks posed by climate change with limited or no input from civil society.

Naturally we should be careful to draw any far-reaching conclusions on the basis of a limited sample of journal articles. The practices of state making are diverse and do not easily lend themselves to generalizations, neither in the developing nor the developed world. As suggested by our process-oriented ontology, the state will always be an instable and unfinished project. This third and final conclusion from our study should not be seen as a problem for political research. On the contrary, efforts to disassemble the state by reflecting on its conditions of existence and rules of transformation may very well open up new political possibilities for the continued study and practice of climate governance. This is good news in a time when the climate challenge is mounting and the state system is struggling to find effective solutions. The long-standing preoccupation with state action on climate change (defined in terms of interstate treaty-making) has indeed restricted the political imagination and the kinds of solutions that are deemed necessary to halt and adapt to the rising concentrations of greenhouse gases in the atmosphere. By identifying new spaces and subjects of climate governance within and beyond the nation-state, scholarly analyses of non-state climate action may help to push the realm of the possible for climate policy practice and hereby take the study of state greening in new directions.

Acknowledgements

This chapter forms part of the research project 'Non-state actors in the new landscape of international climate cooperation', funded by the Swedish Research Council and the Swedish Research Council Formas. We are highly indebted to Naghmeh Nasiritousi at Linköping University for her contributions to an earlier version of this chapter, presented at the 2013 Conference of the International Studies Association in San Francisco.

References

Bäckstrand, K., 2008 Accountability of networked climate governance: the rise of transnational climate partnerships. *Global Environmental Politics* 8(3): 74–102.

Barry, J., 1999 *Rethinking Green Politics*. Sage, London.

Betsill, M., and Bulkeley, H., 2006 Cities and the multilevel governance of global climate change. *Global Governance* 12: 141–59.

Bevir, M., and Rhodes, R., 2010 *The State as Cultural Practice*. Oxford University Press, Oxford.

Bookchin, M., 1982 *The Ecology of Freedom: The Emergence and Dissolution of Hierarchy*. Cheshire Books, Palo Alto, CA.

Bulkeley, H., and Schroeder, H., 2012 Beyond state/non-state divides: global cities and the governing of climate change. *European Journal of International Relations* 18(4): 743–66.

Butler, C., and Gates, S., 2012 African range wars: climate, conflict, and property rights. *Journal of Peace Research* 49(1): 23–34.

Christoff, P., 2005 Out of chaos, a shining star? Toward a typology of green states. In Barry, J., and Eckersley, R., (eds) *The State and the Global Ecological Crisis* 25–52. MIT Press, Cambridge, MA.

Compagnon, D., Sander, C., and Mert, A., 2012 The changing role of the state. In Biermann, F., and Pattberg, P., (eds) *Global Environmental Governance Reconsidered* 237–64. MIT Press, Cambridge, MA.

Dodds, K., 1998 The geopolitics of regionalism: the Valdivia Group and southern hemispheric environmental co-operation. *Third World Quarterly* 19(4): 725–43.

Downie, C., 2012 Toward an understanding of state behavior in prolonged international negotiations. *International Negotiation* 17: 295–320.

Easton, D., 1957 *The Political System: An Inquiry into the State of Political Science*. Alfred A Knopf, New York.

Eckersley, R., 2004 *The Green State: Rethinking Democracy and Sovereignty*. MIT Press, Cambridge, MA.

Fisher, S., 2012 Policy storylines in Indian climate politics: opening new political spaces? *Environment and Planning C* 30: 109–27.

Forsyth, T., 2010 Panacea or paradox? Cross-sector partnerships, climate change, and development. *Wiley Climate Change* 1: 683–96.

Foucault, M., 1991 Governmentality. In Burchell, G., Gordon, C., and Miller, P., (eds) *The Foucault Effect: Studies in Governmentality* 87–104. University of Chicago Press, Chicago, IL.

Jasparro, C., and Taylor, J., 2008 Climate change and regional vulnerability to transnational security threats in Southeast Asia. *Geopolitics* 13: 232–56.

Jessop, B., 2001 Bringing the state back in (yet again): reviews, revisions, rejections, and redirections. *International Review of Sociology* 11(2): 149–53.

Koch, I.C., Vogel, C., and Patel, Z., 2007 Institutional dynamics and climate change adaptation in South Africa. *Mitigation and Adaptation Strategies for Global Change* 12: 1323–39.

Krasner, S.D., (ed) 1989 *International Regimes*. Cornell University Press, Ithaca, NY.

McKenzie, D., Munieas, F., and Siu, L., (eds) 2007 *Do Economists Make Markets? On the Performativity of Economics*. Princeton University Press, Princeton, NJ.

Meadowcroft, J., 2005 From welfare state to ecostate. In Barry, J., and Eckersley, R., (eds) *The State and the Global Ecological Crisis* 3–23. MIT Press, Cambridge, MA.

Meadowcroft, J., 2012 Greening the state? In Steinberg, P.F., and VanDeveer, S.D., (eds) *Comparative Environmental Politics: Theory, Practice and Prospects* 63–88. MIT Press, Cambridge, MA.

Mitchell, T., 1991 The limits of the state: beyond statist approaches and their critics. *The American Political Science Review* 85(1): 77–96.

Mol, A.M., 2002 *The Body Multiple: Ontology in Medical Practice*. Duke University Press, Durham, NC.

Okereke, C., Bulkeley, H., and Schroeder, H., 2009 Conceptualizing climate governance beyond the international regime. *Global Environmental Politics* 9(1): 58–78.

Ophuls, W., 1977 *Ecology and the Politics of Scarcity*. WH Freeman and Company, San Francisco, CA.

Passoth, J.H., and Rowland, N., 2010 Actor-network theory as state theory. *International Journal of Sociology* 25(6): 818–41.

Pattberg, P., 2012 How climate change has become a business risk: analyzing non-state agency in global climate politics. *Environment and Planning C* 30(4): 613–26.

Pattberg, P., and Stripple, J., 2008 Beyond the public and private divide: remapping transnational climate governance in the 21st century. *International Environmental Agreements* 8: 367–88.

Schroeder, H., 2010 Agency in international climate negotiations: the case of indigenous peoples and avoided deforestation. *International Environmental Agreements* 10: 317–32.

Skjærseth, J.B., and Wettestad, J., 2010 Making the EU emissions trading system: the European commission as an entrepreneurial epistemic leader. *Global Environmental Change* 20: 314–21.

Streck, C., 2004 New partnerships in global environmental policy: the clean development mechanism. *Journal of Environment and Development* 13(3): 295–322.

Victor, D., 2011 *Global Warming Gridlock: Creating More Effective Strategies for Protecting the Planet*. Cambridge University Press, Cambridge.

Walters, W., 2012 *Governmentality: Critical Encounters*. Routledge, Abingdon.

Appendix

Table 3.1 List of reviewed journal articles

Author	Title	Journal	Year	State type
Pattberg P.	How climate change became a business risk: Analyzing non state agency in global climate politics	*Environment and Planning C: Government and Policy*	2012	The decentered partnering state
Bulkeley H., Schroeder H.	Beyond state/non-state divides: Global cities and the governing of climate change	*European Journal of International Relations*	2012	The decentered partnering state
Lövbrand E., Stripple J.	Disrupting the public-private distinction: Excavating the Government of carbon markets post-Copenhagen	*Environment and Planning C: Government and Policy*	2012	The decentered partnering state
Downie C.	Toward an understanding of state behavior in prolonged international negotiations	*International Negotiation*	2012	The responsive pluralist state
Vormedal I.	States and markets in global environmental governance: The role of tipping points in international regime formation	*European Journal of International Relations*	2012	The responsive pluralist state
Cadman T., Maraseni T.	The governance of REDD+: An institutional analysis in the Asia Pacific region and beyond	*Journal of Environmental Planning and Management*	2012	The limited post-colonial state
Fisher S.	Policy storylines in Indian climate politics: Opening new political spaces?	*Environment and Planning C: Government and Policy*	2012	The limited post-colonial state
Butler C.K., Gates S.	African range wars: Climate, conflict, and property rights	*Journal of Peace Research*	2012	The limited post-colonial state
Ruddock K., Green D.	What legal recourse do non-state islands have to obtain resources to adapt to climate change?	*Macquarie Journal of International and Comparative Environmental Law*	2011	N/A

continued…

Table 3.1 continued

Author	Title	Journal	Year	State type
Bailes A.J.K.	Institutions and stability: The Arctic case	Nordia Geographical Publications	2011	Outlier
Rae J., Gunther M., Godden L.	Governing tropical forests: REDD+, certification and local forest outcomes in Malaysia	Macquarie Journal of International and Comparative Environmental Law	2011	The limited post-colonial state
Bernstein S.	Legitimacy in intergovernmental and non-state global governance	Review of International Political Economy	2011	The decentered partnering state
Schroeder H.	Agency in international climate negotiations: The case of indigenous peoples and avoided deforestation	International Environmental Agreements: Politics, Law and Economics	2011	The responsive pluralist state
Forsyth T.	Panacea or paradox? Cross-sector partnerships, climate change, and development	Wiley Interdisciplinary Reviews: Climate Change	2010	The decentered partnering state
Dimitrov R.S.	Inside Copenhagen: The state of climate governance	Global Environmental Politics	2010	The decentered partnering state The limited post-colonial state
Skjaerseth J.B.	EU emissions trading: Legitimacy and stringency	Environmental Policy and Governance	2010	The responsive pluralist state
Ingold K., Balsiger J., Hirschi C.	Climate change in mountain regions: How local communities adapt to extreme events	Local Environment	2010	The limited post-colonial state
Skjaerseth J.B., Wettestad J.	Making the EU Emissions Trading System: The European Commission as an entrepreneurial epistemic leader	Global Environmental Change	2010	The responsive pluralist state
Lazarus R.	A huge green win in the 2nd circuit	Environmental Forum	2009	Outlier

Author	Title	Journal	Year	State type
Okereke C., Bulkeley H., Schroeder H.	Conceptualizing climate governance beyond the international regime	*Global Environmental Politics*	2009	The decentered partnering state
Bailey I., Maresh S.	Scales and networks of neoliberal climate governance: The regulatory and territorial logics of European Union emissions trading	*Transactions of the Institute of British Geographers*	2009	The decentered partnering state
Bradshaw M.J.	The geopolitics of global energy security	*Geography Compass*	2009	N/A
Pahl-Wostl C.	A conceptual framework for analysing adaptive capacity and multi-level learning processes in resource governance regimes	*Global Environmental Change*	2009	The decentered partnering state
Boykoff M.T., Goodman M.K.	Conspicuous redemption? Reflections on the promises and perils of the 'Celebritization' of climate change	*Geoforum*	2009	The decentered partnering state
Bäckstrand K.	Accountability of networked climate governance: The rise of transnational climate partnerships	*Global Environmental Politics*	2008	The decentered partnering state
Toly N.J.	Transnational municipal networks in climate politics: From global governance to global politics	*Globalizations*	2008	The decentered partnering state
Pattberg P., Stripple J.	Beyond the public and private divide: Remapping transnational climate governance in the 21st century	*International Environmental Agreements: Politics, Law and Economics*	2008	The decentered partnering state
Levin K., McDermott C., Cashore B.	The climate regime as global forest governance: Can reduced emissions from Deforestation and Forest Degradation (REDD) initiatives pass a 'dual effectiveness' test?	*International Forestry Review*	2008	The decentered partnering state
Jasparro C., Taylor J.	Climate change and regional vulnerability to transnational security threats in Southeast Asia	*Geopolitics*	2008	The limited post-colonial state

continued…

Table 3.1 continued

Author	Title	Journal	Year	State type
Tompkins E.L., Amundsen H.	Perceptions of the effectiveness of the United Nations Framework Convention on Climate Change in advancing national action on climate change	Environmental Science and Policy	2008	The responsive pluralist state
Bailey I.	Neoliberalism, climate governance and the scalar politics of EU emissions trading	Area	2007	The decentered partnering state
Mander S.L.	Regional renewable energy policy: A process of coalition building	Global Environmental Politics	2007	The responsive pluralist state
Koch I.C., Vogel C., Patel Z.	Institutional dynamics and climate change adaptation in South Africa	Mitigation and Adaptation Strategies for Global Change	2007	The decentered partnering state
Betsill M.M., Bulkeley H.	Cities and the multilevel governance of global climate change	Global Governance	2006	The decentered partnering state
Streck C.	New partnerships in global environmental policy: The Clean Development Mechanism	Journal of Environment and Development	2004	The decentered partnering state
Thoms L.	A comparative analysis of international regimes on ozone and climate change with implications for regime design	Columbia Journal of Transnational Law	2003	N/A
Auer M.R.	Who participates global environmental governance? Partial answers from international relations theory	Policy Sciences	2000	The responsive pluralist state
Dodds K.	The geopolitics of regionalism: The Valdivia Group and southern hemispheric environmental co-operation	Third World Quarterly	1998	The limited post-colonial state
Samhat N.H.	International regimes as political community	Millennium	1997	The responsive pluralist state

4 The green state and the prospects of greening sovereignty

Rickard Andersson

Introduction

Michael Saward once asked whether the state is "capable of *systematically* prioritizing the achievement of sustainability" (1998: 345). The modern state and its historical development cannot be dissociated from the concept of sovereignty (Walker 1993; Bartelson 1995); sovereignty is both the organizing principle of the state as a territorially bounded unity, and the ultimate point of reference for the state's claim to legitimate authority. It conditions modern state-based politics. When asking about the state's capability for achieving sustainability, then, one is also asking whether sovereignty is compatible with sustainability. In examining the relationship between the state and sustainability, a key question is whether sovereignty is capable of systematically prioritizing the achievement of sustainability.

In this chapter, I will argue that the theory of the green state needs to be rethought because it does not provide a coherent and conclusive answer to this question, the reason being that the debate on sovereignty and sustainability is currently caught in a restraining impasse. If the state is to be capable of systematically prioritizing sustainability, the concept of sovereignty on which it relies needs to be rethought. I will also suggest how such a rethinking can proceed.

One of the most prominent and well-argued examples of the current efforts to "reinstate the state" (Barry and Eckersley 2005: x) in green political thought, and of the ongoing normative and pragmatic consolidation of the state and state-based sovereignty in the face of environmental crisis, is Robyn Eckersley's *The Green State* (2004), in which she details a transformation of the modern *liberal state* into an ecological *green state*.

Eckersley and other advocates of the green state affirm the capability of statist politics based on the principle of sovereignty to systematically prioritize sustainability (cf. Barry 1999; Lafferty 2000; Lundqvist 2001; Barry and Eckersley 2005; Meadowcroft 2012). In this literature, sovereignty is understood empirically – as a concept referring to the facts of governmental practices.[1] In other words, it refers to what can be called positive political order, by which I mean the actual manifestations of order.

But sovereignty is more than its positive manifestation. In political philosophy, sovereignty is generally treated as the theoretical concept denoting what makes governmental practices possible in the first place. Here, however, interest in the notion of the green state has been limited, with a notable exception in the work of Mick Smith (2009, 2011), who has leveled a critique of sovereignty in general, and the notion of green sovereignty in particular, making his work highly relevant for the rethinking of sovereignty in the debate on the green state.

Smith builds on the theoretical exposition of sovereignty by Carl Schmitt and Giorgio Agamben. Referring to Schmitt's (in)famous definition of the sovereign as "he who decides on the exception" (Schmitt 2005: 5) and to Agamben's (1998) elaboration thereof, Smith claims that the sovereign decision is inherently anti-ecological and anti-political. It is anti-ecological because it always excludes the natural world from political consideration and reduces it to a set of resources, and it is anti-political because its ultimate mark is the suspension of the juridico-political order from within itself and with it the rights of humans as political beings (Smith 2011: xi–xx).

Smith's critique of sovereignty explicitly targets the debate on the green state (2009; 2011: 193–218). Whereas Eckersley's account is a defense of sovereignty because of its inherent capabilities as a principle for democratic ecological politics, Smith's account adds up to its rejection on the same grounds. Accordingly, they arrive at opposed answers to the question regarding the compatibility of sovereignty and sustainability. This opposition constitutes the impasse I claim to be hampering current thinking on the green state.

Below, I revisit Eckersley's and Smith's accounts of sovereignty. I concentrate on Eckersley's work because of her authoritative contribution to the normative endorsement of the green state. Smith continues a long line of anti-statist ecological thought, but his work deserves special attention because of its theoretical rigor and its critique of the contemporary statist turn in green political theory. In the chapter, I show that whereas Eckersley approaches sovereignty as positive order, Smith treats it as the exception of positive order in the form of a sovereign decision, and that each account presupposes the other in order to be meaningful – Eckersley's positive order presupposes Smith's sovereign decision and vice versa. Furthermore, I also claim that whereas sovereignty as positive order can be transformed so as to prioritize sustainability, the sovereign decision constituting that order is indifferent to concerns such as sustainability. I will then proceed to argue that in order to avoid this impasse the seemingly opposed and contradictory takes on sovereignty represented by Eckersley and Smith be reconceived of as equally valid for sovereignty to be fully intelligible. Doing so will reposition their contradiction to sovereignty itself. Being equally necessary for the understanding of sovereignty while also contradicting each other, positive order and sovereign decision emerge as what Kant referred to as antinomies, in this case as the antinomies of sovereignty: equally valid but mutually conflicting principles. I end the chapter by suggesting that this rendering of sovereignty opens up a way beyond the impasse current thinking on sovereignty and sustainability is caught in. Taking Kant as an historical precedent and how he constructs his philosophy through an engagement with antinomies, so too, I argue, can the debate on sovereignty and sustainability move beyond impasse by exploring the gap in-between the antinomies of political order and sovereign decision.

The analysis in this chapter is theoretical. It is situated on the level of theoretical and philosophical concepts, focusing on their definition, construction, and deconstruction. The ambition with this approach is to contribute to and strengthen the conceptual foundation of the current debate on the green state by providing the means for this debate and a philosophical discussion on sovereignty to encounter each other. It goes without saying, however, that the high level of abstraction of this approach is achieved at the expense of empirical analysis.

The green state: sovereignty as positive political order

An important claim engendering the normative affirmation of the green state is that, notwithstanding the dubious environmental track record of the modern state, the state as such is not necessarily anti-ecological and that it can be transformed so as to work for an environmentalist agenda (Eckersley 2006: 127–8; cf. Meadowcroft 2005: 6). Eckersley identifies three structural arrangements pushing the modern liberal state onto unsustainable pathways:

1   international anarchy, which results in international atomism, limited efforts of interstate collaboration, and to the logic of the tragedy of the commons;
2   the state's entanglement with capitalism and economic globalization;
3   administrative state hierarchy, democratic deficits and liberal dogmas of political subjectivity (Eckersley 2004: 19–110).

Opposing these structural arrangements, Eckersley identifies three counter-developments: environmental multilateralism, ecological modernization, and domestic environmental legislation and discursive decision-making designs. These are indications of an ongoing greening of the state, from which Eckersley extrapolates the major properties of a fully green state.

Ecological modernization holds the promise of a *reflexive* ecological modernization (cf. Christoff 1996, 2005) which could rearrange the relations between state and economy so that market activities would sometimes be suppressed by social and ecological norms, turning the green state into a *post-capitalist* state (Eckersley 2004: 83–4).

Regarding domestic policy and institutional arrangements, Eckersley emphasizes the importance of civil society and the fostering of a green public sphere, shared norms and values of democracy and ecological responsibility, as well as the need to institutionalize new forms of decision-making procedures in order to increase public political participation and deliberation (*ibid.*: 139–69).

In terms of international relations, Eckersley stresses the importance of strengthening environmental multilateralism, of pioneering green states acting as good examples (*ibid.*: 201), and of changed norms regarding the rights and responsibilities of states. The international relations of the green state would be of a different character than those of the modern liberal state. Whereas the modern international system is composed of discrete elements of nation states, the environmental multilateral system would be populated by states who would share a sense of belonging, mutuality, and interdependence, and it would be saturated by a culture of responsibility and friendship (*ibid.*: 43–8; Eckersley 2005).

Despite emphasizing the green potential of such evolutionary changes, the most radical transformation of the state emerging from Eckersley's work originates from positing a principle of ecological democracy as the foundation of the green state (Meadowcroft 2006; Vogler 2006).

Eckersley posits ecological democracy as an "ambit claim," stating that "all those potentially affected by a risk should have some meaningful opportunity to participate or otherwise be represented in the making of the politics or decisions that generate the risk" (2004: 111). From this claim emerge a number of properties of the green state. As a decision rule, it situates the principle of risk aversion as normative guidance for political decisions. Practically, risk aversion could be constitutionally entrenched domestically and actively pursued internationally (*ibid.*: 135, 231–6). Further, it situates an all-affected principle as the principle for determining rights of participation, representation, and citizenship. Eckersley does not limit this principle to presently living humans. Instead, it is extended to future generations and to non-human beings (*ibid.*: 112), whereby the constitutive interconnectedness of the political subject and the natural world is affirmed in opposition to modern anthropocentric atomism (cf. Eckersley 1992). In order to include in the decision-making process those affected by it who cannot participate in it themselves, Eckersley (2004: 114) suggests they be represented by trustees. The green state, then, would require new forms of political participation and deliberation, as well as new forms of representation.

The ecocentric all-affected principle has far-reaching implications for the concepts of state and sovereignty. Instead of being determined statically as the citizens of a state within a territory over which the state exercises exclusive authority, the people of the green state would be a fluid entity, constantly changing depending on the determination of risk exposure; it would be an emergent not-only-human community of fate not necessarily contiguous in time and space, and the state itself would be outward-looking, transnational, and cosmopolitan in character, and it would have to give up on the principle of territorial exclusivity (Eckersley 2005: 175–6; 2000).

In all, Eckersley's green state would be a transnational, cosmopolitan, risk averse, discursive participatory and representative democratic, post-liberal, post-capitalist ecological state. Domestically, the green state would still primarily be concerned with law-making, regulation, implementation, and enforcement. Added to this would be an overarching fostering of a democratic culture of ecological responsibility. Internationally, two key aspects of green statism would be multilateral agreements conferring reciprocal rights of citizenship to non-members of a particular state in matters where they would be affected by decisions made by that state (Eckersley 2005: 176), and the pursuit of an interstate culture of ecological concern, reciprocity, responsibility, and belonging.

To summarize, the green transformation of the state would proceed from an ecocentric all-affected principle as a foundational decision rule for the state, the compliance to which would initiate a series of constitutional and institutional rearrangements and innovations. This would loosen the connection between the state and its territory; the people would emerge as fluid communities of fate; ecological concern would not be trumped by security and development, it would be an overriding state imperative; the international system would move away from atomism toward a community of interdependent cosmopolitan states. Ultimately, these transformations would bring about a shared culture of ecological reason, where ethico-political concerns would not be limited to humans, and where belonging and mutuality would replace liberal notions of autonomy and self-determination. In such a world, people and states would assume the roles of stewards of the natural and social world (Eckersley 2004: 249).

In this transformation, the appearances of sovereignty would change, but sovereignty itself would remain intact, one reason being that the changes needed for such a profound transformation of the political landscape are so demanding that "it is difficult to imagine how such changes might occur on the kind of scale that is needed without the active support of states" (*ibid.*: 6). The authority of sovereignty is, according to Eckersley, simply needed. The legislative, regulative, and redistributive capacity of states is required for sustainability, and this capacity arises because the state "enjoys a (virtual) monopoly of the means of legitimate coercion and is therefore the final adjudicator and guarantor of positive law. In short, the appeal of the state is that it stands as the most overarching source of authority within modern, plural societies" (Eckersley 2005: 172).

As it appears in Eckersley's theory of the green state, sovereignty is primarily a term referring to empirical governmental operations made possible by a specific configuration of political authority. Here, sovereignty denotes state conduct, actual practice and exercise of power, the scope and intensity of political authority. Sovereignty is treated as a fact, and as a concept it refers to *positive political order*. Eckersley's reinvention of the state is predominantly concerned with transforming positive political order in terms of international integration as well as constitutional, institutional, and cultural change. Indeed, these transformations alter sovereignty as positive order, but they leave "formal sovereignty" – the legal supremacy and independence of states (Conca 1994: 703) – intact. They even rely, in fact, on the effective power of formal sovereignty. Thus, the project of the green state is a normative theory pursuing the transformation of positive political order in a green direction by a rearrangement of sovereignty as positive order while maintaining formal sovereignty intact, the latter also being the condition of possibility for the former.

Following Litfin (1998b: 7), Eckersley affirms that attempts to green the state are better served by attending to positive order rather than formal sovereignty (2004: 209–10). But, by focusing on the content of sovereignty and ignoring its form, this approach fails to take into account important aspects of political order. When referring to state authority as the original source of the green transformation of the state, Eckersley accepts that there is more to political order than its positive manifestation. What is left out of the analysis is the source of sovereignty itself, the very ordering of political order. And this aspect of order, what brings positive order into existence, is not itself immanent to positive order. This intricacy is exposed in Eckersley's turn to the ambit claim of ecological democracy as the foundation for the green state. The ambit claim is the very source of the green state as positive order, but it does not itself emerge from within it or from the present order. In fact, because of modern political thought, including the concept of sovereignty, being foundationally anthropocentric (Eckersley 1992; Wendt and Duvall 2008), its realization would require the suspension of the current manifestation of anthropocentric statist order. Ecological democracy could emerge only through the suspension of the current anthropocentric order. The ambit claim, then, is an example of what is referred to in political theory as a sovereign decision – the ability to create order by suspending it, and as will be elaborated below, the sovereign decision leaves no ecological guarantees. In line with Smith, it could therefore be concluded that the attempt to green the state presupposes and affirms what it tries to neutralize, namely the ecologically destructive capacity of the state.

The sovereign decision and ecological indifference

Smith maintains that the history of Western society is, by and large, a history of human domination over the natural world, the reason being that Western civilization has always raised humanity above that which is natural. He does so by drawing on Agamben's concept of the *anthropological machine*, defined by Smith as "the historically variable but constantly recurring manufacture of metaphysical distinctions to separate and elevate the properly human from the less-than-fully-human and the natural world" (Smith 2011: xii; cf. Agamben 2004). He refers to this transhistorical domination as *ecological* sovereignty. *Political* sovereignty, in modernity exclusively associated with the state (Smith 2011: 121), while conditioned by ecological sovereignty is also its constant affirmation and reproduction (*ibid.*: xi–xiii). Political sovereignty presupposes and reproduces a world in which humans are elevated over nature, and in which nature is reduced to mere resource. Smith claims that this connection between the metaphysics of humanity's place in the world and political sovereignty is the reason behind the ecological predicament modern society has created for itself.

Whereas advocates of the green state affirm sovereignty, Smith rejects it as the source of political authority. Instead, he pursues a green alternative to the modern political order along the lines of anarchic ethics and politics, the realization of which would establish an ecological concern for the natural world while affirming the relative autonomy of human and non-human modes of being (*ibid.*: 101–34). The ethical stance sought by Smith would position itself in the void left by the abandonment of sovereignty as the infinite responsibility towards the other not to reduce it according to any preconceived principle of determination (*ibid.*: 27–64). Likewise, ecological anarchic politics would be the actualization of the potential of human beings for being political, of their natural ability to act and speak freely, and to respond to a world they can never fully determine. Ecological politics in this vein would "release" nature from the domination of political and ecological sovereignty, and thus "save the natural world" by letting it be in its multiple modes of existence (*ibid.*: 101–34).

In his analysis of sovereignty and sustainability, Smith draws on Agamben's conceptualization of sovereignty and the sovereign decision, itself indebted to Schmitt. Schmitt's definition of the sovereign as he who decides on the exception situates the sovereign as paradoxically both inside and outside the law (Schmitt 2005: 5–7). The law, therefore, is outside itself (Agamben 1998: 15). In relation to the universal application of law, the sovereign positions itself outside of it, since it has the power to suspend it. This decision is necessarily exceptional, since it consists in the suspension of the order of any regular situation (*ibid.*: 17).

Something is always excluded in the sovereign decision, but what is excluded is never fully disentangled from relation to order (*ibid.*: 17–19). Instead, the excluded maintains a relation to order as that which is excluded from it. By maintaining a relation to what it excludes, sovereign order manages to include what it excludes from itself. Sovereignty thus operates by establishing a zone of indistinction between inclusion and exclusion, between inside and outside, between norm and exception (*ibid.*: 18–19). In this zone it becomes possible to determine what order is and is not. What is included in any specific juridico-political order and what is excluded from it gains its meaning through the sovereign decision on the exception (*ibid.*: 25–6). Citizenship, for instance, is only meaningful in a context of sovereignty, since contemporary citizen identity is gained through a sovereign decision on a territorial demarcation of the people.

Smith locates the reason for sovereignty being necessarily irreconcilable with sustainability in the zone of indistinction between inside and outside created by the sovereign decision. The natural world is what is first and foremost held in suspension by political order. Nature is included in politics only by being excluded from it, and through its inclusive exclusion the sovereign decision draws a primordial line between what is political and what is not (Smith 2011: 107, 205–6). In general, nature's inclusive exclusion in politics takes the form of nature being reduced to property or resource. By not acknowledging it as properly belonging to the political realm, nature as resource is subjected to all kinds of governmental practices and makes such practices possible at all. In less abstract terms, nature can, for instance, be inclusively excluded as carbon emission reduction credits, as it has been in the global environmental governance emerging from the Kyoto Protocol. Emissions trading, as a form of political practice, is conditioned by carbon first being rendered meaningful as an object readily available for political tinkering. The environmental governance of emissions trading would not have been possible without the separation of nature and politics and the exclusion of carbon from the political realm.

In his work, Agamben pursues the hypothesis that the historical unfolding of sovereign rule has consisted in the constant foregrounding of the exception, whereby in modernity the state of exception has become the rule (cf. Agamben 1998, 2005). In the state of exception, the subjects of political rule are stripped of their political rights, and political life is reduced to bare life. This is a so-called biopolitical process, a process in which political categories and concepts are replaced by those of biological life as the locus of political order, the result of which is a reduction of politics to the management of the life and death of a population. Since sovereign rule operates by suspending political rights and reducing the political being of humans to bare life, Smith (2011: 201) approaches sovereignty as effectively anti-political.

Smith claims that a similar story can be told about nature and our relation to it. Technological development, he argues, has created the conditions for a technological framing of the natural world, which reduces it to resource and property, to a "standing reserve" (*ibid.*: 103–6). The technological reduction of the natural world to a standing reserve and the biopolitical reduction of humans to bare life are intimately linked and mutually reinforcing, since, according to Smith, both are the historical and logical consequences of the sovereign decision.

Given the anti-ecological and anti-political character of the sovereign decision, a truly ecological politics would, according to Smith, have to reject any notion of sovereignty – including natural sovereignty over politics – and affirm the relative autonomy of the human and the non-human world, which would amount to a dual saving of the natural and political world. Notwithstanding significant differences otherwise, Smith's position is comparable to Eckersley's here. Both emphasize that a greening of politics would direct itself towards the dual emancipation of humans and non-human nature. Whereas Eckersley strives for an ethical care for the natural world in the form of human stewardship of nature based on notions of interdependence, Smith – who discards stewardship as yet another form of sovereign domination (*ibid.*: 13–15) – emphasizes the indispensible need for an ethical stance of letting nature be.

In sum, sovereignty according to Smith is both anti-ecological and anti-political. It is anti-ecological because it necessarily reproduces human domination over nature and reduces nature to a standing reserve, and it is anti-political because it suspends political rights and reduces humans to bare life.

Being sympathetic to Smith's insistence to look beyond positive political order in the analysis of sovereignty and sustainability, I do however think he overstates the negative logic of the sovereign decision, and that this has significant consequences for the judgment of sovereignty vis-à-vis sustainability.

In the genealogy of sovereignty from Schmitt to Agamben to Smith, something is lost along the way. For Schmitt, any juridico-political order grounds itself by reference to its exception. Here, the sovereign decision has a cyclical structure; the functional logic of the sovereign decision is that of a revolving movement: "Sovereignty," as Derrida (2005: 13) notes, "is round"; it always expresses itself as a turn and a re-turn to itself. This return directs attention to the positive effects of sovereignty as a form and force of constitution. Here, sovereignty refers to unconditional self-constitution (cf. Derrida 2009: 66), and this self-constitution functions as a decision on the exception. The sovereign decision on the exception is a suspension of *and* a return to juridico-political order. There is a creative side to sovereignty, its negative operation of suspension functioning positively to establish order anew. Eckersley's ambit claim for ecological democracy is an illustrative example hereof; as a sovereign decision it suspends modern anthropocentric order so as to arrive at a new ecocentric order.

Agamben preserves a positive function for the sovereign decision, but because of his insistence on the intimate connection between the sovereign decision and the historical emergence of biopolitics, this positive function is effectively detrimental. Smith downplays the positive element of the sovereign decision even further, ultimately to such an extent that it becomes insignificant. Here, the sovereign decision is understood rather as a purely negative force, a one-way movement away from order. It becomes equated with a tangible declaration of a state of emergency (cf. Smith 2011: 123–5).

Insisting on a positive dimension of the sovereign decision one is less inclined to dismiss it as altogether anti-political. And in terms of sovereignty being anti-political, the critique does not seem overly devastating. Political sovereignty is anti-ecological, argues Smith, because it reproduces a metaphysical distinction between human and the natural world according to which humanity is hierarchically positioned above the natural world. But even though this distinction constantly reappears in the history of Western thought, its historical manifestations are much too intricate and complex to simply be referred to as a uniform perennial relation of human dominion of nature (cf. Glacken 1976; Williams 1980; Evernden 1992; Hadot 2006). Rather than domination, what is accomplished through the anthropological machine is primarily a drawing of distinctions and an establishing of difference between the natural and the human. Considering the complexity of this conceptual distinction, domination over nature seems to be a contingent rather than necessary result of this process. And by insisting on the importance to uphold the relative autonomy of the political and the natural world, Smith himself affirms a version of the anthropological machine.

To emphasize the way in which the sovereign decision on the exception functions as the source of political authority evidently undermines the green appeal of sovereignty. But rather than demonstrating that sovereignty is necessarily anti-ecological and anti-political, by attending to the positive moment in the sovereign decision I have tried to demonstrate that the sovereign decision is indifferent to any environmental concerns. Since "sovereignty decides upon its own limits, its decision cannot be bound by those limits" (Norris 2000: para. 16), and the sovereign decision is therefore constitutively and logically antecedent to any moral axioms or political imperatives whatsoever, green or otherwise. As such, it is best conceived of as ecologically indifferent.

The antinomies of sovereignty

When political rule is understood only in positive terms and sovereignty as contingent facts of governmental operations – as does Eckersley – there seems to be no insurmountable obstacles for greening the state, for turning sovereignty into something ecologically beneficial, and for affirming that states are in fact capable of systematically prioritizing sustainability. But attending to the very configuration of authority engendering positive order and theorizing it as the sovereign suspension of order from within – as does Smith – discloses sovereignty as indifferent to environmental concerns, which disqualifies the possibility of states being capable of such prioritizing.

But rather than being incommensurable, the two approaches to sovereignty and sustainability represented by Eckersley and Smith presuppose each other, and also reveal each others' limits and shortcomings. The positive order emphasized by Eckersley is only possible if the ability of order to suspend itself from within is present as well, and that such suspension is conditioned by the existence of positive order should be quite evident. And whereas Eckersley is implicitly committed to an ecologically indifferent sovereign decision as constitutive of the green state, the positive outcome of such a decision disqualifies Smith's claim that the sovereign decision only functions negatively.

At this theoretical, and admittedly abstract, level, the question of sovereignty and sustainability reaches an impasse here, for the contradictory conclusion to be drawn is that even though a greening of sovereignty and statist political order is possible it will be conditioned by a configuration of political authority indifferent to such concerns as sustainability.

This impasse, and the contradiction upon which it rests, is the reason why the green state and the question of sovereignty and sustainability need to be rethought. I would like to suggest that this rethinking, rather than trying to avoid the impasse, proceeds from it, and in the remainder of this chapter I will sketch the outlines for how this can be done. Below, I will show how positive order and sovereign decision can be conceived of as antinomies, the way in which Kant used this term. My suggestion for advancing the debate on the green state beyond this impasse is to engage with positive order and sovereign decision in the way Kant engaged with antinomies in his philosophy.

As a first step in this endeavor, I suggest that the two takes on sovereignty represented by Eckersley and Smith be reconceived of and posited as referring to different aspects of political order, both of which are equally valid and necessary for the intelligibility and coherence of the concept and experience of sovereignty. As a consequence, the contradiction they expose is also recast as inherent to sovereignty itself.

Drawing on Prozorov (2005), I propose political order be conceptualized as consisting of a positive manifestation – positive political order – and a sovereign decision relating to positive order as an excess. The excess is something of a Derridean supplement. A supplement is both the addition of a surplus and a compensation for an internal lack (Derrida 1981: 42–3; 1997: 144–5). It is both constitutive and transgressive (Prozorov 2005: 84); it grounds and disrupts, it creates wholes as well as making final self-immanence impossible. As an example, returning once again to the ambit claim suggested by Eckersley, it could be noted that the excess enters as that which suspends the current political order and constitutes an ecological green state. The very constitution of a green state is not part of that green state, this being a result of the circumstance that order itself is not ordered, that a structuring principle is never itself structured. In this sense, the excess constitutes. But it also transgresses; it is also that which disrupts order and historically dissolves it. For instance, should the ambit claim be realized and institutionalized, its realization would proceed from a moment in which the excess would transgress the current political order. Likewise, that power which once had constituted the green state by suspending the old order would throughout its existence threaten its continuation. The same power that once awakened it can always put it back to sleep. Since rule by law can always suspend itself – any law-making body can declare that the laws that it has established no longer apply – political order is always threatened from within. For this reason, the excess is not only constitutive, but also transgressive. Being a necessary excess to positive order, the sovereign decision indicates that there is always something that is not and cannot be captured by order, something that does not belong to it.

Three characteristics define the relation between positive order and its excess (Prozorov 2005). First, the sovereign decision is the condition of possibility of positive order; positive order is founded on the sovereign decision on the exception. Second, positive order functions and is maintained by the constant suppression of the excess. As noted by Agamben, the sovereign decision provides meaning to what is ordered, and thus allows for experience to be ordered by determining it. It entails a move away from indeterminate to determined being, and since the normal functioning of order proceeds as the suppression of its excess, this normal functioning amounts to positive order functioning principally as the complete determination of everything. Third, positive order is always undermined by its excess, which also provides the basis of its eventual suspension and change.

With such a grasp of political order, according to which it necessarily consists of a positive manifestation and a constitutive as well as transgressive excess of that order, positive order and sovereign decision emerge as perennial and irreducible components of any political order whatsoever. Thus, sovereignty as such could be said to consist "in the relation of exteriority between the positivity of order and its constitutive transgression" (*ibid.*: 87). Here, sovereignty becomes a perennial characteristic of politics as such, and political experience becomes fully circumscribed by the traversal functions of the sovereign decision. This relational take on sovereignty also exposes its contradictory nature. For insofar as the sovereign decision entails a move away from indetermination to determination, and positive order in its normal functioning in principle is the complete determination of everything, the excess's constant and necessary undermining of positive order from within affirms the impossibility of final determination. Sovereignty, then, functions as the complete determination of being while also affirming being's indetermination. The sovereign decision puts things in place; it brings order to what would otherwise be unruly chaotic existence, and it has the power to bring order to chaos in any way possible. Therefore, in order for sovereignty to do this, being in general must be indeterminate. Thus, sovereignty, in its operative logic, presupposes and affirms being as indeterminate. I would even venture to suggest that it is this contradiction which pushes current thinking on sovereignty and sustainability towards deadlock, for whereas Eckersley's emphasis on positive order indicates that order can be determined so as to be sensitive towards the natural world, the sovereign decision this presupposes, by confirming that things could always be otherwise, constantly threatens such determination.

To posit positive order and sovereign decision as equally necessary for the intelligibility of political order *tout court* means they are irreducible to each other. Both are needed for the coherence of sovereignty. In order for sovereignty to make sense, one needs to account for both positive political order and the constitution and eventual transgression of that order. But positive order and sovereign decision also engender contradiction, as argued above. They are mutually conflicting, each being the opponent of the other. Because of this uneasy relationship, being both equally necessary for the intelligibility of sovereignty and mutually conflicting, it is reasonable to approach them as antinomies. The way it is used by Kant, antinomies refer to equally valid but mutually conflicting principles. And this, I argue, is what we are dealing with when we are confronting positive order and sovereign decision. They are the antinomies of sovereignty.

Antinomies are crucial in the philosophical methodology Kant deploys in developing his transcendental idealism, and having recast positive order and sovereign decision as perennial and irreducible characteristics of political order as such, I would like to suggest that the second and final step for opening up a way to rethink the green state and sovereignty consists in a return to Kant as a historical precedent for how to constructively engage with antinomy. This return will show that notwithstanding their necessity for the intelligibility of political order, positive order and sovereign decision can be treated as a kind of necessary illusion, and that they do not necessarily exhaust our thinking on politics.

Kant famously claimed that human knowledge of the world is guaranteed by the universal categorical structure of our cognitive faculties. We provide for ourselves the condition of possibility for our own knowledge, he argued, and in this respect we are transcendental subjects. In his philosophy, a correspondence between subject and object is substituted by a view of humans as epistemologically active and constructive. Kant's "essential discovery," writes Deleuze (2008: 12), "is that the faculty of knowledge is legislative ... The rational being thus discovers that he has new powers". Kant's message, Deleuze continues, is "that it is we who are giving orders ... we are the legislators of nature" (*ibid.*).

Kant's antinomies of reason consist of a series of mutually incompatible but internally plausible statements about the natural world. Reason, Kant argues, runs into these contradictions in its incessant push towards and beyond its own limits (Kant 1998: 459–95). In order to avoid such contradictions as 'the world has a beginning' and 'the world has no beginning' (Kant's first antinomy) – for which reason can provide equally valid proofs and disqualifications – one must accept the distinction between things in themselves and things as they appear for the human subject, and further that claims about the world refer only to things as they appear for us, not to things in themselves. The antinomies of reason arise because the world and its appearances are thought to be things in themselves, but once this illusion is abandoned and it is accepted that appearances are "nothing outside our representations" they simply dissolve (*ibid*.: 518–19).

Kant's resolution of this kind of contradiction proceeds neither by proving or rejecting either position, nor by introducing a third alternative in a dialectical synthesis. Instead, it disqualifies them altogether by claiming that their presuppositions are illusions thought to be real. And this disqualification can only be achieved when the contradictory statements are engaged with on their own terms.

But in Kant's philosophy, antinomies do not merely describe contradictory statements about the world, they play a much more important role (cf. Karatani 2003: 50). Transcendental idealism as a whole can in fact be grasped as having been developed through Kant's engagement with rationalism and empiricism as illusory antinomies (*ibid*.: 4). By setting up rationalism and empiricism as antinomies, Kant proceeds from their conflictual relation in order to formulate his transcendental idealism. Likewise, I suggest that the debate on the green state should proceed by treating positive order and sovereign decision in a similar fashion in order to arrive at something new. Therefore, a slight detour in pre-Kantian philosophy is in order.

Rationalism extends knowledge beyond experience by postulating eternal truths, thereby providing knowledge with a foundation securing it from the limitations of finite subjective experience. But such truths cannot be proven, only asserted, and since one can always posit more fundamental truths, the rationalist position ultimately results in an infinite regress of deeper truths or to a dogmatic assertion of God (Williams 1992: 101–2). Empiricism, on its part, limits knowledge to experience. But despite enabling a critique of rationalism, once knowledge is restricted to experience, it becomes impossible to claim any positive truths – especially regarding the future – since that would require extending knowledge beyond experience. And what is even more troublesome, the empiricist refusal to accept truths beyond experience is itself a rationalist claim (*ibid*.: 102–4).

Again, Kant's solution to these predicaments is to accept that objects of human intuition are not things in themselves but rather appearances, and to claim that knowledge is not of things in themselves but of things as they appear for us. According to Kant, human understanding provides to itself its own categories for making sense of the world, which means that cognition does not arise entirely from experience. Instead, it arises as a composite of what we experience and what our own faculties provide out of themselves (Kant 1998: 136). According to this view of an epistemologically creative subject, the antinomies of rationalism and empiricism are disqualified on the basis that they wrongfully ascribe to things in themselves attributes only belonging to things as they appear for us.

It is in this way Kant engages with the antinomies his philosophy intends to solve. Karatani (2003: 4) maintains that Kant was not "simply thinking from a place between" the poles of rationalism and empiricism. Instead, he "performed a critical oscillation":

He continuously confronted the dominant rationalism with empiricism, and the dominant empiricism with rationalism. The Kantian critique exists within this movement itself. The transcendental critique is not some kind of stable third position. It cannot exist without a transversal and transpositional movement.

(Karatani 2003: 4)

Kant refuses to reduce either pole of the confronted antinomies to the other, nor does he synthesize their opposition dialectically. Instead, he oscillates between them, and it is through this movement his own position of transcendental idealism is constructed. As such, the illusions of the antinomies of reason, themselves necessarily occurring due to reason's drive towards and beyond its own limits, are necessary for the emergence of the philosophical position that dissolves them. And the antinomies of rationalism and empiricism are similarly necessary for the development of transcendental idealism.

That which is transcendental exists only as a function (Karatani 2003: 34) – thus, it is not empirical – and the transcendental subject is "the unity of all the conditions under which something appears ... to each empirical subject" (Deleuze 1978). Kant's critical gesture consists in the constant oscillation between two contradictory poles and in the exploration of the gap "that is exposed through difference" (Karatani 2003: 3), and "the 'transcendental' points to something in this gap, a new dimension which cannot be reduced to either of the two positive terms between which the gap is gaping" (Žižek 2006: 21). By affirming the irreducibility of the antinomy of rationalism and empiricism, the irreducibility of the gap between them is also affirmed, and through the explorative transversal oscillation between the two poles, the transcendental subject and Kant's critical philosophy as a whole emerges, and with that a move beyond impasse is made possible. Likewise, a move away from the impasse of greening sovereignty only by affirming it as indifferent to ecological concern is possible, it seems, if positive order and sovereign decision are engaged with in an analogous manner.

The green state beyond the antinomies of sovereignty

The contradiction inherent to sovereignty of functioning as the complete determination of being while also affirming the indetermination of being resonates within the current debate on the green state. It pushes the debate towards the impasse of having to accept that despite sound arguments about the possibility of a green statist political order, that order would be constituted by an ecologically indifferent sovereign decision. According to this view, the state actually does seem incapable of systematically prioritizing sustainability, and for this reason, the green state and its grounding in sovereignty needs to be rethought.

I have suggested that one way to proceed in thinking the green state and sovereignty anew is to recast positive order and sovereign decision as antinomies of political order and to treat them as Kant treated antinomies in his philosophy. Much like Kant's transcendental idealism was constructed by affirming the irreducibility of the antinomies of rationalism and empiricism as well as the gap between them, and like the transcendental subject was extracted from within this gap, I suggest the antinomies of positive order and sovereign decision be treated in the same way in the rethinking of the green state. For Kant, the antinomies of reason were illusions, but they were necessary illusions, necessary because reason is inclined to understand the world in such a way that they arise (Kant 1998: 386), and necessary because without them, Kant's own philosophy and its ability to move beyond paralyzing contradiction would not have been possible (Karatani 2003). Analogously, I suggest the antinomies of positive order and sovereign decision be treated as irreducible necessary illusions. My suggestion is not to abandon sovereignty as a concept in the political theory of the green state. Quite the opposite, since only its affirmation allows for its contradictory composition to be transcended. What should be abandoned, however, is the impression that positive order and sovereign decision fully exhaust the intelligibility of political order. The contradiction of sovereignty can be dealt with through an engagement with positive order and the sovereign decision, proceeding as a constant oscillation between the two. This could provide a way beyond the impasse of greening the state only by affirming the ecological indifference of the sovereign decision. By exploring the gap between positive order and sovereign decision, we might find something in-between them that would engender a conceptualization of a state actually capable of systematically prioritizing sustainability.

Note

1 Litfin (1998a) is an exception.

References

Agamben, G., 1998 *Homo Sacer: Sovereign Power and Bare Life*. Stanford University Press, Stanford, CA.
Agamben, G., 2004 *The Open: Man and Animal*. Stanford University Press, Stanford, CA.
Agamben, G., 2005 *State of Exception*. University of Chicago Press, Chicago, IL.
Barry, J., 1999 *Rethinking Green Politics: Nature, Virtue and Progress*. Sage, London.
Barry, J., and Eckersley, R., 2005 An introduction to reinstating the state. In Barry, J., and Eckersley, R., (eds) *The State and the Global Ecological Crisis* ix–xxv. MIT Press, Cambridge, MA.
Bartelson, J., 1995 *A Genealogy of Sovereignty*. Cambridge University Press, Cambridge.
Christoff, P., 1996 Ecological modernisation, ecological modernities. *Environmental Politics* 5: 476–500.
Christoff, P., 2005 Out of chaos, a shining star? Toward a typology of green states. In Barry, J., and Eckersley, R., (eds) *The State and the Global Ecological Crisis* 25–52. MIT Press, Cambridge, MA.
Conca, K., 1994 Rethinking the ecology–sovereignty debate. *Millennium* 23: 701–11.
Deleuze, G., 1978 Kant: synthesis and time, part I. Lecture held 14 March 1978. Retrieved March 16, 2014 from www.webdeleuze.com/php/texte.php?cle=66&groupe=Kant&langue=2.

Deleuze, G., 2008 *Kant's Critical Philosophy: The Doctrine of the Faculties*. Continuum, London.

Derrida, J., 1981 *Positions*. University of Chicago Press, Chicago, IL.

Derrida, J., 1997 *Of Grammatology*. Johns Hopkins University Press, Baltimore, MD.

Derrida, J., 2005 *Rogues*. Stanford University Press, Stanford, CA.

Derrida, J., 2009 *The Beast and the Sovereign*, vol. I. University of Chicago Press, Chicago, IL.

Eckersley, R., 1992 *Environmentalism and Political Theory: Toward an Ecocentric Approach*. State University of New York Press, Albany, NY.

Eckersley, R., 2000 Deliberative democracy, ecological representation and risk: towards a democracy of the affected. In Saward, M., (ed) *Democratic Innovation: Deliberation, representation and association* 117–32. Routledge, London.

Eckersley, R., 2004 *The Green State: Rethinking Democracy and Sovereignty*. MIT Press, Cambridge, MA.

Eckersley, R., 2005 Greening the nation-state: from exclusive to inclusive sovereignty. In Barry, J., and Eckersley, R., (eds) *The State and the Global Ecological Crisis* 159–80. MIT Press, Cambridge, MA.

Eckersley, R., 2006 The state as gatekeeper: a reply. *Politics and Ethics Review* 2: 127–38.

Evernden, N., 1992 *The Social Creation of Nature*. Johns Hopkins University Press, Baltimore, MD.

Glacken, CJ., 1976 *Traces on the Rhodian Shore: Nature and Culture in Western Thought from Ancient Times to the End of the Eighteenth Century*. University of California Press, Berkeley, CA.

Hadot, P., 2006 *The Veil of Isis: An Essay on the History of the Idea of Nature*. Belknap, Cambridge, MA.

Kant, I., 1998 *Critique of Pure Reason*. Cambridge University Press, Cambridge.

Karatani, K., 2003 *Transcritique: On Kant and Marx*. MIT Press, Cambridge, MA.

Lafferty, W.M., 2000 Democracy and ecological rationality: new trials for an old ceremony. In Lachapelle, G., and Trent, J., (eds) *Globalization, Governance and Identity: The Emergence of New Partnerships* 39–65. Les Presses de l'Université de Montréal, Montreal.

Litfin, K.T., (ed) 1998a *The Greening of Sovereignty in World Politics*. MIT Press, Cambridge, MA.

Litfin, K.T., 1998b The greening of sovereignty: an introduction. In Litfin K.T. (ed) *The Greening of Sovereignty in World Politics* 1–27. MIT Press, Cambridge, MA.

Lundqvist L.J., 2001 A green fist in a velvet glove: the ecological state and sustainable development. *Environmental Values* 10: 455–72.

Meadowcroft, J., 2005 From the welfare state to ecostate. In Barry, J., and Eckersley, R., (eds) *The State and the Global Ecological Crisis* 3–23. MIT Press, Cambridge, MA.

Meadowcroft, J., 2006 Greening the state. *Politics and Ethics Review* 2: 109–18.

Meadowcroft, J., 2012 Greening the state? In Steinberg, P.F., and VanDeveer, S.D., (eds) *Comparative Environmental Politics: Theory, Practice, and Prospects* 63–87. MIT Press, Cambridge, MA.

Norris, A., 2000 Carl Schmitt's political metaphysics: on the secularization of 'the outermost sphere.' *Theory and Event* 4(1). Available from http://muse.jhu.edu/login?auth=0&type=summary&url=/journals/theory_and_event/v004/4.1norris.html.

Prozorov, S., 2005 X/Xs: toward a general theory of the exception. *Alternatives: Global, Local, Political* 30: 81–111.

Saward, M., 1998 Green state/democratic state. *Contemporary Politics* 4: 345–56.

Schmitt, C., 2005 *Political Theology: Four Chapters on the Concept of Sovereignty*. University of Chicago Press, Chicago, IL.

Smith, M., 2009 Against ecological sovereignty: Agamben, politics and globalisation. *Environmental Politics* 18: 99–116.

Smith, M., 2011 *Against Ecological Sovereignty: Ethics, Biopolitics, and Saving the Natural World*. University of Minnesota Press, Minneapolis, MN.

Vogler, J., 2006 Green statehood and environmental crisis. *Politics and Ethics Review* 2: 101–8.

Walker, R.B.J., 1993 *Inside/Outside: International Relations as Political Theory*. Cambridge University Press, Cambridge.

Wendt, A., and Duvall, R., 2008 Sovereignty and the UFO. *Political Theory* 36: 607–33.

Williams, M.C., 1992 Reason and realpolitik: Kant's 'critique of international politics.' *Canadian Journal of Political Science* 25: 99–119.

Williams, R., 1980 Ideas of nature. In his *Problems in Materialism and Culture: Selected Essays* 67–85. Verso, London.

Žižek, S., 2006 *The Parallax View*. MIT Press, Cambridge, MA.

Part II
Performance of the green state in a comparative perspective

5 Green states in Europe

A comparative view

Max Koch and Martin Fritz

Introduction

In its '2020 Strategy,' the European Union (EU) intends to combine Research and Development, education, employment and poverty targets with climate change and energy benchmarks. The EU aims to reduce greenhouse gas emissions by 20 percent by 2020 (30% if the conditions are right) relative to 1990. Energy from renewables and energy efficiency are both planned to increase by 20 percent in the same period (European Commission 2010). To achieve these targets, the EU applies a 'green growth' or ecological modernization approach. The incorporation of environmental goals such as climate change mitigation into the overall growth strategy has led to a renaissance of state socio-economic and environmental regulation and indeed to a 'return to planning' (Giddens 2009). Giddens represents the academic mainstream in regarding an active state as necessary to set goals and targets, manage risks, promote industrial policy, realign prices and counter negative business interests. He argues that, especially in the circumstances of the financial crisis, economic recovery presupposes public investment, and that this should be targeted towards energy security and low-carbon infrastructures. By reducing energy and material costs and the West's reliance on the fragile geopolitics of energy supply, the provision of jobs in the expanding 'green' sector and meeting carbon emission reduction targets, EU policy-makers intend to achieve synergy between economic, ecological and social welfare goals.

When applying the EU 2020 strategy and 'green growth' policies, EU member states have to deal with contradictory goals. While institutional path-dependency and technological lock-in effects bind them to the pursuit of economic growth, governments find themselves having to intervene to protect the common good from the incursions of the market. For example, governments promote consumer freedoms in the quest for economic growth, on the one hand, and protect social goods and defend ecological limits, on the other. Ecological challenges such as climate change suggest a qualitatively different environmental regulation and welfare policy governance, which would need to integrate the redistribution of carbon emissions, work, time, income and wealth (Gough and Meadowcroft 2011). Social policies will not only need to address the inequalities and conflicts that emerge in the circumstances of the financial crisis, it will be increasingly necessary to formulate them in accordance with environmental goals and with acceptance from the electorate. Dryzek *et al.* (2003) argue that social democratic welfare states are better placed to handle the intersection of social and environmental policies than other welfare state types (see also Gough *et al.* 2008); in other words, what we in what follows refer to as the 'synergy hypothesis' claims that in social democratic welfare regimes the relationship between environmental and welfare policies is less conflictual than in conservative and liberal regimes. The green state is assumed to develop on top of and in consonance with already existing state welfare institutions. In order to test this hypothesis we apply correspondence and cluster analyses on macro-structural welfare and ecology indicators for 28 European countries. We investigate two points in time, 1995 and 2010, and are thus able to also track temporal changes: are there indications that social democratic welfare states move towards becoming green states, and, if so, are they doing this in more pronounced ways than conservative and liberal welfare states? And is this reflected in ecological key indicators such as the ecological footprint and CO_2 emissions per capita? First, we review relevant state theories with an emphasis on welfare regimes and environmental performance, and then we scrutinize the synergy hypothesis in comparative empirical research. The following sections deal with the indicators and methods, present the results of the analyses and discuss policy implications as well as possibilities for future research.

Theorizing the state, welfare regimes and environmental performance

In capitalist economies, processes of production and wealth creation are structurally separated from the political processes of exercising coercive power and administrative control (Koch 2008). Karl Marx, in particular, has linked the autonomous existence of the state to the structural prerequisites of an economy based on the circulation of commodities (Marx 1973: 243). The respect of the principle of equivalence in exchange relations depends on a formally independent institution that guarantees the legal and economic independence of the owners of commodities: their equality, legal security and protection. In the case of an advanced division of labor, this guarantee cannot be ensured in accordance with common law but must be institutionalized in an independent third party that, above all, monopolizes the legitimate use of physical force (Weber 1991: 78): the modern state as rule of law. Exchange relations, however, are not reduced to the exchange of material features of use values. They also reproduce social relationships, which involve power asymmetries and social inequalities. The latter originate in different societal domains and take the form of class, race, religion, linguistic or gender characteristics. In a social structure based on a dynamic plurality of exploitative and exclusionary relationships (Koch 2006: 13–16), the state is the main location for the political regulation of conflicts and for the maintenance of social order (Offe 1984). Since, without state regulation, such a society would disintegrate, a further indispensable task of the state is to maintain a minimum of social cohesion and, at the same time, the legitimization of remaining inequalities.

In temporarily harmonizing conflicting group interests and creating consensus (Gallas *et al.* 2011), the state appears as an autonomous political sphere, where social classes and groups represent their interests in indirect and mediated ways. As political parties and interest groups raise variable issues such as religion, age, and the environment, these interests and issues are sometimes in the focus of government action, only to be superseded by others at later points in time. State policies cannot be reduced to the strategic interests of single actors, but rather develop as a result of the heterogeneity and changing dynamic of social forces that influence state institutions. The nature of the composition of social forces that are able to influence state policies in particular historical configurations cannot be defined in general terms, but must be explored empirically.[1] Once such a coalition of relatively powerful actors is formed and has managed to influence the general direction of the state's policies, it takes the character of a relatively homogenous social phenomenon and appears to 'act' as if it were a single actor: the more socially coherent the coalition of forces that influences the state, the lesser the contradictions across its policies (Poulantzas 1978). Hence, the state is an object of agency of the socio-political coalition that creates and recreates it, and, at the same time, a powerful actor, whose policies shape a range of societal fields. It is, to borrow Bourdieu's terms, structured *and* structuring at once.

The welfare state is no exception to this rule. The extent to which labor power is 'decommodified' (Esping-Andersen 1990), and institutional protection of workers from total dependence for survival on employers is provided, reflects power asymmetries in the social structure, particularly class relations, and varies across the OECD world. For example, the provision of an indirect wage such as a minimum income by the state eases the pressure on the direct wage and trade unions in collective bargaining processes. This protection might be negotiated in collective agreements, but is, at least in relation to minimum standards, guaranteed by state regulation. Welfare regimes take different forms and vary, above all, in terms of the particular division of labor of private and public provision (Arts and Gelissen 2002). Relatively generous welfare regimes with correspondingly high extents of 'decommodification' tend to strengthen the position of workers and facilitate the set up and maintenance of institutionally coordinated industrial relations, while less generous regimes often coincide with weakly coordinated and more 'individualized' industrial relations systems (Koch 2005).

From the perspective of materialist state theory, both social and environmental policies appear as political responses to long-term societal trends related to capitalist development, industrialization and (sub)urbanization (Koch 2012). Both modify these processes through regulation, fiscal transfers and other measures. Exploring and analyzing these policy interactions and their complex institutional coordination is a relatively new research field (Gough 2011). A developing body of literature addresses the distributive consequences and implications of environmental policies for social justice and social policy.

Different societal groups have different responsibilities for ecological issues and suffer different impacts. Indeed, responsibilities and impacts sometimes work in opposite ways to constitute a 'double injustice' (Walker 2012), since the groups and populations likely to be most harmed by environmental issues are the least responsible for causing them and have the least resources to cope with the consequences (Büchs *et al.* 2012). There have also been comparative studies to understand state strategies in relation to environmental performances. Even as early as 1999, Scruggs suggested comparative advantages of corporatism as opposed to pluralism in dealing with environmental issues (Scruggs 1999).

More recently, and in relation to greenhouse gas emissions, Christoff and Eckersley (2011) found that domestic political institutions (proportional representation and presence of green parties in parliament and government) and corporatist systems that include business and labor play an important role in the explanation of states' environmental performance. Furthermore, the study pointed out that while national vulnerability to climate change is a poor indicator, both reliance on fossil fuel extraction and energy-intensive industry heightens opposition to carbon reduction. Of further significance are the ideological discourses on environmental issues. Depending on how these discourses are framed at the national level, they can "give rise to quite different cost/benefit calculations" (*ibid.*: 442). More specifically, Görg (2003) asserts that what actually counts as 'environmentally relevant' is variable over time and across space and thus must be identified as an object of research in the context of changing societal integration and regulation patterns. Societal power relations and the corresponding discourse patterns define which ecological facts and processes are perceived as 'problems' and deserve to be tackled. For example, the question of whether climate change is occurring at all, whether it should be viewed as a serious issue and what could be done about it, is part of struggles for hegemony among opposing interest groups with different power resources (Koch 2012: 36–45).

Yet another stream in the existing literature that is of particular relevance for this chapter suggests that different welfare regimes (Esping-Andersen 1990; Arts and Gelissen 2002) implement environmental policies and the 'green' dimension of the state with different rates of success. Esping-Andersen's pioneering research into the different ways in which the state's welfare and social policies 'decommodify' the commodity character of the labor power by guaranteeing a decent standard of living without market participation resulted in three samples or 'worlds of welfare' of OECD countries: he characterized the 'social democratic' countries (for example Sweden, Norway and Austria) by the highest degree of universalism in welfare programs that offered the highest amounts of redistribution and decommodification potential including a weak role of the market in care for children and the elderly; 'liberal countries' such as the US, the UK or Ireland offered the lowest decommodification potential and a corresponding emphasis on individual responsibility in combination with a greater welfare role of private agencies, charities, churches, employers and unions. The primary goal of public welfare is here not redistribution but the restoration of individuals' and families' self-sufficiency; countries with a Bismarckian welfare tradition (for example Germany or Switzerland) were called 'conservative' because state welfare policies, unemployment and pension policies, in particular, were not designed to redistribute market inequalities but tended to confirm and reinforce market-based differences in unemployment and pension benefits. The conservative welfare regime also tended to reproduce the traditional 'male-breadwinner' model. Later welfare regime typologies that included greater numbers of countries confirmed rather than falsified Esping-Andersen's approach, insofar as they proposed four or five regimes instead of the original three, yet with significant overlap in the allocation of countries (Arts and Gelissen 2002).

According to researchers such as Dryzek *et al.* (2003) and Gough *et al.* (2008), social democratic welfare states are better placed to manage the intersection of social and environmental policies than more liberal market economies and welfare regimes. One reason Dryzek *et al.* mention is the discourse on 'ecological modernization' and the idea that environmental policies can be good for business, which they assume to be especially widespread in the Nordic countries. This discourse would presuppose the capacity of the state to coordinate markets. Rather than trusting in the invisible hand of the market, social democratic welfare regimes would generally make a conscious and coordinated effort and regard economic and ecological values as mutually reinforcing. The "contemporary result" would be the "mainstreaming of both environmental and equality concerns across all areas of government in Northern Europe" (Gough *et al.* 2008: 330). However, Gough and colleagues also open up for the possibility that environmental policies do not develop in synergy but in conflict with social policies, thereby weakening traditional concerns of social justice. They emphasize that the 'green state' may "demand a re-allocation of government expenditure to compensate its victims ... or develop low-polluting forms of energy production" (*ibid.*: 334). They also point to the 'double injustice' as described above by suggesting that many policies that make sense from an environmental perspective "hurt the poor disproportionately. Thus a clash between environmental and social policy looms" (*ibid.*).

Similarly, Meadowcroft (2005) argues that there is a range of linkages between social and environmental policies that together have the potential of bringing about sustainable development. Meadowcroft (in Gough *et al.* 2008) outlines that it was four decades ago when advanced states began to "build up highly complex systems of environmental rule." It would therefore make "sense today to refer to the emergence of an environmental state ... much as we talk about the historical development of the welfare state" (*ibid.*: 331). Yet there are also differences in the developments of the welfare state and the green state. The latter state is "new and weakly institutionally embedded. Environmental functions have been grafted onto state structures that were developed for other purposes (security, economic management and welfare provision), and the economic interests associated with environmental protection remain less developed than those in other domains. Unsurprisingly, struggles over the distribution of the costs and benefits of environmental intervention (and non-intervention) form a central feature of environmental politics and policy" (*ibid.*). Meadowcroft stresses that the "environmental state takes somewhat different forms in varied national contexts" and that there is "no elegant typology of environmental states equivalent to the well-known classification of welfare states" (*ibid.*). This is partly due to the fact that the green state has been "layered on top of well-established economic variants ('forms of capitalism'), political-institutional set-ups, and welfare-state types. National environmental states are strongly coloured by what has gone before" (*ibid.*: 331–2).

There are therefore theoretical reasons to assume that social democratic welfare regimes provide a better institutional basis for the introduction and development of the 'green' dimension of the state than conservative and liberal welfare regimes. However, Gough and others seem to agree that the institutional basis provided by social democratic welfare regime is no guarantee that green states de facto develop in synergy with the welfare state. In fact, all authors in Gough *et al.* (2008) mention the possibility of competition, clashes and conflicts between welfare and environmental policies. This possibility is even more emphasized by environmental economists such as Victor (2008), Jackson (2009) and Daly and Farley (2009), who question both the synergy hypothesis of the welfare and green dimension of the state and the 'green growth' policy option that follows from it (Koch 2013). Instead, these authors regard the welfare and environmental performance of a country primarily as a reflection of its development in economic terms, that is, of GDP growth. Hence, while 'green growth' and 'ecological modernization' discourses claim that the pursuit of economic growth can be compatible with sustainable development and the IPCC climate targets by building on existing (welfare) institutions, 'no-growth' and 'degrowth' theories, and the mentioned environmental economists would regard economic growth itself as the problem. GDP growth would need to be deprioritized in policy making across the advanced capitalist world – that is, irrespective of welfare affiliation – in order to allow for efficient environmental policy making and achieve sustainability (Fritz and Koch 2014). Whether or not synergy or conflict prevails, and whether or not social democratic welfare regimes indeed facilitate the creation of such synergy, cannot be decided on a merely theoretical level. It is instead an empirical question how the welfare and green dimensions of the state vary comparatively across Europe, to which we will turn next.[2]

Countries, indicators and method of analysis

We collected data for 28 European countries and two points in time (1995 and 2010). According to Esping-Andersen's original classification, the countries belong to one of the three welfare regimes: *social democratic* countries are Austria, Belgium, Denmark, the Netherlands, Norway and Sweden; *conservative* countries are Finland, France, Germany, Italy and Switzerland; *liberal* countries are Ireland and the UK. In addition, we included Luxembourg, a sample of eastern European countries (Bulgaria, Czech Republic, Estonia, Hungary, Poland, Romania, Slovak Republic and Slovenia), as well as a group of 'southern European' or 'Mediterranean' states (Turkey, Greece, Portugal and Spain).

In order to comparatively explore the relationships between welfare and ecology indicators across European states, we operationalized these two concepts as follows. In relation to the 'welfare' dimension of the state we followed Esping-Andersen's (1990) classical example and considered *stratification/inequality* using the Gini index for income inequality, and the degree of *decommodification* measured by the overall expenditures for social protection as percentage of GDP (see also Arts and Gelissen 2002: 141–2). With respect to the 'green' dimension of the state we measured *ecological performance* in terms of electricity generated from renewable sources as percent of gross electricity consumption, CO_2 emissions per capita and national ecological footprints. While renewable energy and CO_2 emissions are indicators directly linked to climate change, the ecological footprint is a more general indicator assessing the overall environmental impact of countries (or any other entity). Among other things it includes consumption patterns and land use. We further considered *green regulation* in terms of environmental taxes as a percentage of GDP and the share of seats green parties hold in national parliaments (lower houses).[3] Green taxes increase the costs for ecological harmful practices by companies and households and can thus be used to correct market failures (Jacobs 2012). According to the synergy hypothesis, such regulations can be expected to be highest in social democratic and lowest in liberal welfare regimes, where the trust in 'market solutions' is generally stronger. Finally, we considered the parliamentary representation of green parties. Previous studies (Christoff and Eckersley 2011) indicated that the extent to which this is the case has a significant impact on governments' decision to introduce ecological policies.

In order to empirically understand the relations between the welfare and green dimensions at country level we used correspondence analysis. This method allows for visually depicting latent structures and correlations within maps (Blasius and Greenacre 2006; Greenacre 2007). To give every indicator and every country the same weight, the macro data is standardized through the use of the two-step procedure of ranking and doubling.[4] In total, we compiled and analyzed data for seven indicators (two for the welfare dimension and five for the green state, which we collected from Eurostat (2013), the World Bank (2013), the Comparative Political Data Set III (Armingeon *et al.* 2013) and the Global Footprint Network (2013). See Table 5.2 in the appendix to this chapter for further details of the data and their sources.

We interpret the resulting maps as follows (see Blasius and Graeff 2009):

- The greater the distance of a variable or country from the centroid, which depicts the overall average of all 28 countries, the stronger is its contribution to the respective axis within the two-dimensional map. If, for example, the indicator *Ecological Footprint* is on the first dimension furthest from the centroid, this dimension is mostly determined by 'footprint-differences' between the countries.
- The correlation between two indicators is expressed by the angle of their trajectories in the map, whereby a 90° angle reflects complete independence

or the absence of a correlation between variables (0° represents a perfect positive correlation and 180° a perfect negative).

- Both distances between variables and distances between countries are interpreted as associations: the closer two variables or two countries are located in the map the more similar they are. If, for example, *Footprint* is close, that is, similar, to *Environmental Taxes* but far, that is, dissimilar, from *GINI*, this indicates a pattern of the *Ecological Footprint* being higher in countries where also environmental taxes are relative high but where the GINI is lower.
- The doubling and ranking procedure results in two endpoints for each variable/indicator, a positive and a negative one (indicated as _hi and _lo), which are both depicted in the maps and which are perfectly mirrored by the centroid. If, for example, *GINI_hi* (the positive endpoint of inequality indicating the highest degree of inequality) appears at $x = 1$ and $y = 1$ in the map, *GINI_lo* (the negative endpoint of inequality indicating the lowest inequality) is located at $x = -1$ and $y = -1$.

Empirical results

The situation in 1995

Figure 5.1 displays the results for 1995.[5] For better visualization, we inserted two dotted lines, which represent the latent dimensions of the associated indicators. The indicators 'renewable energy' and 'CO_2 emissions' are negatively correlated and appear in the upper right and lower left quadrant of the map. This finding depicts the expectable pattern that higher shares of renewable energy, which are substituting fossil types of energy production, are associated with relatively few CO_2 emissions. We call this relationship 'Climate Friendliness' and illustrate it by the first dotted line. The latent dimension depicted by the second dotted line involves all other indicators. These take the form of a complex interplay we call 'Welfare and Ecological Damage' in the maps. It contains three aspects; first, the well-known welfare relationship between relatively low inequality and relatively high social expenditure. Second, 'Green regulation,' measured by the influence of green parties and the level of green taxes, is positively correlated with welfare. The tendency of more generous welfare states to foster high levels of state regulation also appears to exist in the area of ecology. Hence, up to this point, the synergy hypothesis is supported. This does not apply for the third aspect within the complex nexus of the second latent dimension, since relatively high levels of welfare and green regulation are, at the same time, strongly associated with a huge ecological footprint.

The fact that the ecological footprint as an indicator for human appropriation of ecosystem products and services (Borucke *et al.* 2013) tends to increase where also the welfare dimension is relatively advanced, contradicts the synergy hypothesis rather fundamentally. The opposite seems to be true: advanced welfare regulation reflects an advanced degree of socio-economic development,

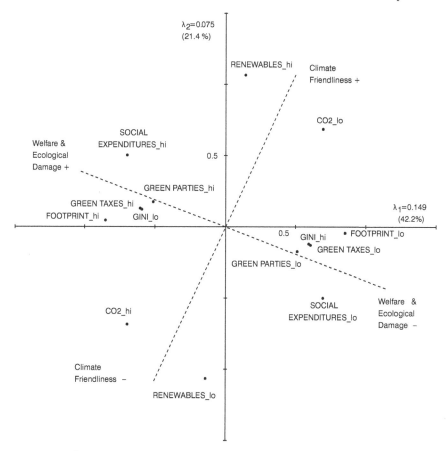

Figure 5.1 Climate friendliness, welfare and ecological damage in Europe in 1995

which has not, at least not yet, been sufficiently decoupled from environmental stress and involves a very high and unsustainable material standard of living. This finding confirms previous studies that found some evidence for relative decoupling (decline in the ecological intensity per unit of economic output) in advanced Western countries, while no evidence whatsoever could be provided for absolute decoupling (where resource efficiencies fall at least as fast as economic output increase; Jackson 2009: 48–50; Koch 2012: 122–5). The nearly 90° angle between the two dotted lines in Figure 5.1 indicates that 'climate friendliness' is statistically independent from the nexus of welfare, state regulation and overall environmental stress. While this indeed suggests the possibility that advanced socio-economic development can be reconciled with ambitious climate goals, it is far more challenging to break the strong link between the (material) standard of living and ecological damages in general.

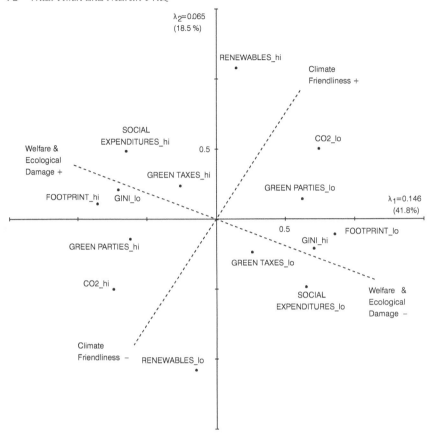

Figure 5.2 Climate friendliness, welfare and ecological damage in Europe in 2010

The situation in 2010

The patterns of indicators and latent dimensions for 2010[6] (Figure 5.2) are very similar to those for 1995. The positions of the welfare and ecological performance indicators towards each other remain largely stable. However, the indicator for the influence of green parties displays some movement. Although higher levels of green seats in parliament are still connected to the welfare, regulation and the ecological damage nexus, this indicator moved downwards along the second dimension 'climate friendliness' and closer to higher levels of CO_2 emissions. This may be explained by the high salience of the topic of climate change and CO_2 emissions in the first decade of the twenty-first century that may have brought more people than previously to vote for parties dedicated to green issues. This especially applies to people in economically advanced countries that featured the highest levels of CO_2 per capita emissions. It is therefore crucial to disentangle environmental *regulation* and *performance*. While one could expect a positive

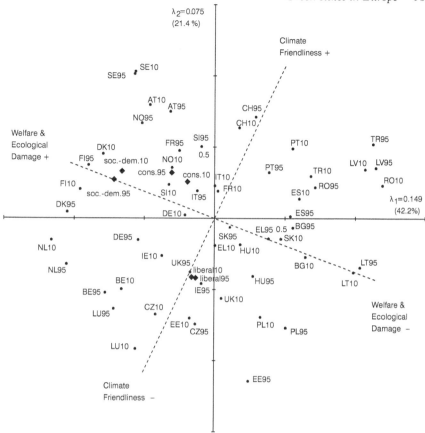

Figure 5.3 Tracking the positional changes of European countries from 1995 to 2010

correlation between the two, the opposite is actually the case: high levels of environmental regulation do not correspond with comparatively good ecological performances and should therefore rather be understood as the result of the need to react to advanced environmental stress.

How the countries and welfare regimes developed from 1995 to 2010

The next theme of our macro-analysis is the positional change in the 28 countries between 1995 and 2010 (Figure 5.3). The hypothesis that social democratic welfare states also perform ecologically well holds for merely two countries: Sweden and, to a lesser degree, Austria. Also Norway figured in this upper left area – but only in 1995. By 2010, the country had become significantly more unsustainable. Yet the development of these countries in socio-economic terms corresponds with comparatively high ecological footprints so that their good ecological performance is largely reduced to relative 'climate friendliness.' Other countries with a social democratic welfare tradition such as the Netherlands and Belgium score below average in terms of 'climate friendliness' and very high on 'ecological footprint.' The ecologically most sustainable countries are located in the upper right quadrant of the map, where 'climate friendliness' is relatively high and ecological damages are comparatively low. Unfortunately, this is inevitably linked with weaker socio-economic development. As a corollary, countries such as Turkey, Latvia, Romania, but also Portugal and Spain, can be found in this region of the map. Switzerland, a representative of the conservative welfare regime, is an interesting case, because it is very 'climate friendly' and features, at the same time, a medium ecological footprint and average welfare provisions. There is finally some 'negative' support for the synergy hypothesis, since the liberal UK and Ireland indeed display much less 'climate friendliness' than the European average; neither do these two countries indicate any sign of improvement during the observed time period. However, their overall ecological performance, that is also considering ecological footprint, is about European average.

By calculating the average values for the respective countries of the three classical welfare regimes, we furthermore inserted their positions in Figure 5.3. In line with Esping-Andersen's original approach, the regimes are ranked according to their level of welfare, with the social democratic regime being located on the left side, closely followed by the conservative regime and the liberal regime. Compared to all 28 European countries, the latter features average levels of welfare. Again and contradicting the synergy hypothesis, welfare is strongly correlated with 'ecological footprint' so that the same regime ranking applies for 'ecological damages.' According to the second dimension of 'climate friendliness' our results support the synergy hypothesis to some extent, even though the social democratic countries are actually less 'climate friendly' than the conservative countries.

Grouping countries according to their welfare and ecology structure

In the final step, we carry out a cluster analysis to explore whether it reinforces the findings from the correspondence analyses. Is advanced socio-economic and welfare development linked to high levels of environmental stress and is this relation accompanied by significantly higher levels of 'green regulation'? The question is whether countries can be grouped into similar clusters according to their 'green state' characteristics. In order to identify such groups of countries the same 28 countries at the same two points in time (yielding 56 cases) were included in the cluster analysis. We used the same seven indicators for welfare, green regulation and performance as in the correspondence analysis above. First, a hierarchical cluster analysis, using the Ward criterion and squared Euclidean distances, led to a solution of four clusters. We then tested the stability of this solution by running several other cluster analyses with different criteria (single linkage, average linkage, etc.). The results verified the finding of the four initial clusters. They are presented in Table 5.1.

The first cluster contains four countries at both points in time. Austria, Norway, Sweden and Switzerland are characterized by a combination of advanced welfare

Table 5.1 Clusters of countries according to their welfare, ecological performance and green regulation

Cluster		Gini	Social expenditures	Renewables	CO_2	Footprint	Green parties	Green taxes
AT, NO, SE, CH	Mean	26.3625	27.1250	68.7250	6.7963	5.1000	4.8023	2.5125
	N	8	8	8	8	8	8	8
	Standard deviation	3.90272	3.73965	19.43000	1.71548	0.57570	3.54790	0.48825
BE, DK, FI, DE, LU, NL	Mean	26.6333	28.0000	11.4000	11.8308	6.3000	5.8136	2.9917
	N	12	12	12	12	12	12	12
	Standard deviation	3.00706	3.65961	11.48643	4.09698	1.36848	3.29329	0.81515
BG95, EE95, PL95, LV, LT, RO, ES, TR95, PT10	Mean	33.4385	18.7538	24.2462	5.5946	3.4385	.0676	1.8000
	N	13	13	13	13	13	13	13
	Standard deviation	3.37874	4.27212	19.45043	2.51408	0.85102	0.17060	0.45826
CZ, FR, EL, HU, IE, IT, SK, SI, UK, BG10, EE10, TR10, PT95, PL10	Mean	30.4826	22.5087	14.2087	7.6048	4.3261	0.6154	2.8391
	N	23	23	23	23	23	23	23
	Standard deviation	4.10827	4.67439	9.09030	2.12310	0.86193	0.90379	.059447
Total	Mean	29.7554	23.4732	23.7250	7.9282	4.6536	2.2003	2.5839
	N	56	56	56	56	56	56	56
	Standard deviation	4.49638	5.40782	23.57234	3.42840	1.37338	3.17223	0.74828

If there is no year in the country abbreviation this indicates that the given country belongs to its respective cluster at both points in time 1995 and 2010.

states (low inequality and high social expenditures), high green regulation in terms of green taxes and green parties in parliament as well as an ambivalent ecological performance. While the share of renewable energy is exceptionally high and CO_2 emissions are on average levels in this cluster of countries, its ecological footprint is significantly higher than the European average. It is in fact mainly the massive use of water power for generating electricity that improves the environmental performance of the countries of this cluster. Without these natural resources their ecological performance would in all likelihood not differ significantly from those of other advanced Western societies and their largely unsustainable production and consumption patterns. Given the great difference that the different provisions with natural resources such as rivers and lakes make for the overall environmental performance of countries, commenters should be accordingly careful with celebrating the ecological 'achievements' of countries such as Sweden.

Cluster 2 likewise illustrates this issue. Belgium, Denmark, Finland, Germany, Luxembourg and the Netherlands are as highly developed as the countries of the first cluster in socio-economic terms, but their ecological performance is much worse. Overall, cluster 2 generates merely 11 percent of its electricity from renewable sources. Accordingly, its CO_2 emissions are the highest in the whole of Europe, and its ecological footprint is the highest among all the 28 countries under observation. Interestingly, this cluster also features the highest values for the two indicators for 'green regulation,' suggesting that people in these countries pay more environmentally related taxes and more often vote for green parties. However, this has as yet not had any significant impact on the ecological performance of these countries. That high levels of environmental regulation are *not* linked to good environmental performances suggests the interpretation that the former are in fact reactions to the existence and perceived significance of ecological issues. Environmental regulation may, in turn, influence performance, but it seems to take longer time than our period of investigation that such regulation starts becoming reflected in lower CO_2 emissions and ecological footprints.

Clusters 3 and 4 consist of weakly developed countries in socio-economic terms, whereby cluster 3 is more ecologically sustainable than cluster 4. Cluster 3 features the lowest CO_2 emissions per capita and ecological footprints in Europe, with almost one quarter of its electricity stemming from renewable sources like solar and water power. It mainly contains eastern European countries (Bulgaria, Estonia, Poland, Latvia, Lithuania and Romania) as well as Turkey, Spain and Portugal. Bulgaria, Estonia, Poland and Turkey belong to this cluster only for the year 1995. By 2010, these countries had shifted to the less sustainable cluster 4, indicating that their ecological performance worsened in the meantime. Conversely, Portugal belongs to cluster 3 only in the year 2010. The country became more sustainable, since it had belonged to cluster 4 in 1995. Furthermore, the most sustainable cluster 3 is characterized by the worst socio-economic development indicators, that is, high inequality and low social expenditures. This finding likewise supports the notion that efforts to decouple advanced levels of socio-economic development and welfare from environmental stress were as yet largely unsuccessful despite more or less far-reaching political efforts in terms of eco-social regulation. This most sustainable cluster actually features the lowest levels of green regulation. We presume this to be the case because the electorate may not perceive the environment as an important political issue in circumstances of relatively good ecological performances and value economic issues higher.

The last cluster is the biggest and combines eastern European, Mediterranean and liberal countries at both points in time. While cluster 4 is slightly more socially equitable than cluster 3, it is much less equitable than the countries in clusters 1 and 2. It does not produce much 'green electricity,' and its CO_2 emissions are relatively high considering the level of socio-economic development – higher even than in the first cluster. The ecological footprint of this cluster is below European average but higher than that of the most sustainable third cluster. It furthermore features a medium extent of green regulation. While the countries of cluster 4 do not display relevant proportions of green parties in parliament, they do raise very high taxes in relation to the environment.

Discussion and conclusion

Reflecting the EU 2020 strategy, authors such as Meadowcroft, Dryzek and Gough expressed some hope in the ability of social democratic welfare regimes to develop the green dimension of the state more successfully than conservative and, especially, liberal welfare regimes, and, consequently, to perform better in terms of ecological key indicators. We called this the 'synergy' hypothesis, which we set out to empirically scrutinize for 28 European countries and over the time period 1995 to 2010. Our results suggest that there is no quasi automatic development of the green state on top of already existing welfare regimes and institutions. Our correspondence analyses revealed that most of the social democratic countries do not display greater associations of the selected welfare and ecology indicators than several of the liberal and eastern European countries. Our cluster analysis demonstrated that representatives of social democratic and conservative welfare regimes are actually spread across all four clusters that summarized states' welfare and environmental performances. However, low empirical scores on ecological performance do not exclude that the existence of the institutional basis of social democratic welfare states is indeed beneficial to the development of the green state; however, this potential would need to be politically actualized much more than currently is the case. The coexistence of environmental problem pressure and high levels of green regulation has, as yet and in itself, not significantly improved environmental performances. One would hope that the political capital that is expressed in green votes, for example, can be used in more efficient ways to initiate the necessary ecological transformation of production and consumption patterns, especially in the most advanced capitalist countries.

Our conclusion is that the links between the welfare and green dimensions of the state are far more complex than suggested by the synergy hypothesis. On the one hand, other factors than welfare regimes, environmental taxation and political representation of green parties may be significant for the explanation of the cross-country differences in ecological regulation and performance. These may include the degree of political decentralization with corresponding different roles and responsibilities for local authorities to develop green politics. While this should be considered in future research, much evidence suggests that the links between the welfare and green dimension of the state are weak and not as envisioned by Dryzek or Meadowcroft. The extent of welfare provision of a country is largely a reflection of its development in economic terms, that is, of GDP. Not only has the welfare state itself a significant ecological footprint, but its redistribution effect, in combination with economic growth, enables vast societal groups to participate in production and consumption patterns that are, all other things being equal, environmentally harmful, not only in terms of CO_2 emissions.

Since the available empirical evidence for absolute decoupling of economic growth, resource input and, consequently, ecological stress is very weak indeed, our results confirm previous studies by Jackson (2009) and Victor (2008) that fundamentally question 'green growth' policy options – the idea that economic growth can be organized in ways that are both socially equitable and ecologically sustainable. In fact, if welfare goals are to be combined with ecological sustainability, it is difficult to see how the top priority of economic growth in policy-making can continue. Ironically, the same mechanism that defuses the socio-economic inequalities inherent to capitalist development appears to ensure the inclusion of an increasing amount of people in social practices that have the potential to undermine the biological reproduction of economy and society. Social scientists can help to develop economic and social models that deprioritize GDP growth and over-consumption as well as associated eco-social policies. In doing so, they are well advised to recognize that any transition towards a non-growing or 'steady state' economy would need to start from the institutional structures of existing capitalist economies and states.

Acknowledgements

The cooperation between the two authors for this chapter is the result of a guest scholarship at the European Data Laboratory for Comparative Social Research (EUROLAB) that GESIS-Leibniz Institute for the Social Sciences awarded to Max Koch in April 2013 ('Attitudes towards Climate Change and Environmental Policies – a Comparative View').

Notes

1   The same applies to the level or scale of state action. Presently, state action is identifiable at local, national and transnational levels (Brenner 2004; Jessop 2007; Koch 2008).
2   For a similar study including also countries from outside Europe see Koch and Fritz (2014).
3   See Table 5.2 in the appendix to this chapter for more detailed information on data sources, missing values, etc.
4   See Greenacre (2007) for statistical details about ranking and doubling and Blasius and Graeff (2009) for an empirical application.

5 The correspondence analysis of the seven macro-level indicators reveals two latent dimensions, which together explain about 64% of the variation in the data.
6 Taken together, the two dimensions explain about 60% of the variation in the data.

References

Armingeon, K., Careja, R., Knöpfel, L., Weisstanner, D., Engler, S., Potolidis, P., and Gerber, M., 2013 *Comparative Political Data Set III 1990–2011*. Institute of Political Science, University of Bern, Bern.

Arts, W., and Gelissen, J., 2002 Three worlds of welfare capitalism or more? A state-of-the-art report. *Journal of European Social Policy* 12: 137–58.

Blasius, J., and Graeff, P., 2009 Economic freedom, wealth and corruption: analyzing their empirical connection by means of correspondence analysis. In Graeff, P., and Mehlkop, G., (eds) *Capitalism, Democracy and the Prevention of War and Poverty* 135–55. Routledge, Abingdon.

Blasius, J., and Greenacre, M., 2006 Multiple correspondence analysis and related methods in practice. In Greenacre, M., and Blasius, J., (eds) *Multiple Correspondence Analysis and Related Methods* 3–40. Chapman & Hall, Boca Raton, FL.

Borucke, M., Moore, D., Cranston, G., Gracey, K., Iha, K., Larson, J., Lazarus, E., Morales, J.C., Wackernagel, M., and Galli, A., 2013 Accounting for demand and supply of the biosphere's regenerative capacity: The National Footprint Accounts' underlying methodology and framework. *Ecological Indicators* 24: 518–33.

Brenner, N., 2004 Urban governance and production of new state spaces in Western Europe, 1960–2000. *Review of International Political Economy* 11: 447–88.

Büchs, M., Bardsley, N., and Duwe, S., 2012 Who bears the brunt? Distributional effects of climate change mitigation policies. *Critical Social Policy* 31: 285–307.

Christoff, P., and Eckersley, R., 2011 Comparing state responses. In Dryzek, J., Norgaard, R., and Schlosberg, D., (eds) *Oxford Handbook of Climate Change and Society* 432–48. Oxford University Press, Oxford.

Daly, H., and Farley, J., 2009 *Ecological Economics: Principles and Applications*. Island Press, Washington, DC.

Dryzek, J., Downes, D., Hunhold, C., Schlosberg, D., and Hernes, H., 2003 *Green States and Social Movements: Environmentalism in the United States, United Kingdom, Germany and Norway*. Oxford University Press, Oxford.

Esping-Andersen, G., 1990 *The Three Worlds of Welfare Capitalism*. Polity, Cambridge.

European Commission 2010 *A Strategy for Smart, Sustainable and Inclusive Growth*. Publications Office of the European Union, Luxembourg.

European Commission 2012 *Taxation Trends in the European Union – Data for the EU Member states, Iceland and Norway*. Publications Office of the European Union, Luxembourg.

Eurostat 2013 Eurostat database. Retrieved April 8–12, 2013 from http://ec.europa.eu/eurostat/data/database.

Fritz, M., and Koch, M., 2014 Potentials for prosperity without growth: Ecological sustainability, social inclusion and the quality of life in 38 countries. *Ecological Economics* 108: 191–9.

Gallas, A., Bretthauer, L., Kannankulam, J., and Stützle, I., (eds) 2011 *Reading Poulantzas*. Merlin Press, London.

Giddens, A., 2009 *The Politics of Climate Change*. Polity, Cambridge.

Global Footprint Network 2013 Country factsheets. Retrieved April 15–19, 2013 from www.footprintnetwork.org.

Görg, C., 2003 *Regulation der Naturverhältnisse: Zu einer kritischen Theorie der ökologischen Krise*. Westfälisches Dampfboot, Münster.

Gough, I., 2011 *Climate Change and Public Policy Futures*. British Academy, London.

Gough, I., and Meadowcroft, J., 2011 Decarbonising the welfare state. In Dryzek, J., Norgaard, R., and Schlosberg, D., (eds) *Oxford Handbook of Climate Change and Society* 490–503. Oxford University Press, Oxford.

Gough, I., Meadowcroft, J., Dryzek, J., Gerhards, J., Lengfield, H., Markandya, A., and Ortiz, R., 2008 JESP symposium: climate change and social policy. *Journal of European Social Policy* 18: 325–44.

Greenacre, M., 2007 *Correspondence Analysis in Practice*. Chapman & Hall, Boca Raton, FL.

Jackson, T., 2009 *Prosperity without Growth: Economics for a Future Planet*. Earthscan, London.

Jacobs, M., 2012 *Green Growth: Economic Theory and Political Discourse*. Working Paper 108. Centre for Climate Change Economics and Policy, London.

Jessop, B., 2007 *State Power*. Polity, Cambridge.

Koch, M., 2005 Wage determination, socio-economic regulation and the state. *European Journal of Industrial Relations* 11: 327–346.

Koch, M., 2006 *Roads to Post-Fordism: Labour Markets and Social Structures in Europe*. Ashgate, Aldershot.

Koch, M., 2008 The state in European employment regulation. *Journal of European Integration* 30: 255–72.

Koch, M., 2012 *Capitalism and Climate Change: Theoretical Analysis, Historical Development and Policy Responses*. Palgrave Macmillan, Basingstoke.

Koch, M., 2013 Welfare after growth: theoretical discussion and policy implications. *International Journal of Social Quality* 3: 4–20.

Koch, M., and Fritz, M., 2014 Building the eco-social state: do welfare regimes matter? *Journal of Social Policy* 43: 679–703.

Marx, K., 1973 *Grundrisse: Foundations of the Critique of Political Economy (Draft)*. Penguin, Harmondsworth.

Meadowcroft, J., 2005 From welfare state to ecostate. In Barry, J., and Eckersley, R., (eds) *The State and the Global Ecological Crisis* 3–24. MIT Press, Cambridge, MA.

OECD 2013 OECD StatExtracts. Retrieved May 15, 2013 from http://stats.oecd.org.

Offe, K., 1984 *Contradictions of the Welfare State*. Hutchinson, London.

Poulantzas, N., 1978 *State, Power and Socialism*. NLB, London.

Scruggs, L.E., 1999 Institutions and environmental performance in seventeen Western democracies. *British Journal of Political Science* 29: 1–31.

Victor, P.A., 2008 *Managing without Growth: Slower by Design, Not Disaster*. Edward Elgar, Cheltenham.

Walker, G., 2012 *Environmental Justice: Concepts, Evidence and Politics*. Routledge, Abingdon.

Weber, M., 1991 Politics as a vocation. In Gerth, H., and Wright Mills, C., (eds) *From Max Weber: Essays in Sociology* 77–128. Routledge, London.

World Bank 2013 World development indicators. Retrieved April 11 and May 7, 2013 from http://data.worldbank.org/products/wdi.

Appendix

Table 5.2 Data table 1995: indicators used in the correspondence and cluster analyses

1995	Gini[1]	Social expendi- tures[8]	Renew- able energy[11]	CO_2 emis- sions per capita[12]	Ecological footprint[13]	Green parties[14]	Environ- mental taxes[15]
Austria	27.0	28.0	72.4	7.77	4.3	5.8	2.1
Belgium	29.0	25.9	0.9	11.15	7.0	8.4	2.2
Bulgaria	31.0[2]	22.2[9]	5.6	6.90	2.9	0.0	1.8
Czech Rep.	25.8[2,3]	16.1	3.9	12.11	4.3	0.0	2.7
Denmark	20.0	31.0	5.2	10.54	9.0	0.0	4.4
Estonia	30.1[2]	15.2[10]	0.1	11.66	4.2	0.3	1.0
Finland	22.0[3]	30.6	27.0	10.34	5.5	4.6	2.9
France	29.0	28.7	17.8	6.60	4.7	0.5	2.5
Germany	29.0	27.2	4.8	10.60	4.6	5.0	2.3
Greece	35.0	19.2	8.4	7.45	4.0	0.0	3.1
Hungary	27.9[2,4]	20.2[10]	0.6	5.81	2.9	0.0	2.9
Ireland	33.0	17.8	4.1	9.11	5.2	0.4	3.0
Italy	33.0	23.1	14.9	7.72	4.2	2.3	3.6
Latvia	31.02	14.9[7]	47.1	3.88	2.5	0.0	1.2
Lithuania	32.3[2,3]	12.7[3]	3.3	4.47	2.6	0.0	1.9
Luxembourg	29.0	20.0	1.7	20.43	5.2	7.7	3.0
Netherlands	29.0	28.9	1.5	11.40	6.6	4.6	3.6
Norway	25.8[2,6]	25.9	104.5	8.01	6.0	0.0	3.4
Poland	32.7[2,3]	19.1[6]	1.4	8.99	3.5	0.0	1.8
Portugal	37.0	18.5	27.5	5.18	4.7	0.0	3.4
Romania	28.2[2,5]	12.7[6]	28.0	5.60	2.7	0.5	1.8
Slovak Rep.	25.8[2,3]	17.9	17.3	8.11	3.1	0.7	2.3
Slovenia	29.2[2,4]	22.8[3]	28.9	7.23	3.5	2.0	4.2
Spain	34.0	20.9	14.2	6.14	4.2	0.0	2.2
Sweden	21.0[7]	33.1	48.1	5.75	5.2	3.7	2.8
Switzerland	33.7[2,6]	21.3	64.1	5.57	4.5	5.3	216
Turkey	41.5[2,5]	22.2[9]	41.9	2.92	2.2	0.0	1.2
UK	32.0	26.1	2.0	9.73	4.4	0.0	2.9

1 GINI Coefficient for income inequality, source if not stated otherwise: EUROSTAT as of 11.4.2013.
2 Source: The World Bank: World Development Indicators as of 7.5.2013.
3 Due to incomplete time series we use data from 1996.
4 Due to incomplete time series we use data from 1993.
5 Due to incomplete time series we use data from 1994.
6 Due to incomplete time series we use data from 2000.
7 Due to incomplete time series we use data from 1997.

8   Expenditures for Social Protection in percent of GDP (all systems and functions), source: EUROSTAT as of 11.4.2013.
9   Replaced with mean due to incomplete time series or otherwise missing value.
10 Due to incomplete time series we use data from 1999.
11 Electricity generated from renewable sources as percent of gross electricity consumption, source: EUROSTAT as of 10.4.2013.
12 Metric tons per capita, source: The World Bank as of 11.4.2013.
13 The Ecological Footprint per person in a country "...measures human appropriation [...] of ecosystem product and services...", in terms of a "world average bioproductive area, referred to as global hectares (gha)." (Borucke *et al.* 2013). It includes cropland, grazing land, fishing ground, forest land, carbon uptake land and built-up land. For details on the construction of that indicator see Borucke *et al.* 2013. Source: Country factsheets of the Global Footprint Network (www.footprintnetwork.org as of 15–19.4.2013).
14 Proportion of seats in parliament held by Green Parties, mean value for the period 1990–2000, source: own calculations based on the Comparative Political Data Set III (Armingeon *et al.* 2013).
15 Total envionmental taxes as percent of GDP, source if not stated otherwise: European Commission (2012, p. 246).
16 Source: OECD.StatExtracts (indicator GG_E41: total environment-related taxes, % GDP) as of 15.5.2013.

Notes for Table 5.3
1   Gini coefficient for income inequality, source if not stated otherwise: EUROSTAT as of 11.4.2013.
2   Due to incomplete time series we use data from 2008, source: The World Bank: World Development Indicators as of 7.5.2013.
3   Expenditures for Social Protection in per cent of GDP (all systems and functions), source: EUROSTAT as of 11.4.2013.
4   Replaced with mean due to incomplete time series or otherwise missing value.
5   Electricity generated from renewable sources as percent of gross electricity consumption, source: EUROSTAT as of 10.4.2013.
6   Due to incomplete time series we use data from 2009, metric tons per capita, source: The World Bank as of 11.4.2013.
7   The Ecological Footprint per person in a country "...measures human appropriation [...] of ecosystem product and services...", in terms of a "world average bioproductive area, referred to as global hectares (gha)." (Borucke *et al.* 2013). It includes cropland, grazing land, fishing ground, forest land, carbon uptake land and built-up land. For details on the construction of that indicator see Borucke *et al.* 2013. Source: Country factsheets of the Global Footprint Network (www.footprintnetwork.org as of 15–19.4.2013).
8   Proportion of seats in parliament held by Green Parties, mean value for the period 2001–2011, source: own calculations based on the Comparative Political Data Set III (Armingeon *et al.* 2013).
9   Total envionmental taxes as percent of GDP, source if not stated otherwise: European Commission (2012, p. 246).
10 Source: OECD. StatExtracts (indicator GG_E41: total environment-related taxes, % GDP) as of 15.5.2013.

Table 5.3 Data table 2010: indicators used in the correspondence and cluster analyses

2010	Gini[1]	Social expenditures[3]	Renewable energy[5]	CO_2 emissions per capita[6]	Ecological footprint[7]	Green parties[8]	Environmental taxes[9]
Austria	26.1	29.5	61.4	7.45	5.3	10.1	2.4
Belgium	26.6	28.4	6.8	9.60	7.0	7.2	2.1
Bulgaria	33.2	17.6	15.2	5.64	3.5	0.0	2.9
Czech Rep.	24.9	19.5	8.3	10.31	5.3	1.1	2.4
Denmark	26.9	32.4	33.1	8.27	8.2	0.0	4.0
Estonia	31.3	17.9	10.8	11.90	4.7	2.1	3.0
Finland	25.4	29.7	26.5	10.03	6.2	6.7	2.8
France	29.8	32.0	14.5	5.61	4.8	0.7	1.8
Germany	29.3	29.4	16.9	8.97	4.5	9.1	2.2
Greece	32.9	28.2	16.7	8.41	4.9	0.0	2.4
Hungary	24.1	22.5	7.1	4.86	3.6	0.8	2.6
Ireland	33.2	28.3	12.8	9.34	6.2	3.1	2.4
Italy	31.2	28.6	22.2	6.66	4.5	0.4	2.6
Latvia	36.1	17.6	48.5	2.95	3.9	0.0	2.4
Lithuania	36.9	18.3	7.8	3.84	4.4	0.0	1.9
Luxembourg	27.9	22.3	3.1	20.38	5.5	10.8	2.4
Netherlands	25.5	30.2	9.3	10.26	6.3	5.6	4.0
Norway	23.6	25.1	90.0	9.75	4.8	0.0	2.6
Poland	31.1	18.6	7.0	7.83	3.9	0.0	2.6
Portugal	33.7	25.5	50.0	5.40	4.1	0.0	2.5
Romania	33.3	17.4	34.2	3.70	2.8	0.0	2.1
Slovak Rep.	25.9	18.0	20.5	6.25	4.7	0.0	1.9
Slovenia	23.8	24.3	33.1	7.50	5.2	0.0	3.6
Spain	33.9	25.2	33.1	6.28	4.7	0.0	1.6
Sweden	24.1	29.9	54.5	4.70	5.7	5.5	2.8
Switzerland	29.6	24.2	54.8	5.37	5.0	8.0	2.0[10]
Turkey	39.0[2]	24.7[4]	26.5	3.87	2.5	0.0	3.9
UK	33.0	27.1	6.7	7.68	4.7	0.0	2.6

6 The 'green' potential of small island states

A comparative study

Marina Povitkina

Introduction

When we think of small island states we imagine small patches of paradise with sandy beaches, warm sun, coconut straw drinks and relaxed happy people. However, there are other attractive images small islands can bring. Recent research has revealed that island states with small populations and territories show an example of successful democratic development (Ott 2000; Srebrnik 2004; Anckar 2006) and good economic institutions (Congdon-Fors 2014). Scholars believe that such developments have been taking place on small island states due to their unique geographical characteristics. The main mechanism is that smallness, isolation and remoteness become unifying factors for island citizens, who all face similar problems related to 'islandness,' and thus tend to develop common values and attitudes, building tight cooperative networks and social capital (Anckar 2006).

This chapter suggests that island-specific characteristics, which are believed to contribute to the advance of democracy on islands, also favor development of a green state under the conditions of environmental vulnerability. Possessing limited resources, being remote, isolated and exposed to various natural hazards, small island states face pressing problems of natural resource management. As a result it was recognized at the World Summit on Sustainable Development in Johannesburg in 2002 that small island developing states (SIDS) "take the lead in the path towards sustainable development" (United Nations 2002: 41). Furthermore, the year 2014 was proclaimed 'International Year of SIDS' in order to attract attention to the need to protect unique environments of small islands (UNESCO 2014). However, there have so far been no efforts to investigate environmental performance of small island states in more detail and explore the mechanisms behind their 'greening' process.

This chapter empirically tests whether small island states have on average better environmental performance than continental countries and large islands. I also unpack which political and social processes contribute to the 'greening' of the state and explain why small islands states are more prone to succeed in this process than their larger counterparts.

In the next section of the chapter I present the main theoretical arguments to why small islands can be expected to become green states. Consequently, I introduce methodology and data followed by empirical testing of small islands' environmental performance. Further on I proceed with the discussion of the main results and conclude what can be learned from the study performed.

Theoretical perspectives

Small island states' characteristics

In this chapter I refer to an island state as "a country with no land borders" (Glassner 1990). Using this definition is convenient for analyzing environmental governance, since it assumes that an island state's government is solely responsible for protecting the whole territory of the country surrounded by water (Congdon-Fors 2014). In a situation when several countries share a border on a single island, such as in the case of Haiti and Dominican Republic, they can face a collective action dilemma when it comes to management of natural resources on the island (e.g. forestry and fisheries). Although governments might care for their own territory, due to the absence of absolute responsibility, they can deviate from sustainable actions, putting all the responsibility for 'cleaning up' on 'the neighbor' or expecting the neighboring country to also deviate.

Smallness usually implies either small land area or small population size, but often both, since these two parameters are highly correlated (World Bank 2014). By small in this chapter I will refer to island states with population below 500,000 inhabitants,[1] as this number is usually used as an upper limit to define a microstate[2] (Hyde and Marinov 2014).

Most small island jurisdictions function under conditions of environmental vulnerability and exposure to natural disasters. Having small in-land zones and large coastal lines, islands tend to suffer more from sea level rise, high winds, tsunamis and other environmental hazards than their continental counterparts do. Environmental vulnerability and limited resources set sustainable development and environmental protection a priority among other political goals (AOSIS 2014).

Facing pressing environmental risks, scarcity of resources, need for good environmental management and resilience building, small island states, which share certain geographical characteristics, are likely to develop social processes favorable to successful collective action in natural resource management (Ostrom 1990; Agrawal and Goyal 2001; Grafton and Knowles 2004; Naidu 2009). Below I will summarize existing theoretical debates on why there are reasons to believe that small island states are more prone to successful management of natural resources.

First of all, small size is believed to create opportunities for closer interaction and cooperation between citizens and the government (Ott 2000), foster responsiveness and accountability (Anckar 1999; Kjaer 2004) and lead to "highly personalized and transparent societies" (Bray 1991: 38–9). For example, if political decisions cause damage to the natural environment, it becomes visible to all and citizens can hold politicians accountable for bad policies, given that a small island state has democratic polity with rule of law (Baldacchino 2004).

Second, living on remote and isolated territories small island citizens tend to develop strong national identity and unity through the shared feeling of belonging to a particular geographically defined territory, which they contrast to the "outside world" (Weale 1992: 81–2; Anckar 2002). This gives islands an advantage of scaling up the mechanisms needed for building social capital onto the national level, rather than strengthening group identity, which could eventually lead to polarization (Baldacchino 2005). Due to a shared sense of fellowship citizens are able to orient themselves towards political life and political apparatus. They may better realize consequences of political actions than citizens on continental states (Anckar 2002).

Third, in their everyday lives island inhabitants all face similar problems that stem from remoteness and isolation, which makes them develop a certain degree of uniformity and homogeneity in attitudes and values (Anckar 1999, 2002; Clague *et al.* 2001). As Hintjens and Newitt (1992: 11) point out, "individual island populations, however small, can easily evolve a strong sense of separate identity. Physical isolation can create a powerful sense of local community and accentuate differences in dialect and custom." In turn Baldacchino (2004: 16) sums up that "island identity thus can in some sense replace ethnicity." Homogeneous populations that share the same norms, traditions and problems to deal with will also tend to develop social trust and cohesiveness, reducing the risk of internal conflicts and building social capital (Dahl 1989; Anckar 2002; Anckar and Anckar 1995; Alesina and La Ferrara 2002; Delhey and Newton 2005). Here, trust becomes "one of the most important synthetic forces" (Simmel 1950: 326), increasing the probability that individuals will engage into cooperation with each other and form civil society groups. Common values, norms, interests and goals therefore become "the glue which holds the complex set of relationships together" (Rhodes 2007: 1246). They help to develop toleration and understanding of the probable effects of each other's actions, which in turn facilitates decision-making and problem solving.

Fourth, territorial fragmentation (many island states have several islands forming the country) favors decentralization processes, which leads to distribution of power and thus usually means better governance corresponding to local needs (Anckar 1996; Schneider 2003).

Finally, water boundaries constrain government leaders and raise the costs of expanding territorial hegemony. The outside threats are therefore reduced, too, leading to less military spending, which in turn leads to decentralization (Clague *et al.* 2001). Due to smallness and isolation, costs of internal conflicts are high, which makes rival groups more prone to cooperate and search for consensus. In turn, a conflict-free setting increases collaboration between all stakeholders.

The mechanisms presented above are believed to contribute both to democratic developments in small island states (Anckar 2002) and to collective action necessary in management of natural resources (Ostrom 1990). In contrast to large islands and continental states, small islands have the opportunity to scale up their local governance mechanisms to the state level due to their small size and shared goals between different community groups to protect the island from

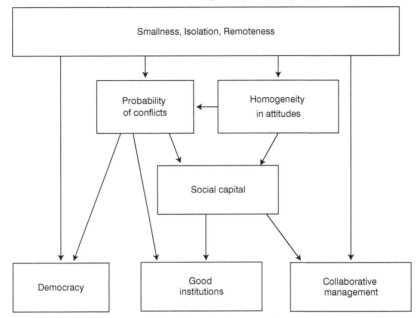

Figure 6.1 Causal links between island-specific factors and prerequisites for a green state

environmental vulnerability. This in turn gives us reasons to believe that small islands have the potential to develop good institutions on the national level for achieving non-corrupt, functioning and reliable polity.

Figure 6.1 summarizes the theoretical links between island-specific characteristics and three preconditions for achieving environmental goals: democracy, good institutions and collaborative management. Such preconditions together with the need for sustainable development and protection of island territories from ecological risks can give the necessary basis for the development of a green state.

Why are democracy, good political institutions and collaborative management important for a green state?

Although there is no comprehensive definition on what constitutes a 'green state,' it has been recognized that the primary task of a green state is to promote environmental protection through laws and regulations and sustainably manage its resources (Eckersley 2004). This implies that both input side of the political system and political processes that lead to the output are involved in 'greening' efforts, with governments being committed to introduce necessary environmental policies, and government administration being effective enough to implement them. The input side of a political system in a democracy is represented by citizens' demands and support for the government's actions (e.g. through voting preferences or work of environmental NGOs and other civil society groups, which lobby environmental interests). In an autocracy, input side is mostly formed by priorities of the ruler and the elite. Political processes in their turn are largely affected by the quality of political institutions and involve policy-making and implementation stages, which translate political decisions into policy outcomes (Easton 1965; Rothstein 2011).

The previous section of the chapter underlined that participatory forms of governance as a type of deliberative democracy create necessary social and political infrastructure for good environmental management and therefore promote sustainable development and the achievement of 'green' goals (Wijkman 1998; Smith 2003; Baber and Bartlett 2005; Bäckstrand *et al.* 2010). Participatory governance suggests decentralization or less formal integration of local communities into environmental management and implies establishing different forms of partnerships between stakeholders in governing natural resources (Newig and Fritsch 2009). Such partnerships have shown to improve quality of decision-making, relationships among players in decision-making processes and capacity for managing environmental problems (Beierle and Konisky 2000; Newig and Fritsch 2009). In small island states, particularly in territorially fragmented islands, local community management can be more efficient than top-down approaches (Rocliffe and Peabody 2012). For example, in Kiribati the distance between the islands can be up to 2,000 kilometers, which makes communication between decision-making center and local authorities problematic. Collaborative governance partnerships between central government structures and local communities in such situations can potentially ensure that environmental management is conducted according to local needs (Ansell and Gash 2007).

However, as Dryzek *et al.* (2003: 196) point out, decentralized environmental governance by local communities or grassroots is not enough, since green political processes are still likely to be dominated by the state in the near future. Therefore, on the input side of political system, democratic features of governments play an important role. Democracies are more responsive to people's environmental demands compared to authoritarian and hybrid regimes. Free media increases public awareness of environmental problems; while participation of green parties and civil society organizations allow citizens' concerns to be represented in the decision-making authorities (Li and Reuveny 2006). Dryzek *et al.* (2003: 195) emphasize the importance of social movements and active inclusion of civil society into decision-making, which can largely contribute to solutions of environmental problems. Bäckstrand *et al.* (2010) underline that such inclusion is likely to promote higher legitimacy of the government. Small island states are prone to have these processes in place, since most of them are well-established democracies and score high on indices of political rights[3] and civil liberties[4] according to the data from Freedom House (2012a, 2012b).[5] Srebrnik (2004: 339) particularly points out that "a significant feature about many small island jurisdictions has been the ability to maintain democratic political systems, something which still eludes many larger countries, particularly in the Third World, where most of these states are located."

While democracy helps voices demanding environmental protection to be heard, government effectiveness, absence of corruption and rule of law are important for ensuring compliance and implementation of environmental laws on the path towards sustainable development (Holmberg *et al.* 2009). Although some of the recent research indeed shows that island states exhibit on average higher rule of law than continental states (Congdon-Fors 2014), studies on small islands' states performance in other institutional indicators are scant. Since there are no existing measurements, which can operationalize environmental management, collaborative governance and stakeholders' involvement, and the lack of data on trust, social capital and quality of government for small island states, it is beyond the scope of this chapter to test for the presence of these factors or test their effect on environmental quality of islands. The aim of this chapter is rather to summarize the existing theoretical arguments and identify the mechanisms behind small islands' potential of developing into green states.

It is possible to measure greening of the political system, however, by means of existing assessments of environmental performance. In the following sections I will test the hypothesis that small island states tend to have better environmental performance than continental states and large islands. The results will indicate whether 'greening' efforts in small islands (if any) result in 'green' outcomes.

Methodology

In the empirical part of the chapter I will test whether small island states tend to have higher scores on major indicators of environmental performance compared to continental states and large islands. Such analysis will help to conclude whether small islands on average perform better in protecting their environments and show indications of 'greener' processes within the state. The sample includes 23 small island states,[6] all of which have fewer than 500,000 inhabitants and a land area less than 1,000 km^2. All of the nations in the sample, except for Iceland, are recognized as SIDS, and are a group of countries which share similar challenges of sustainable development, limited resources, exposure to external shocks, and vulnerable environments.

First, I will analyze descriptive statistics for major indicators of environmental performance of small islands states and compare it to the data on environmental performance of continental countries and large island states. In the analysis I only use those environmental indicators that are available for at least 10 out of 23 small island states to make sure that statistical patterns within the groups are not random and that it is possible to draw justifiable conclusions based on the patterns.

Second, I will perform bivariate Ordinary Least Squares regressions with environmental indicators as dependent variables and small island countries dummy as a single explanatory factor. The analysis will show whether the differences between environmental performance of small island countries and continental states observed during the analysis of descriptive statistics are statistically significant.

Data

In order to measure environmental outcomes of small island states I will use sub-components of Environmental Performance Index (EPI 2012) taken in a single 2012 year. The index is a comprehensive compilation of a wide set of environmental indicators related to air and water pollution, forest, fishery and biodiversity protection, agriculture regulation and climate change. The primary selection is based on the availability of the indicators for at least 10 small island states identified by 12 main indicators for which I will be able to perform further analysis (Table 6.1).

First, these are indicators that account for the effect of environmental quality on human health, such as access to sanitation, access to drinking water, levels of pollution concentrated indoors and child mortality. Second, these are indicators related to ecosystem health, such as protection of marine areas and terrestrial ecosystems (biomes), forest cover change, forest loss owing to deforestation, fishing pressure, fishing stocks overexploitation, pesticide regulation, and change in water quantity as a result of water withdrawals and reservoir constructions. With respect to air pollution, there is not enough data for small island states on such indicators as CO_2 emissions and SO_2 emissions, which makes it problematic to compare their performance to continental states (see Table 6.3 in the appendix to this chapter).

Each of the indicators measures whether a country has reached the level of environmental outcomes desirable by internationally recognized target.[7] They

Table 6.1 Environmental indicators used in the analysis

Type of influence	Indicator type	Indicator
Human health	Air pollution	Indoor air pollution
	Water (effects on human health)	Access to drinking water
		Access to sanitation
	Environmental burden of disease	Child mortality
Ecosystem health	Water (effects on ecosystem)	Change in water quantity
	Biodiversity and habitat	Biome protection
		Marine protection
	Forests	Forest loss
		Forest cover change
	Fisheries	Coastal shelf fishing pressure
		Fish stocks overexploited
	Agriculture	Pesticide regulation

Source: Based on data from EPI (2012)

show how well a country performs in terms of environmental protection policies, based on the observed environmental outcomes, and range from 0 to 100, where 100 means that the policy target has been reached.

Results

The results for the first step of the analysis are reflected in Figure 6.2. The figure presents mean values for each environmental indicator for the sub-category of small island states (dark grey) and sub-category of other countries, which includes continental countries, large island states and countries sharing a border on an island (light grey).

The figure shows that small island states have on average higher performance than the rest of the countries in most of the environmental indicators analyzed (for detailed descriptive statistics see Table 6.3 in the appendix to this chapter). They have higher percentage of people with access to drinking water and sanitation, less indoor air pollution, lower child mortality, smaller change in water quantity, less fishing pressure and smaller change in forest cover compared to other countries. However, compared to continental countries and large

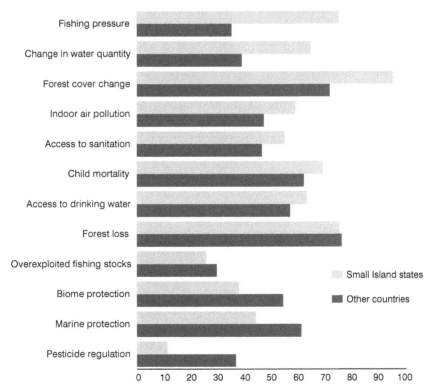

Figure 6.2 Comparative environmental performance of small island states
Note: Higher scores mean better performance

Table 6.2 Environmental performance of small island nations comparing continental countries and large island states

Indicator	Performance
Change in water quantity	better
Forest cover change	better
Coastal shelf fishing pressure	better
Terrestrial protected areas	worse
Marine protected areas	worse
Pesticide regulation	worse

Note: The table is based on calculations presented in Table 6.3 to this chapter

islands, small island states have lower average values in protection of marine and terrestrial areas (biomes). The average for forest loss and exploitation of fishing stocks indicators are roughly the same for both of the sub-groups. Overall, small island states have higher means of most environmental performance indicators than continental states and large islands do.

In the next step I test whether the differences observed during the analysis of descriptive statistics are statistically significant. Table 6.2 presents summary of the results, while Table 6.5 in the appendix to this chapter contains details on regression outputs.

The results show that small island states are significantly less likely to suffer from change in water quantity, are closer to policy targets on restoring their forest cover and exert less coastal fishing pressure. At the same time small islands have lower percentage of their territories (marine and terrestrial) under the status of protected areas compared to continental states. Moreover, they have weaker pesticide regulation, which means that they have banned fewer pesticide substances.[8]

Discussion

The empirical analysis conducted in the previous section shows mixed results. Small isolated communities tend to take a better care of the scarce resources allocated to their territories, such as forest and fresh water, and have stronger protection of their fisheries, which is a resource that they are vitally dependent on. For example, a detailed analysis of the data showed that small island states on average tend to reach international targets for keeping their forest cover unchanged. Most of them have reached or are close to reaching the goal of minimum usage of dangerous fishing gears. In addition, some of the richest islands (such as Antigua and Barbuda, Bahamas, Malta, Seychelles, etc.) have approached minimum levels of indoor air pollution.

However, small island states have shown a weaker track record in agricultural management, and more specifically, in pesticide regulation, which technically means that they do not restrict or ban the use of dangerous pesticides as prescribed by the Stockholm Convention on Persistent Organic Pollutants (EPI 2012; UNEP Chemicals 2003). This can be a result of the fact that small island states do not engage in large-scale agriculture activities, which makes agriculture laws generally underdeveloped. Worse, performance in the biome protection indicator implies that islands tend to have on average smaller percentage of their territories under protection status. This finding is surprising, since one would expect that small islands would vividly engage in protection of their limited biodiversity resources.

Poor performance in marine protection is, at first glance, also unexpected. It is reasonable to assume that island states should care for their water boundaries more than continental states, since they are dependent on the health of their marine ecosystems. As Cicin-Sain and Mangone (2013: 2) point out in linking debates on the green economy to the context of oceans: for island states, "the green economy is the blue economy." However, worse performance in the marine protection indicator simply signifies that a country has a smaller territory under the status of Marine Protected Areas. It does not mean that the marine territory is not under another form of protection, such as, for example, community-based management. In fact, local communities are forbidden to fish in the waters, which are under the status of Marine Protected Areas, and therefore deprived of its primary food source. This forces them to search for alternative solutions for sustainable management of the seas, such as locally managed marine areas. Such forms of partnerships imply either purely local management or management in the form of cooperation between government and local communities (Rocliffe and Peabody 2012). Due to the presence of community-based management regimes in place, bad performance in the marine protected areas indicator does not necessarily mean mismanagement of the marine ecosystems, but rather implies possibilities for less formal and more inclusive forms of governance. This trend is reflected in the result that small islands exert less fishing pressure in their marine areas compared to continental countries and larger island states.

Therefore, the results only partially confirm the hypothesis of the study (i.e. that small island states have better environmental performance than other countries). With such contradictory findings we cannot make a definite conclusion on whether small island states are most likely candidates for green states. However, although environmental performance is a result of environmental legislation and environmental governance in place (depending on the indicator analyzed), the outcomes are also largely affected by vulnerability of islands. Therefore, in the most extreme cases, despite the fact that environmental governance might work well, some outcomes might be 'spoiled' by the consequences of islands' exposure to ecological risks.

In fact, according to theoretical arguments outlined in the first section of this chapter there are reasons to believe that mechanisms of good environmental governance in small islands are precipitated by certain geographical characteristics. The scholarly work on small island states and governance systems shows that we can expect isolation and smallness to foster dialogue between government and the citizens, facilitate inclusion of civil society groups into politics, as well as nurture responsiveness, transparency and accountability by the government. Isolation and remoteness are also expected to help islanders develop uniformity in values and attitudes, facilitate decision-making and problem solving as well as make them more prone to develop trust and social capital, necessary for successful collective action in natural resource management. High costs of internal conflicts are likely to encourage dialogue between stakeholders, making them more prone to search consensus and cooperation. Democratic features of small islands are expected to make them more attuned to citizens' environmental activism and prone to include green parties and environmental civil society organizations in decision-making.

Conclusions

The contribution of this chapter is twofold. First, it has put forward a number of theoretical arguments for why small island states have a potential of conforming to normative ideals of the green state. Second, it has tested the hypothesis that small island states have stronger environmental performance compared with continental and large island states.

The theoretical claims advanced in this chapter suggest that geographical characteristics of small island states, such as isolation, remoteness and smallness, make them more likely to emerge as green states. Living on closed and remote territories, islands' citizens tend to develop social trust, cohesiveness, homogeneity in attitudes, values, interests and a common shared goal to protect their environmentally vulnerable country from ecological risks. These factors facilitate solving of collective action dilemmas in natural resource management and constitute prerequisites for the development of collaborative governance and good institutions, therefore being favorable for 'greening' of the state. Additionally, on the input side, democratic features of small island states leave room for environmental voices within civil society to be heard and addressed in decision-making. On the output side, the results of the empirical analysis show mixed results. Small island states demonstrate better performance in managing resources that are vital for islanders, such as water, fisheries and forests. However, at the same time, they exhibit a weaker performance in measurements related to protection of marine and terrestrial areas as well as regulations for safety of agriculture activities.

Both theoretical and empirical analysis showed that island states have the prerequisites and the potential to emerge as green states, but there is a need for in-depth studies on whether this potential is realized and whether these processes are indeed in place. Although research on the governance systems of small island states predicts that they are likely to develop into green states, the empirical analysis of their environmental performance provides mixed evidence. Hence, whether small island states are more likely to develop as green states, more empirical investigation is needed before any definite conclusion can be reached.

Notes

1 These include 23 countries: Antigua and Barbuda, the Bahamas, Barbados, Dominica, Grenada, Iceland, Kiribati, the Maldives, Malta, Marshall Islands, Micronesia, Nauru, Palau, Samoa, São Tomé and Principe, Seychelles, Solomon Islands, Saint Kitts and Nevis, Saint Lucia, Saint Vincent and the Grenadines, Tonga, Tuvalu and Vanuatu. With the exceptions of Samoa, Vanuatu, Iceland and Bahamas, all the listed countries have land area less than 1,000 km².

2 The World Bank sets the upper limit for the population of a microstate at 1.5 million inhabitants. In order to avoid uncertainty about the results, I perform the analysis for both samples and compare the results between the groups.

3 Political rights include the right to vote in free and fair elections, compete for public office and join parties.

4 Civil liberties include freedom of expression and belief, rights to form and participate in associations and organizations, rule of law, and personal autonomy, with no interference from the state.

5 In fact, 18 out of 23 small island states used in the analysis are full democracies, the Maldives, the Seychelles, Solomon Islands, Tonga, and Antigua and Barbuda being the only exceptions.

6 Countries used in the analysis are listed in note 1 above.

7 The targets present a guidance for countries to reach the following standards: provide access to clean water and sanitation to 100% of their populations, approach zero probability of a child dying in the age between 1 and 5, non-negative or zero percentage change in forest cover, 0% of overexploited fish stocks, 0% of population with high indoor air pollution, 10% of marine territory under the status of marine protected areas, and 17% of terrestrial biomes under protection status. Targets also abide to restrict the use of all pesticides prescribed by Stockholm Convention on Persistent Organic Pollutants and ban the use of trawling and dredging gears in fishing activities.

8 Since there is no strict definition on how large the island should be to be considered 'small,' I performed the same analysis for island states with the population below 1.5 million inhabitants, according to the definition used by World Bank for treating small economies (World Bank 2014). Apart from the 23 countries analyzed previously, the sample included: Bahrain, Comoros, Fiji, Trinidad and Tobago, Cape Verde, Mauritius, and Cyprus. Adding new observations slightly influenced the size of the effect of the indicators (β-values), but generally the results have shown to be almost identical to the results of a smaller sample. New selection allowed for adding new variables into the analysis, due to the availability of more data for small island states. New variables included forest growing stock change, critical habitat protection and agricultural subsidies. The findings have shown that island status is significantly and negatively correlated with critical habitat protection, which means that small islands tend to have a smaller percentage of their territories recognized by the Alliance for Zero Extinction. The results for the other two indicators were insignificant.

References

Agrawal, A., and Goyal, S., 2001 Group size and collective action: third-party monitoring in common pool resources. *Comparative Political Studies* 34(1): 63–93.

Alesina, A., and La Ferrara, E., 2002 Who trusts others? *Journal of Public Economics* 85: 207–34.

Anckar, D., 1996 Noncontiguity and political architecture: the parliaments of small island states. *Political Geography* 15(8): 697–713.

Anckar, D., 1999 Homogeneity and smallness: Dahl and Tufte revisited. *Scandinavian Political Studies* 22: 29–44.

Anckar, D., 2002 Why are small island states democracies? *The Round Table: The Commonwealth Journal of International Affairs* 91(365): 375–90.

Anckar, D., 2006 Islandness or smallness? A comparative look at political institutions in small island states. *Island Studies Journal* 1(1): 43–54.

Anckar, D., and Anckar, C., 1995 Size, insularity and democracy. *Scandinavian Political Studies* 18(4): 211–29.

Ansell, C., and Gash, A., 2007 Collaborative governance in theory and practice. *Journal of Public Administration and Theory* 18: 543–71.

AOSIS 2014 Alliance of Small Island States. Retrieved October 11, 2014 from http://aosis.org.

Baber, W.F., and Bartlett, R.V., 2005 *Deliberative Environmental Politics: Democracy and Ecological Rationality*. MIT Press, Cambridge, MA.

Bäckstrand, K., Khan, J., Kronsell, A., and Lövbrand, E., 2010 *Environmental Politics and Deliberative Democracy: Examining the Promise of New Modes of Governance*. Edward Elgar, Cheltenham.

Baldacchino, G., 2004 Sustainable use practices, including tourism, in/for island states. *INSULA International Journal of Island Affairs* February: 15–20.

Baldacchino, G., 2005 The contribution of social capital to economic growth in small states: lessons from island jurisdictions. *Round Table* 94(1): 31–46.

Beierle, T.C., and Konisky, D.M., 2001 What are we gaining from stakeholder involvement? Observations from environmental planning in the Great Lakes. *Environment and Planning C: Government and Policy* 19(4): 515–27.

Bray, M., 1991 *Making Small Practical: The Organization and Management of Ministries of Education in Small States*. Commonwealth Secretariat, London.

Cicin-Sain, B., and Mangone, G.J., 2013 The way forward: next steps in the context of global ocean developments. Paper presented at session 5, EU–ES Sustainable Oceans: Reconciling Economic Use and Protection conference no. 3, Good Governance for Sustainable Marine Development, Cascais, Portugal, June 3–5.

Clague, C., Gleason, S., and Knack, S., 2001 Determinants of lasting democracy in poor countries: culture development and institutions. *Annals of the American Academy of Political and Social Science* 573: 16–41.

Congdon-Fors, H., 2014 Do island states have better institutions? *Journal of Comparative Economics* 42(1): 34–60.

Dahl, R.A., 1989 *Democracy and its Critics*. Yale University Press, New Haven, CT.

Delhey, J., and Newton, K., 2005 Predicting cross-national levels of social trust: global pattern or Nordic exceptionalism. *European Sociological Review* 21(4): 311–27.

Dryzek, J., Down, D., Hernes H-K., and Scholosberg, D., 2003 *Green States and Social Movements: Environmentalism in the United States, United Kingdom, Germany, and Norway*. Oxford University Press, Oxford.

Easton, D., 1965 *A systems Analysis of Political Life*. John Wiley, New York.

Eckersley, R., 2004 *The Green State: Rethinking Democracy and Sovereignty*. MIT Press Cambridge, MA.

EPI 2012 Environmental Performance Index. Yale Center for Environmental Law & Policy, Center for International Earth Science Information Network, Columbia University, World Economic Forum, Joint Research Centre of the European Commission. Retrieved April 16, 2013 from http://epi.yale.edu/Home.

Freedom House 2012a *Freedom in the World*. Freedom House, Washington, DC. Retrieved April 10, 2013 from https://freedomhouse.org/report/freedom-world/freedom-world-2012#.VN40QS70x-w.

Freedom House 2012b *Freedom of the Press*. Freedom House, Washington, DC. Retrieved April 10, 2013 from https://freedomhouse.org/report/freedom-press/freedom-press-2012#.VN4z_i70x-w.

Glassner, M., 1990 *Neptune's Domain: A Political Geography of the Sea*. Routledge, London.

Grafton, R.Q., and Knowles, S., 2004 Social capital and national environmental performance: a cross-sectional analysis. *The Journal of Environment Development* 13: 336–70.

Hadenius, A., 1992 *Democracy and Development*. Cambridge University Press, Cambridge.

Héritier, A., and Lehmkul, D., 2008 Introduction: the shadow of hierarchy and new modes of governance. *Journal of Public Policy* 28: 1–17.

Hintjens, H.M., and Newitt, M.D.D., 1992 *The Political Economy of Small Tropical Islands: The Importance of Being Small*. University of Exeter Press, Exeter.

Holmberg, S., Rothstein, B., and Nasiritousi, N., 2009 Quality of government: what you get. *Annual Review of Political Science* 12(1): 135–61.

Hyde, S., and Marinov, N., 2014 National Elections across Democracy and Autocracy (NELDA). Yale University, New Haven, CT. Retrieved March 5, 2014 from http://hyde.research.yale.edu/nelda/#codebook.

Kjaer, A.M., 2004 *Governance*. Polity Press, Cambridge.

Li, Q., and Reuveny, R., 2006 Democracy and environmental degradation. *International Studies Quarterly* 50(4): 935–56.

Naidu, S.C., 2009 Heterogeneity and collective management: evidence from common forests in Himachal Pradesh, India. *World Development* 37(3): 676–86.

Newig, J., and Fritsch, O., 2009 Environmental governance: participatory, multi-level – and effective? *Environmental Policy and Governance* 19(3): 197–214.

Ostrom, E., 1990 *Governing the Commons*. Cambridge University Press, Cambridge.

Ott, D., 2000 *Small is Democratic: An Examination of State Size and Democratic Development*. Garland, New York.

Rhodes, R.A.W., 2007 Understanding governance: ten years on. *Organization Studies* 28: 1243–64.

Rocliffe, S., and Peabody, S., 2012 Locally-managed marine areas: towards a global learning network. Workshop report, World Conservation Congress, Jeju, South Korea, September. Blue Ventures, London.

Rothstein, B., 2011 *The Quality of Government: Corruption, Social Trust and Inequality in International Perspective*. University of Chicago Press, Chicago, IL.

Schneider, A., 2003 Decentralization: conceptualization and measurement. *Studies in Comparative International Development* 38(3): 32–56.

Simmel, G., 1950 *The Sociology of Georg Simmel*. Free Press, New York.

Smith, G., 2003 *Deliberative Democracy and the Environment*. Routledge, London.

Srebrnik, H., 2004 Small island nations and democratic values. *World Development* 32(2): 329–41.

UNEP Chemicals 2003 *Master List of Actions on the Reduction and/or Elimination of Releases of Persistent Organic Pollutants*, 5th edn. United Nation Environmental Programme Chemicals, Geneva.

UNESCO 2014 International Year of Small Island Developing States 2014. Retrieved February 3, 2015 from www.unesco.org/new/en/sids_2014.

United Nations 2002 Report of the World Summit on Sustainable Development Johannesburg, South Africa, 26 August–4 September 2002, A/CONF. 199/20. United Nations Publications.

Weale, D., 1992 *Them Times*. Institute of Island Studies, University of Prince Edward Island, Charlottetown, Canada.

Wijkman, A., 1998 Does sustainable development require good governance? *UN Chronicle* 35(1): 86.

World Bank 2014 The World Bank Institute. Retrieved March 10, 2014 from http://wbi.worldbank.org.

Appendix

Table 6.3 Descriptive statistics of environmental indicators for small island states

Variable	Obs.	Mean	Std. Dev.	Min.	Max.
Child mortality	14	68.645	15.971	32.38	100
Indoor air pollution	19	58.588	45.345	1.21	100
Particulate matter	1	100.000	.	100	100
Access to drinking water	20	62.649	28.275	18.22	100
Access to sanitation	20	54.754	35.671	6.45	100
Sulfur dioxide emissions per capita	2	7.180	10.154	0	14.36
Sulfur dioxide emissions per GDP	2	27.420	7.552	22.08	32.76
Change in water quantity	15	64.099	23.096	12.3	100
Biome protection	23	37.821	37.044	0	100
Marine protection	23	43.964	24.700	0	100
Critical habitat protection	9	29.762	42.383	0	100
Agricultural subsidies	6	55.470	40.120	7.04	100
Pesticide regulation	23	11.265	29.834	0	95.45
Growing stock change	7	71.429	48.795	0	100
Forest loss	16	74.856	22.719	40.39	100
Forest cover change	21	94.693	16.881	37.94	100
Fishing stocks overexploited	23	25.713	29.523	0	100
Coastal shelf fishing pressure	23	74.393	26.335	10.83	100
CO_2 per capita	2	42.570	1.527	41.49	43.65
CO_2 per GDP	2	55.530	9.815	48.59	62.47
CO_2 emissions per electricity generation	2	45.335	64.113	0	90.67
Renewable electricity	2	49.995	70.704	0	99.99

Table 6.4 Descriptive statistics of environmental indicators for continental states and large island states

Variable	Obs.	Mean	Std. Dev.	Min.	Max.
Child mortality	171	60.021	29.259	3.55	100
Indoor air pollution	164	44.439	43.096	0	100
Particulate matter	154	89.207	18.936	0	100
Access to drinking water	166	54.850	32.352	2.72	100
Access to sanitation	164	44.468	34.613	2.02	100
Sulfur dioxide emissions per capita	135	38.909	22.090	0	88.38
Sulfur dioxide emissions per GDP	135	41.251	20.920	0	85.82
Change in water quantity	168	35.436	21.577	0	100
Biome protection	176	53.967	34.520	0	100
Marine protection	131	64.307	28.085	0	100
Critical habitat protection	69	46.517	37.858	0	100
Agricultural subsidies	144	60.196	32.310	0	100
Pesticide regulation	177	43.348	41.052	0	95.45
Growing stock change	144	80.623	33.616	0	100
Forest loss	158	75.837	25.631	0.95	100
Forest cover change	169	68.396	37.149	0	100
Fishing stocks overexploited	128	31.400	20.302	0	100
Coastal shelf fishing pressure	133	27.885	21.940	0	98.92
CO_2 per capita	134	62.013	33.617	0	100
CO_2 per GDP	134	45.012	21.182	0	87.01
CO_2 emissions per electricity generation	134	15.824	18.543	0	100
Renewable electricity	134	31.229	31.689	0	100

Table 6.5 The effect of being a small island state on environmental performance

	Variables	Small island states	Error	Constant	Error	Obs.	R^2
1	Child mortality	8.624	(7.928)	60.02***	(2.181)	185	0.006
2	Indoor air pollution	14.15	(10.5)	44.44***	(3.383)	183	0.01
3	Access to drinking water	7.798	(7.564)	54.85***	(2.48)	186	0.006
4	Access to sanitation	10.29	(8.225)	44.47***	(2.712)	184	0.009
5	Change in water quantity	28.66***	(5.847)	35.44***	(1.674)	183	0.117
6	Biome protection	−16.15*	(7.718)	53.97***	(2.624)	199	0.022
7	Marine protection	−20.34***	(6.245)	64.31***	(2.413)	154	0.065
8	Pesticide regulation	−32.08***	(8.857)	43.35***	(3.004)	200	0.062
9	Forest loss	−0.982	(6.661)	75.84***	(2.02)	174	0
10	Forest cover change	26.30**	(8.225)	68.40***	(2.734)	190	0.052
11	Fishing stocks overexploited	−5.687	(4.962)	31.40***	(1.936)	151	0.009
12	Coastal shelf fishing pressure	46.51***	(5.108)	27.89***	(1.961)	156	0.35

Standard errors in parentheses; *** $p < 0.001$, ** $p < 0.01$, * $p < 0.05$.

7　Greening the state, American style

Elizabeth Bomberg

Introduction

Over the last decade questions about the nature of the state and whether it can address contemporary global environmental challenges – especially those of sustainability and climate change – have preoccupied theoretical and practical debates. Some international relations scholars suggest globalization has rendered the state impotent and that other actors – multinational corporations, NGOs, international organizations, have become more important in determining whether and how such issues will be addressed (Held and McGrew 2002; see also Chapter 3, this volume). Meanwhile many greens deeply distrust the state and the centralization and authoritarianism it implies (Torgerson 2005); some, especially those drawn towards eco-anarchism, would even advocate its abolition (Bookchin 1991). Other theorists, however (Eckersley 2004; Paehlke and Torgerson 2005; Connelly *et al.* 2012), have argued compellingly that the state is here to stay *and* that there is much promise in the idea of reforming (or transforming) the state so that it can respond to environmental challenges (see also Chapter 1, this volume). These green state scholars suggest the possibility of developing genuinely ecologically sensitive states that can fulfill the role of a "public ecological trustee" (Eckersley 2004: 12) and coax their polity toward addressing domestic and global environmental challenges. This chapter examines the prospects of and barriers to such a transformation in the United States.

The green state

A green state is one capable of developing policies and practices designed to limit harmful emissions and achieve a sustainable future for its citizens. Such a state would assume responsibility for environmental harm domestically but also seek to develop ecologically responsible statehood globally. In this chapter particular attention is paid to the state's ability to address climate change.

In her seminal work, Eckersley (2004) identified some key challenges to greening the state (including the dominance of sovereignty, capital accumulation and democracy deficit), but also countervailing positive trends (multilateral agreements, rise of ecological modernization, and deliberative democratic practices). Complementing Eckersley's work, other writers have investigated these challenges and opportunities in more depth (Chapter 2, this volume). Ecological modernization scholars have demonstrated how states can 'green' by developing economic strategies linked to reform of the market economy and production processes (Mol 1996; Hajer 1995). Dryzek *et al.*'s (2003) comparative study identifies the state and societal features most amenable to greening strategies. They find that greening the state is more likely when environmental strategies are linked to state imperatives such as security or economic growth. Paehlke (2005), Smith (2005), Meadowcroft (2004) and Eckersley (2004) focus particularly on the role of deliberative democracy in pushing a state forward.

Despite different arguments and emphases within green state literature there is a consensus that the contemporary US lags well behind others in the development of green statehood. This chapter shares that view: the US has not achieved the domestic or global role outlined above and is not close to green statehood as defined above. The main concern of the chapter is to explain that laggard development as well as exploring how a transformation may be achieved. Most explanations for America's laggardness focus on either institutional (constitutional separation of powers; multiple veto points) or ideological barriers (neoliberalism or individualism) to greening the state. This chapter demonstrates that both institutions and ideology are important, but suggests they gain full potency only when embedded in public discourse. How the state and the challenges of climate and sustainability are understood by policymakers and the public are crucial to understanding the limits of the US as a green state, as well as the possibilities of a transformation.

To examine these barriers and their interaction, this chapter adopts a hybrid framework combining an emphasis on institutions, ideology and discourse. It uses those insights to identify the institutional and ideological barriers stymieing progress towards green statehood. It then examines how each barrier is underlined and enforced by powerful frames that currently favor anti-state, anti-climate advocates. The subsequent section explores how these institutional, ideational and discourse barriers might be overcome to allow a transformation of the state. It considers first arguments that the US central state could, by adopting a weak form of ecological modernization, develop into a potential 'environmental neoliberal state' which would focus on promoting national economic activity and technological innovation (Christoff 2005; MacNeil and Paterson 2012). The chapter counters this claim, arguing instead that any transformation must come from below the state level and must involve a change in discourse as much as in policy and practice.

Framework

This chapter draws first on new institutionalist literature to help identify and analyze the institutional factors constraining US state action. Writers in this school suggest institutional structures and norms operating in the US constrain policy action in powerful ways (Weaver and Rockman 1993; Nivola and Jones

2008). These structures include formal institutions (e.g. legislative structures, constitutional and voting rules, federalism) as well as informal institutions – behavioral norms such as adversarialism – which shape actors' political behavior. I also draw on other institutionalists who focus more on ideology (Checkel 2005), especially the norms and values of neo-liberalism and individualism. I then supplement this institutionalist literature with insights from discourse analysis, which places greater emphasis on how problems are defined, framed, argued and debated.[1] Drawing on studies of media and public opinion data, I show how attention to discursive frames provides an important supplement for understanding public acceptance of state action and transformation.

Institutional barriers

The institutional barriers to positive US state action are many. Chief among formal institutional constraints is the federal legislative system, which is "deliberately designed to restrain the scale and pace of change" (Nivola and Jones 2008: 13). The constitutional separation of powers makes policymaking difficult and gridlock more likely, especially on politically divisive issues such as climate change. Competition between the executive and congressional branches of government is built into the US policymaking system, and judicial action – either pushing or resisting environmental change – is a further powerful dynamic. More generally the US political system is characterized by its multiple veto points: actors occupying positions (in different institutions, different branches of government and at different levels of governance) can block action at several points in the policymaking process. Each point creates an opportunity for some interest or constituency to demand a concession or to block progress. In the US, a plethora of organized interests can further stagnate change and can render any reform – especially the sort required by greening – particularly difficult (Kleiman and Teles 2006: 642; Christoff and Eckersley 2011: 440). Entrenched interests are apparent in US climate and environmental policy, which is marked by vociferous constituencies on either side of a given issue (Bomberg and Schlosberg 2008; Nijhuis 2014).[2]

In recent years, climate and other environmental legislation has faced additional institutional hurdles as adversaries within Congress employ institutional rules to block executive action. The use of filibuster – an on-going speech in the Senate intended to block legislative action – has increased sharply and has been invoked to block climate and environmental legislation. More recently, its use was threatened by Republicans keen to block Obama's appointments to head the Environmental Protection Agency (EPA) (Peters 2013). These strong veto players make it more difficult to re-evaluate existing policies and even harder to change them. The resulting 'path dependency' means that it is hard to change strategy or policy, even when it outlives its usefulness, because of entrenched interests but also because of the 'sunk costs' (time and resources) already invested. It is an especially powerful explanation of current dilemmas of greening, and helps explain, for instance, the continuation of subsidies for fossil fuels, or the difficulty of developing more sustainable forms of transport (Paterson 2007).

These institutional dynamics have become more apparent in recent environmental and climate policy. The promise of transformational change in environmental and climate issues under an Obama presidency (Bomberg and Super 2009) soon reverted to legislative stagnation as congressional–executive relations soured and blockages increased. Although a modest proposal for climate legislation made it through the House in 2009 it did not survive the Senate and soon slipped off the federal (both congressional and presidential) agenda. The setback sparked dismay from environmentalists who complained of presidential broken promises and neglect. But the setback was more a product of institutional barriers rather than any personal presidential betrayal.

Accompanying these structural constraints are informal norms such as increasing and intensified partisanship, entrenched adversarialism and severe fragmentation. In the US the constitutional brakes on policymaking described above are ever present, but they have been exacerbated in recent administrations by a fiercely adversarial atmosphere. The Obama administration promised to bring to Washington not just stronger environmental policy but a new mood of bipartisanship and working across the aisle. Obama stressed that US "efforts to create jobs, achieve energy security and combat climate change demand integration among different agencies, cooperation between federal, state and local governments and partnership with the private sector" (Obama 2010), but cooperation among government, private and public actors remained elusive. By some measures the level of partisanship in US government today is the highest on record (Abramowitz 2013). Aspirational, positive environmentalism is easily sabotaged in this adversarial milieu. It means, for instance, that the veto points and institutional blocks mentioned above are invoked more often and with more vigor. Such adversarialism was rife during earlier climate change bill debates[3] but also present in more recent debates on Keystone XL oil pipeline and, especially, executive attempts to regulate carbon emissions. Using its authority under the Clean Air Act, the EPA issued rules in 2014 compelling new electricity utilities to limit emissions of any new facilities.[4] The move sparked fierce, immediate opposition from Republican opponents who, insisting the rules would decimate coal industry and harm the economy, vowed to thwart further executive action.

Ideological barriers

A closely linked set of explanations for America's 'un-green' state focuses on ideological barriers, which exacerbate institutional constraints. The most dominant of these is a neoliberal ideology, which favors markets over state action and makes it difficult for governments to take a proactive role. Peter Christoff (2005: 304), for example, notes how neoliberalism leads states to eschew responsibility for natural resources protection and instead shift control and ownership to the private sector. In their comparison of the potential of states to achieve green statehood, several authors conclude that EM strategies are easier to pursue in social democratic welfare states (Mol and Spaargaren 2000; Hajer 1995; Christoff 2005). Similarly the varieties of capitalism literature (Hall and

Soskice 2001) draw useful distinctions between coordinated market economies and liberal market economies and suggest that the latter is less likely to develop state-led environmental leadership because of a highly antagonistic relationship between markets and state. In his explanation of the US's comparatively laggard pace on climate change, for instance, Driesen (2010: 112) underlines a culture of market fundamentalism and an "ideological climate that embraced free markets as the solution to all economic and social issues and regarded vigorous government action as anathema." Meanwhile a neoliberal preference for "more market, less state" has become especially evident in congressional voting patterns in the last decade (MacNeil and Paterson 2012: 236).

Linked to neoliberalism is a strong emphasis on individualism, a distrust of the state, and a limited conception of the public good (Bomberg 2003). Foley (2007: 37) outlines American's deep historical emphasis on individualism and distrust. American liberty, he writes, acquires its meaning through the agency of the individual rather than social classes or nationality: "In American eyes it is a matter of simple logic that a society dedicated to liberty should have as its hallmark the freedom of the most fundamental constituent unit of that society – the individual citizen." That logic is reflected in the constitutional blueprint that intentionally ring-fences state power with prohibitions and constraints. But the belief also underlines public attitudes towards the scope of government action, which is often summed up as: "freedom preserved by the state must always be qualified by guarantees of freedom *from* the state" (*ibid.*: 40). Put bluntly, greening initiatives (to reduce harmful emissions, to ensure sustainability) are most likely to succeed when they do not invoke the central state.

In sum, institutional constraints and ideology defining US environmental policies and politics has led to a seemingly dysfunctional – or at least a severely challenged – green state. Its neoliberal ideology and adversarialism, in particular, seem to suggest the US would be far less likely to take a green lead compared to other, especially Nordic, welfare states characterized by greater cooperation among business, government and environmental groups (MacNeil and Paterson 2012: 234; see also the other chapters in this volume).

Yet these barriers alone do not explain US laggardness. First, the institutional barriers outlined above are not unique to the US; analysts of European Union (EU) policy have revealed a similarly rich vein of institutional hurdles, contestation and policy convolution (see Peterson and Shackleton 2012). Yet the EU has been able to take a significant leadership role on climate and sustainability (Bomberg 2009; Schreuers and Tiberghien 2007). Second, despite long-standing entrenched ideologies and barriers, the US has showed itself capable of far reaching environmental action, including under Republican presidents (Bomberg 2003). Nor must neoliberalism itself be a barrier. Christoff (2005: 304), for example, refers to Australia as a possible "neoliberal environmental state" active in promoting economic growth through environment-related state funding and activity. The hurdles facing the current US, in other words, are neither unique nor new. What is distinctive is the extent to which these hurdles are accompanied by an increasingly powerful anti-state discourse, which renders pro-active state action extremely difficult. We explore below how actors opposed to state action have successfully framed environmental action – and especially climate change – as an unimportant problem, and the state's role on climate as negative, intrusive and even 'un-American.'

Discursive barriers

Discourse analysis focuses on how problems are defined and debated, and how through that process an overall narrative (or story) emerges (Hajer 1995). In the area of climate change, opponents to action have sought to construct an overall narrative of *climate denialism* which acts as a discursive barrier to state action on climate. Key to this narrative-building is the act of framing which refers to how actors select and emphasize particular aspects of an issue according to an overarching shared narrative and set of assumptions (Miller 2000: 211). Frames can be used to draw attention to a problem (or solution), but also to deflect attention away from an issue (Baumgartner and Jones 2009).[5] In the discourse battle surrounding climate change, one of the most powerful frames employed by opponents of climate action is the 'doubt frame.' Corporate interests threatened by more rigorous climate legislation have long employed such a frame in an effort to downplay the link between greenhouse gases and warming temperatures and thus call into question the need for state action or regulation. A range of scholars (see Christoff and Eckersley 2011; Dunlap and McCright 2011; Jacques 2009; McCright and Dunlap 2003) have outlined how corporate funded organizations generate intentionally conflicting or misleading knowledge to underpin the doubt frame, and use the media links to limit and mold available information about climate change (Norgaard 2011).

The use of the doubt frame is evident in opponents' response to the Obama Administration's recent efforts to reduce emissions through EPA regulations. An example is provided by the Environmental Policy Alliance (it has intentionally appropriated the acronym of the federal Environmental Protection Agency), which was created in 2014 by a public relations firm representing large corporate interests opposed to legislation on energy or climate. On their website, the Alliance repeats claims of the well-known climate-denying Heartland Institute that the International Panel on Climate Change's (IPCC) science is "seriously flawed," the link between emissions and changing climate is "still unclear" and that alarmists have created a "fictitious global warming crisis" (Heartland Institute 2014).

According to discourse analysts, a narrative is successful if it achieves discursive dominance in public debate. Such dominance is reflected in public opinion polls and media reporting or government pronouncements (Hajer 1995). According to several criteria it appears that the climate opponents' narrative of climate denialism has taken hold in the US public debate and consciousness. Opinion polls show significant skepticism surrounding the science of climate change. Compared to citizens in most other countries Americans show much greater doubt about the existence and severity of climate change and its anthropogenic causes.

That trend is well documented by Gallup and Pew opinion polls, which have tracked the percentage of Americans agreeing that "there is no solid evidence for global warming" (Gallup Organization 2014). Although the percentage doubting the existence of climate change has decreased since 2008–9, it still remains over a quarter of the population. A much greater percentage continues to deny that humans are responsible for that change.[6]

Media portrayals, too, illustrate a dominant narrative of denialism communicated through frames of doubt.[7] A recent study analyzing television coverage of both national and international climate change reports showed that coverage of climate by major networks is low overall (an IPCC report received a total of two minutes on CNN), with an overall emphasis on doubt and even superstition. A Fox News announcer introduced the scientific consensus on climate change as "the oldest superstition around" (Media Matters 2014). According to other studies, most networks also tend to feature false balance by providing equal time and credibility to scientists confirming or denying climate change (see also Boykoff and Boykoff 2004). Similarly the doubt frame is reflected in US media's increasing use of hedging words (such as perhaps, speculative, controversial, blurry and disagreement) when reporting on climate scientists' reports. In their comparative study of coverage of the 2014 IPCC report, Bailey *et al.* (2014) note how US newspapers increased their utilization of such words even as the scientific consensus that climate change is real and humans are contributing to it has substantially strengthened.

Although scholars have given much attention to this sort of climate framing, fewer have focused on the framing of the state and how that might shape public understanding of climate and environmental policy (but see Antonio and Brulle 2011). In their public discourse many opponents of green or climate action often portray the state as oppressive, stifling prosperity and infringing economic and individual liberty. This "oppressive state" frame is highly resonant in current debates and illustrated in the Environmental Policy Alliance's full page advert in the *Wall Street Journal* (July 3, 2014) warning that "Obama's EPA ... is moving full steam ahead with oppressive energy regulations to make higher costs a reality." Similarly, opponents to climate initiatives in Congress accused the administration not just of imposing an economic burden, but of executive branch "suffocation," "over-reach" and a President "hell bent on adding layer after layer of harmful red tape," in the words of a Republican Congressman quoted in the *Washington Post* on July 15, 2014.

Although the resonance of the anti-state frame is often overlooked, it can be powerful. One telling indicator is the consecutive Gallup polls which gauge over time Americans' view of the state, business and trade unions. Asked in 2013 which will be the biggest threat to the country – business, labor or government – an overwhelming 72 percent believed big government posed the gravest threat. Moreover that percentage has risen significantly in the last decade (Gallup Organization 2013).[8] In sum, according to several indicators an anti-climate and anti-state narrative currently enjoys discourse dominance in US debate. Such dominance suggests a different sort of transition may be needed to green the state, one that tackles institutional and ideological barriers, but also reframes climate, the state, and citizens' relationship to both.

Transformation of the state?

The institutional and ideological barriers to a green US state are formidable. Crucially, these features gain potency when combined with a narrative eschewing action on climate generally, and especially action by the state. But we also know the US system can feature dynamism, and the ability to change, innovate and adapt. It has done so in the past on issues linked to the environment (Bomberg 2003). Moreover the state, and our conceptions of it, can transform and have done so throughout history (Micklethwait and Wooldridge 2014). So how might the US state be greened? What are prospects for a transition? While the barriers outlined above cannot be entirely removed, several avenues for reform are possible and under way.

Empowering the central state

One way to bypass veto points outlined above has already been attempted: it involves the executive taking a more active unilateral role in promoting climate care and sustainability. As mentioned above, the Obama administration has used enacting legislation to pursue carbon reduction objectives through unilateral authority in the form of federal greenhouse gas reduction regulations (Kahn 2014). The measure is an example of how the administrative state has been able to use powerful direct state intervention to reduce harmful pollutants and improve public health. However, this top-down move is politically unpopular and subject to considerable pushback.

Likely to be more successful are executive actions reframed not as climate or carbon reduction initiatives but as economic opportunities. Echoing descriptions of Christoff's (2005) environmental neoliberal state, this ecological modernization approach shifts the "capital accumulation imperative" from acting as a hurdle (Eckersley 2004) to a key tool in shifting to a low carbon society. The shift is in evidence within the Obama administration. His earlier global emphasis on the need to protect the environment and avoid a "Planet in Peril" (Obama 2009) has shifted to a frame of economic opportunity for the nation. Similarly Fletcher (2009) tracks the development of a positive "opportunity frame" (the 'Apollo' frame) with an emphasis on industrial transformation, technological innovation, and economic opportunity.[9] MacNeil and Paterson (2012: 241) also note the Obama administration's increasing tendency to present climate initiatives (such as renewables) as a technologically savvy, neoliberal economic opportunity.

Similarly, central state action could be further empowered if climate and environmental goals were couched in terms of national security. Schlosberg and Rinfret (2008) note how reframing climate as security issue makes clear the links between climate and the need for government action. For the US that security frame would encompass security of lives and livelihoods. Such a shift is now more relevant following recent dramatic weather events, which proponents of climate action can link to climate change. This "scary weather" frame – invoking a threat to American infrastructure, farm land and lives – is very pertinent when conveyed as an immediate economic threat. The third US National Climate Assessment (NCA), which was released by the federal government in May 2014, outlined the direct consequences for the US economy if no action were taken. With a heavy emphasis on US producers it warned:

> Climate change, once considered an issue for a distant future, has moved firmly into the present. Corn producers in Iowa, oyster growers in Washington State, and maple syrup producers in Vermont are all observing climate-related changes that are outside of recent experience …
>
> (US Global Change Research Program 2014: 1)

A tandem security frame – that of energy security or independence – held promise in the early 2000s. This frame stressed the need to conserve and limit fossil fuel use to avoid dependence on dodgy foreign energy sources. But this frame is no longer as resonant following the recent boon in shale gas, which has increased remarkably the US access to domestic energy. Exploitation of shale gas through hydraulic fracturing (or fracking) is not new, but it has experienced an astonishing revival in the US. Despite profound environmental concerns, fracking operations have increased dramatically, with yields jumping from less than 1 percent in the late 1990s to 20 percent of domestic gas production by 2010 (EIA 2012). While its contribution to low carbon state remains controversial,[10] shale gas has certainly rendered far less powerful the notion that energy conservation and climate reduction is the key to ensuring US energy security. Nonetheless, wider national security framing remains potentially potent.

For its proponents such reframing could herald a wider, much more fundamental reframing of green issues away from a vaguely altruistic goal to a central organizing principle of the state's domestic and foreign policies. Some writers have suggested these measures herald the emergence of an "American style" ecological modernization (Schlosberg and Rinfret 2008). But there are limits to this strategy and its contribution to a US green state. First, while the Administration's focus on unilateral action is understandable, Obama's measures will be subject to challenge (they already are), not just by corporate interests but other organs of the state (including Congress and perhaps also the Courts). Also, while this strategy involves rethinking and reframing climate change and its effects, it does not rethink the state. Nor does it involve citizens or change their view of the state. Finally, this reframed narrative has become strikingly inward looking and does not focus on a direct global role for US. Proponents argue that the US acting domestically would inevitably address global responsibilities, but this domestic focus calls into question the green state requirement of multilateral action and engagement (see Eckersley 2004). In short, this path alone will not lead to an American green state.

Relocating the state

Another approach is not to empower the state but to relocate its locus of power. Americans' view of a/the central state is distrustful, and becoming more so (Micklethwait and Wooldridge 2014). But views of their own state (e.g. California, Wisconsin, New Hampshire) or local governments tend to be much more charitable (McKay 2013: 66). Thus empowering the sub-state and local level is a way to reshape citizens' views of government and state action. It might, in other words, form part of a slow move to rehabilitating the state in the eyes of its citizens and counter opponents' depiction of state action as oppressive and threatening. Moreover, while the federal institutional obstacles outlined above are not absent on the state level, they are more easily overcome. The expanding literature on US cities, states and climate suggests how on the subnational level climate advocates are creating new initiatives or expanding existing ones (Selin and VanDeveer 2009: 309). Barry Rabe (2004, 2010) and others have documented a plethora of state-led collaborative initiatives to combat climate, including greenhouse gas (GHG) inventories, mandatory caps, and multi-state carbon cap and trade programs. These same measures have struggled to gain acceptance on the federal level. Also significant is the extent to which these government-led initiatives are (partially) able to circumvent the partisanship and adversarialism of the federal level. In contrast to federal-level stagnation, state government climate initiatives have been generally bipartisan and consensual (Rabe 2004). Also striking is states' growing willingness to engage beyond the nation-state to forge international networks of climate initiatives and ideas (Selin and VanDeveer 2009: 312; Climate Group 2014; Chapter 11, this volume). Of course states vary significantly in their embrace of green policies and it is easy to overstate the sub-state green transformation. While Vermont, California and others have introduced far-reaching innovative climate measures, other states remain inactive if not downright hostile to climate action.[11]

Empowering the citizens

Relocating state power down to a level closer to citizens is also a way to empower greater citizen action, whatever their home state. Eckersley's vision of the green state is based on notions of citizen input because "all those potentially affected by ecological risks ought to have some meaningful opportunity to participate, or be represented in the determination of politics of decisions that may generate risks" (Eckersley 2004: 243). Similarly, Dryzek *et al.*'s (2003) comparative study underlined the core role of social movements and NGOs. In the American context, citizen action to green the state will be most powerful when framed in a distinctly American context. In particular it will be strongest when wedded to two powerful trends in US political culture that were first observed by de Tocqueville in the nineteenth century. The first is an appeal to the individual as an agent of social dynamism (Foley 2007: 43). But the second American trend is equally important. It involves tapping the ethos of communal responsibility through the building of community groups and organizations. That appeal would both moderate the effects of the individual and create an intermediary organization that would resist the intrusion of "any large scale organized force" (i.e. the state) (de Tocqueville quoted by Foley, *ibid.*: 45). Americans are individualists but they are also joiners. Both strands can be harnessed for climate action (see Paehlke 2005).

In short, an ecological modernization approach – reframing climate as economy-boosting, technology-rich, security-enhancing project aiding America's current and future generations – is an important step in the construction of a green state. But equally important is reframing the state, society and individual as outlined by Christoff (1996) in his version of strong ecological modernization. How citizens view the state, and their own role within it, will be crucial. In practical terms that means action must come from below. We have already seen such initiatives in the area of city or local measures on climate mitigation (Gore and Robinson 2009). These mitigation initiatives are small scale and most are non-binding, but they allow local actors to shape policy and behavior on day-to-day activities and thus can alter citizens' conceptions of climate and climate action. Such activity resembles what transition theorists refer to as micro niches: protected spaces for experimental activity and developments, which can over time, challenge or transform dominant practices (Chapter 1, this volume; Berkhout *et al.* 2003).

While such micro mitigation activities are well documented, less attention has been given to climate adaptation initiatives, perhaps because adaptation measures do not combat climate change and thus are not immediately seen as part of greening or low carbon transition. Yet adaption projects can play an important role in reframing how citizens view climate and the state. Crucially, recent activity in the area of climate adaptation has involved federal authorities, but not in a visible role. Federal authorities have worked with local governments and groups, providing funding and expertise for adaption projects. Because that federal action is low profile it tends to sidestep high profile political battles. As one observer noted, "the idea is to get this conversation on climate change into town halls and city halls and planning boards and zoning board where it's not partisan: it's just very practical" (quoted in Khan 2014: 2). This reframing strategy is indirect but vital. First, it counters the climate denial narrative: climate change is real and these are its impacts. Second, it encourages and builds partnerships: you need to develop common sense strategies to deal with climate change (and we can help). These programs are growing in strength and number (CEQ 2014) and suggest how communities, towns, cities and states might act as incubators of new policies or ideas which may eventually lead to a major federal shift. The next challenge is how to enact that shift – how to scale up sub-state initiatives to the federal or central state or, in the language of transition theorists, how to ensure norms and practices adopted in the niche become practiced more widely (Berkhout *et al.* 2003).

Conclusion

Efforts to green the US state have been bogged down by features distinctive to the US: these include specific institutional pathologies, competition between entrenched interests, a privileging of the economy, and a limited conception of the public good. This chapter has identified several such barriers but has also suggested how each is cemented by powerful frames and a discourse dominance currently enjoyed by opponents of any green state action. Overcoming such barriers requires bypassing veto points but also – as advocated by ecological modernization proponents – reframing climate in terms of economic opportunity and security. This chapter has suggested further, however, that this ecological modernization approach is not enough to green the state because it ignores the role of citizens. Reframing climate initiatives as economy-boosting does little to assuage citizen concerns of an overweening state, or involve them in a transition. Efforts to green the American state will thus need to reframe the state and citizens' role within it. In the US, at least, it will mean ensuring green initiatives are not concentrated at central level but are relocated to the subnational level and citizens themselves. In short, greening needs to come from below. It needs to be reframed not as a centralized green state endeavor but as a bottom up, citizen-inspired venture.

While this chapter has focused on the US and highlighted its distinctive role, the analysis offers wider insights into the nature of green state transformation. First, attention to institutional and ideological factors is clearly important; they can spur or block sustainability and climate initiatives. But equally important is an understanding of how climate, sustainability and the state are themselves understood and framed by citizens, interests and policymakers. Second, any analysis of the state's role must include attention to its citizens. Ecological modernization accounts often neglect this aspect of green state development. The chapter has thus underlined the argument made by Eckersley, Paehlke, Smith and others: green measures are unlikely to be successful without opportunities for democratic participation. Further, this chapter has shown not only that participation is important, but that citizen and grassroots niche activity can thrive even when the central state is stymied. That suggests grassroots action might not only supplement, but could even trigger or spark broader initiatives. Finally while this chapter has made much of the US's distinctive, if not exceptional, characteristics, every state is distinct and greening solutions must recognize that diversity. There is, in other words, no one way to green or transform the state, but rather a mix of framing strategies and initiatives which should reflect individual state characteristic even while seeking common global solutions.

Notes

1 New Institutionalists do not ignore discourse but it is not usually central to their analysis (see Schmidt 2008).
2 For a recent example of seemingly implacably opposed interests clashing over environmental issues, see Nijhuis's (2014) coverage of on-going debates concerning

the Keystone XL pipeline, which, if approved, would create a direct link between the Alberta oil sands and the Gulf of Mexico.

3 Typical was John Boehner's (House Republican leader) heated claim that the proposed climate change bill's cap and trade "will increase taxes on all Americans who drive a car, who have a job, who turn on a light switch, pure and simple" (quoted in the *Economist* 7 March 2009: 48).

4 Under the Clean Air Act (as interpreted by subsequent court rulings) federal executive agencies have the power to regulate CO_2 emissions. The new rules announced by the Obama administration in 2013 and unveiled by the EPA in 2014 require all new power plants to cut carbon emissions by 30% by 2030.

5 Frames and narratives are sometimes used interchangeably in the discourse literature. In this chapter, narratives refer to the overarching idea or story being portrayed (e.g. climate denialism), while framing (e.g. the doubt frame) is the technique used by actors to simplify and communicate that wider narrative.

6 The results indicate sharp partisan differences, with over 50% of Republicans in the 'skeptic' camp compared with only 15% of Democrats (Gallup Organization 2014; see also Pew Research Center 2013).

7 While this section is concerned primarily with the media as reflecting or representing public understanding, its role is of course interactive: the media not merely reflects but can also shape public perceptions (see Boykoff and Boykoff 2004).

8 The precise question asked was: "Which will be the biggest threat to the country in the future: big business, big labor or big government?"

9 The Apollo metaphor compares the task of controlling climate to the America's successful 1960s effort to put a man on the moon.

10 Advocates promote shale as a 'transition' fuel: cleaner than coal and therefore a step towards a more sustainable energy future. Opponents note that coal will simply be shipped and burned elsewhere, however. They also highlight the risk during drilling operations of escaped methane, a greenhouse gas more potent than CO_2 (see Small *et al.* 2014).

11 To illustrate, Louisiana and Texas have introduced state measures requiring educators to teach climate change denial as a valid scientific position (Bidwell 2014).

References

Abramowitz, A., 2013 *The Polarized Public: Why American Government is So Dysfunctional*. Pearson, New York.

Antonia, R., and Brulle, R., 2011 The unbearable lightness of politics: climate change denial and political polarization. *The Sociological Quarterly* 52: 195–202.

Bailey, A., Giangola, L., and Boykoff, M., 2014 How grammatical choice shapes media representations of climate (un)certainty. *Environmental Communication* 8 197–215.

Baumgartner, R., and Jones, B., 2009 *Agendas and Instability in American Politics*, 2nd edn. University of Chicago Press, Chicago, IL.

Berkhout, F., Smith, A., and Stirling, A., 2003 *Socio-technological Regimes and Transition Contexts*. SPRU Working Paper 106. June. Science Policy Research Unit, Brighton.

Bidwell, A., 2014 Climate change debate: coming soon to a school near you. June 20. Retrieved June 13, 2014 from www.usnews.com/news/articles/2014/06/20/how-the-climate-change-debate-is-influencing-whats-taught-in-schools.

Bomberg, E., 2003 Environmental policy in a divided democracy. In Singh, R., (ed) *Governing America: the Politics of a Divided Democracy* 302–20. Oxford University Press, Oxford.

Bomberg, E., 2009 Governance for sustainable development: the US and EU compared. In Schreurs, M., Selin, H., and VanDeveer, S., (eds) *Transatlantic Environmental and Energy Politics* 21–40. Ashgate, Burlington, VT.

Bomberg, E., and Schlosberg, D., 2008 US environmentalism in comparative perspective. *Environmental Politics* 17: 337–48.

Bomberg, E., and Super, B., 2009 The 2008 US presidential election: Obama and the environment. *Environmental Politics* 18: 424–30.

Bookchin, M., 1991 *The Ecology of Freedom*, 2nd edn. Black Rose Books, Montreal.

Boykoff, M., and Boykoff, J., 2004 Balance as bias: global warming and the US prestige press. *Global Environmental Change* 14: 125–36.

CEQ 2014 State, local, and tribal leaders task force on climate preparedness and resilience. Retrieved June 13, 2014 from www.whitehouse.gov/administration/eop/ceq/initiatives/resilience/taskforce.

Checkel, J., 2005 International institutions and socialization in Europe: introduction and framework. *International Organization* 59: 801–26.

Christoff, P., 1996 Ecological modernization, ecological modernities. *Environmental Politics* 5: 476–500.

Christoff, P., 2005 Green governance and the green state: capacity building as a political project. In Paehlke, R., and Torgerson, D., (eds) *Managing Leviathan. Environmental Politics and the Administrative State* 289–310. Broadview Press, Plymouth.

Christoff, P., and Eckersley, R., 2011 Comparing state responses. In Dryzek, J., Norgaard, R., and Schlosberg, D., (eds) *The Oxford Handbook of Climate Change and Society* 431–48. Oxford University Press, Oxford.

Climate Group 2014 States and regions alliance: what we do. Retrieved May 9, 2014 from www.theclimategroup.org/programs/states-and-regions.

Connelly, J., Smith, G., Benson, D., and Saunders, C., 2012 *Politics and the Environment: From Theory to Practice*, 3rd edn. Routledge, Abingdon.

Driesen, D., (ed) 2010 *Economic Thought and US Climate Change Policy*. MIT Press, Cambridge, MA.

Dryzek, J., Downs, D., Hunold, C., Schlosberg, D., and Hernes 2003 *Green States and Social Movements*. Oxford University Press, Oxford.

Dunlap, R., and McCright, A., 2011 Organized climate change denial. In Dryzek, J., Norgaard, R., and Schlosberg, D., (eds) *The Oxford Handbook of Climate Change and Society* 144–60. Oxford University Press, Oxford.

Eckersley, R., 2004 *The Green State: Rethinking Democracy and Sovereignty*. MIT Press, Cambridge, MA.

EIA 2012 *Annual Energy Outlook*. Energy Information Administration, Washington, DC.

Fletcher, L., 2009 Clearing the air: the contribution of frame analysis to understanding climate policy in the US. *Environmental Politics* 18: 800–16.

Foley, M., 2007 *American Credo: The Place of Ideas in US Politics*. Oxford University Press, Oxford.

Gallup Organization 2013 Record high in US say big government greatest threat. December 18. Retrieved June 13, 2014 from www.gallup.com/poll/166535/record-high-say-big-government-greatest-threat.aspx.

Gallup Organization 2014 One in four in US are solidly skeptical of global warming. April 22. Retrieved September 20, 2014 from www.gallup.com/poll/168620/one-four-solidly-skeptical-global-warming.aspx.

Gore, C., and Robinson, P., 2009 Local government response to climate change: our last, best hope? In Selin, H., and VanDeveer, S.D., (eds) *Changing Climates in North*

American Politics: Institutions, Policymaking and Multilevel Governance 138–58. MIT Press, Cambridge, MA.

Hajer, M., 1995 *The Politics of Environmental Discourse: Ecological Modernization and the Policy Process*. Oxford University Press, Oxford.

Hall, P., and Soskice, D., 2001 *Varieties of Capitalism: The Institutional Foundations of Comparative Advantage*. Oxford University Press, Oxford.

Heartland Institute 2014 Myths busted at climate conference. July 18. Retrieved July 21, 2014 from http://news.heartland.org/newspaper-article/2014/07/18/myths-busted-climate-change-conference.

Held, D., and McGrew, A., 2002 *Globalization/Anti-globalization*. Polity Press, Oxford.

Jacques, P., 2009 *Environmental Skepticism: Ecology, Power and Public Life*. Ashgate, Burlington, VT.

Kahn, A., 2014 The surprising way Obama is trying to tackle climate change. *PBS Frontline* February 27. Retrieved March 28, 2014 from www.pbs.org/wgbh/pages/frontline/environment/climate-of-doubt/the-surprising-way-obama-is-trying-to-tackle-climate-change.

Kleiman, M., and Teles, S., 2006 Market and non-market failures. In Moran, M., Rein, M., and Goodin, R., (eds) *The Oxford Handbook of Public Policy* 624–50. Oxford University Press, Oxford.

MacNeil, R., and Paterson, M., 2012 Neoliberal climate policy: from market fetishism to the developmental state. *Environmental Politics* 21: 230–47.

McCright, A., and Dunlap, R., 2003 Defeating Kyoto: the conservative movement's impact on US climate change policy. *Social Problems* 50: 348–73.

McKay, D., 2013 *American Politics and Society*, 8th edn. Blackwell, London.

Meadowcroft, J., 2004 Participation and sustainable development: modes of citizen, community and organisational involvement. In Lafferty, W., (ed) *Governance for Sustainable Development: The Challenge of Adapting Form to Function* 162–90. Edward Elgar, Cheltenham.

Media Matters 2014 Top cable news coverage of federal climate change report cast doubt on science. May 9. Retrieved February 15, 2015 from http://mediamatters.org/research/2014/05/09/study-top-cable-news-coverage-of federal-climat/199247.

Micklethwait, J., and Wooldridge, A., 2014 *The Fourth Revolution: The Global Race to Reinvent the State*. Penguin, London.

Miller, C., 2000 The dynamics of framing environmental values and policy: four models of societal processes. *Environmental Values* 9: 211–33.

Mol, A., 1996 Ecological modernisation and institutional reflexivity: environmental reform in the late modern age. *Environmental Politics* 5: 302–23.

Mol, A., and Spaargaren, G., 2000 Ecological modernisation theory in debate: a review. *Environmental Politics* 9 17–41.

Nijhuis, M., 2014 Rethinking the keystone pipeline. *New Yorker* June 25. Retrieved June 2014 from www.newyorker.com/tech/elements/rethinking-the-keystone-pipeline.

Nivola, P., and Jones, C., 2008 'Change' or plus ça change …? Pondering presidential politics and policy after Bush *Brookings Issues in Governance Studies* Paper 20. Retrieved February 15, 2015 from www.brookings.edu/papers/2008/09_change_nivola_jones.aspx.

Norgaard 2011 Climate denial: emotion, psychology, culture and political economy. In Dryzek, J., Norgaard, R., and Schlosberg, D., (eds) *The Oxford Handbook of Climate Change and Society* 399–413. Oxford University Press, Oxford.

Obama, B., 2009 From peril to progress White House address. Retrieved November 9, 2009 from www.whitehouse.gov/blog_post/Fromperiltoprogress.

Obama, B., 2010 Press statement on energy & environment: a new foundation. Retrieved November 9, 2009 from www.whitehouse.gov/issues/energy-and-environment.

Paehlke, R., 2005 Democracy and environmentalism: opening a door to the administrative state. In Paehlke, R., and Torgerson, D., (eds) *Managing Leviathan: Environmental Politics and the Administrative State* 25–46. Broadview Press, Plymouth.

Paehlke, R., and Torgerson, D., (eds) 2005 *Managing Leviathan: Environmental Politics and the Administrative State*. Broadview Press, Plymouth.

Paterson, M., 2007 *Automobile Politics: Ecology and Cultural Political Economy*. Cambridge University Press, Cambridge.

Peters, J., 2013 Republican drive to block cabinet picks may spur change to senate rules. *New York Times* May 16. Retrieved May 7, 2014 from www.nytimes.com/2013/05/17/us/politics/obama-appointees-fight-may-change-senate-rules.html?_r=0.

Peterson, J., and Shackleton, M., 2012 *The Institutions of the European Union*, 2nd edn. Oxford University Press, Oxford.

Pew Research Center 2013 GOP deeply divided over climate change. November 1. Retrieved May 7, 2014 from www.people-press.org/2013/11/01/gop-deeply-divided-over-climate-change/#trends-in-views-on-global-warming.

Rabe, B., 2004 *Statehouse and Greenhouse: The Merging Politics of American Climate Change Policy*. Brookings Institution Press, Washington, DC.

Rabe, B., (ed) 2010 *Greenhouse Governance: Addressing Climate Change in America*. Brookings Institution Press, Washington, DC.

Schlosberg, D., and Rinfret, S., 2008 Ecological modernization – American style. *Environmental Politics* 17: 254–75.

Schmidt, V., 2008 Taking ideas and discourse seriously: explaining change through discursive institutionalism as the fourth 'new institutionalism.' *European Political Science Review* 2: 1–25.

Schreuers, M., and Tiberghien, Y., 2007 Multi-level reinforcement: explaining European Union leadership in climate change. *Global Environmental Politics* 7: 19–46.

Selin, H., and VanDeveer, S., 2009 North American climate governance: policymaking and institutions in the multilevel greenhouse. In Selin, H., and VanDeveer, S., (eds) *Changing Climates and Institution Building across the Continent* 305–25. MIT Press, Cambridge, MA.

Small, M.J., Stern, P.C., Bomberg, E., Christopherson, S.M., Goldstein, B.D., Israel, A.L., Jackson, R.B., Krupnick, A.K., Mauter, M.S., Nash, J., North, D.W., Olmstead, S.M., Prakash, P., Rabe, B., Richardson, N., Tierney, S., Webler, T., Wong-Parodi, G., and Zielinska, B., 2014 Risks and risk governance in unconventional shale development. *Environmental Science and Technology* 48: 8289–97. Retrieved July 7, 2014 from http://pubs.acs.org/doi/full/10.1021/es502111u.

Smith, G., 2005 Democratic deliberation and environmental policy: opportunities and barriers in Britain. In Paehlke, R., and Torgerson, D., (eds) *Managing Leviathan: Environmental Politics and the Administrative State* 209–34. Broadview Press, Plymouth.

Torgerson, D., 2005 Obsolescent Leviathan: problems of order in administrative thought. In Paehlke, R., and Torgerson, D., (eds) *Managing Leviathan: Environmental Politics and the Administrative State* 11–24. Broadview Press, Plymouth.

US Global Change Research Program 2014 *Climate Change Impacts in the US*. 3rd NCA report. Retrieved June 13, 2014 from http://nca2014.globalchange.gov.

Weaver, R.K., and Rockman, A., (eds) 1993 *Do Institutions Matter? Government Capabilities in the United States and Abroad*. Brookings Institution Press, Washington, DC.

Part III
Transforming the state toward climate objectives

Nordic experiences

8 Blue and yellow makes green?

Ecological modernization in Swedish climate policy

Paul Tobin

Introduction

Climate change increases distributional conflicts, creates tension between policy objectives, and challenges the viability of the existing dominant economic model (Gough and Meadowcroft 2011: 493–95). Eckersley (2004: 91) argues that "[g]iven the seriousness and urgency of [climate change] ... building on the state governance structures that already exist seems to be a more fruitful path to take" than dissolving the existing patchwork quilt of states. A green state builds on existing capitalist structures and adds environmental principles to the core aims of the state (*ibid.*: 83). At the formation of the United Nations Framework Convention on Climate Change (UNFCCC) in 1992, 23 states, all capitalist, were identified as 'developed,' thus sharing the greatest responsibility to reduce greenhouse gas emissions (UNFCCC 2014a). Sweden is one of the 23 states and has frequently been identified as a pioneer regarding its environmental policies (Lafferty and Meadowcroft 2000; Lundqvist 2004) and its climate legislation (Friberg 2008; Burck *et al.* 2009). Thus, if any state may be considered a green state regarding climate change, it is likely to be Sweden. However, being a relative leader is not the same as becoming a green state.

Meadowcroft (2005) argued that it would be at least 15 to 20 years before a green state would be realized. To avoid the two degree increase in global temperatures, identified as the maximum change the world can endure, however, states must adopt the properties of the green state much sooner. According to Christoff's (2005) typology of states' environmental performance, Sweden was classified as only one 'level' short of being defined as a green state in 2005. In 2006, Sweden saw a change in government from the traditionally dominant Social Democrats (*Socialdemokraterna*) to the Conservative/Liberal Alliance (*Alliansen*) of four center-right parties (Aylott and Bolin 2007: 621). I use Christoff's typology to analyze the new government's response to climate change during its first term of office, until 2010, and ask whether Sweden evolved to become a green state. Climate policy has been selected for exploration as climate change arguably represents the greatest current environmental threat (DiMento and Doughman 2007), yet has been neglected in the current green state literature.

To become a green state, it is increasingly argued that a state must exhibit the characteristics of ecological modernization (EM) (see also Eckersley 2004; Barry and Eckersley 2005; Christoff 2005; Meadowcroft 2005). For Christoff (2005: 41) *strong* EM must be present in a green state, which is EM in combination with biocentric values. As such, this chapter will begin by outlining the theoretical foundations of EM and the green state. Next, a cursory methodology of how to measure whether Sweden was a green state will be developed. The bulk of this chapter assesses how the Alliance government dealt with four key climate policy areas during 2006–10, according to the principles of strong EM. The primacy of the policy areas – overall emissions reductions, renewable energy production, energy efficiency, and renewable transport development – is evident as they are prioritized in the four headline goals of Sweden's 2009 Energy Bill, which was the standout piece of legislation during the Conservative/Liberal Alliance's first term of office. Finally, it will be argued that Sweden did not become a green state during the period studied, but instead continued to be what Christoff (2005) has termed an 'ecological welfare state': sufficiently ambitious to be a global leader, but not a green state regarding climate change.

Ecological modernization and the green state

Ecological modernization is presented as a means by which capitalism can accommodate the environmental challenge (Chapter 1, this volume; Gouldson and Murphy 1997: 75). Due to the reliance of EM on the market, the concept has been seen as a tacit endorsement of pre-existing economic inequalities (Eckersley 2000: 239). Additionally, as the paradigm seeks to improve efficiency, rather than reduce overall consumption, environmental degradation is almost certain to occur; "[i]n short, it seeks more environmentally efficient ways of expanding output" (Barry and Eckersley 2005: 262). Expansion of output is clearly incompatible with mitigating climate change. EM has been described as ineffective for transboundary issues because economies are not transformed as much as polluting industries are simply relocated to states with weaker environmental legislation (Schnaiberg et al. 2002: 21). Moreover, according to Davidson (2012: 32) and Gouldson and Murphy (1997), the presumption that sufficiently effective technology will be developed is technologically deterministic, necessitating that a degree of biocentrism is at least partly employed in order to avoid drastic resource shortages, and transform weak EM into strong EM (Christoff 2005). Biocentrism emphasizes equality between the species by challenging assumptions of anthropocentrism; all aspects of nature are argued to possess an inherent value, regardless of their utility to humanity (Taylor 1981; Sterba 2011). Thus, policies that protect the environment because of its intrinsic value, rather than instrumental benefits for humanity, will be seen as biocentric. This chapter therefore posits that if a country is to become a green state, policies reflecting the principles of strong EM must be developed.

For Eckersley (2004: 3), the green state is a normative idea as well as a theoretical framework, and thus she helps us conceptualize how states 'should' act in order to achieve sustainability. Yet while localized issues may be more easily addressed by the state, transboundary challenges such as climate change require a green state that is willing to pursue policy solutions for both localized and international environmental challenges (Meadowcroft 2005: 5). Although climate change may be complex, its high-profile status draws greater awareness to environmental threats, and has pushed the environment up the political agenda. Eckersley (2004: 169) acknowledges that the green state she theorized may never be finalized, because of inherent conflicts between environmental and developmental priorities. Christoff (2005: 44) argues that states which *almost* exhibit the necessary criteria for being a green state – namely 'environmental welfare states' – "engage in weak ecological modernization," of which an example was Sweden, alongside Netherlands. They have already achieved a high commitment to human welfare environmentalism, underpinned by moderate budgetary commitment and state capacity regarding ecological issues (*ibid.*: 40). Therefore, in order to minimize the inherent weaknesses within EM described above, a state must develop a high commitment to biocentric values (i.e. *strong* EM; *ibid.*: 41).

Methodology

'Environmental policy' concerns many areas of a state's activity, such as biodiversity protection, air and water pollution mitigation, and the minimization of greenhouse gases, among others. As such, determining whether Sweden may be considered a green state across all of these areas is beyond the scope of this chapter. Climate policy is not a proxy for the green state, but rather a single – yet highly significant – constituent part and has been selected because of the many threats posed by climate change if left unchecked (DiMento and Doughman 2007). More specifically, the four headline policy areas identified within the 2009 Energy Bill are examined, as their prominence in the Bill demonstrates their significance to climate change mitigation. While it is unlikely that any state would become a green state in the space of one term of government, Christoff's (2005) identification of Sweden as an environmental welfare state suggests that if any state made the transition during 2006–10, it would be Sweden.

I share Christoff's (2005) argument that in order for a state to be considered a green state, it must exhibit the features of strong EM. Therefore, this chapter interprets EM as a means of technological adjustment in narrow terms, and so EM is assumed to be inadequate for a green state. Thus, for Sweden to be considered a green state, it must have employed not only the pro-capitalist and pro-technology principles of EM, but also a biocentric concern for nature in its own right (Sterba 2011; Taylor 1981). In order to be a green state, overall consumption levels and the production of greenhouse gases must not merely be made more efficient, but reduced in absolute terms (Eckersley 2004: 76).

Swedish climate policy

Sweden has long been seen as an environmental leader (cf. Chapter 9, this volume), having been the first state in the world to create an Environmental Protection Agency in 1967. By 2006, Sweden had halved greenhouse gas emissions from electricity and district heating since the 1970s, thanks in part to an energy portfolio dominated by hydropower (45%) and nuclear energy (44%) (Regeringskansliet 2009: 20–21; Sarasini 2009: 639). Electricity production was almost carbon-free by the start of the period under investigation, reflecting Sweden's pioneering approach to climate change. Sweden was found to be the most ambitious state in the world in 2009 for its climate policy (Burck *et al.* 2009).

In 2006 there was a change in government from the traditionally dominant Social Democratic Party to a center-right coalition that remained in power throughout the period covered in this chapter, before being replaced by a minority Social Democrat government in September 2014. The willingness of the center-right parties to co-operate as a new Conservative/Liberal Alliance was a shift in Swedish politics. In June 2006, the Alliance agreed a common position on energy policy, which ended the Centre Party's long-held opposition to nuclear power (Aylott and Bolin 2007: 626). The Alliance won the 2006 election comfortably, becoming the first surplus majority coalition government in Sweden since 1981 (Widfeldt 2007: 1118). Even prior to the election of the more pro-market Alliance in 2006, climate change had already begun to be seen as a means of providing economic development in Sweden and not just a constraint on existing lifestyles. Political parties across the spectrum were building a narrative that "more and more construct[ed] climate change as an Opportunity rather than a Sacrifice" (Lundqvist 2004: 104). The chapter will assess four policy areas to determine the extent to which the principles of EM and biocentrism have been married.

Overall emissions reductions

The Social Democrats, in government until 2006, demonstrated a strong commitment to both environmental protection and economic growth, with an ambitious overall greenhouse gas emissions reduction target for 2020 of 25 percent from a 1990 baseline. The Coalition Government built on the ambition of Energy Bills passed in 2002 and 2006 and raised this target considerably, to a world-leading 40 percent in the 2009 Energy Bill. The 40 percent target related to emissions produced outside the EU Emissions Trading Scheme, in sectors such as housing, transport and waste (Regeringskansliet 2009: 2). "The former opposition, now in government, here seemed to have higher ambitions (40 percent versus 25 percent) than the former Social Democratic government" (Zannakis 2009: 118).

The bold increase from 25 percent to 40 percent may initially suggest that the Conservative/Liberal Alliance was demonstrating much greater climate ambition than both its Social Democrat predecessor and contemporary governments around the world (UNFCCC 2014b). Yet Zannakis (2009: 118) notes that while the 25 percent target of the Social Democrat government referred to greenhouse gas reductions made purely in Sweden, one third of the Alliance's 40 percent target could be met by flexible mechanisms, such as the Clean Development Mechanism (CDM) and Joint Implementation (JI). CDM and JI are market based emissions reductions tools, whereby CDM refers to the funding of emissions reductions in developing states, and JI encompasses joint projects between two developed states (UNFCCC 2014c). The ability to use CDM or JI to meet the 40 percent target was not well received by opposition parties, the Church or environmental groups, as it was seen as a disincentive to the development of more radical domestic policies (Zannakis 2009: 119). The perception of the Alliance was that policy-makers must make ambitious goals, but that these must be affordable to the Swedish population in the short term and not facilitate a loss of industry to states with less strict emissions goals.

By enabling investments via JI or CDM to count towards the state's 40 percent target, Sweden only slightly increased its overall target for domestic emissions reductions. Indeed, under the EU's 'burden-sharing agreement' as part of the Kyoto Protocol, those states that failed to meet their emissions reductions goals were required to make up for the remaining emissions via JI and CDM. The instruments were thus associated with less radical attempts to reduce emissions, and were seen by some as not counting towards 'genuine' emissions reductions. As such, the inclusion of flexible mechanisms reflected a paradigm shift regarding attitudes towards climate change in Sweden. Zannakis (2009: 150) argues that, "[t]he shift of Government in 2006 … slightly marked Swedish climate policy, which is manifested in the Climate Commission report from 2008" that led to the Energy Bill of 2009. This "slightly marked" change of approach reflected movement towards the greater flexibility and market assumptions of EM. Such a change was in keeping with the more market-friendly ideologies of the Coalition Government.

In sum therefore, it must be remembered that the 40 percent goal, despite including flexible mechanisms, equated to a 26.6 percent reduction in domestic emissions, which was greater than the 25 percent reduction goal introduced by the Social Democrats, and still placed Sweden at the forefront of global climate policies. The geographical location of reductions makes little difference to a transboundary issue such as climate change, in which catastrophic climate change may only be prevented if global emissions levels are reduced. However, when seeking to assess the extent to which an individual state lives up to ideals of the green state, such decisions play a crucial role. By including flexible mechanisms, the pressure for greater domestic climate ambition was reduced, thus weakening Sweden's progress towards becoming a green state. Had a more biocentric commitment been present, Sweden would have employed flexible mechanisms as additional tools, rather than including them with the emissions target. Instead, little domestic change was required, as a third of the emissions reductions could be simply 'purchased' through CDM and JI. A fear of being exploited by free riders engenders more incremental policy responses to climate change, which in turn stymies the development of the green state. As such, the realization of the green state may be more challenging for transboundary environmental issues, such as climate change, than more local environmental issues. For overall emissions reductions goals, therefore, while Sweden was world-leading, its target reflected the principles of weak rather than strong EM.

Renewable energy policy

The production of hydropower and nuclear energy alongside a lack of coal in the Swedish energy mix had already placed the state in an unusually low-carbon position prior to 2006. Underlining his support for technological investment, Moderate Prime Minister Reinfeldt stated alongside European Commission President Barroso that climate change could be a 'profit machine' for Sweden and Europe (Sarasini 2009: 645). Such statements emphasize the pro-market foundations of EM; Sweden continued to invest in renewables technology over 2006–10, which in turn supported the state's exports across the world (Regeringskansliet 2011). With solar power able to offer little due to Sweden's geography and climate, this section will survey the state's renewables policy with regard to hydropower and wind power, before turning to how nuclear energy policy decisions affected renewables development.

By 2006, Sweden already had over 700 large hydropower stations, each with capacity over 1.5 MW, while 1200 small stations collectively generated 1.5 TW (Wang 2006: 1211). However, as expansion of hydropower is constrained by the number of previously untapped free-flowing rivers, by 2006, the possibility of expanding hydropower generation into 'untouched rivers' was almost impossible (Zannakis 2009: 138). As a result, the 2009 Energy Bill sought neither to increase nor decrease hydropower provision, despite EU pressure to increase renewables. However, Sweden did invest in a small-scale hydropower plant in Malaysia to reduce its greenhouse gas emissions production, as another example of more flexible solutions being favored in Sweden when facing a politically challenging domestic situation (Regeringskansliet 2009: 55). In a boost to domestic transformation, the Swedish Electricity Certificate System (ECS) was expanded in 2009, such that consumers were required to buy renewables certificates corresponding to 15.1 percent of their electricity use (cf. *ibid.*: 42; Chapter 9, this volume). The investment in a Malaysian hydropower plant and expansion of the ECS reflect small policy changes to a sector that had already received significant support for several decades prior to 2006. Regarding hydropower, therefore, I argue that Sweden demonstrated the hallmarks of the green state. By balancing the expansion of renewable energy production elsewhere via hydropower with the protection of remaining rivers, Sweden reflected a strong commitment to technological innovation and biocentric values. In order to 'expand' renewable energy provision, however, Sweden was forced to look beyond hydropower.

Wind power offered the only means for Sweden to increase significantly its renewables provision. Decision-making on turbines in the state was already highly decentralized, essentially giving veto power to those affected locally by the installations. As Söderholm and Petterson (2011: 523) argued, decentralized decision-making made offshore wind production much more favorable than onshore installation. Therefore, relying on the market to determine whether people would choose to pay a premium for wind power and also accept the construction of turbines in their local area would not be effective (Ek 2005: 1688). As such, the 2009 national planning framework to increase wind power to 30 TWh by 2020 demonstrated a strong example of leadership on climate change by giving greater municipal powers. Additionally, the 2010 Bill (2009/10:1335) to extend the existing ECS until 2035 gave greater stability to the market – thus stimulating investment – and reflected ambitious and long-term policy-making by the Conservative/Liberal Alliance (see Energimyndigheten 2010a: 10).

Without subsidies, however, the Swedish wind market was perceived as too unstable to be worthy of investment (Wang 2006: 1217). The Alliance met this challenge by investing SEK 20 million directly into a network for wind producers each year (Rudberg *et al.* 2013: 3). The Bills simplifying the concession-granting process (2008/09:146) and aiding the connection of wind power to the national grid (2009/10:51) further introduced stability into the domestic wind market. More could have been done to support offshore construction financially (see Söderholm and Petterson 2011: 524) – suggesting the financial constraints associated more with an environmental welfare state rather than a green state – but overall, the Alliance expressed a strong commitment to developing wind energy through a variety of measures. As such, the Alliance successfully demonstrated principles grounded in strong EM, as required to be considered a green state (Christoff 2005: 40). In addition to Sweden's status as a green state regarding hydropower during 2006–10, therefore, Sweden exhibited the credentials of the green state towards wind power as well.

Yet an analysis of renewables policy would not be complete without considering Sweden's other dominant energy source: nuclear power. The 1980 moratorium on the expansion of nuclear energy necessitated strong support for the renewables sector, in order to prevent a shortfall of energy for the growing economy (cf. Chapter 9, this volume). However, the decisions of the Conservative/Liberal Alliance on nuclear policy during 2006–10 highlighted a sharp divergence from its Social Democrat predecessors. The 1980 referendum was seen at the time as a partial victory for nuclear power, as the moratorium did not require an immediate phase-out, such as that of Austria in 1978 (see Marshall 2007: 148; Martinovsky and Mareš 2012: 349). Moreover, the fears over nuclear safety that once dominated the environmental-political agenda were replaced during the 1990s by the threat of climate change. This reprioritization posed a dilemma; Nordhaus (1997: 44) argued in 1997 that "[i]f Sweden chooses to phase out its nuclear power plants, meeting… [its Kyoto Protocol] commitment will go from difficult to near impossible." As such, nuclear power rapidly regained acceptance in a new guise as a climate-friendly energy source (Sailor *et al.* 2000).

The Conservative/Liberal Alliance reflected the change of perception towards nuclear power as a low-carbon energy source in 2009. The government overturned the 1980 moratorium on Sweden's nuclear portfolio enabling the construction of replacement reactors for pre-existing plants (see Sarasini 2009: 639). With the Centre Party and Christian Democrats having previously expressed opposition to nuclear power, low electricity prices were cited as a key factor in their decision (see Zannakis 2009: 141). The desire to reduce prices via nuclear power in order to protect industry does not bear the hallmarks of strong EM outlined earlier (Eckersley 2004: 76). While nuclear power may enable emissions per unit of electricity to be reduced, the energy source does not facilitate a reduction in overall consumption. As Eckersley (*ibid.*: 77) argues regarding the green state, "many industries are inherently environmentally degrading, such as the nuclear and fossil fuel industries, and therefore must be phased out rather than merely modernized." Furthermore, by enabling newer, more efficient nuclear power stations to replace older reactors, the need to invest in further renewables was reduced. Therefore, the nuclear U-turn significantly dented the likelihood of Sweden going beyond its 50 percent renewables target. The U-turn can thus be seen as a missed opportunity in hastening the development of the green state. Regarding renewable energy policy overall, while hydropower and wind power reflected a successful merger of biocentric values with technological innovation, Sweden remained an ambitious 'environmental welfare state' due to the U-turn over nuclear energy production.

Energy efficiency

Improvements in energy efficiency are problematic with regard to the green state, as improved energy efficiency does not necessarily entail a reduction in overall emissions. When seeking to mitigate climate change, it is vital that overall emissions are reduced, rather than their production simply becoming more efficient, if a state is to progress from an environmental welfare state to a green state (Eckersley 2004: 76). With a low population density and low temperatures, Swedish energy consumption is likely to be higher than that of other states. As with the previously discussed policy areas, the Conservative/Liberal Alliance ensured that Sweden remained a pioneer by building on existing ambition, but did not facilitate significant structural transformations. This incremental ambition will be analyzed regarding the state's policy decisions on district heating, industry and housing.

First, Sweden generates much of its heating and some of its electricity from Combined Heat and Power (CHP) (cf. Chapter 9, this volume). Almost half of all houses are heated using district heating, with around half of this energy sourced from biomass (Jewert 2012: 15). Increasing the percentage provided by biofuels would reduce the greenhouse gas production resulting from CHP. As the Government stated in 2009 (Regeringskansliet 2009: 6), "[d]istrict heating has been … crucial in enabling national policy instruments for renewable energy to bring about the extensive phasing-out of fossil fuels." CHP electricity generation grew steadily from 11.43 TWh in 2006 to 15.07 TWh by 2011, yet it can be argued that this was more to do with previous policies than Alliance leadership (Eurostat 2011). Sweden failed to implement the policies that had led Finland to becoming a world leader in biofuel production (see Ericsson *et al.* 2004). Indeed, there were no further policies to hasten the transition towards biofuels during 2006–10, suggesting that while energy efficiency in CHP was not undermined, the reduction in absolute consumption that is necessary to translate weak EM into its stronger form (Eckersley 2004: 76), was neglected.

Second, a voluntary program for energy efficiency in energy-intensive industry was introduced in 2005, in which companies were exempted from the national energy tax for five years in exchange for implementing an energy management system (see Energimyndigheten 2011). As such, from December 2009, energy audits in energy-intensive companies were subsidized by up to 50 percent (with a maximum SEK 3 billion budget overall). However, the government was reluctant to force businesses to cut emissions too quickly for fear of harming competitiveness. For example, while the original program reduced emissions by around 1.45 TWh across 180 power-intensive industries, its successor featured only 90 such industries (Swedish Institute 2013). As a result, the program showed all the hallmarks of EM by facilitating industry reductions, but failed to introduce a state-required obligation to make significant overall cuts. Moreover, the scheme essentially placed a price on emissions, whereby companies could simply pay to continue existing energy practices, rather than acknowledge an intrinsic value for nature. With industry representing around 45 percent of the country's electricity consumption, the reduction of emissions in this sector was crucial to overall greenhouse gas levels, yet few policies were developed over the period. As such, protection of the status quo for industry – and the jobs and profits it offered – continued to be the dominant paradigm around which the Alliance based its policies, reflecting the lack of biocentric values.

Finally, two new building efficiency policies were introduced in 2008. Prior to 2006, Sweden had already possessed ambitious housing standards, whereby renovated buildings needed to meet the same efficiency requirements as new buildings. The first of the Conservative/Liberal Alliance's responses was a new energy declaration law – in force since January 1, 2008 – that built upon an EU Directive and was designed to raise awareness of a building's energy consumption (see Swedish Institute 2013). The second was the first National Energy Efficiency Action Plan or NEEAP (a successor followed in 2011), set in November 2008 that sought to realize energy savings of 41 TWh by 2016 across buildings and also transport and small industries (SOU 2008: 11). However, the Alliance did not formulate a plan to support zero energy buildings, indicating a similar complacency to that found regarding industrial efficiency policies (see WWF 2010). Housing therefore represented another area of incremental improvements, when significant policy changes were needed to reduce overall consumption rather than merely improve efficiency while building more houses and watching energy consumption within these houses rise.

As such, it can be seen that the government of 2006–10 built on pre-existing efficiency policies rather than reversing them, thus incrementally increasing climate ambitions. Yet in many ways these exploited rather than consolidated Sweden's existing status as a pioneer, thus failing to continue previously high levels of ambition at the same rate. Sweden's high proportion of renewable energy arguably lessened the pressure to reduce consumption of electricity. Overall, Sweden performed poorly regarding efficiency throughout the period, and by 2011, total energy consumption in Sweden was still 55 percent above the EU average at 5.1 ton per capita, while electricity consumption per capita was around 2.5 times higher than the EU average (ABB 2013). As such, Sweden's attitude to energy efficiency – despite a call for a 20 percent improvement by 2020 and the biocentric views of 90 percent of its population – prioritized industry and growth over a reduction in consumption. Indeed, Sweden's continued high consumption levels placed the state at the less ambitious end of the 'environmental welfare state' capacity, let alone close to progressing to the green state.

Transport policy

Since the oil crisis of 1973, Sweden has sought to develop alternative fuels to support its domestic infrastructure, which is heavily reliant on the transportation sector (Hillman and Sandén 2008: 1287). Due to its location on the 'edge' of Europe, cheap transportation is crucial for the Swedish economy. As a result, transport remains the fastest growing sector regarding emissions in Sweden (Åkerman and Höjer 2006: 1944) and accounted for around 40 percent of Swedish CO_2 emissions in 2008 (Friberg 2008: 171). Despite a growth in the use of biofuels that has given Sweden the largest fleet of hybrid vehicles in the world, transportation remains heavily dependent upon fossil fuels, which in turn makes Sweden dependent on imports (Nordic Energy 2012). However, as Lindfeldt *et al.* (2010: 1843) argue, Sweden "is comparably rich in terms of biomass and renewable electricity… [meaning that] an import-independent road transport system based on renewable energy sources is realistic." More than 75 percent of all person kilometers travelled in Sweden were made by car in 2010 (*ibid.*: 1840), ensuring that small changes in this crucial sector could make a significant difference to emissions. At the national level, some progress was made during the period that reflected strong EM, but the norm of individual freedom and the role of market incentives to drive policy decisions maintained the dominance of car ownership and thus ensured that overall consumption remained high (Zannakis 2009: 187).

The most significant policy to reduce car emissions was the April 2007 introduction of a SEK 10,000 rebates on all purchases of 'environmentally friendly' hybrid cars. By September 2008, such vehicles accounted for 41 percent of Swedish new car sales. This approach again highlighted the presence of the principles of EM in policy decisions, as individuals' preferences in the market were allowed to shape the number of green vehicles in the national fleet (albeit with some direction from the state). Indeed, by encouraging individuals to buy new cars, Sweden offered a classic techno-fix to the issue, rather than seeking to radically change lifestyle behaviors regarding transportation. Moreover, in December 2008, it was announced that SEK 875 million would be provided to facilitate research and development of second-generation biofuels and other energy sources over a period of three years by the government, again demonstrating a long-term commitment to renewable transport policies, with the potential bonus of increasing exports (Energimyndigheten 2010b). By requiring all biofuels used in transport to be sustainable in line with the Renewable Energy Directive, a more top-down, regulatory approach was also developed by the government, which sought to facilitate a reduction in overall emissions production.

It can be argued that Swedish transport policy between 2006 and 2010 demonstrated innovative policies at the national level. These policies represented a mixture of theoretical underpinnings, from the more ecological modernization-aligned pro-market and individualized focus of the tax rebate for green vehicles and research into biofuel technologies, to the more biocentric principles of strong EM that ensured that all biofuels be proved sustainable. Therefore, steps were taken towards reducing emissions in the sector responsible for the largest share of Swedish CO_2 emissions. Yet these steps were not sufficient to transform Sweden into a green state during 2006–10. The Government has estimated that emissions from the transport sector will continue to increase between 2007 and 2020 (Regeringskansliet 2009: 10), meaning that while efficiency was improving, overall consumption was not. The overall share of biofuels – although growing – remained small (Lindfeldt *et al.* 2010: 1840). As such, the findings in this section support Åkerman and Höjer's (2006: 1955) argument that "[i]mproved technology in conjunction with renewable fuels is important, but transport volume growth also has to be curbed." As long as car ownership continues to be seen as a rite of passage in Sweden, a societal transformation of the kind needed to become a green state will not have occurred. Although the transport sector demonstrated perhaps the biggest improvement of the four areas explored in this chapter, it also remained the area where the most work was needed to reduce overall consumption, and thus, during 2006–10, continued to represent the principles of weak, rather than strong, EM.

Conclusion

Climate change poses a catastrophic threat to the planet and its inhabitants. Yet with the world's biggest greenhouse gas emitters almost exclusively capitalist, this chapter has sought to assess the extent to which a capitalist economy can become a green state. The chapter began by summarizing the principles of ecological modernization and the green state. It was argued that while EM may be a crucial feature of the green state, a strong version of EM must be pursued, alongside biocentric values, such as the protection of remaining river areas and reductions in overall consumption levels. This chapter examined the extent to which Sweden displayed the characteristics of the green state with regard to the most significant environmental threat, climate change. The chapter analyzed policy action in each of the four main emissions reductions areas prioritized between 2006 and 2010, according to the principles of strong EM.

First, the headline goal of the 2009 Energy Bill was the 40 percent greenhouse gas emissions reduction target which clearly increased ambition, yet the inclusion of flexible mechanisms enabled 'business-as-usual' policies to be pursued domestically while exporting reductions abroad. Next, renewable energy policy was examined, in which the pro-growth benefits of renewables technologies were highlighted by the Prime Minister as well as by policies incentivizing their introduction domestically. By not expanding hydropower while investing in wind power during 2006–10, Sweden could thus be said to reflect the biocentric yet technologically advanced requirements of the green state. Yet these developments clashed with the Government's 2009 U-turn over nuclear energy, which tacitly weakened the renewables sector and facilitated the continued production of nuclear waste. Third, regarding energy efficiency, support for CHP and voluntary measures for reducing emissions in heavy industry showed progress, but not at the rate required to see a transformation to the green state. To be considered a green state regarding climate change, not only should energy efficiency be improved, but overall emissions should be reduced significantly. Sweden's policies did not facilitate such a reduction to take place. Finally, transport policy showed the greatest amount of improvement during the five-year period, thanks to a requirement that all biofuels be renewably sourced and the introduction of rebates on environmentally friendly cars. However, this quick progress was partially due to the sector's weak starting point. Carbon emissions continued to grow in the Swedish transport sector, ensuring that any policy successes were far from sufficient to consider Sweden a green state on the issue.

During the first term of the Conservative/Liberal Alliance Government, Sweden continued and developed many policy decisions that drew from weak EM, while also reflecting some of the principles of strong EM. This mix was sufficient to protect Sweden's status as a climate pioneer, while also offering additional development opportunities for its economy via exports, but not enough to facilitate a transition from environmental welfare state to green state. If Sweden had produced more ambitious policies, however, businesses may have moved abroad, while other states could have exploited Sweden's ambition by failing to reduce their greenhouse gases as significantly. These problems reflect the challenges faced by a potential green state in responding to transboundary issues such as climate change. Future theorization of the green state must therefore seek to conceptualize how the framework can respond to transboundary issues. If even the most climate-friendly states, such as Sweden, are not yet green states regarding climate change, avoidance of the catastrophic two-degree increase in global temperature appears unavoidable. Sweden may be a green state regarding other environmental policy areas. However, regarding climate change, it appears that the argument of Dryzek (*et al.* 2003: 2) remains valid: "[a]t present there are no green states. But some states are greener than others."

References

ABB 2013 *Sweden: Energy Efficiency Report*. Retrieved March 2, 2014 from www05. abb.com/global/scot/scot380.nsf/veritydisplay/8f166ef5fbcf55a7c1257be9002bb822/ $file/Sweden.pdf.

Åkerman, J., and Höjer, M., 2006 How much transport can the climate stand? Sweden on a sustainable path in 2050. *Energy Policy* 34: 1944–57.

Aylott, N., and Bolin, N., 2007 Towards a two-party system? The Swedish parliamentary election of September 2006. *West European Politics* 30(3): 621–33.

Barry, J., and Eckersley, R., 2005 W(h)ither the green state? In Barry, J., and Eckersley, R., (eds) *The State and the Global Ecological Crisis* 255–72. MIT Press, Cambridge, MA.

Burck, J., Bals, C., and Ackermann, S., 2009 *The Climate Change Performance Index 2009*. Retrieved January 22, 2013 from http://germanwatch.org/klima/ccpi09res.pdf.

Christoff, P., 2005 Out of chaos, a shining star? Toward a typology of green states. In Barry, J., and Eckersley, R., (eds) *The State and the Global Ecological Crisis* 25–51. MIT Press, Cambridge, MA.

Davidson, S., 2012 The insuperable imperative: a critique of the ecologically modernizing state. *Capitalism, Nature, Socialism* 23(2): 31–50.

DiMento, J.F.C., and Doughman, P., 2007 Climate change: what it means to us, our children, and our grandchildren. In DiMento, J.F.C., and Doughman, P., (eds) *Climate Change: What it Means for Us, Our Children, and Our Grandchildren* 181–92. MIT Press, Cambridge, MA.

Dryzek, J.S., Downes, D., Hunold, C., Schlosberg, D., and Hernes, H.K., 2003 *Green States and Social Movements: Environmentalism in the United States, United Kingdom, Germany, and Norway*. Oxford University Press, Oxford.

Eckersley, R., 2000 Disciplining the market, calling in the state: the politics of economy–environment integration. In Young, S.C. (ed.) *The Emergence of Ecological Modernisation: Integrating the Environment and the Economy?* 233–52. Routledge, London.

Eckersley, R., 2004 *The Green State*. MIT Press, Cambridge, MA.

Ek, K., 2005 Public and private attitudes towards "green" electricity: the case of Swedish wind power. *Energy Policy* 33: 1677–89.

Energimyndigheten 2010a Sweden energy 2010. Retrieved July 25, 2013 from http://webbshop.cm.se/System/TemplateView.aspx?p=Energimyndigheten&view=default&id=b4cea7b00212456b9bdbdbe47a009474.

Energimyndigheten 2010b Seabased receives SEK 139 million for wave power project. Retrieved March 4, 2013 from www.energimyndigheten.se/en/About-us/Press-/Press-releases/Seabased-Receives-SEK-139-Million-for-Wave-Power-Project.

Energimyndigheten 2011 The programme for improving energy efficiency in energy intensive industries "PFE." Retrieved March 2, 2013 from www.energimyndigheten.se/en/Sustainability/Companies-and-businesses/Programme-for-improving-energy-efficiency-in-energy-intensive-industries-PFE.

Ericsson, K., Huttunen, S., Nilsson, L.J., and Svenningsson, P., 2004 Bioenergy policy and market development in Finland and Sweden. *Energy Policy* 32: 1707–21.

Eurostat 2011 Combined heat and power (CHP) data 2005–2011. Retrieved March 2, 2013 from www.google.co.uk/url?sa=t&rct=j&q=&esrc=s&source=web&cd=3&cad=rja&ved=0CDcQFjAC&url=http%3A%2F%2Fepp.eurostat.ec.europa.eu%2Fportal%2Fpage%2Fportal%2Fenergy%2Fdocuments%2FCHPdata.

xlsx&ei=jG8TU6fXIc-VhQfe7oGgDQ&usg=AFQjCNGco4FnkcuS5Sv0VarYhX1d7fs oZw.

Friberg, L., 2008 Conflict and consensus: the Swedish model of climate politics. In Compston, H., and Bailey, I., (eds) *Turning Down the Heat: The Politics of Climate Policy in Affluent Democracies* 164–82. Palgrave Macmillan, Basingstoke.

Gouldson, A.P., and Murphy, J., 1997 Ecological modernisation: restructuring industrial economies. In Jacobs, M., (ed) *Greening the Millennium: the New Politics of the Environment* 74–86. Blackwell, Oxford.

Hillman, K.M., and Sandén, B.A., 2008 Exploring technology paths: the development of alternative transport fuels in Sweden in 2007–2020. *Technological Forecasting and Social Change* 75: 1279–1302.

Jewert, J., 2012 Swedish climate policy: lessons learnt. Retrieved July 20, 2013 from http://en.globalutmaning.se/?p=2885.

Lafferty, W.M., and Meadowcroft, J., 2000 Patterns of governmental engagement. In Lafferty, W.M., and Meadowcroft, J., (eds) *Implementing Sustainable Development. Strategies and Initiatives in High Consumption Societies* 337–421. Oxford, Oxford University Press.

Lindfeldt, E.G., Saxe, M., Magnusson, M., and Mohseni, F., 2010 Strategies for a road transport system based on renewable resources – the case of an import-independent Sweden in 2025. *Applied Energy* 87: 1836–45.

Lundqvist, L.J., 2004 *Sweden and Ecological Governance: Straddling the Fence.* Manchester University Press, Manchester.

Marshall, K.E., 2007 Sweden, climate change and the EU context. In Harris, P.G., (ed) *Europe and Global Climate Change* 139–60. Edward Elgar, Cheltenham.

Martinovsky, P., and Mareš, M., 2012 Political support for nuclear power in central Europe. *International Journal of Nuclear Governance, Economy and Ecology* 3(4): 338–59.

Meadowcroft, J., 2005 From welfare state to ecostate. In Barry, J., and Eckersley, R., (eds) *The State and the Global Ecological Crisis* 3–24. MIT Press, Cambridge, MA.

Nordhaus, W.D., 1997 *The Swedish Nuclear Dilemma: Energy and the Environment.* Resources for the Future Press, Washington, DC.

Nordic Energy 2012 Renewables and nuclear. Retrieved March 2, 2014 from www.nordicenergy.org/thenordicway/country/sweden.

Regeringskansliet 2009 *Sweden's Fifth National Communication on Climate Change.* Retrieved July 8, 2014 from http://unfccc.int/resource/docs/natc/swe_nc5.pdf.

Regeringskansliet 2011 *Environmental Technology – 13 Swedish Solutions.* Retrieved March 2, 2014 from www.regeringen.se/content/1/c6/17/61/39/67ff1a10.pdf.

Rudberg, P., Weitz, N., Dalen, K., and Haug, J.J.K., 2013 *Governing Growing Wind Power: Policy Coherence of Wind Power Expansion and Environmental Considerations in Sweden, with Comparative Examples from Norway.* Stockholm Environment Institute, Stockholm. Retrieved February 16, 2015 from www.sei-international.org/publications?pid=2329.

Sailor, W.C., Bodansky, D., Braun, C., Fetter, S., and van der Zwaan, B., 2000 Nuclear power: a new solution to climate change? *Science* 288(5469): 1177–8.

Sarasini, S., 2009 Constituting leadership via policy: Sweden as a pioneer of climate change mitigation. *Mitigation and Adaptation Strategies for Global Change* 14: 635–53.

Schnaiberg, A., Pellow, D.N., and Weinberg, A., 2002 The treadmill of production and the environmental state. *Research in Social Problems and Public Policy* 10: 15–32.

Söderholm, P., and Petterson, M., 2011 Offshore wind power policy and planning in Sweden. *Energy Policy* 39: 518–25.

SOU 2008 *Ett energieffektivare Sverige: Nationell handlingsplan för energieffektivisering* [An Energy Efficient Sweden: National Action Plan for Energy Efficiency]. Statens

Offentliga Utredningar. Retrieved March 2, 2014 from www.regeringen.se/content/1/c6/10/01/75/31e3b45a.pdf.

Sterba, J.P., 2011 Biocentrism defended. *Ethics, Policy and Environment* 14(2): 167–9.

Swedish Institute 2013 Energy use in Sweden. Retrieved March 2, 2014 from http://sweden.se/society/energy-use-in-sweden.

Taylor, P.W., 1981 The ethics of respect for nature. *Environmental Ethics* 198(3): 197–218.

UNFCCC 2014a Annex, II., *Full Text of the Convention*. Retrieved March 2, 2014 from http://unfccc.int/key_documents/the_convention/items/2853.php.

UNFCCC 2014b Appendix, I., – quantified economy-wide emissions targets for 2020. Retrieved March 2, 2014 from http://unfccc.int/meetings/copenhagen_dec_2009/items/5264.php.

UNFCCC 2014c The mechanisms under the Kyoto Protocol: emissions trading, the Clean Development Mechanism and joint implementation. Retrieved March 2, 2014 from http://unfccc.int/kyoto_protocol/mechanisms/items/1673.php.

Wang, Y., 2006 Renewable electricity in Sweden: an analysis of policy and regulations. *Energy Policy* 34: 1209–20.

Widfeldt, A., 2007 Sweden. *European Journal of Political Research* 46: 1118–26.

WWF 2010 *Climate Policy Tracker for the European Union 2010*. Brussels: World Wide Fund for Nature. Retrieved March 2, 2014 from www.ecofys.com/files/files/wwf%20climate%20policy%20tracker%20final%20report_03%2011%2010_02.pdf.

Zannakis, M., 2009 *Climate Policy as a Window of Opportunity: Sweden and Global Climate Change*. University of Gothenburg Press, Gothenburg.

9 Towards a decarbonized green state?

The politics of low-carbon governance in Sweden

Roger Hildingsson and Jamil Khan

Introduction

Climate change governance is changing and shifting in emphasis from regulating reductions in carbon emissions towards promoting low-carbon development and decarbonization. In recent years, state actors and institutions have been active in developing a number of initiatives and national strategies for supporting low-carbon development. Such decarbonization strategies imply a different kind of direction for climate policy and represent, we argue, steps in the direction towards a decarbonized green state, i.e. a state engaged in greening society through decarbonizing societal structures and systems. In this chapter we ask what the politics of a low-carbon transition might imply for such a state and explore how the state engages in governing transformative change through various arrangements of public policy and governance by examining insights from the case of Swedish climate policy.

In the latest climate and energy bill the Swedish government addressed a long-term vision that "Sweden by 2050 will have no net emissions of greenhouse gases in the atmosphere" (SweGov 2009: 13). This policy vision could be seen as an ambition to achieve a low-carbon transition within the next 40 years. The Swedish Environmental Protection Agency has presented a draft low-carbon roadmap for realizing this vision (SEPA 2012), commissioned by the Government in anticipation of the 2010 Cancun Agreements, the 2011 EU Low-Carbon Roadmap (EC 2011) and similar national strategies elsewhere (e.g. in the UK and Denmark).

These policy developments indicate political agreement on the long-term objective of low-carbon societal development, although the policy landscape is fuzzier regarding what strategies are implied and how they are to be achieved. Low-carbon scenarios entail phasing out fossil fuels and shifting towards energy efficiency, renewable energy and other low-carbon technologies (for a recent review see Söderholm *et al.* 2011). Such low-carbon transitions require major transformations of key economic sectors in society such as transport, industry, energy and housing. Still, there is uncertainty and disagreement on, for example, how much to rely on technological change and to what extent our societies also need to be reshaped towards less harmful behaviors.

Ambitious long-term goals are being formulated but climate policy is still locked into the Kyoto mind-set of achieving emission reductions at the lowest possible cost. For low-carbon developments it is unlikely sufficient to only deploy policy measures that allocate the reduction of greenhouse gas (GHG) emissions in the most cost-efficient way. There is no one solution, or silver bullet, but much speaks in favor of a broader portfolio of approaches (Prins and Rayner 2007). This implies that climate policy has to be reconsidered and widened to assemble a range of efforts encompassing relevant policy areas and societal goals in order to spur and support the required processes of change.

The overarching objective in this chapter is to explore ways in which a decarbonized green state might develop by using Sweden as an example. We will examine what the politics for a low-carbon transition imply in that respect and empirically assess to what extent the present climate governance arrangements in Sweden support decarbonization and low-carbon transitions. In focus for the analysis are national climate policy strategies and the potential impact of state-sanctioned interventions and efforts to reduce emissions, spur innovation and enter new policy pathways towards decarbonization.

We compare policies in four sectors – electricity, heating, transport and industry – as they are central in transforming the society and economy towards low-carbon trajectories. The empirical analysis is based on an examination of government reports combined with secondary sources such as policy evaluations and peer-reviewed articles on Swedish climate policy. In addition, the analysis is informed by an interview study with nearly 60 national policy actors involved in climate policy-making that has provided deeper insights into the Swedish policy practice (see Kronsell *et al.* 2012).[1]

Climate-relevant policies in the four sectors are analyzed through the lens of theoretical perspectives on transformative change, sustainability transitions and policy change. Informed by our argument that a decarbonized green state represents a state engaged in promoting transformative social change, our analysis departs from (1) innovation studies dealing with questions about sociotechnical system innovation and sustainability transitions, and (2) policy studies that emphasize path dependency and the creation of policy pathways for carbon lock-out. These perspectives are used for analyzing the potential impacts of climate policy strategies central in the Swedish polity for steering and enabling low-carbon transitions.

The transformative agenda of the decarbonized state

As set out in Chapter 1 of this book, the green state is a generic concept that can mean many things. The green state could be seen as either a normative or an analytical construct, as a counterfactual ideal of ecological responsiveness to strive for (Eckersley 2004) or an evolving institutionalization of ecological responsibilities that can be empirically assessed (Meadowcroft 2005). Our approach here is that the green state is not only a normative ideal or an end-state to strive for, but a process that we can empirically research. The green state is already in the making through public policy arrangements targeting ecological challenges and through political commitments to steer society towards ecological sustainability. Engaging in the quest for greening the state is to engage public actors and state institutions in processes of transformative social change. In a similar vein, a decarbonized state is understood as emerging through its commitment to prevent climate change and through state-sanctioned governance strategies striving towards deep emission reductions and the decarbonization of societal structures and social practices.

So far, the responses to climate change have been dominated by mitigation strategies aimed at short-term emission reductions and market-based approaches for cost-efficient emissions abatement. However, it is uncertain whether such a market-liberal agenda is sufficient to address the ecological challenges associated with climate change and the structural change needed for reversing the current patterns of unsustainability. Liberal regulatory regimes might provide room for strengthening environmental regulation in terms of limiting harmful behavior and setting mitigation requirements through emissions standards or by other means. In climate governance, it might be defended on market-liberal grounds to internalize external costs for GHG emissions through carbon pricing mechanisms such as emissions trading and carbon taxation. But for decarbonizing the economy in advanced welfare states it is doubtful whether such weak ecological modernization strategies (Christoff 1996) will ever do the job. Market-liberal approaches can rather be criticized for not being reflexive enough to the ecological challenge (Eckersley 2004) and lacking the capacity to generate the kind of systemic change associated with what Meadowcroft (2012: 77) calls the third maxim of the green state: to "transform societal practices to respect ecological limits." This provides legitimation for state authority to actively intervene in the economy for regulating and promoting new patterns of production and consumption; for supporting innovation and facilitating system change; and for organizing and institutionalizing the societal restructuring required. A green, decarbonized state is represented by the assembled efforts by state institutions and public policy actors to steer and enable processes of transformative change aimed at both greening and decarbonizing the economy and society. Hence, such a state is committed to decarbonize societal structures and practices in sustainable ways to make society respect ecological limits.

New theoretical perspectives have emerged that in different ways study how transitions towards a low-carbon economy and sustainable societal development can be achieved and supported, and what role the state might play in such developments. For our analysis in this chapter, we will depart from two perspectives: what innovation studies tells us about instigating and enabling sustainability transitions and what policy studies has to say about the creation of policy pathways for steering transformative change.

Innovation studies and sustainability transitions

Theories on sustainability transitions assign the state an important role in creating incentives and supporting arenas for the emergence of new low-carbon innovations, technologies and practices (Markard and Truffer 2008; Chapter 10, this volume). As also discussed in Chapter 1 of this volume, the multi-level perspective (MLP) emphasizes technological transitions as "interactive processes of change at the micro-level of niches and the meso-level of socio-technical regimes both embedded in a broader landscape of factors at the macro-level" (Markard and Truffer 2008: 601; see also Geels 2002, for example). Transitions occur when a dominant socio-technical regime (i.e. rules, accepted norms and established practices) is challenged and replaced by a new regime. Niches are protected spaces where radical innovations, technologies and practices emerge, are developed and grow mature in order to challenge existing regimes. The MLP framework has inspired policy recommendations and prescriptive governance approaches such as strategic niche management and transition management (Kemp *et al.* 2007; Frantzeskaki *et al.* 2012). Technological innovation systems (TIS) studies provide another approach related to transition studies that focuses on the different phases of technological development and structural factors supporting innovation and the emergence of new technologies (Bergek *et al.* 2008). A key insight from TIS studies is that successful policies are directed to all innovation phases, from emergence to diffusion, which provides arguments for employing a broad spectrum of innovation policies adjusted over time in relation to technological maturity, for example (*ibid.*).

In transition studies, non-state actors such as innovators in low-carbon energy are seen as main drivers of socio-technical change, while the state has a pivotal role in nurturing and facilitating innovation. While the main focus in transition management is how to facilitate the involvement and networking of frontrunners (Kemp *et al.* 2007; Frantzeskaki *et al.* 2012), the main focus in TIS studies is how strategic support structures (i.e. systems of innovation) and innovation policies can create markets in which new technologies might develop (Bergek *et al.* 2008). The key implication for a decarbonized state is to develop policies and governance arrangements that support innovation and development of low-carbon technologies and practices.

Policy studies on transformation pathways

In policy studies, some scholars have started to ask questions about how policy making can be redirected to support transformative change in response to long-term challenges such as climate change. A prominent example is found in Levin *et al.* (2012). Building on Cashore and Howlett (2007) they go beyond traditional forms of policy analysis to elaborate concepts of path-dependency and mechanisms for policy change with the aim to explore plausible policy logics "that may trigger and nurture path-dependent processes that lead to transformative change over time" (*ibid.*: 131). They argue that, instead of relying on single-shot policy interventions, a series of incremental policy improvements and reforms is more apt to gradually attract political acceptance and create conditions for change. For entering transitional pathways towards decarbonization, they identify four types of mechanisms generating path-dependency (i.e. lock-in, self-reinforcement, increasing returns and policy feedbacks) that could be revised and exploited for path creation. It includes crafting policy strategies that are sticky and hard to reverse, that may entrench support over time and that can be expanded to cover many areas to make an impact. This bears resemblance to arguments brought forward by Compston and Bailey (2008), for example, about designing political strategies for climate policy in ways that lower political risks for resistance by incumbents while building momentum for more radical policy change over time. This literature tells us that a decarbonized state not only needs to deploy policies that reduce GHG emissions by supporting innovative technologies and practices. Policies also need to be strategically designed in order to reinforce and generate policy paths towards low-carbon transitions that support longer-term processes of transformation and decarbonization.

Towards a politics for low-carbon transitions in Sweden?

In this section we assess to what extent climate governance in Sweden contributes to promote low-carbon transition processes. The empirical analysis is guided by the theoretical perspectives discussed above and studied in four policy sectors (electricity, transport, industry and heating) by asking the questions: to what extent has Swedish climate policy and governance reduced GHG emissions, supported low-carbon innovations, and enabled transitional policy paths towards decarbonization?

As noted in Chapter 1 of this volume, Sweden has a strong track record in environmental and climate policy and is in many ways regarded a frontrunner (OECD 2014) by reaching its climate policy objectives guided by a benevolent win–win policy discourse (Zannakis 2009; see also Chapter 8, this volume). According to official national assessments Sweden has decreased its GHG emissions by 16 per cent between 1990 and 2011 (SweGov 2013a) and thereby overachieved its commitment of 4 per cent emission reductions by 2008–12. Projections based on existing and decided policy measures show that total GHG emissions will decrease further to 19 per cent below the 1990 year baseline until 2020 and 21 per cent until 2030 (*ibid.*: 26). The long-term objective to have no net GHG emissions by 2050 basically requires a transition to a low-carbon society (SweGov 2009), which would imply near-zero emissions. The Swedish Environmental Protection Agency (SEPA) has recently presented the basis for a Swedish low-carbon road map to 2050, in which they envision such decarbonization in main economic sectors such as electricity, transport, industry and heating (SEPA 2012).

Although total emissions have decreased since 1990 the picture looks different sector by sector. In Table 9.1 we see that the lion share of the decrease in emissions has been achieved in the energy sector. The emission reductions are mainly due to the transition from fossil fuels to bioenergy in the heating sector, while the electricity sector has had low emissions for a long time due to early investments in hydropower and nuclear power. More recently, investments in new energy sources such as wind and biomass energy have increased substantially.

Table 9.1 Historical emissions 1990–2011 and projected emissions of greenhouse gases 2011–2030 per sector (Mt CO_2-equivalent)

Sector	1990	2011	1990–2011	1990–2030
Energy (heat and electricity)	22.3	15.5	–30%	–36%
Transport	19.3	20.0	+4%	–3%
Combustion in manufacturing industry	12.1	9.5	–21%	–17%
Industrial processes	6.3	6.7	+6%	–2%
Other (agriculture, waste)	12.7	9.8	–23%	–35%
Total emissions	72.8	61.4	–16%	–21%

Source: SweGov (2013a: 27, 39)

Emissions from the transport sector have leveled out and are today down to almost the same level as in 1990. But the transport sector is particularly challenging considering its strong dependence on petroleum products with trends pointing towards increased transport volumes for both passenger and goods. Emissions from the industry sector emanate both from industrial processes and from energy use. While energy-related emissions from industrial combustion have decreased, industrial process emissions have increased slightly. The latter is to a large extent still dependent on fossil fuels and fluctuates with the global economic situation.

Swedish policy instruments and low-carbon developments

The Swedish climate policy landscape has evolved in a step-wise fashion since the early 1990s and is primarily based on a mix of market-based and general economic instruments (see Table 9.2). The CO_2 tax introduced in 1991 is regarded a flagship of Swedish climate policy (SweGov 2013b: 40; Kronsell *et al.* 2012). The tax has increased over time and is differentiated across sectors.[2] In 2005 the EU emissions trading scheme (EU ETS) was introduced to regulate GHG emissions from electricity producers and energy-intensive industries (thus exempted from the CO_2 tax since 2011). These carbon-pricing mechanisms have over the last decade become accepted as key climate policy measures across the political spectrum. According to economic theory the advantage of economic policy instruments is that they contribute to cost-efficient emission reductions. However, the evidence that they promote innovation and instigate long-term transitions is weak, especially in the context of low emission prices in the EU ETS (Egenhofer *et al.* 2011; Calel and Dechezleprêtre 2012; Gullbrandsen and Stenqvist 2013).

   Mechanisms to support investments in renewable energy are other important policies. Since 2003 a market-based scheme that obliges electricity distributors to obtain a certain quota of renewable electricity generation in their portfolio – the electricity certificate system – has been in place. Between 1998 and 2012 government-led climate subsidy programs supported municipal investments in bio-fuelled district heating systems, ecological refurbishment, energy efficiency and sustainable mobility projects. Subsidies have also supported offshore wind, solar power, heat pumps, eco-cars, and transport biofuels. Other policy measures include support to research and development, technological procurement, planning and infrastructure, energy labeling, and regulatory initiatives through the Environmental Code (e.g. emissions permits and standards, etc.) and the Building Code (e.g. energy efficiency standards).

In Table 9.2 we present an overview of the main climate policy instruments introduced over the last 20 years. This is based on the ways in which climate policy is constituted in Swedish national communications to the UNFCCC (SweGov 2010, 2013b) and the European Commission(SweGov 2013a). The main findings of the analysis are summarized in Table 9.3. But first we provide an analysis of the studied sectors.

Table 9.2 Policy instruments in Swedish climate policy

Cross-sectoral	Electricity	Heating	Industry	Transport
Climate information (national campaign 2002–2003)	Emissions trading (EU ETS)	Emissions trading (EU ETS), large-scale thermal plants	Emissions trading (EU ETS)	CO_2 requirements on new vehicles (EU regulation)
Environmental Code (1999–)	Energy tax (1957–)	CO_2 tax (1991–)	Energy tax (minimum; EU)	CO_2 tax; CO_2 differentiated vehicle tax
Planning and Building Act	Green Electricity Certificates (renewable obligation quotas)	Building regulations and energy declarations (EU EPBD)	CO_2 tax (non-ETS industries), phasing out differentiation	Tax exemption for biofuels
Local investment subsidies (LIP, KLIMP, SustCities)	Investment support solar power	Eco-Design Directive and Energy Labeling (EU)	*Program for improving energy efficiency (PFE), incl. tax exemption*	Green car rebate; and 5-year vehicle tax exemption for new green cars
Research and development	*Investment support wind power (offshore, etc.)*	Technology procurement		Infrastructure and spatial planning
		Local and regional energy advice		Local mobility management projects

Note: Finished policies are italicized

Sources: SweGov (2010, 2013a, 2013b)

Electricity

Two main climate policy instruments target the electricity sector: the EU ETS and the electricity certificate system. While EU ETS addresses a broad variety of activities the electricity certificates are designed to increase the diffusion of renewable electricity generation. The Swedish electricity system is today almost fully decarbonized, however the ambition to phase-out nuclear, which is politically contested, would require a transition to renewable energy sources. The electricity certificate system has been effective in terms of cost-efficiency and in achieving the goals of introducing new renewable energy and low-cost technologies (Bergek and Jacobsson 2010). Interestingly, the system provides for path dependency as the annual renewable energy obligations are successively escalated by design and could, thus, be regarded as an instance of a sticky and progressively incremental policy reform that is hard to reverse once introduced.

Does the certificate scheme contribute to technology development? In theory, the certificates are technology neutral since a wide range of technologies are eligible such as wind power, small scale hydro power, bioenergy, solar power, wave energy and geothermal energy. However, in practice the scheme creates competition among renewable technologies. This leads to a situation where more mature technologies are favored while emerging technologies are locked out. The outcome is that bioenergy, hydropower and onshore wind power have received the bulk of certificates while e.g. solar power has not received any support. Bergek and Jacobsson contend that the certificate system seems to be "designed to *avoid* forming nursing and bridging markets" (*ibid.*: 25, emphasis added). That indicates a gap in Swedish climate and energy policy between supporting fundamental research and demonstration, on the one hand, and market deployment, on the other. In their perspective, more strategic innovation policies in between these phases could help create niche markets for emerging technologies (see also Söderholm 2012). Dedicated subsidies for market introduction are available (e.g. for wind power in difficult locations and for solar power), but they are inadequate to create viable nursing and bridging markets (about offshore wind power, see Söderholm and Pettersson 2011).

So, while current policies in the electricity sector support low-carbon transitions by means of expanding mature technologies for renewable electricity generation, they do not promote the emergence and innovation of new energy technologies. As long as the potential for biomass energy and onshore wind power is sufficiently high to accommodate future supply of electric power, that might not be problematic. However, when such resources get utilized at larger scale, their potential gets exhausted and the currently broad acceptance of such investments might change. For onshore wind installations there are already such contestations.

Heating

The heating sector represents a case where policy strategies have been successful in promoting transition processes, with district heating as the most apparent

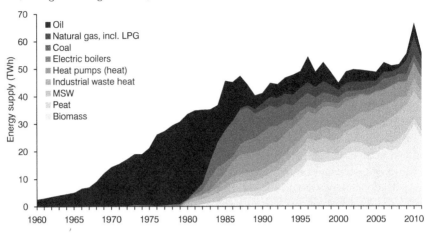

Figure 9.1 District heating production in Sweden 1960–2011, broken down into fuels and energy sources (source: Di Lucia and Ericsson, 2014: 16)

example. The Swedish district heating system has experienced two transformations since the 1960s (see Figure 9.1). First, the system has expanded in volume from less than 5 TWh in 1960 to around 60 TWh in 2011, and today district heating accounts for almost 90 per cent of heating in multi-dwelling buildings. Second, the fuel mix has been completely restructured from being totally dependent on fossil fuels in the early 1980s to become almost decarbonized due to a gradual increase of biomass and municipal solid waste. In 2011 fossil fuels accounted for only 14 per cent of the production while biomass had increased to 45 per cent and municipal solid waste to 19 per cent (Di Lucia and Ericsson 2014: 16).[3] The main factors explaining this transition is a combination of policies such as municipal infrastructure planning, government investment subsidies and the CO_2 tax introduced in 1990 (Ericsson 2009; Di Lucia and Ericsson 2014). The gradual expansion of district heating has been facilitated by public ownership of local energy companies and the CO_2 tax, which made biomass energy the most competitive fuel for district heating purposes. Government subsidies have also been important to support investments in production capacity, retrofitting and grid expansion (Di Lucia and Ericsson 2014). Although these policies have varied over time, collectively they have provided enduring policy support and resulted in successful transitions towards decarbonization (Ericsson 2009).

Transport

Transport is perhaps the most challenging sector to decarbonize considering the dominance of road-based modes of transportation and the high dependence on petroleum fuels. Transport-related carbon emissions have continued to increase since the 1990s, although at a slower rate. In the transport sector, the main policies are the CO_2 tax on vehicle fuels and specific instruments directed to promote alternative fuels and vehicle technologies. This includes the tax exemption for biofuels, subsidies for eco-car purchases, and research and development support for new generations of biofuels and engine technology. Policy measures in the transport sector are also largely dependent on EU policy such as the regulation of CO_2 emissions from new vehicles and the promotion of biofuels under the RES Directive. While existing policies have slowed down growth in carbon emissions from transport, stimulated energy-efficient vehicles and facilitated the introduction of transport biofuels (SweGov 2013b: 49), decarbonization has been limited.

The Swedish government has addressed further ambitions as expressed in the vision for a vehicle fleet independent from fossil energy by 2030. Being a contested target, a governmental inquiry has recently presented a thorough assessment of how to achieve this target and proposed a broad policy package aimed at, for instance, increasing biofuels blending (e.g. ethanol) and promoting energy-efficient vehicles (SOU 2013). Key insights from the inquiry relate to the inconsistency in choice and design of policy measures and the lack of attention to transport planning and demand-sided measures.

Swedish transport planning is locked-in to a mobility paradigm with increased transportation as the central policy objective. Sustainability and decarbonization concerns are secondary objectives, resulting in a focus on vehicle technologies, new fuels and railway as appropriate solutions (Pettersson 2014). More promising is the ongoing contestation about the meaning of sustainable transport, as part of which the mobility paradigm is being challenged by alternative views on reducing transport volumes and car use. This is reflected even within the Swedish Transport Administration (STA), the government agency responsible for transport planning. In 2010 STA suggested as part of their broad climate strategy to radically reduce GHG emission from transports by means of promoting energy efficiency, renewable energy and, most importantly, efforts to reduce transport demand and support modal shifts from road traffic to railway, bicycle and public transport (STA 2010). However, this perspective has not yet influenced mainstream planning within the STA. In April 2012 the STA published a study on future capacity needs in the Swedish transport system commissioned by the government (STA 2012). Based on a traditional prognosis of transport development assuming car traffic to increase substantially,[4] the study analyzed how to accommodate such an increase while neglecting transport policies to reduce transport demand. This mismatch between climate policy and other societal objectives has been criticized by the National Audit Office (Riksrevisionen 2012).

Due to the dominant mobility paradigm, current national policies on urban planning and infrastructure planning are not well devised to affect change towards low-carbon mobility patterns. Although policy reforms and changes in planning regulation have been suggested in order to put more requirements on local governments and provide progressive cities with more planning tools, few national policy instruments have been implemented (STA 2010). Policy innovation in this area rather emanates from local governments responsible for urban planning, and several cities in Sweden are working to promote sustainable mobility. These city initiatives can be seen as niches or sites for experimentation where new innovations and practices are developed, however, so far without the support of government policies and with limited effect on traditional planning.

Industry

Industry is responsible for around 40 per cent of energy use and 25 per cent of GHG emissions in Sweden (SEA 2013). The main part of this originates from energy-intensive industries such as pulp and paper, iron and steel, mineral and chemical industries, which are particularly important for Swedish exports. Carbon pricing, through EU ETS or CO_2 tax, is the main policy targeting the industry sector. However, in anticipation of the risk for harming industrial competitiveness in global markets, policy makers have restrained from introducing stringent measures, which has hampered the effectiveness of such carbon pricing mechanisms. A large part of Swedish industry is regulated by the EU ETS and currently 800 facilities are covered by the scheme. Although the EU ETS has the potential of being an effective policy instrument, its steering capacity and influence on emission reductions and low-carbon innovation are in practice low since the allocation of allowances to companies has been far too generous (Gullbrandsen and Stenqvist 2013). Non-ETS industries are subject to carbon taxes but have enjoyed discounted tax rates motivated by international competitiveness concerns, a differentiation currently being dismantled. Industries are also subject to regulatory requirements through the Environmental Code, but legislative action is not actively used by authorities to regulate GHG emissions.

A few distinctions are necessary when studying the effect of climate policy in industry. First, while the pulp and paper industry has gone through a transition and is almost fully decarbonized, other industries (e.g. iron and steel, mineral and chemical industry) are still largely dependent on fossil fuels. The government agency Growth Analysis has recently analyzed the transition in the pulp and paper industry (Tillväxtanalys 2014). The shift from fossil fuels to bioenergy has been a long process beginning with the oil crisis in the 1970s. A combination of higher oil prices and government policies spurred the industry to search for new sources of energy. There are clear parallels to the development of district heating. However, in this case climate policies have been weaker due to competitiveness concerns (e.g. lower carbon taxes for industry, generous EU ETS allowances) and, thus, the transition has to a large extent been driven by other factors such as energy prices and concerns about environmental reputation. The public voluntary Program for improving energy efficiency (PFE) is in this view an interesting governance strategy targeting energy-intensive industries. Companies engaged in PFE agreed to implement energy efficiency schemes in exchange for exemption from the energy tax on electricity. The PFE started in 2005 and includes energy management, auditing and implementation of energy efficiency measures. While the EU ETS and the tax scheme have been criticized for generating low incentives for emission reductions and innovation, judgments on the effects of the PFE are mixed. While the Swedish National Audit Office argue the program to be less successful in achieving substantial emission reductions (Riksrevisionen 2013), other evaluations prove the PFE to have had positive effects both concerning emission reductions and in terms of organizational change and the priority for energy efficiency innovation within companies (Stenqvist and Nilsson 2012; Stenqvist 2013).

Second, industrial emissions from combustion and industrial processes differ in trends. Combustion emissions have shown a slow downward trend mainly due to an increased use of biofuels in the pulp and paper industry together with energy efficiency measures, while emissions from industrial processes are slightly higher than in 1990 (see Table 9.1). When it comes to industrial process emissions there is a lack of policies as well as technology options. The current policy framework is clearly insufficient to facilitate technological innovation towards an economically viable *and* low-carbon energy-intensive industry (Åhman *et al.* 2012). There is a lack of technology-specific policies fostering innovation and, more fundamentally, established ideas about how to support low-carbon industrial development while dealing with the risk of loss of competitiveness and carbon leakage (*ibid.*). So far, research on industrial emissions has focused on energy efficiency and not on new innovations and technology options.

Sweden towards a decarbonized green state?

Overall, the analysis of Swedish climate policy, which is summarized in Table 9.3, provides a mixed picture of policy change in support of low-carbon transition pathways. The emission reductions achieved since 1990 (16%) are to a large extent due to the conversion from fossil fuels to bioenergy for combustion purposes in the heating and industry sectors. Swedish climate policy is strongly geared towards supporting short-term and tangible emission reductions by means of general economic incentives that alternate marginal abatement costs. It is designed to be cost-effective and technology neutral, while delegating the selection of measures to market actors. This approach has to some extent been complemented with more designated policy instruments designed to support specific technologies or developments.

Policy interventions have been successful in enabling transitions in the energy sectors (electricity and heating), which are on their way to become fully decarbonized. The Swedish electricity certificate scheme represents a long-term policy framework creating lock-in to investments in mature renewable energy technologies at a successively increasing pace. The scheme has, however, proven less fit to support innovation and deployment of new technologies. Whether existing policies will be sufficient for decarbonizing the power sector also in a context of a future nuclear phase-out is a moot point. The Swedish heating sector, and the transformation of the district heating system in particular, represents a clear-cut example of the kind of progressive incrementalism that Levin *et al.* (2012) discuss. A series of innovative and incremental policy changes introduced and unfolding over a longer period of time have collectively contributed to generate self-reinforcing processes, increasing returns and policy feedbacks supporting decarbonization.

Table 9.3 Assessment of climate governance in four sectors in Sweden

Policy sector	Emission reductions	Support to niches and innovation	Policies for low carbon policy pathway
Electricity	No (because already near zero emissions), but strong increase in renewable energy	No, support mainly to mature renewable technologies	Yes, electricity certificate contributes to gradual expansion of renewables in the system
Heating	Yes, substantial (near decarbonization)	Yes, mainly in district heating	Yes, mix of policy instruments contributed to transition of heating system
Transport	No, but stabilization	Partially for technologies (biofuels, vehicle technology); not yet for behavior, but experimentation with e.g. mobility management	No, transport policy and planning still locked-in to the 'old' mobility paradigm
Industry	Yes, but marginal	No, but potential technical solutions yet to be developed; PFE mainly supports low-hanging fruit	No

In the transport sector and for industrial processes, however, emissions have remained around 1990 levels, and there are few signs of a trend towards decarbonization. For these sectors there are no comparatively easy solutions (such as the fuel shift in the heating sector) and policies have so far not been able to induce any major transformations in behavior or technology. General policy instruments, such as carbon pricing, have been insufficient in these sectors compared to in the energy sector. This provides argument for combining such incentives with more specific policies (e.g. industrial and innovation policy) in order to provide support for the innovation of new technologies and practices or to correct for other market failures than externalized emissions costs (Söderholm 2012). For instance, the PFE case shows how information asymmetries can be overcome by energy management schemes. Other examples mentioned above are transport and infrastructure planning, support to niche technologies for electricity production, and industrial policies. There is also a lack of national policy strategies for transforming transport behavior, something that is only promoted at the local level, where policy makers lack authority over infrastructure developments.

In an international comparison it is clear that Sweden has come a long way in reducing its GHG emissions; emission trends since 1990 as well as the present per capita emissions[5] set Sweden at a front position compared to other industrialized countries. It should be noted that Sweden is in a privileged position with large assets of renewable energy sources such as hydro, biomass and wind as well as investments in nuclear energy, which account for around 40 percent of the electricity production. Swedish governments have taken advantage of such available resources, and promoted policy interventions and incentives towards low-carbon development. It is less certain that Sweden retains its frontrunner position when it comes to long-term decarbonization strategies. Quite contrary, the primary focus on cost-efficient measures to secure short-term emission reductions has not proven successful in spurring low-carbon pathways in more problematic sectors such as transport and industry. Rather other countries have gone further in institutionalizing decarbonization as a core policy goal, an issue discussed further in the next section.

Institutionalization of low-carbon governance in Sweden?

Our analysis of Swedish climate policies should be understood in the context of the broader institutionalization of decarbonization as a long-term societal objective. While Swedish climate and energy policy developments have changed the courses of action and entered low-carbon pathways in some policy areas and sectors, decarbonization is not institutionalized as a core objective for Swedish climate governance, nor operationalized in terms of targets, policy strategies and governance initiatives in other sectors (e.g. industry and transport). This might appear paradoxical in the face of a broad political consensus on ambitious long-term climate objectives. However, it can be explained by contestations in policy-making circles over the means for governing the low-carbon transition, if climate governance merely entails regulating emission reductions by means of carbon pricing or whether it should also foster decarbonization by transforming societal structures and systems.

The results from an interview study carried out in 2011 with nearly 60 policy actors confirm that the notion of a low-carbon transition beyond 2020 has not yet been institutionalized in Sweden (Kronsell *et al.* 2012). Instead policy making has mainly focused on achieving short-term emission reductions in the most cost-efficient way. Hildingsson (2014) identifies two main policy discourses on climate governance competing for dominance. On the one hand there is a dominant market-liberal policy discourse emphasizing the policy problem as a market failure to be corrected by carbon pricing. On the other hand, a counter-discourse stresses the challenge as an energy system problem to be handled by decarbonizing society. The decarbonization narrative is gaining ground but has not yet taken root in policy-making circles. In this respect, Swedish climate governance differs from other countries such as the UK, Germany and Denmark. In the UK, the Climate Change Act manifested such an orientation and introduced a broad package of new policy initiatives. In Germany and Denmark, long-term commitments to an energy transition away from both nuclear and fossil energy are being operationalized through programs such as the Energiwende and the Energiaftale respectively.

In 2011 the Swedish government commissioned the SEPA to prepare the basis for a Swedish roadmap for the low-carbon transition. The SEPA presented its proposals in December 2012 (SEPA 2012). This has yet to be followed by a parliamentary process including all political parties in order to create political support for a low-carbon road map. Such an initiative could have the potential of attracting wider legitimacy for the transition by initiating public deliberations among a broad set of societal actors. However, at time of writing (October 2014) it remains to be seen how this process will unfold.

Conclusions

The chapter has provided new empirical insights on the experience and progress of the politics and governance of a low-carbon transition in Sweden, both in terms of achievements and challenges for such decarbonization strategies. While being successful in achieving substantial emission reductions and supporting low-carbon transition processes in some sectors, neither a general trend towards decarbonization nor an institutionalized political commitment on decarbonization can be observed. Thus, Sweden could be characterized as an advanced climate-mitigating state rather than a decarbonizing green state. The climate mitigation strategy has proven effective in sectors where mature technological alternatives have been present (i.e. energy) but has so far been less successful in more complex sectors with stronger needs for innovation and changed patterns of behavior (i.e. process industry and transportation).

Beyond the analysis if current climate policies live up to goals of decarbonization, our chapter provides more general insights on the ways to develop a decarbonized state. First of all, for a decarbonized state to emerge as a green state it has to address climate change in relationship to other ecological challenges. That implies that the scope of climate policy has to be reconsidered and widened towards including a broader array of strategies to support decarbonization and steer low-carbon transitions in ecologically sustainable ways. Second, as "ecologism in one country" is an impossibility (Lundqvist 2004: 20), the international dimension and the difficulties for small states to instigate low-carbon transition processes in some areas have to be considered. In those sectors where decarbonizing processes have been more successful, Swedish authorities possess a larger degree of national control and autonomy. But the industrial and transport sectors are much more sensitive to international developments. For the industry, international competitiveness is essential, while transport patterns are largely determined by global trends. Technology development is to some extent also beyond the control of individual states. Still, there are a number of policy measures available that have not been deployed in the Swedish case. For instance, the prospect for innovation policy to foster low-carbon technologies and promote industrial competitiveness simultaneously is largely untapped. For the transport sector there is a clear lack of national priority on planning issues in order to support niche experiments at the city level around sustainable mobility.

Finally, this ties further to our main argument that a decarbonized green state is a state committed to and engaged in promoting transformative social change. So far, climate policy has been dominated by the market-liberal norm of cost-efficiency and has focused on short-term climate mitigation, while lacking a strategic focus on long-term decarbonization strategies. Our analysis shows how market-based policies alone are insufficient to incentivize low-carbon transitions. Thus, to generate the kind of transformative change implied, a decarbonizing state has to engage more actively in fostering innovation and supporting policy pathways towards low-carbon and sustainable patterns of production, distribution and consumption.

Notes

1 The Swedish case study is based on research conducted within the LETS 2050 project (www.lets2050.se), which explored political and societal challenges for reaching near-zero carbon emissions in Sweden by 2050.
2 Households, services and heating plants pay the full tax rate, while non-ETS industry, agriculture, forestry and combined heat and power plants only pay 21 percent of the tax. Electricity producers pay no CO_2 tax at all.
3 The remaining energy supply came from industrial waste heat and heat pumps.
4 From 2006 to 2050 the estimated traffic increases (in person kilometers) were 67% for car traffic, 80% for rail and 91% for domestic aviation. Total personal transport increase was estimated to 63%, while for freight 61% (STA 2012: 11–12).
5 In 2010 Sweden emitted 7.1 metric tons of GHG per capita which can be compared to the European level of 9.2 metric tons and the OECD average of 13.0 metric tons (OECD 2013).

References

Åhman, M., Nikoleris, A., and Nilsson, L.J., 2012 *Decarbonizing Industry in Sweden: An Assessment of Possibilities and Policy Needs.* Report no. 77. Environmental and Energy Systems Study, Lund University.
Bergek, A., and Jacobsson, S., 2010 Are tradable green certificates a cost-efficient policy driving technical change or a rent-generating machine? Lessons from Sweden 2003–2008. *Energy Policy* 38(3): 1255–71.
Bergek, A., Jacobsson, S., Carlsson, B., Lindmark, S., and Rickne, A., 2008 Analyzing the functional dynamics of technological innovation systems: a scheme of analysis. *Research Policy* 37: 407–29.
Calel, R., and Dechezleprêtre, A., 2012 *Environmental Policy and Directed Technological Change: Evidence From the European Carbon Market.* Fondazione Eni Enrico Mattei, Milan.
Cashore, B., and Howlett, M., 2007 Punctuating which equilibrium? Understanding thermostatic policy dynamics in Pacific Northwest forestry. *American Journal of Political Science* 51(3): 532–51.
Christoff, P., 1996 Ecological modernization, ecological modernities. *Environmental Politics* 5(3): 476–500.
Compston, H., and Bailey, I., 2008 *Turning Down the Heat: The Politics of Climate Policy in Affluent Democracies.* Palgrave Macmillan, Basingstoke.
Di Lucia, L., and Ericsson, K., 2014 Low-carbon district heating in Sweden: examining a successful energy transition. *Energy Research and Social Science* 4: 10–20.
EC 2011 *Roadmap for Moving to a Low-Carbon Economy in 2050.* European Commission, Brussels.

Eckersley, R., 2004 *The Green State: Rethinking Democracy and Sovereignty*. MIT Press, Cambridge, MA.

Egenhofer, C., Alessi, M., Georgiev, A., and Fujiwara, N., 2011 *The EU Emissions Trading System and Climate Policy towards 2050: Real Incentives to Reduce Emissions and Drive Innovation?* Centre for European Policy Studies, Brussels.

Ericsson, K., 2009 *Introduction and Development of the Swedish District Heating Systems: Critical Factors and Lessons Learned*. Report for the IEE project. RES-H Policy, Lund University, Lund.

Frantzeskaki, N., Loorbach, D., and Meadowcroft, J., 2012 Governing societal transitions to sustainability. *International Journal of Sustainable Development* 15(1–2): 19–36.

Geels, F., 2002 Technological transitions as evolutionary reconfiguration processes: a multi-level perspective and a case-study. *Research Policy* 31: 1257–74.

Gullbrandsen, L.H., and Stenqvist, C., 2013 The limited effect of EU emissions trading on corporate climate strategies: comparison of a Swedish and a Norwegian pulp and paper company. *Energy Policy* 56: 516–25.

Hildingsson, R., 2014 Too many targets or too few measures? Discourses on decarbonisation in Swedish climate policy-making. In Hildingsson, R. (ed.) *Governing Decarbonisation: The State and The New Politics of Climate Change*. Lund Political Studies 172. Lund University, Lund.

Kemp, R., Loorbach, D., and Rotmans, J., 2007 Transition management as a model for managing processes of co-evolution towards sustainable development. *International Journal of Sustainable Development and World Ecology* 14(1): 78–91.

Kronsell, A., Hildingsson, R., and Khan, J., 2012 *Intervjustudie om förutsättningar för en svensk klimatomställning* [Interview Study on the Conditions for a Swedish Low-Carbon Transition]. LETS Report, Lund University, Lund.

Levin, K., Cashore, B., Bernstein, S., and Auld, G., 2012 Overcoming the tragedy of super wicked problems: constraining our future selves to ameliorate global climate change. *Policy Sciences* 45(2): 123–52.

Lundqvist, L.J., 2004 *Sweden and Ecological Governance: Straddling the Fence*. Manchester University Press, Manchester.

Markard, J., and Truffer, B., 2008 Technological innovation systems and the multi-level perspective: Towards an integrated framework. *Research Policy* 37(4): 596–615.

Meadowcroft, J., 2005 From welfare state to ecostate. In Barry, J., and Eckersley, R., (eds) *The State and the Global Ecological Crisis* 3–23. MIT Press, Cambridge, MA.

Meadowcroft, J., 2012 Greening the State? In Steinberg, P., and VanDeveer, S., (eds) *Comparative Environmental Politics: Theory, Practice and Prospects* 63–87. MIT Press, Cambridge, MA.

OECD 2013 *Environment at a Glance 2013: OECD Indicators*. OECD Publishing, Paris.

OECD 2014 *OECD Environmental Performance Reviews: Sweden 2014*. OECD Publishing, Paris.

Pettersson, F., 2014 Swedish Infrastructure Policy and Planning: Conditions for Sustainability. PhD thesis, Environmental and Energy Systems Studies, Lund University, Lund.

Prins, G., and Rayner, S., 2007 *The Wrong Trousers: Radically Rethinking Climate Policy*. James Martin Institute for Science and Civilization, University of Oxford, Oxford.

Riksrevisionen 2012 *Infrastrukturplanering: På väg mot klimatmålen?* [*Infrastructure Planning: Towards the Climate Objectives?*]. RiR 2012:7. Riksrevisionen, Stockholm.

Riksrevisionen 2013 *Energieffektivisering inom industrin* [*Energy Efficiency in Industry*]. RiR 2013:8. Riksrevisionen, Stockholm.

SEA 2013 *Energy in Sweden 2013*. Swedish Energy Agency, Eskilstuna.

SEPA 2012 *Underlag till en svensk färdplan för ett Sverige utan klimatutsläpp 2050* [*Basis for a Swedish Roadmap for a Sweden without Climate Emissions 2050*]. Report 6487. Swedish Environmental Protection Agency, Stockholm.

Söderholm, P., 2012 *Ett mål flera medel: Styrmedelskombinationer i klimatpolitiken* [*One Target Several Measures: Policy Mixes in Climate Policy*]. Report 6491. Swedish Environmental Protection Agency, Stockholm.

Söderholm, P., and Pettersson, M., 2011 Offshore wind power policy and planning in Sweden. *Energy Policy* 39(2): 518–25.

Söderholm, P., Hildingsson, R., Johansson, B., Khan, J., and Wilhelmsson, F., 2011 Governing the transition to low-carbon futures: a critical survey of energy scenarios for 2050. *Futures* 43(10): 1105–16.

SOU 2013 *Fossilfrihet på väg* [*Fossil Free on the Road*]. 2013:84. Swedish Government, Stockholm.

STA 2010 *Trafikslagsövergripande planeringsunderlag för begränsad klimatpåverkan* [*Cross-Sectoral Planning Basis for Reduced Climate Impact of Transport*]. Report 2010:95. Swedish Transport Administration, Borlänge.

STA 2012 *Transportsystemets behov av kapacitetshöjande åtgärder* [*The Need for Measures to Increase Capacity in the Transport System*]. Summary of final report 2012:101. Swedish Transport Administration, Borlänge.

Stenqvist, C., 2013 Industrial Energy Efficiency Improvement: The Role of Policy and Evaluation. PhD thesis, Environmental and Energy Systems Studies, Lund University, Sweden.

Stenqvist, C., and Nilsson, L., 2012 Energy efficiency in energy-intensive industries: an evaluation of the Swedish voluntary agreement PFE. *Energy Efficiency* 5(2): 225–41.

SweGov 2009 *En sammanhållen klimat och energipolitik – Klimat* [*An Integrated Climate and Energy Policy*]. Bill 2008/09:162. Swedish Government, Stockholm.

SweGov 2010 *Sweden's Fifth National Communication on Climate Change under the UNFCCC*. Ds 2009:63. Ministry of the Environment, Stockholm.

SweGov 2013a *Report for Sweden on Assessment of Projected Progress*. March. Ministry of the Environment, Stockholm.

SweGov 2013b *Sweden's Sixth National Communication on Climate Change*. Swedish Government, Stockholm.

Tillväxtanalys 2014 *Styrmedlens betydelse för en grön omställning av näringslivet* [*The Significance of Policy Instruments for a Green Transition of Industry*]. Tillväxtanalys, Östersund.

Zannakis, M., 2009 *Climate Policy as a Window of Opportunity: Sweden and Global Climate Change*. Gothenburg Studies in Politics 121. University of Gothenburg, Gothenburg.

10 Negotiating green growth as a pathway towards sustainable transitions in Finland

Tuula Teräväinen-Litardo

Introduction

Recent global economic turbulences and the concerns over energy security and climate change have led national governments and international organizations such as the World Bank, the Organisation for Economic Co-operation and Development (OECD), the United Nations (UN), and the European Union (EU) to develop new suggestions of greener and more sustainable socio-economic development paths (OECD 2009; EC 2010). Many of these have emphasized the promotion, development, and utilization of clean technologies as an inherent element in transitions towards sustainable production and consumption. At the same time, scholars of innovation studies, sociology, and political science have increasingly argued that incremental changes in the established socio-technical systems may not be sufficient in terms of generating the kind of profound transformations throughout all levels and sectors of a society that internationally agreed climate policy targets would necessitate. Therefore, debate has emerged around the idea of system-level transitions, with references to systemic innovations that would entail a transition from one socio-technical system to another and have profound implications for the entire systems of production, consumption, and governance (Geels and Kemp 2007; Geels 2010; Chapter 1, this volume). This has also had important implications on the role of the state in governing technology, innovation, environmental, and economic development policies (Lovell 2007; OECD 2009). In particular, a holistic and integrated view of innovation, sustainability and governance has been called for (EC 2010; OECD 2011). A key question in this respect has concerned the ways in which national governments could best support and advance system-level sustainable transitions and adopt ideas of a green state (Eckersley 2004; Kemp *et al.* 2007; Lovell 2007; Chapter 1, this volume).

In this chapter I focus on the recent Finnish policy debate concerning green growth and innovation. The Finnish green growth approach can be seen as one example of on-going national level policy initiatives that aim at accelerating system-level changes to achieve sustainable socio-technical transitions. In the following, I discuss the construction of legitimacy for and competing interpretations of green growth at the national level as well as the implications these have on the role of the state in governing and facilitating sustainable transitions. I argue that the ways in which policy discourses reassure and depart from the established polity and policy have important implications to the opportunities and constraints for system-level sustainable transitions in the green state.

Empirically, I use qualitative content analysis to scrutinize the recent debate concerning green growth in Finland. I draw from the results of a broader research project entitled Global and Local Policies, Institutions, and Experiences in Finland and in Emerging Economies. This project ran during 2012–14 and was part of the Green Growth research program funded by the Funding Agency for Technology and Innovation in Finland (Tekes). The data consist of official policy documents, stakeholder statements and press releases concerning climate, energy, environmental, technology and economic policies, particularly in relation to policies, initiatives and policy measures concerning green growth, green economy, and clean technology in Finland (2010–12). In addition, the data include 14 personal semi-structured expert interviews among civil servants, companies, policy-makers, and NGOs, carried out in 2012. The analysis was conducted in several phases and it followed a qualitative inductive content analysis approach (Mayring 2000). Accordingly, the data were carefully read through several times and organized first into thematic categories and then further into broader themes, which formed the basis for the identification of key lines of argumentation in the policy debate and for analyzing the construction and legitimation of green growth as a new broad storyline at the national level. Through this data-oriented method the categories and themes were allowed to emerge directly from the empirical data rather than being forced into predefined framework or fixed categories.

In the following, I first discuss the notion of green growth and its relationship to sustainable development and ecological modernization. I then describe my theoretical framework and the Finnish context for green growth policies. In the empirical sections, I analyze the construction of green growth as a new, broad storyline and then identify four more specific interpretations that have emerged in the Finnish debate. Finally, I conclude by discussing the implications that the recent debate has had on the ideas of the green state, political inclusion and system-level transformations.

Policy debates on green growth: the context for the Finnish program

The recent efforts of greening the state – in the context of the EU, for instance, most visibly through the objective of introducing "smart, sustainable and inclusive growth" (EC 2010) – have been accompanied by the emergence of new policy concepts and state strategies like green economy (UNEP 2011) and green growth (OECD 2011). According to the United Nations Environment Programme (UNEP), green economy refers to "improved human well-being and social equity, while significantly reducing environmental risks and ecological scarcities" (UNEP 2011). This formulation emphasizes the social dimension of sustainability through aiming at poverty reduction at the global level, and views economic growth as a favorable condition for sustainable development rather than primary objective of its own. The OECD's green growth strategy, which Finland has recently adopted as a broad policy guideline for greening the economy and society, takes green growth to mean "fostering economic growth and development while ensuring that natural assets continue to provide the resources and environmental services on which our well-being relies" (OECD 2011: 9).

Green growth has a stronger emphasis on economic and environmental aspects of sustainability with its explicit objectives of boosting economic growth through innovation and directed public policies. The OECD (2011) also recognizes the dual nature of natural capital as providing both an input to economic production and a contribution to human well-being. In this view, a transition to green growth requires that resources are more efficiently used to secure sustained long-term economic growth and societal well-being. Moreover, the OECD highlights that public policy intervention can be an important factor in accelerating comprehensive transitions towards a more sustainable economy and society (*ibid.*).

The discussion on the optimal ways to organize the relationship between the environment and economy as well as concerning the scale of economic activities, however, date back to the 1970s when discussion began to emerge about ultimate limits to economic growth and the preconditions of sustainable development. Sustainable development was introduced as a way to harmonize these objectives to promote present and future social well-being (WCED 1987). Ecological modernization emerged later and had a stronger emphasis on economic and technological aspects but, more importantly, stressed that environmental and economic goals were mutually reinforcing (Jänicke 2008; Langhelle 2000; Dryzek 2005; Baker 2007). The core goal of Green growth combines environmental and economic development objectives and thus reflects ideas expressed earlier in sustainable development. Moreover, it builds on the economically oriented ideas of ecological modernization by seeking to respond to "the dual global challenges of (1) expanding economic opportunities for a growing population; and (2) mitigating the environmental pressures that otherwise could undermine our ability to take advantage of these opportunities" (OECD 2013: 21) through greater resource efficiency and the development and utilization of green innovation.

Similar ideas from the late 1990s and early 2000s surface in EU-initiated concepts such as integrated innovation policy and knowledge-based economy (Teräväinen 2012). These views have largely reflected the increasing preoccupation among national decision-makers and supranational organizations with the 'grand challenges of our time,' such as the threat of climate change. Establishing holistic and integrative view on innovation-related policies has also been adopted as a guiding principle at the national level in many EU member states. In Finland this is reflected for instance in the government's STI strategies and policy programs calling for cross-sectorial governance and the integration of climate, technology, and economic development policies into a coherent national approach. Following the OECD and the EU guidelines, this has also entailed efforts to develop policies and instruments that would balance supply-and-demand-side innovation policies in responding to broad cross-sectorial policy challenges in an integrative way.

State orientations and political opportunities framing policy debates

Studies of sociology and political science have often sought explanations for political processes and policy change from varying combination of structures (polity) and agency (discourses) (Hansen and Sørensen 2005; Hay 2008; Schmidt 2008). One structurally oriented strand in research addressing the importance of particular politico-economic and historic-cultural contexts in policy design, implementation, and outcomes is the political opportunity structure (POS) literature. In this literature, the relative openness of a society and certain societal conditions, such as formal decision-making structures, elite strategies towards challengers, political cleavages, and cultural features are seen to foster and constrain political opportunities and mobilization (Gamson and Meyer 1996; Tarrow 1996; Koopmans and Statham 1999; Kriesi 2004). The structural features of a polity, whether formal/informal or stable/volatile, are in this research strand seen as having a formative influence on policy negotiation in a given historical moment. Political inclusion has been a particularly relevant aspect as the specific politico-institutional structures and historically developed modes of negotiation have tended to define the boundaries, legitimate participants, and credible forms of argumentation.

Dryzek *et al.* (2003) studied the relation between the state and society. To do this they build on the POS literature, and develop the idea of state inclusion by identifying active and passive forms of inclusion and exclusion. On this basis, they formulate a fourfold categorization of state inclusion types: actively inclusive (expansive corporatism), passively inclusive (pluralism), passively exclusive (legal corporatism), and actively exclusive (authoritarian liberalism) (*ibid.*: 7). In this typology, the Nordic countries can be characterized as actively inclusive states with expansive corporatist traditions and relatively open and inclusive political systems (*ibid.*; Teräväinen 2012). In the Finnish context, the active state inclusion has been manifested particularly in the structures of the formal decision-making system. The Finnish multi-party system based on proportional representation, the majority coalition governments that since the 1980s have mostly been in office for the entire four-year electoral terms, and the history of collective agreements among labor market organizations, the state, and industry have contributed to generating stability and continuance to national politics and encouraged active stakeholder inclusion at least in the formal structures of policy making.

In particular, the relatively broad-based interest group representation in policy preparation, parliamentary committee work, and expert and stakeholder hearings – together with informal communication among policy makers and indirect means of regulation – have been characteristic for the Finnish political system. These features have been accompanied with integrative and non-confrontational state strategies, which have reflected the historically constituted mode of consensus-oriented policy negotiations typical for an actively inclusive state (cf. Kriesi 2004; Dryzek *et al.* 2003). The consensus-seeking nature of Finnish decision-making processes in climate and energy policies has also been strengthened by the state ownership in large national energy companies, which has provided indirect means of regulating the energy sector and reduced open political conflicts.

Yet the active political inclusion has largely taken place within the formal structures of the national political system. Unlike other actively inclusive states such as the Netherlands and Denmark, for instance, democratic experiments like consensus conferences and participatory technology assessment exercises have been lacking from Finland. Another distinct feature in the Finnish polity has been the lack of a critical public space that would operate independently in relation to the actively inclusive state. Together with the consensus-seeking policy negotiations, expansive corporatism and the relatively strong public trust in state authorities and institutions has contributed to legitimating national policy objectives such as sustaining national welfare through economic competitiveness and high technology-driven policies, ensuring good operational conditions for the national heavy industry, and reducing import dependency as key responsibilities of the state (Teräväinen *et al.* 2011). Throughout decades, the role of the national heavy industry in guiding Finnish energy and climate policies has been particularly strong, while alternative expertise has typically remained relatively weak in the national policy debate. This points to a degree of selectivity in active inclusion. The broad-based interest group representation in formal structures of policy making has often remained ineffective in terms of political influence and outcomes due to the relatively strong political power of the highly selected energy and technology policy elite. Moreover, the successive governments' continued commitment to investment and support to the development of research and development (R&D) in general and in environmental and energy technologies in particular has resulted in a rather strong national technology-driven climate and energy policy approach. The Finnish state orientation can thus be characterized as 'technology-and-industry-know-best,' where sustainable transitions are seen as best achieved by facilitating the development and use of green innovation and market-based mechanisms (*ibid.*).

The POS and state orientation theories have, however, been criticized for being incapable of addressing change over time and of providing too static explanations concerning politics. Moreover, most of research utilizing these models has tended to focus on scrutinizing how the structural features of a polity shape policy discourses and outcomes and thereby have failed to recognize the potential of policy discourses and political action to transform the polity. I argue that addressing the dynamics of politics requires complementing the structural understanding of polity by recognizing the two-way relationship between polity and politics (see also Teräväinen 2012). From this perspective, policy structures and discourses are seen as mutually constitutive elements in politics.

Drawing from constructivist neo-institutionalism (Hay 2008; Schmidt 2008), I take institutions in a broad meaning, as composed of "regulative, normative and cultural-cognitive elements that, together with associated activities and resources, provide stability and meaning to social life" (Scott 2008: 48). They can be formal, like regulations and standards, or informal, like norms and generally accepted values. In addition, I complement the institutional dimension of a polity by discursive approach and argue that discursive practices play a significant role in understanding the dynamics of politics. In this respect, I combine the POS analysis with Hajerian discourse theory (Hajer 1995) and argue that discourses are not only shaped by their respective polities but also importantly shape them through competing interpretations concerning key policy concepts and practices.

Towards a national green growth strategy

Recent efforts to establish a national green growth strategy for Finland can be seen to exemplify the interplay between policy discourses and structures. The tightening climate policy regulation together with the concern over the security of energy supply, inexpensive energy and sustained economic growth (MEE 2013) have made the OECD's green growth an appealing policy strategy for Finnish policy makers as a pathway towards a more sustainable and competitive carbon-neutral innovation economy (*ibid.*). Initiatives relating to green growth have included the government's inter-ministerial clean tech program coordinated by the Ministry of Employment and the Economy (MEE), and the broader export-oriented 'Team Finland' initiative with a high-level steering group chaired by the Prime Minister. These have been accompanied by strong government support for environmental and energy-related R&D activities including the Strategic Centre for Science, Technology and Innovation (SHOKs), the large multidisciplinary research programs Green Growth and Groove (funded by Tekes), and the national cluster of expertise in environmental technology (Cleantech cluster). At the same time, discussion has emerged on new policy instruments and initiatives, such as public procurement of green innovation, which would combine demand- and supply-side policies as suggested by the OECD's green growth strategy.

The Finnish inter-ministerial clean technology program launched in 2012 forms the key framework for national green growth policies. It seeks to enhance policy coherence among national technology, innovation, environmental, and economic development policies, and to strengthen linkages between environmental and economic development policies that in Finland have historically operated as relatively separate policy spheres with often confronting objectives (see Teräväinen 2012). The clean tech program follows the ideas of the recent national climate and energy strategy (MEE 2013) and another government program in 2011, which identified climate change as a key driver for innovation-driven economic growth and also suggested that a strategic program of clean technology be established. At the same time, being steered by the MEE, which is responsible for technology, innovation, and energy policies, the program reflects the key premises of the established national innovation policy approach, where the crucial role of high technology and innovation in all societal development has been strongly emphasized.

The aim of the clean tech program is to create at least 40,000 new jobs to the sector and double the turnover of Finnish clean tech companies from 20 billion to 50 billion euros by 2020 (MEE 2013). It contains five key strategic themes aiming at developing a favorable operational environment for the acceleration of clean tech in Finland across different sectors and levels of operation. The themes include:

- strategic influence entailing sectoral and intersectoral government strategies;
- sustainable mining with a national mining program;
- clean energy with a program promoting the development and commercialization of clean technology, energy efficiency and self-sufficiency;
- the funding of clean technology including the allocation of R&D resources and cooperation with funding agencies and the private sector; and
- promoting international business activities particularly in the form of the Team Finland initiative and cooperation with the clean tech cluster.

With these strategic themes, the government seeks to establish an integrated approach at the national level for greening the state and accelerating sustainable socio-technical transitions. Key elements visible in these strategic themes and in related policy documents include a support for new and promising techno-economic openings, the prioritization of selected fields of innovation in areas where Finland already has competence (e.g., water technology, waste management and biomass), combining economic, environmental and societal objectives through strategic, thematically oriented and cross-sectorial innovation initiatives, promoting technological and economic cooperation and business at the national and global levels, and – largely in line with the model of active inclusion (Dryzek *et al.* 2003) – emphasizing multi-stakeholder inclusion in policy negotiations. Moreover, the Finnish debate on green growth largely draws from and builds on earlier environmental policy discourses and the historically developed national innovation-driven climate and energy policy approach. As I discuss in the following sections, this embeddedness of the green growth strategy in the Finnish polity contributes to the construction of its political legitimacy and to the formation of a broad, integrative green growth storyline at the national level. At the same time, the new elements included in this approach imply a need for new kinds of policy practices and challenge the established modes of negotiation and policy formulation.

Constructing legitimacy for green growth

The clean tech program has largely drawn its legitimacy from certain cultural, historical, and politico-economic features of the Finnish society. One important feature in this respect has been the relatively strong technological orientation in national politics in comparison to other Nordic and European countries. Whereas the political weight of energy technologies and green technological innovations were not recognized in some other European countries such as the UK until the 2000s, in Finland they have been seen as an important part of national technology-led economic growth for decades (Teräväinen 2012). Following the rapid industrialization and urbanization processes since the 1950s and the state-led program of 'managed structural change' since the late 1980s, successive governments have pursued a state-led growth-oriented policy approach and highlighted the role of technology and R&D investment in creating world-class performance in selected industrial areas such as energy and the environment. The green growth approach continually emphasizes the Finnish technological orientation within this policy sphere by stressing the importance of R&D investment and of public sector support to promoting clean energy innovations (e.g. MEE 2013). Policy makers and business actors do perceive the state as an important facilitator and an enabler of green innovation, particularly in clean technology areas that are economically promising but where the current market demand is not fully developed. The potential to use public procurement to create demands for clean technology is one example; other measures recommended in fostering green transitions are standards and directed regulative measures.

Unlike the earlier formulations of national technology and innovation policy, the framework of green growth entails an explicit effort to integrate the objectives of environmental, technology, and economic development policies into a coherent national approach. This integration takes place while maintaining the expansive corporatist and actively inclusive mode of policy design and negotiation. The Finnish climate and energy policy discussion has previously organized around three broad storylines and respective discourse coalitions, namely economic rationalism, consensus reformism, and progressive environmentalism, having their emphasis mainly on the national economic performance and competition, institutions and broad-based consensual policy negotiations, or the global environment and social justice, respectively (Teräväinen 2011). They have also suggested a varying degree of societal change, ranging from an effort to foster gradual and sector-based transformations within techno-social and economic systems (or sub-systems) to a focus on profound transitions of the system as a whole (see also Clapp and Dauvergne 2005).

A key aspect in the recent green growth discussion has been an effort to overcome the divisions between the previous storylines, namely the historically controversial divisions between environmental, economic, and social objectives on the one hand and between regional, national, and global interests on the other hand. In this respect, a new green growth storyline seems to be evolving among key actors and institutions across policy sectors. The core of this storyline entails generating a new kind of green consensus at the national level by simultaneously promoting job creation, environmental protection, regional development, and international market opportunities along the lines of the OECD strategy. In this process, a new discourse coalition is also emerging. The integrative storyline of green growth has mobilized an unprecedented range of actors across policy sectors and fields of business (cf. Chapters 5 and 8, this volume). A key advocate in this respect has been the national technology and innovation funding agency Tekes, which has had a key facilitating role, not only as a funding organization but also in bringing various actors together and actively engaging in the development of a national vision and action plan. Drawing from the Finnish tradition of the relatively strong trust in state authorities and state-led policies, one form of building political legitimacy for green growth has also been the several Tekes-initiated green growth events and seminars with high-level political representation, high public visibility, and the involvement of international experts. The consensus-building form of policy negotiation has also been strengthened in that these initiatives have emphasized political inclusion and dialogue and thereby broadened the understanding concerning relevant stakeholders in the policy process.

Alongside the state-led orientation in the governance and development of the national high technology-driven policy approach and the effort to foster integrative, multi-stakeholder and cross-sectorial policies, the relative strength of the economically important heavy industry has remained significant in national policy documents and negotiations. Finnish climate and energy policies have been historically conditioned by industrial concerns, which has at some point generated conflicts between national and international levels, particularly in terms of national energy policy interests and the tightening EU emission reduction obligations. In recent green growth discussion, the national technological policy orientation, the 'technology-and-industry-know-best,' has importantly shaped the terms of the debate. The green growth rhetoric has focused on the importance and the potential of high technology and innovations in solving broad societal problems. This has entailed suggestions of creating new 'green Nokias' within selected technological areas, emphasizing small and medium-sized companies, particularly in initiatives aiming at developing new technological niches within the field of clean energy. At the same time, greening the production methods and processes of traditional heavy industrial sectors such as pulp and paper industries are often mentioned among the priorities of the national approach, not least because of recent global economic fluctuations and their impact on the operational conditions of heavy industry.

The compatibility of the green growth rhetoric with the long-term innovation policy approach has also been visible in that the recent discussion has indicated continuity in terms of the relative strength of competition discourse (see also Teräväinen 2011, 2012), wherein international competitiveness, technological leadership, and the functioning of the market have been raised as normative principles guiding all national policies. At the same time, the historically developed concentration of power within the Finnish energy sector (see e.g. Litmanen 2009) around a few large partly state-owned energy companies has contributed to legitimizing the industrial and market-based arguments in the national debate. Particularly the idea of successfully combining the objectives of economic growth and environmental protection has chimed rather well with the dominant competition discourse, and highlighting the economic opportunities of the green growth strategy has proved a successful strategy for engaging economic actors to the green growth process. A contributing factor in this respect has also been the government's commitment to the EU-initiated ideas of knowledge-based economy and broad-based innovation policy since the late 1990s and early 2000s.

In this respect, green growth rhetoric has indeed largely drawn from the established structures and vocabulary of a competitive innovation economy that has become almost a non-negotiable imperative (Blühdorn 2007). Finnish decision-makers and stakeholders tend to see the OECD's green growth strategy as providing a broad framework for designing national policies and introducing new policy instruments to foster the development, adoption, and commercialization of environmental and energy technologies. At the same time, the idea of perceiving economic and environmental policy objectives not only in some way compatible but also mutually reinforcing has gained a broad acceptance and support among Finnish decision-makers and stakeholders and reflected a 'win–win' situation (Hajer 1995; Dryzek 2005) in terms of simultaneously promoting environmental protection and economic growth. Yet the Finnish 'technology-and-industry-know-best' approach (Teräväinen *et al.* 2011) has pointed to a form of techno-corporatist eco-modernism (Hajer 1995), as the 'win–win' ideas of environmental and economic benefits have largely excluded the social dimension of green growth. This has further strengthened the dominance of competition discourse in the national debate through mechanisms of discourse structuration (*ibid.*): the green growth language has inherently formed into an economic one.

Multiple meanings of green growth

Beyond the generic acceptance of the core principles of the green growth storyline, the recent debate points to differences among actors concerning the more exact meaning and content of green growth. There seems to be unanimity concerning green growth vocabulary, and different actors tend to use varying and multiple concepts relating to the promotion of green technology and innovation. Green growth is a relatively new policy concept, it is still 'in the making,' and its definition a subject of competing interpretations. While some actors see green growth primarily as a response to the recent global economic crisis, for others it is more of a matter of resource management in terms of efficient use of natural, human, technological and economic resources. Moreover, some actors perceive green growth as a continuum for national innovation policy and see its rationale particularly from the viewpoint of the potential of creating new business opportunities and activities.

The ways in which various actors understand and interpret green growth is an indication of its potential for generating sustainable transitions. They also imply differing understandings concerning the role of the state in governing these transitions. In the recent debate, four key lines of interpretation concerning green growth can be found:

- green growth as an umbrella concept for various green practices, processes and policies;
- green growth as an extension of national technology/innovation policy;
- a resource management perspective to green growth; and
- green growth implying a system-level change throughout the economy and society.

For those seeing green growth as *an umbrella concept*, it is not much more than a new label for established practices, a business-as-usual state of affairs. The historically developed state support for clean technology, the expansive corporatist governance, and the national competence and know-how in selected areas of green innovation indeed are quite compatible with the green growth strategy in its broadly defined umbrella concept sense. In this respect, adopting green growth as a national policy guideline does not require large socio-technical or politico-institutional changes as many already established government policies and business practices fit rather easily under the 'green' or 'sustainable' label. This perspective also exemplifies how green growth has been a relatively difficult concept to define: many interviewees found it hard to make a difference between sustainable development and green growth. Yet, at the same time, many saw green growth as a more positive and dynamic concept in comparison to the old notion of sustainable development and therefore more appealing to a variety of actors across administrative and industrial branches.

Largely building on ideas of ecological modernization and nationally almost hegemonic competition rhetoric, many actors perceive green growth primarily as providing a potential for the creation of new clean tech business activities in the global market. In this perspective, green growth is seen as *an extension to national technology/innovation policy* and interpreted, as for instance a trade union confederation representative put it, as directing new growth towards sustainable development by utilizing technological innovations that may simultaneously open new markets for Finnish companies and provide solutions to environmental problems nationally and internationally. The state is typically seen as facilitator and enabler of green innovation, advancing the development of clean tech through new demand side innovation policy measures such as public procurement. Yet, as some ministerial representatives mentioned, a common view seems to be that public policies should not intervene in making technological choices as that is seen to best take place through competition and market selection. As most national, sectorial strategies and international initiatives as well as the *Team Finland* adhere to this understanding of green growth, it seems to be the dominant interpretation of green growth in the recent debate.

The resource management perspective to green growth draws from the OECD strategic guidelines and emphasizes the efficient use of natural, human, technological and economic resources. The perspective underscores the need to manage natural resources in a more efficient way. Many policy documents contain suggestions of sector-specific policy measures such as improving energy efficiency in the construction sector, developing better cultivation methods for agricultural production or enhancing waste management practices. The resource management perspective is the most practically oriented understanding of green growth as it often entails concrete suggestions about specific policy measures and their implementation. In comparison to the relatively static understanding of green growth as an umbrella concept and to the idea of green growth as an extension to national innovation policy which only call for small or gradual changes in the current socio-technical and politico-economic practices, the resource management perspective suggests more substantial changes in the established technological and institutional arrangements. However, the changes called for are sector-based and thus remain limited in terms of accelerating large, society-wide socio-technical transitions. As regards to the role of the state, however, this perspective confers to the state a stronger regulative and strategic role in governing green growth than the two other perspectives.

Finally, the idea of green growth as implying *a system-level change* throughout the economy and society has been advocated by some strategic policy documents and influential actors like Tekes, but this has not translated into concrete policies, or into what Hajer (1995) calls discourse institutionalization. In this view, current patterns of production and consumption are seen as unsustainable and potentially causing serious problems such as water crisis, global poverty and the loss of biodiversity. The established technology and economic policy measures traditionally designed to correct market failures are considered insufficient for solving such complex and multi-level problems. Instead the call is for profound socio-technical and politico-economic changes at all levels of a society. Given the inadequacy of market mechanisms to solve the urgent problems, this perspective emphasizes the crucial role of the state to actively promote and accelerate sustainable transitions. In addition, it has a strong emphasis on intersectoral, multi-level and multi-stakeholder cooperation and in this way it builds on and further develops the tradition of active inclusion in the national polity. The inclusion suggested by this perspective would indeed entail opening the policy making and negotiation structures vertically and horizontally in a way that would allow not only broader but also politically more influential stakeholder inclusion in strategically important matters. In this way, it calls for new political openings, such as bottom-up initiatives and new stakeholder alliances also beyond and outside the formal structures of the state.

These four understandings of green growth suggest a varying degree of socio-technical and politico-economic change with different implications on political inclusion (Table 10.1). They can thus be seen as specifying the Finnish model of active inclusion in terms of entailing varying suggestions on the actors, levels, modes and sectors of inclusion. The umbrella concept perspective views green growth as a relatively static approach that contains little or no new elements in relation to the established policies. As regards to the state, it suggests a business-as-usual understanding of the political system with formal inclusion (expansive corporatism) that takes place within the established structures. The umbrella concept thus takes green growth as legitimating current policies, negotiation structures and business practices – and justifying existing patterns of production and consumption under a green label. The understanding of green growth as an extension to national technology/innovation policy contains somewhat more socio-technical and politico-economic transformation potential in terms of the development and utilization of clean technology. It calls for stronger investment in clean technology and environmental innovation, but beyond this techno-economist modernization agenda, it also largely remains a reassuring discourse for established policy practices. In this perspective, political inclusion is network-based with an emphasis on fields and actors directly related to clean technology and environmental innovation.

The resource management view instead suggests some concrete policy changes particularly in strategically important and economically potential sectors and calls for a more coordinated effort to socio-technical transformations. In terms of political inclusion, new actors are invited to policy negotiations also from sectors such as agriculture that traditionally have not been seen as belonging to the core fields of clean technology. Unlike the extension to national technology/innovation policy perspective that emphasizes horizontal coordination, however, the active inclusion of this view is largely sector-based. It lacks a comprehensive view concerning intersectoral and multi-level changes and thus remains limited in its transformative potential. The systemic changes perspective suggests the most radical form of societal transformation, calling for profound changes throughout sectors and levels of the society and economy as a whole. It calls for extended political inclusion accompanied with integrated and multi-level governance. Rather than simply increasing inclusiveness in terms of inviting more participants in policy making, extended inclusion calls for both vertical and horizontal dimensions in policy negotiations and encourages greater transparency, openness, and new forms and channels of political influence. In practice, however, advocates of this perspective have so far been unable to define concrete measures through which such changes could be achieved. Sectorial strategies and measures to promote clean tech activities have been developed but a comprehensive national strategic approach aiming at systemic changes seems still to be lacking. In this sense, the systemic changes perspective seems to be in need of clarification in order to move from rhetorical level and discourse structuration to discourse institutionalization and concrete policy changes.

Despite the varying interpretations about its definition and detailed content, green growth has been represented as a broad national project with broad political acceptance at the national level due to a number of stakeholder consultations and the broad-based committee work in the preparatory phases of national policy. Yet one can ask to what extent the formally open and inclusive state orientation that has so far rather effectively legitimized the economic growth-oriented green growth storyline at the national policy debate is capable of taking into account alternative strategies, critical voices, and emerging counter-discourses such as de-growth and politics of unsustainability. The green growth storyline's interpretative flexibility has proved appealing to a broad range of stakeholders, but different understandings have emerged about its meaning and content beyond its generic principles. Moreover, since most policy documents

Table 10.1 The degree of political and socio-technical change in the interpretations of green growth in Finland

Understanding of green growth	Degree of change	Mode of active inclusion
Umbrella concept for green processes	–	Formal inclusion
Extension to national innovation policy	– / +	Network-based inclusion
Resource management perspective	+	Sector-based inclusion
System-level change	+ +	Extended inclusion

and stakeholders seem to understand green growth as an extension to established national technology/innovation policy rather than a new policy approach with substantial transformative potential, one can ask whether this approach is capable of generating the kinds of transitions that the OECD guidelines and international climate policy agreements would require.

Conclusion

The discursive compatibility of green growth with the national innovation policy approach has made it relatively easy to accept among a range of actors and contributed to generating a new national level 'green consensus.' Drawing from the historically developed active inclusiveness of the Finnish polity together with the 'technology-and-industry-know-best' state orientation, the storyline of green growth has proved an appealing policy approach for actors across administrative and industrial sectors. Its flexibility and loose definition, however, have allowed different actors to interpret green growth – and related policies – largely through their own lenses, which has led to ambiguity in terms of defining a more detailed national vision and an action plan that would enable systemic changes throughout the economy and society. Beyond the generic principles of green growth as suggested by the government policy documents, the four lines of interpretation indeed suggest rather different development paths for sustainable transitions with substantially differing views regarding the role of the state in these processes.

In this respect, legitimating green growth in the national context by its compatibility with the established high technology-driven innovation economy approach and the dominant economist vocabulary does not imply an emergence of a holistic and integrative approach to green transitions that both the OECD and the UNEP suggestions have called for. The relatively narrow focus on clean technology (versus green growth as a comprehensive societal strategy) contributes to the development, utilization and export of green innovation but does not as such indicate system-level transformations. With its emphasis on economic, technological and environmental aspects, the Finnish green growth storyline thus largely remains a kind of loose framework for environmentally informed and technology-driven economic growth that focuses on international competitiveness and good techno-economic performance, but at the same time lacks for instance social and cultural dimensions of sustainability.

In terms of a potential transformation towards a green state, the recent debate contains little elements that would have the potential of changing the current policy and governance practices. In this sense, the Finnish version of green growth indicates gradual and sector-based changes within socio-technical and politico-economic (sub-)systems rather than transforming these systems as a whole. It thus can be asked whether green growth is only yet another rhetorically appealing and politically powerful discursive strategy for maintaining the current patterns of unsustainability and reassuring the established polity – and under which conditions it could be harnessed to challenge and modify the dominant policy approach towards genuinely sustainable transitions. The integrative approach suggested by the systemic perspective might have some potential in this respect, but it would require rethinking the balance between different dimensions of sustainability at multiple levels instead of conditioning all policy objectives by technological and economic concerns, and shifting the focus from the development of clean technologies to their utilization and demand. In terms of political inclusion and (an ideal of) the Green State, achieving sustainable transitions in the sense of system-level changes might require replacing the consensus-seeking orientation and selective inclusiveness with more open, dialogical and even confrontational policy-making style, and incorporating ideas like adaptive governance and critical public sphere into policy making – in other words, moving from the static 'technology-and-industry-know-best' orientation towards a more dynamic, multi-level and multi-dimensional approach.

References

Baker, S., 2007 Sustainable development as symbolic commitment: declaratory politics and the seductive appeal of ecological modernisation in the European Union. *Environmental Politics* 16(2): 297–317.

Blühdorn, I., 2007 Sustaining the unsustainable: symbolic politics and the politics of simulation. *Environmental Politics* 16(2): 251–75.

Clapp, J., and Dauvergne, P., 2005 *Paths to a Green World: The Political Economy of the Global Environment*. MIT Press, Cambridge, MA.

Dryzek, J.S., 2005 *The Politics of Earth: Environmental Discourses*. Oxford University Press, Oxford.

Dryzek, J.S., Downes, D., Hunold, C., Schlosberg, D., and Hernes, H.K., 2003 *Green States and Social Movements: Environmentalism in the United States, United Kingdom, Germany and Norway*. Oxford University Press, Oxford.

EC 2010 *Europe 2020: A Strategy for Smart, Sustainable and Inclusive Growth*. European Commission, Brussels.

Eckersley, R., 2004 *The Green State: Rethinking Democracy and Sovereignty*. MIT Press, Cambridge, MA.

Gamson, W., and Meyer, D.S., 1996 Framing political opportunity. In McAdam, D., McCarthy, J.D., and Zald, M.N., (eds) *Comparative Perspectives on Social Movements* 275–90. Cambridge University Press, Cambridge.

Geels, F.W., 2010 Ontologies, socio-technical transitions (to sustainability), and the multi-level perspective. *Research Policy* 39: 495–510.

Geels, F.W., and Kemp, R., 2007 Dynamics in socio-technical systems: typology of change processes and contrasting case studies. *Technology in Society* 29(4): 441–55.

Hajer, M., 1995 *The Politics of Environmental Discourse*. Oxford University Press, Oxford.

Hansen, A.D., and Sørensen, E., 2005 Polity as politics: studying the shaping and effects of discursive polities. In Howarth, D., and Torfing, J., (eds) *Discourse Theory in European Politics: Identity, Policy and Governance* 93–116. Palgrave Macmillan, Basingstoke.

Hay, C., 2008 Constructivist institutionalism. In Rhodes, R.A.W., Binder, S.A., and Rockman, B.A., (eds) *The Oxford Handbook of Political Institutions* 56–74. Oxford University Press, Oxford.

Jänicke, M., 2008 Ecological modernisation: new perspectives. *Journal of Cleaner Production* 16(5): 557–65.

Kemp, R., Loorbach, D., and Rotmans, J., 2007 Transition management as a model for managing processes of co-evolution for sustainable development. *The International Journal of Sustainable Development and World Ecology* 14: 78–91.

Koopmans, R., and Statham, P., 1999 Ethnic and civic conceptions of nationhood and the differential success of the extreme right in Germany and Italy. In Giugni, M., McAdam, D., and Tilly, C., (eds) *How Social Movements Matter* 225–51. University of Minnesota Press, Minneapolis, MN.

Kriesi, H., 2004 Political context and opportunity. In Snow, D., Soule, S.A., and Kriesi, H., (eds) *The Blackwell Companion to Social Movements* 67–90. Blackwell, Malden, MA.

Langhelle, O., 2000 Why ecological modernisation and sustainable development should not be conflated. *Journal of Environmental Policy and Planning* 2(4): 303–22.

Litmanen, T., 2009 The temporary nature of societal risk evaluation: understanding the Finnish nuclear decisions. In Litmanen, T., and Kojo, M., (eds) *The Renewal of Nuclear Power in Finland* 192–217. Palgrave Macmillan, Basingstoke.

Lovell, H., 2007 The governance of innovation in sociotechnical systems: the difficulties of strategic niche management in practice. *Science and Public Policy* 34: 35–44.

Mayring, P., 2000 Qualitative content analysis. *Forum: Qualitative Social Research* 12: art. 20.

MEE 2013 *National Energy and Climate Strategy*. Government Report to Parliament on March 20. Ministry of Employment and the Economy of Finland, Helsinki.

OECD 2009 Declaration on green growth. Adopted at the Council Meeting at Ministerial level on 25 June 25. Retrieved March 15, 2014 from www.oli.oecd.org/olis/2009doc.nsf.

OECD 2011 *Towards Green Growth*. Paris: Organisation for Economic Co-operation and Development. Retrieved March 15, 2014 from www.oecd.org/greengrowth/48224539.pdf.

OECD 2013 OECD green growth studies: putting green growth at the heart of development. Retrieved March 15, 2014 from www.oecd.org/dac/environment-development/greengrowthand development.htm.

Schmidt, V.A., 2008 Discursive institutionalism: the explanatory power of ideas and discourse. *Annual Review of Political Science* 11: 303–26.

Scott, W.R., 2008 *Institutions and Organizations*. Sage, Thousand Oaks, CA.

Tarrow, S., 1996 States and opportunities: the political structuring of social movements. In McAdam, D., McCarthy, J.D., and Zald, M.N., (eds) *Comparative Perspectives on Social Movements* 41–61. Cambridge University Press, Cambridge.

Teräväinen, T., 2011 Representations of energy policy and technology in Finnish and British newspaper media: a comparative perspective. *Public Understanding of Science* July 13: 0963662511409122.

Teräväinen, T., 2012 *The Politics of Energy Technologies: Debating Climate Change, Energy Policy, and Technology in Finland, the United Kingdom, and France.* Into, Helsinki.

Teräväinen, T., Lehtonen, M., and Martiskainen, M., 2011 Climate change, energy security and risk – debating nuclear new build in Finland, France and the UK. *Energy Policy* 39(6): 3434–42.

UNEP 2011 Towards a green economy: pathways to sustainable development and poverty eradication. Retrieved March 15, 2014 from www.unep.org/GreenEconomy.

WCED 1987 *Our Common Future.* Report of the World Commission on Environment and Development ('the Brundtland Report'). Oxford University Press, Oxford. Retrieved March 15, 2014 from http://conspect.nl/pdf/Our_Common_Future-Brundtland_Report_1987.pdf.

Part IV
Transforming the polity toward climate and sustainability objectives

11 Greening the state of California

Governmentality and the subjectification of the polity through climate governance

Matthew Cashmore and Jaap G. Rozema

Introduction

The green state is a notion that engenders largely positive associations for many actors with an interest in sustainable development (cf. Eckersley 2004; Chapter 1, this volume). Yet like any other academic concept, the green state needs to be approached critically for there is a danger that such positive associations obfuscate power dynamics and political practices that may be less progressive. This chapter examines climate policy within the State of California using governmentality. This is as an analytical perspective on power that has proven particularly strong at focusing attention on the specificity of the operation and effects of public policy. The application of governmentality surfaces how the values, beliefs and world views of parts of the polity are discursively constituted by actors in positions of relative authority in purposeful attempts to 'conduct conduct' through climate policy. Such attempts constitute a phenomenon known as subjectification in governmentality scholarship.

We focus on California – a federal, rather than a nation, state – for several reasons. First, California is known for having a reasonably progressive approach to a number of sustainability concerns, including air quality, waste management and hazardous chemical usage (London *et al.* 2013). Significantly in the context of this book, it has been viewed as a frontrunner in terms of climate change policy implementation, nationally and arguably internationally (Bedsworth and Hanak 2013; Urpelainen 2009). California's Global Warming Solutions Act of 2006 (Assembly Bill 32) established ambitious targets for reducing greenhouse gas emissions. Climate change mitigation initiatives have included action to promote renewable energy, green building design, emission reductions from cars, and efficiency gains in urban water usage, which is a notably energy-intensive sector (Bedsworth and Hanak 2013). In 2009 a statewide 'Climate Adaptation Strategy' was adopted, marking the formalization of policy on adaptation to climate change. Their policy implementation record, therefore, suggests California may be a frontrunner in greening of the state.

Second, the level of economic activity in California makes it highly important in terms of sustainability at the global scale. California would have the ninth largest economy in the world if it were a country. Thus, with a similar GDP to the Russian Federation, Italy and Brazil, plus many nation states-like functions attributed to it under the US system of government, California forms an important site for exploring transformations to green statehood, and potential implications for the polity therein.

Like much governmentality scholarship, our specific empirical focus is a largely overlooked and seemingly fairly innocuous locus of power and authority in climate governance: non-binding guidance documents. While guidance implies that compliance is based upon free choice, norms of appropriate conduct that often remain implicit problematize its apparently voluntary character. The analysis of guidance thus provides a detailed empirical account of institutional responses by the state to climate change and the particularities of the identities presupposed for specific actors in and through such initiatives (Dean 2010).

More specifically, the analysis focuses on a series of guidance documents that address climate change adaptation planning practices. Although the level of attention given to climate change adaptation has increased over time, it still garners less consideration than mitigation. The reasons for this are many and varied, but most significantly there is a lingering concern that adaptation is "ethically inferior because it connotes acquiescence" (Landy 2010). Yet in the US context where congressional debates are mired in controversy, climate change adaptation may appear rather less confrontational and threatening than mitigation. This may explain why the State of California has produced guidance on adaptation but not mitigation. Furthermore, it has been suggested that given the obstacles to regulatory intervention by the federal government, the Obama administration has pursued action through less visible (and hence less controversial) strategies, including providing technical assistance to individual states (Kahn 2014). Rendering climate change adaptation practical in California through the planning system may constitute one such mechanism by which the Obama administration can circumvent, to a certain degree, political deadlock at the federal level. Nevertheless, an aim to render climate change practical, and hence taken for granted, raises important questions about legitimacy and authority in the governance of green initiatives, issues which may "often get obscured by the urgency of trying to save the planet" (Death 2014).

In applying governmentality to study apparently progressive policies, our analysis diverges somewhat from what have arguably been the core concerns of many green state scholars (e.g. Eckerlsey 2004; Dryzek 2005; Paehlke 2005). The application of governmentality leads us to examine the microphysics of the mechanisms through which rule is accomplished in a context where the California state appears strongly committed to some level and form of greening. Our focus is then more on opening up questions about how power and authority are exercised in the process to green the state, and the appropriateness of such situated practices in the light of the normative axioms contained in green state scholarship.

The chapter commences with a succinct introduction to governmentality as an analytical perspective on power and its application within environmental politics in general, and climate governance in particular. After introducing the research design, we use the case analysis to explore the account of adaptation planning policy, and the desired values and conducts of specific parts of the Californian polity involved in this policy field, that can be mounted through the application of governmentality. The chapter concludes with an examination of the value of governmentality in enriching discussions upon the green state as a site of climate and sustainability transitions.

Governmentality

Around the mid-1970s the focus of Foucault's scholarship expanded to include the government of populations as an object of inquiry. Governmentality as a critical perspective was introduced initially to analyze the mechanisms through which populations in nation states were regulated by public authorities – government in its more traditional sense. Over the course of his lectures at the Collège de France between 1977 and 1979, Foucault developed the concept to encompass the notion of government as all procedures intended to direct human conduct. It became an analytical perspective for the study of relations of power in general, and an antecedent to Foucault's later work on the ethics of the subject (Senellart 2009).

Governmentality is based upon a premise that government involves calculated attempts to shape the beliefs and conducts of individuals towards particular ends; to govern is to "structure the possible field of action of others" according to a particular rationality (Foucault 2002: 341). Rationality is conceived in governmentality as any form of reasoning that is reasonably clear about the ways things are and should be (Dean 2010).

Governmentality focuses, therefore, on the microphysics of power, as played out through particular modes and techniques of governing. Particular emphasis is placed on the relations between power and knowledge, and on the subjectification of the polity (Rose and Miller 2010; Dean 2010), so that citizens "do as they ought" (Scott 2005: 34, paraphrasing Jeremy Bentham).

A governmentality, then, is the rationality underpinning, and immanent to, micro-power (Senellart 2009), and power is interpreted as a productive force: "power produces: it produces reality: it produces domains of objects and rituals of truth. The individual and the knowledge that may be gained of him belong to this production" (Foucault 1995: 194).

Through the complex and often subtle shaping of the 'conduct of conduct,' individuals have a central role in defining their own subjectivities. They are conceived not merely as 'subject to' power for they play a fundamental role in its operation through their own self-regulation. Power is interpreted as "not so much a matter of imposing constraints upon citizens as of 'making up' citizens capable of bearing a kind of regulated freedom" (Miller and Rose 2008: 53). Political power under the governmentality perspective thus depends on the deployment of technologies that promote self-regulation by apparently autonomous subject citizens.

Governmentality emphasizes the ubiquity of government in social relations, the dispersed nature of power, and the significance of the individual to the neoliberal project, but also the ability of individuals to act in ways other than expected. Government is interpreted as a congenitally failing exercise. This means, among other things, the value of governmentality is as a diagnostic tool rather than a predictive one; it is used to surface representations of what subject citizens might be, rather than what they actually are (Hacking 1986). The limited consideration given to empirical realities in governmentality research is often perceived to be one of the key limitations of this body of scholarship (McKee 2009).

Foucault's work on governmentality has given rise to "a veritable cottage industry of material" (Elden 2007: 29) within the social sciences, and environmental concerns now feature fairly prominently in this literature. Scholars have applied a governmentality perspective to, among other things, environmental policy in international development (Goldman 2004; Cashmore *et al.* 2014), biodiversity conservation (Waage and Benediktsson 2010), and various dimensions of the urban environment (Kevin 2009). Through such analyses, governmentality has contributed to a critique of green or eco-governmentalities emergent in policy initiatives that are said to be based on environmental or sustainability ethics (e.g. Luke 1999; Rutherford 2007).

Governmentality has also gained some traction in climate change research, albeit such work remains at the margins of scholarship on climate governance. The work of governmentality scholars has contributed to evidencing how techniques of notation and inscription serve to make the climate amenable to programmatic government (e.g. Lövbrand *et al.* 2009; Paterson and Stripple 2010). It has also documented the emergence of a phenomenon which Stripple and Bulkeley (2014) label the 'conduct of carbon conduct,' with specific impetus given to shaping carbon subjectivities. This phenomenon concerns programmatic interventions intended to reform behavioral norms among energy end-users, for example in seeking to value certain social practices pertaining to energy consumption as more virtuous than others (e.g. Paterson and Stripple 2010).

Case study and methods

Our analysis focuses on the use of guidance to 'conduct conduct' within California. Various guidance documents on climate change adaptation have been issued by Californian governmental agencies in recent years, supported by periodic impact and vulnerability assessments. The guidance examined in this study is the 2012 California Adaptation Planning Guide, published jointly by the California Emergency Management Agency and the California Natural Resources Agency (hereafter CEMA/CNRA). The guidance consists of a main document (CEMA/CNRA 2012a, on planning for adaptive communities) and three supplementary ones (CEMA/CNRA 2012b, on defining local and regional impacts; CEMA/CNRA 2012c, on understanding regional characteristics; and CEMA/CNRA 2012d, on identifying adaptation strategies; see Table 11.1).

The analysis of these four documents facilitates the reconstruction of the virtual reality projected through the guidance. In particular, it provides insights into the values, beliefs and behaviors which are expected of certain actors,

Table 11.1 Overview of the California Adaptation Planning Guide series

Document (citation code)	Overview of content	Length in pages
Planning for adaptive communities (CEMA/CNRA 2012a)	Key guidance document outlining and explaining a process for adaptation planning	48
Defining local and regional impacts (CEMA/CNRA 2012b)	Supplemental documentation on climate change impacts which intended to support the conduct of vulnerability assessments	81
Understanding regional characteristics (CEMA/CNRA 2012c)	Describes environmental and socio-economic characteristics at a regional scale	114
Identifying adaptation strategies (CEMA/CNRA 2012d)	Presents examples of potential adaptation strategies as input to plan preparation	55

and hence the rationality underpinning governmental action in this field. Our focus on non-binding guidance, which by definition need not be adopted by its target audience, represents a belief that the political dimensions of this governmental technology are underexplored, presumably because non-binding guidance is viewed as a weak, mundane or asessentially benevolent form of policy intervention. It also reflects a desire to highlight the potentially diverse societal implications of emerging climate change policy regimes.

A premise of our analytical approach is that ideas about the conduct of the polity are written into guidance documents in ways that may be explicit and transparent in the text, such as particular actions that 'shall' or 'ought to be' taken, but they can also be implicit. Purposeful attempts to reshape actors' ways of knowing and acting through planning practices may then be more or less overt in such documents. Methodologically, the rationality underpinning and subjectivities embedded in the guidance under consideration are reconstructed through a textual analysis framework, which draws strongly upon the work of Alexander (2009). The textual analysis framework draws attention to, for example, terms of praise and of belittling (personalization for these implies a choice of affiliation and loyalty); naturalizing of concepts, beliefs and practices; and omissions, for what is not discussed can provide insights into how issues are framed (*ibid.*).

Adaptation planning in California

The need for governmental intervention on climate adaptation in California is based around a problematization that draws upon a number of factors, but central to it is the notion that adverse impacts from climate change are unavoidable. It is noted that climate change impacts might only be perceived as relatively minor at the present time, nevertheless "the longer communities wait, the greater the costs of the impacts and the costs to react to these impacts" (CEMA/CNRA 2012a: 4). Prudent government, therefore, prioritizes an early response to climate impacts based on economic considerations. This strategy of presenting particular patterns of behavior as being in the citizen's or a society's best interest, and thereby naturalizing such behaviors among a specific target group, is referred to as 'responsibilising' actors by Oels (2013).

The guidance also proclaims that many adaptation measures can generate additional social and economic benefits, thereby invoking a comparison to the notion of 'win-win' in the climate change mitigation discourse. Not only then is adaptation planning economically prudent in terms of unavoidable climate change impacts, and hence a responsibility of a dutiful adaptation planner, but it can also create additional desirable spillover effects for society.

The California Adaptation Planning Guide is described as providing advice for the community, but exactly what 'community' means in the context of this guidance is unclear. While the term community is used consistently throughout the guidance, it appears that the primary audience is those individuals most directly involved in adaptation planning. This is said to include individuals working in local (and in some cases regional) government functions, local non-governmental organizations and professional organizations (CEMA/CNRA 2012a).

The composition of the climate change adaptation team that will lead the preparation of the adaptation plan is defined in terms of considerations of expertise. Local government staff have a prominent place in this team for they are said to hold expert knowledge on, among other things, physical and natural hazards, public utilities, public health, and the emergency services. The adaptation team might also include professional and non-governmental organizations, but their participation is defined in terms of the expertise they hold, as opposed to democratic or other considerations. The guidance thus seeks primarily to conduct the conduct of the expert adaptation team members, who in turn may affect the conduct of the public through the ways of knowing and acting that they promote and the societal expectations contained therein.

Problem framings and appropriate policy responses

Adaptation to climate change is presented as a societal necessity due to the inevitability of change, but adaptation planning does not call into question prevailing political, sociocultural or economic trends. As such it does not necessitate significant behavioral transformations within government nor the public. Politically, adaptation planning is aligned with popular thought on good government. The importance of decentralized government is reaffirmed through arguments that it is local government that is "best positioned to assess and address the implications of climate change at the local level" (CEMA/CNRA 2012a: 4). National and regional government are to be interpreted as too large and distant to comprehend local particularities, such as the situated impacts of climate change. Local self-determination is emphasized through the repeated emphasis placed on the design of the guidance. The guidance is said to "allow flexibility in the commitment of time, money, and scope" (*ibid.*: 8). Local government is encouraged to "use it in a way that best serves their needs" (*ibid.*: 2) and do "as much or little as they desire" (*ibid.*: 8). The mentality of government intervention is then one of implicit support of the rights of self-determination of local government and a criticism of so-called big government.

While the fundamental norms of local self-determination within a federal state are supported, extant governance practices are not operating as efficiently as possible. A criticism of government as too fragmented and lacking co-ordination is invoked in several places in the guidance. This critique is accompanied by proposals for relatively modest governance reforms: for example the pooling of data, and ensuring new initiatives to raise awareness about climate change impacts and adaptation are linked to existing or planned governmental actions (i.e. policy coherence).

A similar logic is applied to the economic and sociocultural implications of adaptation planning. Where climate change impacts put at risk economic interests, the appropriate adaptation strategy is to strengthen what is termed community resilience through economic diversification. An example is provided in the guidance of a community reliant on tourism based around snow sports that identified the need to diversify economic activity due to the assessment of "hazards to the economy" (CEMA/CNRA 2012a: 33). Consideration of the fundamental resilience and appropriateness of economic assumptions underpinning the political economy, which is a core element of some constructions of what it means to be a green state (see the framework in the Chapter 1, this volume), is thus simultaneously omitted and devalued. Continuing economic prosperity can be ensured through foresight.

Special attention needs to be given to communities that are marginalized by virtue of, for example, their race, economic status or linguistic capacities, for such communities should be understood as particularly vulnerable to the impacts of climate change and less resilient. Nevertheless, the exposure of poor and marginalized parts of the population does not lead to proposals for adaptation at any spatial scale that might alter socioeconomic institutions that produce or sustain inequalities. The special needs are to be addressed instead through reformed planning practices, wherein greater consideration is given to their concerns and requirements to participate in policy debates.

In this way adaptation to climate change impacts, which could potentially be interpreted to require constraining or even transforming extant social and economic institutions, is rendered compatible with the dominant rationality of rule in California. While it is stated in the guidance that climate change mitigation and adaption "should be pursued in parallel" (CEMA/CNRA 2012a: 6), at the same time it is reasoned that local climate policies should primarily serve the needs of the community. Arguably, the implication is that adaptation serves more immediate needs than does the mitigation of greenhouse gas emissions. This leads to the ordering of clear policy priorities, as "[f]or each strategy considered to address a climate adaptation need, GHG [greenhouse gas] reduction should be viewed as a desirable co-benefit" (*ibid.*: 7).

The art of adaptation planning

A similarly orthodox position is taken in the guidance on the nature of adaptation planning *vis-à-vis* popular representations of the role of knowledge in society. Adaptation planning is to be understood as an essentially technical and managerial process involving the application of a risk management ethos to systematically address vulnerability within the green state. A procedural heuristic guides adaptation planning. The heuristic comprises two main functions: an analytical vulnerability assessment (drawing on the science of climate change impacts and a risk assessment methodology); and the formulation of an adaptation plan (drawing upon principles of risk management). Successful implementation of an adaptation strategy is similarly dependent upon a systematic and programmatic approach wherein a "responsible or lead department, staff member, or entity should be defined as responsible for implementation, a phased program should be established; a funding source should be identified and obtained; and a monitoring program should be developed" (CEMA/CNRA 2012a: 40).

The vulnerability assessment is based on a stepwise assessment of factors contributing to risk and exposure to risk. The adaptation planner is invited to address the following question in determining vulnerability:

- What climate change effects will a community experience?
- What aspects of a community (people, structures and functions) will be affected?
- How will climate change affect points of sensitivity?
- What is currently being done to address the impacts?
- How likely are the impacts and how quickly will they occur?

(CEMA/CNRA 2012a: ii)

This systematic approach is both universally applicable and should be used irrespective of the context. An example of an assessment of the potential impacts for a municipal marine safety building built on the beach is provided in the guidance to illustrate what such an assessment might look like (see Table 11.2). The building is already exposed to damage during high winter tides. Yet its extreme vulnerability to even a small increase in sea level (that is to say its self-evident vulnerability and unsustainability) does not override the value of systematically plotting and rating impacts and sensitivities.

The vulnerability analysis draws extensively on technical processes of "inventorying and mapping" (CEMA/CNRA 2012b: 30). Despite emphasizing that the gross uncertainty inherent in predictions of climate change impacts makes a quantitative assessment of risks untenable at the local scale, it is nevertheless emphasized that "accurately describing potential impacts" (CEMA/CNRA 2012a: 23) involves expert input from the adaptation planning team. Uncertainty does not render expert knowledge less useful; it should merely be applied in a particular way (i.e. qualitative analysis as opposed to quantitative analysis).

Table 11.2 Extract from a spreadsheet charting potential impacts resulting from sea level rise to a marine safety building

Potential impacts	Sensitivity	Temporal extent	Spatial extent	Rating
Water damage and destruction of marine safety building	Marine safety building	4 years +	One area (marine safety building)	High
Service-level impacts				
Loss of on-site offices; staff less able to respond to public emergencies	Potential impact on any of 2.5 million visitors to the beach	4 years +	Entire beach	High
Loss of on-site supervision and oversight	Potential impact on any of 2.5 million visitors to the beach	4 years +	Entire beach	High
Loss of advanced first aid facilities for the public	Impact on injured citizens	4 years +	One area (marine safety building)	High
Loss of hot showers for hypothermic patients and lifeguards	Impact on public and employees	4 years +	One area (marine safety building)	High
Loss of building providing public walk-in assurance	Impact on public and employees	4 years +	One area (marine safety building)	Medium
Loss of training facilities/ class room for junior lifeguards	Impact on 650 students annually	4 years +	One area (marine safety building)	Medium
Loss of swimmer observation facility	Impact on approximately 30% of beach population	4 years +	One area (marine safety building)	High
Loss of public beach clock visible to 50% of beach	Impact on approximately 30% of beach population	4 years +	50% of beach	Low

Source: CEMA/CNRA (2012a: 25)

Adaptation planning is thus to be understood as being programmable. Plan development and implementation are achieved through the systematic application of a sequence of steps and methods by experts (see Figure 11.1). Values, ethics and forms of knowing other than expert knowledge have limited roles to play in this process. Repeated acknowledgement that in reality the nine steps which the procedural heuristic is said to consist of are "iterative," "ongoing" and "overlap" (CEMA/CNRA 2012a: 14) does not discount or even apparently devalue the notion of programmatic government or the utility of the heuristic. Adaptation planning is then a process of systematic analysis by experts within a risk management framing.

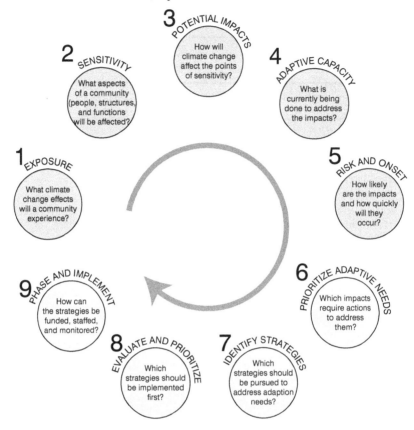

Figure 11.1 The nine steps of climate adaptation strategy development (source: CEMA/ CNRA 2012a: ii)

Within this construction of planning in California, a lack of political support, the availability of funding, or societal recalcitrance are not fundamental barriers to adaptation planning for "[c]ommunities that *understand* these impacts can prepare climate adaptation policies and programs" (CEMA/CNRA 2012a: 15, emphasis added). Rather, the barriers to effective planning are technical: adaptation is problematic because scientific capacity to accurately predict future impacts is limited (*ibid.*: 34).

Knowing the public

Inclusive, deliberative and accountable democratic practices are central axioms in much writing on the green state (e.g. Dryzek 2005; Eckersley 2004; Meadowcroft 2004) and the environmental movement in general. In the Californian guidance, however, the adaptation planning team should view the public's role in adaptation planning as limited. Local communities have an instrumental role to play in adaptation planning, for they are "key for gathering and analyzing local information, developing robust climate adaptation strategies, building political support, and creating a more informed and active community" (CEMA/CNRA 2012a: 9). But the public is typically misguided in its understanding of climate change, for example, viewing it as a "global rather than local" phenomenon (*ibid.*) and having a limited appreciation of how it impacts upon humans. Constraints upon a more active role for citizens and other community groups in climate adaptation is caused essentially by a knowledge deficit in their understanding of scientific matters (cf. Sturgis and Allum 2004). In consequence, public engagement in adaptation planning can be seen within the context of providing an opportunity to educate an essentially uninformed public. Educational activities therefore become a cornerstone of adaptation strategies.

Public engagement and education also provide a mechanism for building social acceptance for a climate change adaptation strategy, which is essential to the efficient implementation of strategies. Strategies that garner limited public support even after education are not to be automatically ruled out, but adaptation planners should emphasize any social benefits above and beyond climate change adaptation in engagements with the public. Furthermore, "[a]n informed and committed community can maintain adaptation actions even with turnover in political leadership" (CEMA/CNRA 2012d: 10).

Discussion

As opposed to some kind of benevolent assistance to befuddled planning practitioners, under a governmentality lens guidance has been interpreted as a purposeful attempt to subjectivize parts of the polity to think and act in particular ways. An account of the rationality adaptation planners are expected to bring to bear on efforts to address climate change impacts has been constructed from the case study guidance documents. This has emphasized, among other things, the centrality of risk assessment and management to planning for adaptation in California, as has been reported for adaptation planning activities elsewhere (Oppermann 2011); the instrumental values attributed to public involvement in policy making; a faith in expertise; a belief in programmatic government; and an implicit conviction that adaptation does not threaten existing values and practices. Particularly significant within the context of the USA, one of the key values concerned flexibility in interpreting the need for strong governmental action in addressing climate adaptation.

The application of governmentality to this particular sphere of climate policy activity in the State of California indicates that its greening is a case of '*plus ça change, plus c'est la même chose*', for these are, broadly speaking, received values in policy making. In this case of climate adaptation guidance, actions are to be implemented by incumbent bureaucratic elites and in accordance with policies in the socioeconomic domain. Arguably, the state-wide approach is to ensure that climate change as the new discursive reality in local governance will not problematize the existing economic ethos. This is an interesting power play in part because adaptation can be considered a potentially destabilizing policy topic, for it is a concept replete with questions concerning social development (O'Brien *et al.* 2007). The Californian case, thus, provides an example of the dynamics through which an emergent and potentially destabilizing policy topic has been recruited to actively reinforce the status quo. Furthermore, the apparent greening of the State of California is to be implemented in a way that appears incompatible with certain core values in many conceptions of the green state, such as those pertaining to public involvement, accountability and transparency.

Within the analysis, we have indicated that maintenance of the *status quo* in the case study applies not only to politics and power relations, but also to economic and social realities that support the extant political system. The guidance examined thus constitutes an attempt to maintain the existing way of life, while accepting the need for climate change policy initiatives. For example, the economic system is to be understood as inherently durable, and governmental norms and practices, if not perfect, are resolvable. A predetermined set of responsibilities and sphere of action at each level of governance (local, regional, national) is maintained as the framework through which the adverse impacts of climate change can be managed. Where change is required in planning practices, it is limited to a broadening of analytical horizons (i.e. to include climate change adaptation) and to adopt a longer-term perspective.

Transformations are not ruled out, but the notion of risk management through preparatory planning foregrounds changes in those specific community variables deemed at risk or vulnerable to impacts, rather than the system itself. The issue of potentially necessary system transformation for good governance of adaptation is circumscribed in setting out a strategy of incremental change. Thus, where economic prosperity is at risk, economic activity is to be diversified; vulnerable land may be relinquished to the sea; the monitoring and management of natural resources is to be reformed to accommodate increased hazard risk; and, the public is to be educated so that they accept the need for change (CEMA/CNRA 2012d). This framing implies the need for adaptation, and the specter of climate change more generally, does not fundamentally endanger California's way of life, for either the privileged or the marginalized.

Reinforcement of the status quo occurs through the naturalization of particular ideas about the world within which government planners exist, including particular representations of the public, and of the responsibilities of planners to the polity and their profession. Naturalization, in turn, is expected to produce certain tendencies in terms of self-regulation or the 'conduct of conduct' within the governmental bureaucracy. These may include, for example, criticizing colleagues who fail to systematically estimate vulnerability or who view the public's role in adaptation planning in any other light than an essentially instrumental one. Furthermore, the focus on adaptation planners' analytical and managerial roles places political questions outside the scope of planning, and perhaps even rational expert thought. That societal inequalities exist is a given; governmental planners are expected to interpret their existence in terms of the implications inequality brings to bear in assessing vulnerability, to actor engagement, and in terms of public education strategies. It is technical expertise within a structured field of practice that is the key to planning, not questions of values or ethics. According to Li (2011), this is a phenomenon that renders politics technical.

The purpose of this analysis is not to suggest that California has failed to embrace some form of green statesmanship, or even that there is something necessarily wrong with the status quo in California. The value of governmentality lies in the opportunity for opening up debate on governmental practices it can provide by analyzing how government is to be achieved at the micro level. Relating our observations back to the questions about the green state posed in the introductory chapter, we may then ask are these institutions and governance practices appropriate for societal goals of low-carbon and sustainability transitions? And how do they fit with different conceptualizations of the green state?

Conclusions

In California, we have elucidated a power play in an emergent policy field (climate change adaptation) intended to reinforce extant political and cultural norms. It is a power play, we suggest, that subverts and subsumes what could potentially constitute a transformative agenda in support of a barely modified version of the status quo. The rationality embedded in the Californian climate adaptation guidance indicates that greening of the state is understood in terms of dominant Western political ideology and the technical, economic and social practices that this tends to encompass. In terms of its policy implementation record, California appears to be something of a frontrunner in climate change policy, particularly so in the context of the federal nation state of which it is part (see Chapter 7, this volume). Yet in the miniature of this particular climate policy initiative, California appears quite far removed from Eckersley (2004) and other scholars' normative vision of the green state.

A particular analytical perspective on power, popularly called governmentality, has been used in this chapter to shed light on the power dimensions of the greening of California. Our ambition has been to open up new research questions, and perhaps even new research directions, for green state scholarship around the analytical and normative dimension of political power. A key value of the governmentality perspective, which differentiates it from an approach producing merely thick description, is in clarifying the conditions under which society, or particular components therein, think and act (Dean 2010). This is typically where a governmentality analysis stops. It is a critical perspective in the sense of surfacing the microphysics of power, rather than involving a critique of the rights and wrongs of situated power dynamics. In contrast, green state scholarship has tended to be strongly normative, but partial in its understandings of, and engagement with, power analytics. An important direction for future development should be the marrying of analytical perspectives on power with approaches for assessing the normativity of situated power dynamics in theorizing and studying the green state.

References

Alexander, R.J., 2009 *Framing Discourse on the Environment: A Critical Discourse Approach.* Routledge, Abingdon.

Bedsworth, L.W., and Hanak, E., 2013 Climate policy at the local level: insights from California. *Global Environmental Change* 23: 664–77.

Bulkeley, H., and Stripple, J., 2014 Conclusions: towards a critical social science of climate change? In Stripple, J., and Bulkeley, H., (eds) *Governing the Climate: New Approaches to Rationality, Power and Politics* 243–59. Cambridge University Press, Cambridge.

Cashmore, M., Richardson, T., and Axelsson, A., 2014 Seeing power in international development co-operation: environmental policy integration and the World Bank. *Transactions of the British Institute of Geographers* 39: 155–68.

CEMA/CNRA 2012a *California Adaptation Planning Guide: Planning for Adaptive Communities.* California Emergency Management Agency, Mather, CA/California Natural Resources Agency, Sacramento, CA.

CEMA/CNRA 2012b *California Adaptation Planning Guide: Defining Local and Regional Impacts.* California Emergency Management Agency, Mather, CA/California Natural Resources Agency, Sacramento, CA.

CEMA/CNRA 2012c *California Adaptation Planning Guide: Understanding Regional Characteristics.* California Emergency Management Agency, Mather, CA/California Natural Resources Agency, Sacramento, CA.

CEMA/CNRA 2012d *California Adaptation Planning Guide: Identifying Adaptation Strategies.* California Emergency Management Agency, Mather, CA/California Natural Resources Agency, Sacramento, CA.

Dean, M., 2010 *Governmentality: Power and Rule in Modern Society.* Sage, London.

Death, C., 2014 Can we save the planet? In Edkins, J., and Zehfuss, M., (eds) *Global Politics: A New Introduction.* Routledge, London.

Dryzek, J.S., 2005 *The Politics of the Earth.* Oxford University Press, Oxford.

Eckersley, R., 2004 *The Green State: Rethinking Democracy and Sovereignty.* MIT Press, Cambridge, MA.

Elden, S., 2007 Rethinking governmentality. *Political Geography* 26: 29–33.

Foucault, M., 1995 *Discipline and Punish: The Birth of the Prison.* Vintage, New York.

Foucault, M., 2002 The subject and power: why study power? The question of the subject. In Faubion, J.D., (ed) *Michel Foucault Power: Essential Works of Foucault 1954–1984,* vol. 3, 326–48. Penguin Books, London.

Goldman, M., 2004 Imperial science, imperial nature: environmental knowledge for the World (Bank). In Jasanoff, S., and Martello, M.L., (eds) *Earthly Politics: Local and Global in Environmental Governance* 55–80. MIT Press, Cambridge, MA.

Hacking, I., 1986 Making up people. In Heller, T.C., Sosna, M., and Wellbery, D.E., (eds) *Reconstructing Individualism: Autonomy, Individuality, and the Self in Western Thought* 222–36. Stanford University Press, Stanford, CA.

Kahn, A., 2014 The surprising way Obama is trying to tackle climate change. *PBS Frontline* February 27. Retrieved March 28, 2014 from www.pbs.org/wgbh/pages/frontline/environment/climate-of-doubt/the-surprising-way-obama-is-trying-to-tackle-climate-change.

Keskitalo, E.C.H., Juhola, S., and Westerhoff, L., 2012 Climate change as governmentality: technologies of government for adaptation in three European countries. *Journal of Environmental Planning and Management* 55: 435–52.

Kevin, G., 2009 Rethinking the nature of urban environmental politics: security, subjectivity, and the non-human. *Geoforum* 40: 207–16.

Landy, M., 2010 Adapting to climate change: problems and prospects. In Rabe, B., (ed) *Greenhouse Governance: Addressing Climate Change in America* 204–26. Brookings Institution Press, Washington, DC.

Li, T.M., 2007 *The Will to Improve: Governmentality, Development, and the Practice of Politics.* Duke University Press, Durham, NC.

Li, T.M., 2011 Rendering society technical: government through community and the ethnographic turn at the World Bank in Indonesia. In Mosse, D., (ed) *Adventures in Aidland: The Anthropology of Professionals in International Development* 57–80. Berghahn Books, Oxford.

London, J., Karner, A., Sze, J., Rowan, D., Gambirazzio, G., and Niemeier, D., 2013 Racing climate change: collaboration and conflict in California's global climate change policy arena. *Global Environmental Change* 23: 791–9.

Lövbrand, E., Stripple, J., and Wiman, B., 2009 Earth system governmentality: reflections on science in the Anthropocene. *Global Environmental Change* 19: 7–13.

Luke, T.W., 1999 Environmentality as green governmentality. In Darier, E., (ed) *Discourses of the Environment* 121–51. Blackwell, Oxford.

McKee, K., 2009 Post-Foucauldian governmentality: what does it offer critical social policy analysis? *Critical Social Policy* 29: 465–86.

Meadowcroft, J., 2004 Participation and sustainable development: modes of citizen, community and organisational involvement. In Lafferty, W., (ed) *Governance for Sustainable Development: The Challenge of Adapting Form to Function* 162–90. Edward Elgar, Cheltenham.

Miller, P., and Rose, N., 2008 *Governing the Present: Administering Economic, Social and Personal Life.* Polity Press, Cambridge.

O'Brien, K., Eriksen, S., Nygaard, L., and Schjolden, A., 2007 Why different interpretations of vulnerability matter in climate change discourses. *Climate Policy* 7: 73–88.

Oels, A., 2013 Rendering climate change governable by risk: from probability to contingency. *Geoforum* 45: 17–29.

Oppermann, E., 2011 The discourse of adaptation to climate change and the UK Climate Impacts Programme: de-scribing the problematization of adaptation. *Climate and Development* 3: 71–85.

Paehlke, R., 2005 Democracy and environmentalism: opening a door to the administrative state. In Paehlke, R., and Torgerson, D., (eds) *Managing Leviathan: Environmental Politics and the Administrative State* 25–46. Broadview Press, Plymouth.

Paterson, M., and Stripple, J., 2010 My space: governing individuals' carbon emissions. *Environment and Planning D: Society and Space* 28: 341–62.

Rose, N., and Miller, P., 2010 Political power beyond the state: problematics of government. *The British Journal of Sociology* 61: 271–303.

Rutherford, S., 2007 Green governmentality: insights and opportunities in the study of nature's rule. *Progress in Human Geography* 31: 291–307.

Scott, D., 2005 Colonial governmentality. In Inda, J.X. (ed) *Anthropologies of Modernity: Foucault, Governmentality, and Life Politics* 23–49. Blackwell Publishing, Oxford.

Senellart, M., 2009 Course context. In Senellart, M., (ed) *Michel Foucault Security, Territory, Population: Lectures at the College de France 1977–1978* 369–401. Palgrave Macmillan, Basingstoke.

Stripple, J., and Bulkeley, H., 2014 Introduction: on governmentality and climate change. In Stripple, J., and Bulkeley, H., (eds) *Governing the Climate: New Approaches to Rationality, Power and Politics* 1–23. Cambridge University Press, Cambridge.

Sturgis, P., and Allum, N., 2004 Science in society: re-evaluating the deficit model of public attitudes. *Public Understanding of Science* 13: 55–74.

Urpelainen, J., 2009 Explaining the Schwarzenegger phenomenon: local frontrunners in climate policy. *Global Environmental Politics* 9: 82–105.

Waage, E.R.H., and Benediktsson, K., 2010 Performing expertise: landscape, governmentality and conservation planning in Iceland. *Journal of Environmental Policy and Planning* 12: 1–22.

12 The green state and the design of self-binding

Lessons from monetary policy

Åsa Knaggård and Håkan Pihl

Introduction

The green state debate (e.g. Eckersley 2004; Barry 2008; Dryzek *et al.* 2003) emphasizes the continued importance and power of the state to reach a sustainable future. Eckersley (2004: 80), in her book *The Green State*, discusses needed changes at four different levels – changes in (1) policy instruments, (2) policy goals, (3) the hierarchy of policy goals, and (4) the role of the state. She argues that in order to reach a green state, reflexivity and change are required at all levels. Further, the state is unable to manage this on its own but needs to be both pushed and bound to achieve necessary changes. Eckersley, therefore, focuses on a green public sphere coupled with a green constitutional design. Others, like Torgerson (1999: 20), emphasize the importance of a green public sphere, which he defines as an open space for meaningful disagreement, necessary for creating the reflexivity needed in order to enable change at deeper levels. Dryzek *et al.* (2003: 169) argue that without a green public sphere there could only be a light greening of the state; hence, both are needed to push and bind the green state.

In the green state debate, deliberation is seen as crucial for a public green sphere. Some see deliberation as connected with the green state at a principle level – deliberation fosters reflexivity and through that an appreciation of the needs of others, even that of non-human species and future generations (e.g. Dryzek 2000: 141–8). Others are more skeptical about the ability of deliberative processes to reach green ends (e.g. Goodin 1992; Smith 2003). They argue that we have to separate the discussion on means (type of system) and ends (green or other outcomes). Thus, there is no agreement on whether deliberation is sufficient for the development of the green state; the optimists' claims are so far unproven (Lövbrand and Khan 2010).

Eckersley (2004) is more optimistic about the potential of deliberation. However, she argues that a green public sphere needs to be supported by some form of green constitutional design, or green constitutionalism (cf. Barry 2008). The purpose of the constitutional design is "to provide a structure that enables, and where necessary enforces, ecological responsibility on behalf of the broader community at risk" (Eckersley 2004: 245). Green constitutionalism builds upon the idea of constitutional democracy, which in essence is about creating safe-guarding mechanisms that constrain the behavior of those in power – in other words, how "the nation can bind 'itself'" (Elster 1979: 93). Eckersley (2004: 243) presents "a broad sketch of what might be included in a green constitution." It could incorporate some form of substantial claims on the state, for example responsibilities to protect biodiversity, life-support systems and ecosystems. It could incorporate procedural claims, including rights to environmental information and information about risk-generating proposals; rights to participate in decision-making processes on impact assessments and environmental standards; responsibilities to use the precautionary and 'polluter pays' principles; and the responsibility of an independent public authority to represent public environmental interests in political and legal processes (*ibid.*: 243–4). Eckersley points out that these are merely examples.

Eckersley opens up for a discussion of how a green constitution could be designed to bind the polity in a certain direction. In this chapter, we will contribute to this discussion by comparing the climate and the monetary policy areas, using the example of Sweden. We argue that the self-binding design of monetary policy can provide important lessons for the green state in terms of constitutional design. In Sweden, the monetary policy is based on a constitutional delegation of power from parliament to the independent Central Bank. The bank is responsible for price stability, expressed as an inflation target, and controls the major policy instrument in the form of the interest rate. The monetary policy focuses predominantly on the effectiveness in reaching price stability, at the cost of democratic influence. A rationale for this is to reduce the influence of short-term vested interests. Thereby, the delegation of power from the parliament to an expert body is seen as justified. In the climate policy area this justification can be more difficult to accept (cf. Dryzek 2000; Eckersley 2004; Torgerson 1999). However, even though constitutional support to a green public sphere might in the longer term be the most effective strategy for reaching deep changes to the state, it is a less certain short-term strategy. The need for prompt action on many environmental problems, including climate change, implies that we need to consider alternatives. Some states have decided on climate laws, including the UK, Denmark, Finland, and Ireland, to make their climate policy more effective in reaching certain ends. So far, no states have incorporated ideas from this legislation into their constitutions. We propose how this could be done through a constitutional change that establishes an independent expert authority with a mandate to make decisions on climate policy.

In this chapter we will discuss similarities and differences between the climate and monetary policy areas. We will pay particular attention to the design features of the two policies and the self-binding potential within them. The chapter is a thought experiment to investigate what it would mean to design climate policy according to monetary policy. It is not the feasibility of the suggestion which is our priority, but rather to discuss if such a design could be seen as a first step towards a green state. The last part of the chapter will scrutinize this issue. Before introducing the two policy areas, we will present the idea of self-binding in more detail.

Self-binding

From the perspective of new institutional economics (see North 1990; Williamson 2000), a constitution provides society with fundamental rules of the game that constrain behavior and determine incentives. The state is seen as a coercive force with the potential to serve the public interest. The power of the state, however, needs to be constrained to prevent the risk for mismanagement. The constitution can be regarded as a safe-guarding mechanism, an institution created at a specific point in history to constrain the behavior of those in power.

As was early observed by Elster (1979), people – and politicians – can behave irrationally due to inconsistent time preferences and endogenous changes of preferences. In his book *Ulysses and the Sirens*, Elster discusses solutions to such problems and identifies binding oneself, as Ulysses did, as a solution to the problem. Self-binding, or the 'Ulysses strategy', is a credible pre-commitment to a future behavior. It consists of structural constraints to guard against future deviations from an intended direction. Thus, it is a decision to constrain oneself that is difficult to alter even if one should want to at a later stage. Constitutionalism can be understood as such a self-binding that makes commitments credible and resistant to future undesirable or unintended behaviors.

Elster discusses different possibilities for the constitutional democracy to bind itself politically, including the removal of responsibility for achieving political decisions from the polity, which can be codified in the constitution or not. A constitutional change is a rigid form of self-binding, whereas changes made through law or administrative regulation are more flexible (Buchstein 2013: 66–7). In modern democracies several institutions can be interpreted as such devices for pre-commitment. One example is the organization of monetary policy in many western states, with a free-standing Central Bank.

Self-binding for the green state

One of the difficult aspects for the green state, and a reason for self-binding, are the time horizons involved in climate policy. Short-term costs for reducing emissions stand against long-term gains and there are several reasons why the short-term might be valued over the long-term. One such problem is reflected in the use of discount rates, which is discussed in environmental economics (see e.g. Nordhaus 2007). Another problem is time inconsistencies in political decision-making over election periods, and a tendency of voters to evaluate politicians on a short-term basis. An associated problem is a tendency among politicians to be influenced by small and well-organized interest groups, at the expense of decisions to protect broader general interests. These problems have been discussed by the public-choice school of economics (for an overview, see Buchanan 2003). A related problem is that the interests of non-human species and future generations, which stand for long-term interests, are not organized and lack voice (e.g. Eckersley 2004; Dryzek 2000).

Swedish monetary policy: self-binding through delegation

In monetary policy, self-binding means that decision-making power has been delegated to an independent expert body, equipped with political instruments for reaching long-term objectives. To understand the mechanisms of self-binding we turn to the example of Swedish monetary policy.

The economic crisis in the beginning of the 1990s became a turning-point for Swedish monetary policy (Heikensten 1999). The Swedish economy had severe structural problems with persistent high inflation. To lower the inflation to a level that was aligned with the surrounding world had been a political priority for decades, but the political system had shown itself unable to deliver such an outcome. The crisis in 1992 led to a political awareness of the need for structural reforms. An assigned commission suggested, among several things, that the Central Bank should be given an independent standing and that monetary policy should focus on price stability (SOU 1993). The Central Bank, as the independent expert body, was granted the prerogative to use the interest rate as an instrument to reach price stability (Heikensten and Vredin 1998).

This new monetary policy was inspired by similar changes in other countries. In 1993, the Parliament decided that the long-term objective of the Central Bank should be to maintain price stability. The Central Bank then set the fixed short-term target to stabilize yearly inflation to 2 percent with a tolerance of ±1 percentage point. The inflation target was based on the consumer price index corresponding to a level that also other countries had chosen (Bernanke *et al.* 1999; Berg 2005). The law stated that the Central Bank should be governed by an 11 member General Council from the Parliament that would appoint an Executive board of six members including the chairman and governor of the Central Bank. The Executive Board should not be politically appointed but selected on merits of expertise. The independence of the Central Bank was strengthened through amendments to the Riksbank Act in 1999 (SFS 1998:185) and was later insribed in the Instrument of Government (2011:109, chapter 9, article 13). Hence, the political system constrained itself and delegated responsibility to experts, to be immune to influence by public authorities or politicians (Heikensten 1999). The policy successfully curbed inflation. After earlier periods with high inflation, from the mid-1990s Sweden experienced stable prices. However, after the financial crisis in 2008 monetary policy, foremost in the USA, the Central Bank was criticized for contributing to the crisis. It was argued that low interest rates had inflated asset prices and encouraged excess lending, and critics argued that not only price stability but unemployment and resource use should be considered (Reichlin and Baldwin 2013). As a response, the Swedish Central Bank has increasingly come to emphasize its role in contributing to growth and employment, still with the inflation target as the overarching objective (Swedish Central Bank 2013). Another criticism against the Swedish Central Bank is that the yearly target should be decided politically and not by experts in an executive board (Calmfors 2013).

Climate change policy: no constitutional self-binding

Swedish climate policy is not based on self-binding but on objectives. The overarching objective, decided in 1998, is formulated as 'a reduced climate impact' (Government Bill 1997/98) specified as a global warming of two degrees over pre-industrial levels (Government Bill 2008/09). The objective also includes a concentration target of 400 ppm greenhouse gases in the atmosphere. A problem with these objectives is that they are concerned with global warming and the global level of concentrations. As decreases in Swedish emissions only have a very marginal effect on global levels, the climate objectives are of little guidance to what targets and policy instruments should be put in place. To do so, specific objectives for Sweden have been formulated. One objective is to decrease Swedish emissions by 40 percent by 2020 compared to the levels in 1990 (Government Bill 2009/10).[1] Further objectives are: a larger share of renewables in the energy mix (50% by 2020), more renewables in the transport sector (20% by 2020), a fossil-free transport sector (by 2030) and increased energy efficiency (20% by 2020). The Government has also formulated an objective for 2050 of no net emissions of greenhouse gases to the atmosphere (Government Bill 2008/09).[2] The Swedish climate policy is thus formulated in terms of a set of long-term objectives. These objectives are not coupled to any structural constraints but are, over the years, open to political renegotiation. There is thus no constitutional self-binding in Swedish climate policy.

In order to reach the formulated objectives a variety of policy instruments are used. Two important instruments are the carbon tax and the EU Emission Trading System (EU ETS). The carbon tax was introduced in 1991 (SFS 1990:582). The full tax is paid in areas such as transport and heating, whereas industries in international competition have a reduced tax, and some are exempted. The most energy-intensive part of the industry is covered by EU ETS and is not included in the tax scheme. Further taxes are an energy tax, a tax on the consumption of electricity, and a vehicle tax calculated on emissions of carbon dioxides. Other policy instruments include electricity certificates to increase the amount of renewable energy in the production of electricity, and different subsidies. Beside these market-based instruments there are demands in the Environmental Code (SFS 1998:808) and the Planning and Building Act (SFS 2010:900) to take climate change into account.[3] Hence, a broad set of policy instruments are used in climate policy.

The responsibility for reaching the climate objectives and targets is dispersed on a number of actors (Government Bill 2009/10), such as public authorities on national level (foremost the Swedish Environmental Protection Agency) and regional level (County Administrative Boards). In 2010 a new public commission – the Environmental Quality Objectives Commission – was given the responsibility for suggesting new targets and policy instruments for climate and other environmental issues. This commission was set up by the Government with representatives from the Parliament, ministries, regional and local political levels, as well as interest organizations. Also municipalities are emphasized as highly important for the obtainment of environmental objectives, including climate (Government Bill 2009/10). The municipalities are responsible for planning land and water use, which is crucial both for climate mitigation and adaptation. Municipalities do not have any formal responsibility to work towards the climate objectives, and the minimum demands set up by the Environmental Code and the Planning and Building Act are insufficient. National public authorities and the County Administrative Boards lack efficient policy instruments to influence the behavior of municipalities, business and individuals. This leads to a fundamental problem regarding who takes responsibility and who can be held accountable for the climate objectives (cf. Swedish National Audit Office 2013).

Comparison between climate and monetary policy

There are many weaknesses with the climate policy and as a remedy there have been suggestions for more self-binding policies, based on lessons that can be drawn from monetary policy (Pihl 1997; Helm *et al.* 2003; Nilsson and Kahn 2010). Climate acts adopted in some states can also be understood in this light. Even if they do not constitute constitutional changes, they still bind the state to a certain policy direction, although in a flexible manner. In the case of the UK Climate Change Act of 2008, the long-term objective is connected to binding five-year carbon budgets. These targets are suggested by an independent expert authority, but decided by the Parliament, and are chosen so that the long-term objective can be reached.

Self-binding institutions, such as in monetary policy, can increase credibility and reduce uncertainty. However, climate policy also needs to maintain democratic legitimacy and flexibility to adapt to changing conditions. Brunner *et al.* (2011) discuss how this trade-off in climate policy can be handled. They identify legalization, delegation and securitization as underlying rationales for instruments that increase the credibility of commitment. Again, monetary policy is used as an illustration of such arrangements, by the separation of politics and administration, and by the legal constraints that insulate agents from political pressure. However, the authors do not further develop how climate policy could be designed based on lessons from monetary policy. To study this, similarities and differences between climate and monetary policy have to be analyzed in greater detail.

Similarities between the climate and monetary policy areas

The monetary policy area shares a number of traits with the climate policy area and they are outlined in the following discussion. Both policy areas are characterized by a situation where short-term and special interests can push more long-term general interests aside. Avoiding climate change can compete with more short-term interests such as low unemployment and growth. Vested interests that may support a short-term orientation can be illustrated by energy-intensive industries that see their competitive advantages threatened. The long-term public interest of price-stability is also challenged by more short-term interests. Long-term price stability can conflict with short-term goals of low unemployment and high growth. Various vested interests may support short-termism, with the examples of labor organizations that want higher wages, or owners of real-estate that want lower interest rates.

Another similarity between the two areas is that they are both related to widespread activities throughout the economy. Decisions made by myriads of people in their capacity as households, consumers and producers, employees and employers, result in emissions of greenhouse gases and affect prices. In both cases, there are some actors that are more central than others. In the case of climate change, large energy producers and energy intensive industries are crucial.[4] For price stability, the organizations in the labor market are central. The employer organizations' interest in a low increase in wages coincides with the long-term public interest of low inflation. In the case of climate change, there are few special interests that coincide with the long-term interest since alternative energy producers and industries are not yet established, and there is no constitutional guarantee that the interests of non-human species and future generations are considered.

There are also similarities regarding the formulation of objectives. Both in the climate and monetary policy areas, objectives are formulated based on what is considered politically and economically feasible, rather than what is optimal. A problem in both policy areas is that the optimal level is not known.[5] The implication is that objectives are formulated as 'good round numbers' that are easy to remember and communicate.

A final similarity is that the objectives have been decided without a clarification of what price society is willing to pay in order to attain them. In order to reach a certain level of inflation or minimize climate impact, costs are incurred that may vary and can be difficult to accept. This is not considered in the objectives; their formulation indicates that they should be reached at any cost. However, in both areas the cost of the policy is discussed. In the monetary policy area the focus on low inflation has been questioned. In the climate policy area cost efficiency has been an issue in the debate about the flexible mechanisms and about environmental objectives (see Government Bill 2009/10; see also Swedish National Audit Office 2013).

Differences between the climate and policy areas

We have shown that there are similarities between the climate and monetary policy areas. There are also some differences. One difference is that Swedish climate policy has only limited influence on the ultimate goal of mitigating climate change. Swedish reductions have a marginal effect on global levels, and the future climate change affecting Sweden depends on what other countries do, although as a part of the EU the influence is larger. Swedish monetary policy, on the other hand, has a large influence on the ultimate goal of long-term price stability in Sweden, even if part of the inflation is imported and the international business cycle also has an impact.

Another difference is that climate policy aims at transforming a system towards a low-carbon path, whereas monetary policy strives to stabilize an existing system. In transforming a system, climate policy has to overcome path dependencies and historical lock-ins in different parts of the economy and in the public administration. There is no consensus on what such transformation actually would imply (see e.g. Clapp and Dauvergne 2005). The green state literature is however clear – a transformation of not only policy instruments and objectives but also of the role of the state is necessary (e.g. Dryzek 2000; Eckersley 2004). Monetary policy does not aim at transforming the financial system, but to stabilize the overall level of on-going price changes.

It is apparent from the above discussion that there are fundamental similarities between the two policy areas. These similarities suggest similar principles of policy design. However, when it comes to how the political system actually has dealt with these policy areas, the differences are striking as is evident in the following.

Differences in design of climate and monetary policy

As part of our effort to evaluate the potential of self-binding for climate policy in the green state, we discuss differences between the design of the climate and monetary policies in different dimensions.

First, there is a difference regarding the time horizon. The climate objectives are formulated as long-term objectives with years such as 2020, 2030 and 2050 as end points. It is not specified when, during the time interval, emission reductions need to be made; the emissions are allowed to vary over time. The monetary objective is connected to short-term targets, limiting the inflation to 2 percent every year. An advantage with the short-term target is that control becomes more rigorous. Short-term deviation calls for immediate action. The long-term climate objectives allow short-term variations; costly measures can be postponed which decreases the possibility of reaching the objectives. In monetary policy, the long-term outcome is not in focus – if short-term is under control the long-term outcome will follow. The target is inflexible and does not allow for adjustments to changing economic conditions.

Second, which actor has the responsibility for deciding on objectives and the autonomy of these actors differ between the two areas. The inflation target is decided by the Central Bank, whereas climate objectives are decided by the Parliament. The Central Bank is an authority under the Parliament with a unique, independent position protected by the constitution (SFS 2011:109). Therefore, there is no direct democratic influence over the monetary policy. Climate policy is under parliamentary control and is also under more influence from lobbyist and interest organizations than is the case for monetary policy.

Third, the allocation of responsibility differs between the two areas. Responsibility for attaining the climate objective is shared. A number of actors are expected to take on responsibility for the implementation of the climate objective, such as the Ministry of the Environment, the Environmental Protection Agency, the parliamentary commission, County Administrative Boards, municipalities, and the EU. In monetary policy, the Central Bank is the only actor given responsibility over the inflation objective. There are no veto points for the parliament, the government, or actors that are affected by its decisions on how the overall objective should be reached.

Fourth, there are differences concerning the choice of policy instruments. The Central Bank controls the interest rate, which is one of the strongest political instruments for controlling the economy. In climate policy a mix of different policy instruments are used, including taxes, subsidies, legislation, and information. The EU emissions trading system and a post-Kyoto agreement are also regarded to be crucial instruments for success.

Fifth, there is a difference in how general the policy instruments are. The level of the key interest rate is the same for everyone, without consideration of the particular situations of different actors.[6] In climate policy the situation is much different. Due to the number of policy instruments used, different actors are subject to different conditions. One of the negative consequences of using different instruments selectively is that the costs for reducing emissions vary among sectors and actors (cf. Swedish National Audit Office 2012). The total reduction is thus not cost-efficient. Furthermore, in a recent assessment of the Swedish environmental policy, a conclusion is that there is a lack of coherence and clarity in the way the environment is managed at different levels of government (OECD 2014).

Sixth, the predictability of the development within each policy area differs. The Central Bank works to create a high level of predictability in the economic sector and announces its predictions and assessment of how the key interest rate will evolve. This has an effect on expectations. If policies are believed to be generally applicable, far-reaching and stable, they are more likely to influence behavior. Within the climate policy area the predictability is lower. Changes in taxes, subsidies and regulations are continuously made. If market actors have doubts and think that political shifts in priorities will be made, from low employment to price stability or from sustainable to unsustainable growth, it will negatively affect their willingness to change behavior, and make new investments less likely.

Seventh, the possibility to evaluate the effectiveness of policy instruments and to hold authorities accountable varies between policy areas. It is easier, as within the monetary policy area, to evaluate the effect if a single policy instrument is used. When multiple policy instruments are used, as within the climate policy area, it is complicated to assess the impact of single instruments making it difficult to adjust the system. Further, it is easier to hold someone accountable if the distribution of responsibility is clear, than if it is vague and distributed on a large number of actors. Therefore, it is easier both to evaluate the effect of policy instruments, and to pinpoint accountability, in monetary policy. However, in elections citizens have a possibility to hold governments accountable for the climate policy, even though elections are fairly blunt tools as it is the entire political program of the government that is assessed.

Finally, decisions on and implementation of climate objectives and policy instruments involve a large number of actors at multiple levels of which many are politically appointed. Within monetary policy it is experts that make decisions and they are by the constitution forbidden to seek advice or acceptance.

A thought experiment: climate policy as monetary policy

As we have demonstrated, there are similar conditions for climate and monetary policy, but there are large differences in the design of policies. In sum, climate policy has, compared to monetary policy, a high level of democratization and flexibility but a low level of credibility and regulatory predictability (cf. Brunner *et al.* 2011). We now turn to how climate policy could be designed if it was organized according to the principles of monetary policy. We then elaborate on how this corresponds to the idea of the green state.

If climate policy was designed as monetary policy, an autonomous expert authority would be created and inscribed in the constitution. It would be given the full authority to decide on targets and policy instruments. A board of experts would take decisions both on objectives and policy instruments. This would decrease the veto points for interest groups and policy-makers. A viable solution would be to follow the UK example with experts in the field of climate change, science, and economics included in the expert committee (see Committee on Climate Change 2014). However, even if the board would be chosen on the basis of expertise and integrity, their advice and decisions could always be questioned. We note that in the Central Bank there are often different opinions on the correct level of the key interest rate. In the climate policy area there is currently no real consensus on emission and target levels.

If modeled on monetary policy, climate policy would have a short-term fixed target, which would be set to correspond with long-term objectives. Power over the target would be delegated to an autonomous climate authority led by experts and safe from direct political influence. The climate authority would be in charge of a policy instrument with enough potency for reaching the target. It would be used without selectivity or exceptions. The use of the instrument should be predictable and the effect would be evaluated on a short-term basis. Sectors or special interests influenced by climate policy would not be invited to participate in the decision-making process.

Instead of formulating long-term objectives such as 40 percent reductions by 2020 or no net emissions by 2050, yearly targets of emission reductions or, perhaps better, yearly targets for the price of emissions could be set. An advantage with short-term targets is that evaluations are easier and more conclusive. An argument against such targets is that in the climate policy area it is less crucial to keep a continuous stability in the pace of quantitative reductions. Here, long-term reduction is what matters, whereas in the monetary policy area a continuing stable price level is important. Another argument is that yearly emissions vary with business cycles, cold winters and so on, which motivates acceptance for variations in yearly reductions. Against these arguments stands the fact that long-term objectives are more difficult to evaluate than short-term ones. Long-term objectives provide more uncertainty; will the goals really be reached; when are the changes going to be implemented: are politicians going to change the policy? Long-term objectives, thus, provide weaker incentives for change.

The policy instrument used could be a tax on greenhouse gases, which would control the price on emissions in a similar way as the interest rate controls the price of money. Alternatively, a cap and trade scheme could be introduced, or a hybrid between the two (cf. Whitesell 2011). An instrument that provides a price on all emissions could replace the wide variety of climate policy instruments used today. It could enhance the possibility to actually reach the objective, as the climate authority would have full control over the instrument. If the target is a quantitative yearly reduction, a climate tax could be continuously adjusted to reach the target.

A general price on emissions would lead to more cost-effective reductions, the profitability of new green innovations would be less uncertain, and the relative advantages of alternatives would increase. The tax on greenhouse gases should be general, a price for emissions equal for everyone without differentiations or exceptions. The higher predictability would create more credibility for the climate policy and, through that, stronger incentives for actors in the private sector to reduce emissions. Further, the possibility to evaluate the effect of policy instruments would increase. However, a general price on emissions would affect some sectors more than others. For example, if Sweden introduces a tax on greenhouse gases without other countries taking similar actions, the Swedish energy-intensive industry lose competitive advantages. On the other hand, tax revenues from greenhouse gas emissions can replace revenue from other distorting taxes and Sweden could set an example that would persuade other countries to move in the same direction.

Discussion

The comparison and the thought experiment has showed that there are some important benefits with the self-binding practiced in monetary policy that can serve as lessons for how to conduct climate policy. The inscription of an independent climate authority in the constitution and the emphasis placed on price stability can contribute to a change at Eckersley's third level – in the policy hierarchy. The success of this policy does not rely only on the independent status of a Central Bank-like institution, but the close coupling of ends and means is another crucial factor in its success. The fact that the Central Bank controls both targets and policy instruments is what really demonstrates the potential of self-binding and shows that politicians are willing to commit themselves. In turn, this creates credibility and reduces uncertainties among market actors.

However, the major disadvantage with this form of self-binding is that it decreases democratic influence and control, and limits flexibility to deal with new circumstances. In a democracy it is questionable if large parts of policy-making should be in the hands of experts rather than elected politicians, as emphasized in the green state literature. The main argument is that without reflexive decision-making processes a green state cannot be developed. These scholars argue that reflexivity and concern about non-human species and future generations, which are crucial for deeper level changes, become possible only through deliberative processes. Does this imply that the type of self-binding that has been discussed could never become a tool for increasing reflexivity? Its mission is to steer the development towards certain ends without questioning or initiating debate. It is likely to lead to deeper changes than we have witnessed so far, but it is unlikely that it will generate changes at Eckersley's fourth level – the role of the state.

The conflict highlighted here is that between efficient policy-making and democracy. It goes to the heart of the debate on climate change and sustainable development (cf. Brunner *et al.* 2011; Lövbrand and Khan 2010). We need to achieve major emission reductions in the near future (see e.g. New Climate Economy 2014). At the same time, we need to make a deeper transformation of society, which is dependent on democratic (and deliberative) processes and therefore slow in progress. If speed and efficiency is important, there is a case for self-binding and an independent expert authority. The question remains whether such a design could promote democratic and deliberative processes.

A solution to this problem is to keep objectives as well as short-term targets within democratic control, and limit the power of the expert authority to the operation of a pre-defined policy instrument. This more limited delegation of power would still increase efficiency, but the decision on the short- and long-term direction would remain democratic. This would strengthen the possibility for a green public sphere to critically debate the role of the state. However, having the democratic system deciding on short-term targets could bring back problems of time inconsistences, changing preferences and increasing uncertainties. A way to mitigate this problem is to make experts responsible for giving advice on targets so that they are aligned with the long-term objective, as in the UK. If limited to more narrow issues an expert authority would not have any major negative impacts on the space for a green public sphere and the possibility to increase reflexivity in political decision-making. One could even argue that the change could enable the growth of a strong green public sphere, at least in the Swedish context. The model practiced today by the Swedish polity, to incorporate interest organizations in a consensus-building process in commissions, could be seen as impairing a green public sphere. Dryzek *et al.* (2003) have shown that this kind of system runs the risk of coopting green social movements and thereby of delimiting the possibilities for a public sphere to grow strong.

Conclusion

The creation of a green state includes changes at several levels. We argue that more self-binding designs are needed to mitigate problems of political time-inconsistences and changing preferences. This would enable changes on deeper levels than we have witnessed so far, but would not be sufficient for reaching a green state.

The decision in Sweden in the early 1990s to redefine the role of the Central Bank illustrates how self-binding can be designed, and shows that self-binding is possible. This chapter compares monetary policy with climate policy and concludes the following possible lessons:

- Rather than having a climate policy with only long-term objectives, a climate policy could also have short-term, stable and measurable targets.
- Rather than involving many authorities at various levels with shared responsibilities for the result, the responsibility for climate policy could be concentrated to one authority held responsible for the outcome.
- Rather than having political control over the authority, it could be led by experts outside direct political control.
- Rather than using a variety of different instruments, more or less effective, the authority could possess one effective instrument (i.e. a greenhouse gas tax).
- Rather than using instruments selectively, treating different sectors in different ways, the instrument could be used similar to all and without exceptions.
- The long-term objective and independence of the authority could be written into the constitution.

Such changes to climate policy would increase credibility, predictability and efficiency – it would create a stronger self-binding.

We have argued that such changes would not necessarily be in opposition of a green public sphere, but could in fact, in the Swedish case, create space for it. To let the political system decide on short-term targets would strengthen democratic influence and provide possibilities for flexibility. To evaluate the realism of these suggestions in Sweden and other states lies beyond the aim of this chapter. However, we note that several states have already moved towards self-binding through decisions on and implementation of climate acts. These attempts fall short of our suggestions, but could be seen as a first step towards them.

Notes

1 This objective includes the use of flexible mechanisms.
2 For the 2050 objective the Swedish Environmental Protection Agency (2012) has formulated a roadmap, which is currently being processed by a commission (Commission Directive 2014: 53, Klimatfärdplan 2050 – strategi för hur visionen att Sverige år 2050 inte har några nettoutsläpp av växthusgaser ska uppnås).
3 For a more extensive discussion of Swedish climate policy see the Government Office (2014).
4 The transport sector has the largest share of Swedish greenhouse gas emission with 32.5 percent in 2011. The emissions from industry were in the same year 26.3 percent (here the energy-intensive industry is included). The energy-producing

industry emitted 17.4 percent of total emission, based on data from the Swedish Environmental Protection Agency (2013).

5 The IPCC has decided to see the optimal level as a political decision that should not be decided by climate experts (see Moss 1995; Knaggård 2009: 250; cf. IPCC 2014).

6 The interest rates that different actors pay of course differs depending on the level of risk, but the key interest rate is still the same for all types of actors.

References

Barry, J., 2008 Towards a green republicanism: constitutionalism, political economy, and the green state. *The Good Society* 17: 1–10.

Berg, C., 2005 Experience of inflation targeting in 20 countries. *Economic Review* 1: 20–47.

Bernanke, B.S., Laubach, T., Mishkin, F.S., and Posen, A.S., 1999 *Inflation Targeting: Lessons from the International Experience.* Princeton University Press, Princeton, NJ.

Brunner, S., Falchsland, C., and Marschinski, R., 2011 Credible commitment in carbon policy. *Climate Policy* 12: 255–71.

Buchanan, J., 2003 *Public Choice: The Origins and Development of a Research Program.* Center for Study of Public Choice, George Mason University, Fairfax, VA.

Buchstein, H., 2013 The concept of 'self-binding' in constitutional theory. In Peruzzoti, E., and Plot, M., (eds) *Critical Theory and Democracy* 56–80. Routledge, Abingdon.

Calmfors, L., 2013 Våga ompröva Riksbankens mål [Dare to reconsider the·objective of the Central Bank]. *Dagens Nyheter* April 3.

Clapp, J., and Dauvergne, P., 2005 *Paths to a Green World: The Political Economy of the Global Environment.* MIT Press, Cambridge, MA.

Committee on Climate Change 2014 Membership of the Committee. Retrieved September 23, 2014 www.theccc.org.uk/about/structure-and-governance/committee-on-climate-change.

Dryzek, J.S., 2000 *Deliberative Democracy and Beyond: Liberals, Critics, Contestations.* Oxford University Press, Oxford.

Dryzek, J.S., Downes, D., Hunold, C., Schlosberg, D., and Hernes H.-K., 2003 *Green States and Social Movements: Environmentalism in the United States, United Kingdom, Germany, and Norway.* Oxford University Press, Oxford.

Eckersley, R., 2004 *The Green State: Rethinking Democracy and Sovereignty.* MIT Press, Cambridge, MA.

Elster, J., 1979 *Ulysses and the Sirens: Studies in Rationality and Irrationality.* Cambridge University Press, Cambridge.

Goodin, R.E., 1992 *Green Political Theory.* Polity, Cambridge.

Government Bill 1997/98 *Svenska miljömål: Miljöpolitik för ett hållbart Sverige* [Swedish Environmental Quality Objectives. Environmental Policy for a Sustainable Sweden]. 1997/98: 145. Government Office, Stockholm.

Government Bill 2008/09 *En sammanhållen klimat och energipolitik: klimat* [A Coherent Climate and Energy Policy: Climate]. 2008/09: 162. Government Office, Stockholm.

Government Bill 2009/10 *Svenska miljömål – för ett effektivare miljöarbete* [Swedish Environmental Quality Objectives – for More Effective Environmental Work]. 2009/10: 155. Government Office, Stockholm.

Government Office 2014 *Sweden's Sixth National Communication on Climate Change: Under the United Nations Framework Convention on Climate Change.* Fritzes, Stockholm.

Heikensten, L., 1999 The Riksbank's inflation target – clarification and evaluation. *Sveriges Riksbank Quarterly Review* 1: 5–17.

Heikensten, L., and Vredin, A., 1998 Inflationsmålet och den svenska penningpolitiken – erfarenheter och problem [The inflation target and the Swedish monetary policy – experiences and problems]. *Ekonomisk Debatt* 26: 573–93.

Helm, D., Hepburn, C., and Mash, R., 2003 Credible carbon policy. *Oxford Review of Economic Policy* 19: 438–50.

IPCC 2014 *Climate Change 2014: Mitigation of Climate Change*. IPCC working group III contribution to AR5. Geneva: IPCC.

Knaggård, Å., 2009 *Vetenskaplig osäkerhet i policyprocessen: en studie av svensk klimatpolitik* [*Scientific Uncertainty in the Policy Process: A Study of Swedish Climate Policy*]. Lund University, Lund.

Lövbrand, E., and Khan, J., 2010 The deliberative turn in green political theory. In Bäckstrand, K., Kahn, J., Kronsell, A., and Lövbrand, E., (eds) *Examining the Promise of New Modes of Governance* 47–64. Edward Elgar, Northampton.

Moss, R.H., 1995 Avoiding 'dangerous' interference in the climate system: the roles of values, science and policy. *Global Environmental Change* 5: 3–6.

New Climate Economy 2014 Better growth better climate. Retrieved September 23, 2014 from http://newclimateeconomy.report.

Nilsson, L.J., and Khan, J., 2010 Politiken och omställningens konst [Politics and the art of transition]. In Johansson, B., (ed) *Sverige i nytt klimat: våtvarm utmaning* [*Sweden in New Climate: A Moist Heated Challenge*] 363–75. Formas, Stockholm.

Nordhaus, W.D., 2007 A review of the Stern Review on the Economics of Climate Change. *Journal of Economic Literature* 45: 686–702.

North, D., 1990 *Institutions, Institutional Change and Economic Performance*. Cambridge University Press, Cambridge.

OECD 2014 *OECD Environmental Performance Review Sweden: Assessment and Recommendations*. OECD, Geneva/Ministry of the Environment, Sweden.

Pihl, H., 1997 *Miljöekonomi för en hållbar utveckling* [*Environmental Economics for a Sustainable Development*]. SNS Förlag, Stockholm.

Reichlin, L., and Baldwin, R., (eds) 2013 *Is Inflation Targeting Dead? Central Banking after the Crisis*. Centre of Economic Policy Research, London.

Smith, G., 2003 *Deliberative Democracy and the Environment*. Routledge, London.

SOU (1993) *Nya villkor för ekonomi och politik: Ekonomikommissionens förslag: betänkande* [*New Conditions for Economy and Policy: The Proposition of the Economy Commission*]. 1993:16. Allmänna förlag, Stockholm.

Swedish Central Bank 2013 *Account of Monetary Policy 2012*. Sveriges Riksbank, Stockholm. Retrieved March 7, 2013 from www.riksbank.se/Documents/Rapporter/ RPP/2013/rap_rpp2012_130327_eng.pdf.

Swedish Environmental Protection Agency 2012 *Underlag till en färdplan för ett Sverige utan klimatutsläpp 2050* [*Support for a Roadmap for a Sweden without Climate Emissions 2050*]. Report 6537. Swedish Environmental Protection Agency, Stockholm.

Swedish Environmental Protection Agency 2013 Utsläpp till luft per bransch [Emissions to air per line of business]. Retrieved March 20, 2013 from www.naturvardsverket.se/ Sa-mar-miljon/Klimat-och-luft/Luft/Utslapp-till-luft-per-bransch.

Swedish National Audit Office 2012 *Klimatrelaterade skatter – vem betalar?* [*Climate-Related Taxes – Who Pays?*]. RiR 2012:1. Swedish Environmental Protection Agency, Stockholm.

Swedish National Audit Office 2013 *Climate for the Money? Audits within the Climate Area 2009-2013*. RiR 2013:19. Swedish Environmental Protection Agency, Stockholm.

Torgerson, D., 1999 *The Promise of Green Politics: Environmentalism and the Public Sphere.* Duke University Press, Durham, NC.

Whitesell, W.C., 2011 *Climate Policy Foundations: Science and Economics with Lessons from Monetary Regulation.* Cambridge University Press, Cambridge.

Williamson, O.E., 2000 The new institutional economics: taking stocks, looking ahead. *Journal of Economic Literature* 38: 595–613.

13 The green state and empathic rationality

Annica Kronsell and Helena Olofsdotter Stensöta

Introduction

Our concern in this chapter is how state institutions can be reformed to realize a sustainable society. State institutions are highly relevant in accomplishing a transition toward climate, environmental and sustainability goals because of their responsibility for decision making, implementation and evaluation of the strategies, policies and decisions that are designed to accomplish these goals. However, we argue that a different rationale for making policy is needed to enhance the capacity for green policy making and suggest that feminist theory can make an important contribution to normative ideals of the green state as well as principles for steering.

Our argument draws attention to patterns of behavior and conduct of the state, i.e. its rationality (Kronsell and Bäckstrand 2010). In using feminist theory to develop thinking on the green state in the realm of policy and decision-making we argue for the notion of empathic rationality. Empathic rationality is a pattern of behavior and conduct that is based on conceptions related to feminist ethics of care theory (Stensöta 2004). The relevance of empathic rationality for sustainability is based on the insight that problems and solutions recognized by feminist ethics of care theory are relevant for the important challenges confronting the state with ambitious climate and sustainability goals.

The aim of this chapter is to first, argue why ethics of care is highly relevant for state transformation toward sustainability and climate goals and second, to develop empathic rationality as a normative foundation for governance in the green state. The empathic rationality should be seen as a concretization of an important dimension, ethics of care, for the green state or the state that cares. To do so, the chapter introduces feminist ethic of care theory through the core notions; interdependence, context sensitivity and responsiveness which we find relevant for advancing the green state. These core notions all imply that humans exist in relation to each other and the world, which includes the ecosystem, and to future generations and that acknowledging and nurturing these relations is a central feature of human society. We argue for empathic rationality as a normative foundation for the green state as well as a principle for steering. We begin with a brief discussion of the commonalities between how feminist theory and green political theory conceptualize the role of the state.

The welfare state is a state that cares

The role and importance of the state has been debated in green as well as feminist theories with diverging views among scholars as to the potential of the state to promote green or feminist values. As within green political theory there is no consensus among feminist scholars on the role of the state. Those who have studied liberal states consider the state as infused with patriarchal power and patriarchal bureaucratic logics and the state does not hold any transformative potential for gender relations (Ferguson 1984; Weir 2005). Instead we have to rely on initiatives in civil society and other societal organizations. In contrast, the state-friendly Scandinavian tradition of feminist research argues that the building of the welfare state provided many new opportunities and brought positive changes to women's lives. The welfare state became the 'women-friendly' state where private care-assignments were made public through welfare state provisions, increased employment and greater economic autonomy for women (Hernes 1987). This feminist scholarship has maintained a focus on problems of the welfare state (Daly and Rake 2003) and, for example, debated the policy reforms that are needed in order to make care a public issue rather than a private concern for women.

In comparison to the feminist discussion, the debate on the welfare state in the green state scholarship is more recent. Green state scholars such as Robyn Eckersley (2004), James Meadowcroft (2005) and Peter Christoff (2005) regard the welfare states in Scandinavia as particularly well suited to adopt environmental norms (see Chapter 1, this volume). This is due, they argue, to an environmental pragmatism embedded in the welfare state. The welfare state has mechanisms for negotiating its state authority and can intervene in different and new areas in society, much like it has with social policy. The welfare state is experienced in safeguarding against many types of risks, which makes it more adaptable to environmental and climate challenges. Moreover, according to Meadowcroft (2005) due to this pragmatism, the welfare state has the potential to develop incrementally to embrace ecological values. We note that in this debate, the transformative potential is associated with how the welfare state has been able to mediate the effects of production and handle the externalities of ecological problems through strategies of ecological modernization (Chapters 5 and 8, this volume). This seems particularly relevant and significant when the focus is on how the state can decarbonize in response to the challenge of global climate change (Gough and Meadowcroft 2011).

We suggest, however, that there is a need to reframe the welfare state in the expanding green state scholarship, and not focus narrowly, as these green scholars seems to do, on how the welfare state has handled the externalities of production. For our purposes the welfare state is important to study because it is the kind of state that 'cares.' We argue that on the whole the welfare state can be seen as a construct that handles the problem of care. It is, further, this caring capability that provides the potential to deal with sustainability and climate concerns. To investigate the role of care in the green state we need to bridge theories of green state with feminism. In feminist theory the discussion on how the welfare state can promote gender equality is to a large extent a discussion on how the problem that humans are in need of care can be handled in a public way, which diminishes inequalities both in relation to who performs the care work, but also in relation to who receives care. Different welfare states may be distinguished by how extensive the state's responsibility in providing and facilitating care is, as well as the institutional forms in which care is provided. The encompassing welfare state is most extensive in providing general benefits and services (Daly and Rake 2003). While the caring in the welfare state has been limited to caring for children, the sick and elderly and through welfare provision such as unemployment benefits and social services, we are particularly interested in the potential of caring for transforming state practices and behavior toward climate and sustainability objectives and a caring for the planet. To do so we turn to a specific scholarship within feminist theory, ethics of care theory.

Ethics of care theory

Ethics of care became a concept through Carol Gilligan's research on moral development, where she argued that care is a form of moral development distinct from the justice-oriented moral dimension stemming from Enlightenment thinking (Gilligan 1982). The political dimension of ethics of care has been highlighted through the second generation of care ethical scholars, starting with Joan Tronto who defined care as a species activity that includes "everything we do to maintain, continue and repair our world so that we can live in it as well as possible" (Tronto 1994: 103). This definition clearly broadens the view of care from something that proceeds between humans to include our relation to the environment as 'the world.' However, subsequent scholarship has mostly dealt with welfare state problems and to care between humans (Hankivsky 2004; Sevenhuijsen 1998; Stensöta 2004; Williams 2001). The broader feature of 'caring for the world' has not been dominant but interesting new theoretical development transgress the national welfare state by a focus on international care chains (Robinson 2006) on peacekeeping (Tronto 2008) but research that expands 'the world' to include the environment is largely absent in the work by ethics of care scholars.

The research on the political importance of ethics of care has evolved to problematize care as not attached to women. Ethics of care is mainly used as a critical lens on the position of care in institutional arrangements. Care is then understood broader than in an everyday sense, applying an image of a four-phased process; caring about, which put attention to a care need; taking care of, which makes arrangements for the need to be met; care-giving which is what we in everyday life understand as caring; and care-receiving, which includes the issue on whether the care need was met (Tronto 1994: 106–7). One strand of research has explored how the perspective of care can be used to argue for inclusive welfare state policies (Engster and Stensöta 2011; Williams 2001) while another strand investigates more theoretically, collisions between an ethics of care perspective and traditional views on policy and public administration (Sevenhuijsen 1998; White 2000).

It can further be noted that the ethics of care perspective, when situated in research based in the US context, often refers to care provision beyond the state (Weir 2005). In the Scandinavian context it is more common to frame issues of care in the welfare state context, where the focus is more on the macro institutional solutions to problems of care, than on the particular detailed demands of care provision. We want to integrate the insights of care-provision mechanisms provided by this research into the general welfare state discussion but expand the scope to ecological interdependence and relations beyond human-to-human.

Within green political theory the care perspective has surfaced but developed separate from the feminist debate and from welfare state research. Val Plumwood proposes a caring ethics, which is, on the one hand about a care for the self, in relation to the individual lifestyle of prudence that sustainability calls for. On the other hand, it is about a care for others which is not restricted to kin or other human beings, as in feminist care ethics, but includes the caring for 'earth others.' Through the notion of 'earth others,' nature is not perceived as an object for human manipulation, but as a subject, that deserves recognition and respect (i.e. care; Plumwood 2006: 66). Writers on animal ethics, argue that ethics of care is a good starting point to re-evaluate human relations with animals (Donovan and Adams 2007). Other green theorists (Cheney 1987) and ecological feminist scholars have used the ethics of care in their work but have also been criticized for essentializing white women's experiences when linking motherhood and reproductive labor with caring for the environment (Thompson 2006; Gaard 2011). Sherilyn MacGregor (2004) considers this use of caring as a problematic celebration of women that has the effect of depoliticizing caring.

It is our conclusion that the ethics of care perspective used by eco-feminist scholars, remains largely within the first generation perspective on ethics of care, meaning that care is attached to women and seen in opposition to justice-reasoning. Within the ethics of care research, the problems of contextualizing from where one speaks has been discussed intensely among scholars who apply a perspective of intersectionality or who argue that ethics of care theory needs to incorporate some of the ideas from intersectionality (Hankivsky 2014). Further, and more importantly for our argument, the theoretical tradition in eco-feminist research has not engaged with the state, institutions, and practices of policy making. An exception is MacGregor (2006) who suggests the use of care as a political principle, as a civic virtue for example in relation to citizenship.

By using the latest development within research on ethics of care heuristically, and learning from how the welfare state has handled the problem of care, we suggest that it is possible to advance thinking on how the state might handle problems relating to climate and sustainability transitions. In the next section we present core notions of an ethics of care perspective that we will build on to suggest how emphatic rationality can be a guiding normative principle for the green state.

Core notions of ethics of care

In this section we present three core notions of ethics of care theory that we think summarizes basic concepts common to several approaches within this theoretical realm: interdependence, context sensitivity and responsiveness. We then proceed to discuss how they are perceived in green political thought. Hence we start in notions identified in ethics of care theory that we argue has bearing on problems of the green state, and bring them into the discussion of the latter. We choose not to start in existing concepts in the green state scholarship, such as justice or the concept of inclusion. Instead we propose that it is the ontological notion of *interdependence* identified in ethics of care theory, that can be conceived as the founding normative principle of the empathic rationality and which is central in our argument of how ethics of care theory can advance green state theory. From that starting point it is then possible to include discussions on justice and inclusion.

Interdependence

Central to ethics of care theory is an ontological notion of humans as interdependent, meaning that humans are seen as both dependent and independent. This refutes the idea that some people are dependent (for example disabled people, sick people, women, children and elderly) whereas others are not. This ontology further relies on an important stance to the goal of *establish*, *nurture*, *sustain* and *protect* relationships of different kinds, which involves contributing to their healthy development and growth, and guarding these relationships from harm. If dependency is considered as part of normality, the act of caring is put more at the center. People do not exist in isolation from each other but in relation to each other and the world. To care is conceived of as a way to grow as a person, a growth that is regarded as central to becoming a part of the human web and society (Stensöta 2015).

Interdependence is important to green political theory as well but in a slightly different way. Human beings are considered dependent on a web of relations but the emphasis is on human dependence on ecological systems and physical and biological resources like air, water, forests and other species. This idea has not been a focus in the discussion of interdependence within ethics of care. Thus, in our interpretation there is a common worldview on interdependence that informs both the ethics of care perspective and the perspective of green political theory, which is why they can be combined. However, the two theoretical fields have emphasized different things, which is why they may also stimulate one other.

Deep green and bio-centric perspectives on interdependence see humans mainly as dependent and an integral part of natural ecosystems. The cognitive base of green political theory is system ecology but different versions of green political theory emerged, from deep eco-philosophical ecologism (Devall and Sessions 1985; Goodin 1992) to more anthropocentric green political theory, like environmentalism and ecological modernization (Hajer 1995; Weale 1992; Mol *et al.* 2009). Humans and societies are considered an integral part of ecological systems, dependent on functioning ecosystems for their life and livelihoods but also enabled and made independent by its resources (Capra 1982; Dobson 1990; Mathews 1991). This is important also in green state theory, in typologies like Christoff's (2005: 42–3) the green state is one that demonstrates a commitment to and institutionalization of biocentric and ecological values (see also Chapter 8, this volume). Hence, green state politics ought to be conducted based on this and the insight that humans will affect ecosystems for generations to come. Since the 1970s there is a fairly widespread understanding of this among policy makers (Dryzek and Dunleavy 2009: 244). What seems to be lacking are ideas about how policy practice can take into account this interdependence on ecosystems. We argue that ethics of care can be helpful here.

In the ethics of care literature, interdependence has mainly been used to highlight interdependence between humans, however, we argue that it does not have to be this way. Inherent in the definition of care by Tronto, is care as a process that includes everything we do to "maintain, continue and repair our world" (Tronto 1994: 103) so that we can live in it as well as possible. The world can incorporate the surrounding non-human world of life and the socio-ecological system. The ethics of care perspective does a great deal in promoting the perspective of care to humankind and includes what is closely connected to us, but also in remote places or as future generations, yet this potential has not been exhausted in previous ethics of care theory.

Green political thought can be used to widen the scope of ethics of care theory to endorse an interdependent view of human life conditions, including the interdependence with nature. This involves for example, the not-yet-born generation, animals as well as nature. Using Tronto's definition above it seems possible to include also human interaction with the environment. Through 'maintain, continue and repair' we can incorporate the concepts of sustainability, environmental protection, ecosystem conservation, which are central to environmental policy-making in the ethics of care. As we comprehend humans as standing in relation also to the environment and future and unborn generations, it becomes important to *establish, nurture, sustain* and *protect* also these relationships.

We propose that the ethics of care can contribute by informing an emphatic rationality for policy making for climate, environmental and sustainability goals. We argue that the ontological view of humans and nature as interdependent leads to a rationality that on the individual level promotes a shared experience of being interdependent. This mechanism can, on a general level, affect local environments as well as global problems.

Context sensitivity

One of the main merits of ethics of care is that it points at the importance of considering the context. Context is about space and the importance of locally anchored and decentralized practices that are highlighted both in green political theory and in ethics of care theory. Green thinking emphasizes the salience of the local context in relation to the importance of grassroots movements, democratization, decentralization and citizen engagement both in gaining knowledge about environmental processes and conditions and to advance environmental responsibility which is understood to be more likely in the local context (Carter 2007; Dryzek 2013). From a policy perspective, the local context and the engagement of civil society can be critical to promote implementation.

Virginia Held (2010) has argued for contextuality, basing her argument on how the standardization of welfare state support may lead to qualifying access to such benefits, in ways that might work against the goals of the policy. Virginia Held illustrates this by referring to the state's expectation that women (or men) who are subject to domestic violence are expected to leave their partners before or while receiving help. As Held (*ibid.*) notes, this puts many victimized people under severe stress and can even make them reluctant to seek support. A care-oriented perspective would, in contrast, pay attention to contextuality and support these people regardless of whether or not they choose to leave the battering party, according to Held.

Stensöta (2004), who traces ideas of care in day-care and law enforcement policy, provides a policy account of what a care-perspective that incorporates contextuality entails. Here, to protect and care for a local context where relations between persons are vivid is understood as a goal from a care perspective. This perspective addresses the nurture and protection of connections between local welfare state and private families, but also civil society organizations. Further, the preventative and locally anchored law enforcement institution is regarded as an example of the local care-oriented state. Citizens are thought of as contextually anchored within their local environment (*ibid.*).

While the local in the care perspective tells us that local is not a homogenous civil society, green political theory advanced another understanding of context. It can be illustrated through the slogan 'think globally, act locally' originating in and frequently used by the environmental movement and green parties to imply that we should consider the effects on the whole planet while taking action in the local community. This can fruitfully be combined with 'caring for the world' in ethics of care thinking. To think globally and act locally implies 'doing caring' in the local context while at the same time paying attention to and caring about the global dimension. The green context sensitivity implies to act in the local context, in such a way that allows local actions to include the caring for people and the treatment of resources and non-humans in remote places where production of products that we consume in Europe takes place (see also Robinson 2006). This implies acquiring knowledge about how our individual acts and actions in the local setting affect other people in different parts of the globe through the globalized chain of production and consumption (Newell 2012) in ecological unequal exchange patterns (Hornborg 1998) and then act differently.

There is further a need for care-thinking about consumption chains, in terms of what constitutes sustainable consumption (Fuchs 2013), how resources are used, what wastes are generated as well as how people are treated along the consumption chain (Acker 2004). While the green and the care perspective both point to the need to contextualize humans in relationship to the local, this should be expanded to include a sensitivity to the 'world' also in terms of attention to the connected relations between the global and the local in systems of consumption, production and resource use that are intimately tied to socio-ecological systems.

To make these insights inform environmental policy-making, changes in existing strategies are likely to be needed, for example in the policies that steer toward ecological objectives or are based on precaution. Eckersley (2004: 135–6) suggests that the precautionary principle is a useful policy mechanism because it shifts the focus to potential harm and potential risks when it is used as a guiding principle for policy making. Similar ideas are also included in more recent care theory, which says that caring includes not only the harm done, but also to prevent the harm from happening in the first place (Engster 2009). This is the difference between care as a cleaning-up activity at the periphery of the world, and care as a central anticipatory principle. The precautionary principle carries a potential for looking into future harms and risks as well as including 'earth others.' The principle has been adopted widely by regional and national governments (Wiener *et al.* 2011) and provides an example of how environmental policy can build on context sensitivity.

In sum, context sensitivity is important for both the green and the ethics of care perspectives and as a normative basis for our articulation of emphatic rationality. The relation to context or to space is crucial because it is constitutive of our experiences. Through context we gain knowledge about the complex socio-ecological system of which we are a part and we learn to respect everyone's uniqueness and foster a preservation of variety and diversity.

Responsiveness

In feminist care theory responsiveness highlights whether the action undertaken to meet a care need actually satisfied this need. Responsiveness stresses the importance of the care-giver being sensitive to the person in need and demands the care-giver makes sure that the needs have been met, before the act of caring can be considered complete (Tronto 1994). In subsequent care ethics theory the problem of paternalism has been increasingly discussed in relation to needs satisfaction. White (2000) proposes that deliberative institutions are used for defining needs, where the care-recipient is given a chance to define his or her needs. A delicate problem is, however, when the care recipient is not able to articulate his or her needs, something that is frequently the case (Barnes 2012). When these problems are discussed within the realm of the state, responsiveness and deliberate structures can be seen as a kind of accountability arrangement (Stensöta 2015).

White (2000) offers concrete examples of how institutional solutions for responsiveness may be designed. She argues that if we want to provide care through the state we need to redefine the concept of paternalism. If we understand paternalism as the process of speaking for others in the course of defining needs, we may be able to criticize domination in the practices of care without simultaneously threatening the prospect of collective responsibility for care. White concludes by suggesting deliberative structures in policies that aim at providing care, where the persons in need of care are asked to participate in defining their needs. This is an argument for responsiveness as more inclusive practices in the provision of care.

In the ethics of care tradition, Young (2000) discusses how the experiences of certain repressed groups necessarily should be represented by politics because these experiences are clearly not included in the 'universal' aspects of citizenship,[1] yet she argues it is crucial to do so if we want to understand the problem of these oppressed groups and find out how to be responsive to their needs (see also Haraway 1987).

Elena Pulcini (2009) has argued that the only theoretical way to arrive at solidarity with future generations is through the framework of an ethics of care. Her account specifically criticizes what she calls unlimited individualism in today's world. Her account of an ethics of care makes feelings central and she argues that we can transform 'fear' and 'anxiety,' which are the emotions that predominate, through care. This act goes through the comprehension of humans as interdependent to a larger context.

A distinguishing feature of green versions of democracy is the responsiveness to a wider political community (Ball 2006; Goodin 1992). Thus, it is important to find ways to be responsive to current interest of nature, non-human species and to take into account the needs of future generations. The emphasis on the care for future generations in the definition of sustainable development (WCED 1987) is such an example. In a similar vein, many of the subjects in green political thought are not able to articulate demands, as they are not yet born, or are not generally viewed as political subjects that should be given a voice.

We argue that responsiveness can include future generations. The care perspective has been used to argue for a focus on the wellbeing of children (Engster and Stensöta 2011). The inclusion of the care of living children, who are not full political subjects, may well be expanded to future generations. From the care perspective, future generations and nature can be comprehended as policy recipients that have difficulties making their claims heard in the way we are used to hearing claims. We need to find ways for the entity in need to define the needs. Responsiveness is needed to account for future generations, nature and non-human species.

This has also been argued by thinkers in green political thought. According to Eckersley, responsiveness requires "that the opportunity to participate or otherwise be represented in the making of risk generating decisions should literally be extended to all those potentially affected, regardless of social class, geographic location, nationality, generation, or species" (Eckersley 2004: 112). As such groups are not represented in contemporary democratic politics, ways for non-human and long-term interests to be accounted for need to be worked out (Ball 2006; Saward 2006: 183–5). There are suggestions on how this can be done. Through forms of political trusteeship or stewardship (Berry 2006) or by treating other species as well as future generations as communities that potentially can be harmed by current industrial practices and political decisions (Saward 2006: 187). Val Plumwood (2006: 71) speaks about the design of political and administrative systems, that they should be set up in a way that make non-human needs and the contribution of 'earth others' both visible and known. Deliberative democratic processes that include processes of judgment, preference formation and transformation in the context of informed and respectful dialogue have been argued to be useful procedures to arrive at shared understandings on the needs of other species or future generations (Dryzek 2010; Lövbrand and Khan 2010).

We argue that responsiveness to the broader political community and future generations can be achieved through the application of ethics of care in the green polity. Responsiveness is central to our articulation of empathic rationality. It requires deliberation with a broad range of actors involved in inclusive processes that are sensitive to care needs of subjects in a broader political community, including present and future generations, nature and non-human species. By taking into account the problems of paternalism, discussed in the care perspective, it can also help ecological responsiveness to steer away from domination and potential power abuse.

The empathic rationality of the green state

Based on the three principles – interdependence, context sensitivity and responsiveness – advanced in this chapter we propose empathic rationality as a core rationality and normative foundation for the green state. It is a contribution that develops normative ideals of governance in line with Eckersley's ideal of the post-liberal green state and Christoff's green state type. Empathic rationality is concerned with the general aim of environmental governance (i.e. of promoting societal change through governance that leads to environmental performance and effectiveness while transforming state and society towards sustainable and environmental behavior). Rationality is defined as the underlying logic of governance and the reasoning behind which action proceeds (Kronsell and Bäckstrand 2010). Action may mean reproduction but it may also incorporate change.

Different rationalities make different assumptions about how to bring about societal change and how to govern effectively. That is also what makes them intriguing for thinking about advancing governance in the green state. In order to develop empathic rationality we systematically compared three rationalities – bureaucratic, market and deliberate rationality – with emphatic rationality, across the core principles. This comparison is developed more extensively elsewhere (Stensöta and Kronsell 2014) and is briefly outlined in Table 13.1.

Empathetic rationality centers on the view of humans as interdependent. This notion builds on an understanding of what holds human communities together. Whereas the bureaucratic rationality builds on participation in formal democratic systems, and the deliberative rationality centers on shared understandings being the outcome of deliberation in smaller groups, emphatic rationality sees

Table 13.1 Empathic rationality in comparison to bureaucratic, market and deliberative rationality

State-level dimension	Bureaucratic rationality	Market rationality	Deliberative rationality	Empathic rationality
Problem-capturing	Problems are translated into general rules	Problems are translated into costs	Problems are translated into 'tragedy of the commons'	Problems are translated into 'interdependent relations'
Mechanisms for change	Rules	Incentives	Institutions for deliberation	Experience of interdependence
Main conflict	The values defended by the majority; ecological concerns	Economic–ecological interests	The values reached by deliberation; ecological values	Growth, standardization; caring/ecological values

solidarity as emanating from a first-hand but also shared experience of how we are both dependent and independent simultaneously. This connection deepens the relation between people in very concrete ways, which leads to an experience of the mutuality in interdependent relations. This deeper interdependence as part of the human condition is not emphasized by any of the other rationalities. Solidarity with the future generation may be established through the experience of interdependence.

Empathetic rationality conceives of environmental problems as problems of interdependent relations that need to be *established, nurtured, sustained* and *protected*. This applies to relationships between people, but also encompasses humans' relationship to natural ecosystems and future generations. In sum 'the world' is comprehended as consisting of interdependent relations.

The mechanism for change emanating from this notion broadens and deepens the understanding of interdependence, for example, through policies that extend the caring of humans to nature, other species and future generations. The way the green state may advance these concerns is to make the experience of interdependence more broadly acquired in society by advocating a generalist view of task division in society, especially in regard of care assignments. Shared parental leave is an example of a policy that works in this direction, but also initiatives that make us aware of the importance of caring for our relations to the world, nature and the future unborn generations. The green state should allow and encourage people to step into the experience of being interdependent in different relationships, to each other and to 'the world,' including nature.

The transformative process of interdependence does not proceed solely intellectually but is rooted in the experiences of meeting other people's needs as well as having one's own needs met. The importance of experience spills over to the core notion of contextuality – locally anchored experiences is a form of contextualization. Sensitivity to context is of core importance and people are seen as anchored in relationships and circumstances of different kinds. In contrast to deliberative rationality, where unification in consensus is a goal, the context of empathic rationality helps preserve uniqueness. Rather, it builds on acceptance for variety and the respect for diversity in experience.

Uniqueness refers to how each individual is embedded in different social categories and power relations (i.e. Intersectionality). For example, how sustainably we live depends on our material resources, our place in the world and on social categories like class, ethnicity and age. Even for citizens in advanced industrialized states, some cannot afford to buy ecological food or upgrade to an environmentally friendly car. The extent to which an individual acts sustainably depends, for example, on economic status. In a similar vein, gender is important for ecology. Women use fewer resources and leave smaller ecological footprints compared to men (Johnsson-Latham 2007). This may be due to an active choice or lack of economic power, meaning that women would expand their footprints if they had the opportunity to consume more. Concrete policy actions that are important from this perspective are enabling strategies that make the sustainable alternative the most economically sound and the easiest path to follow. This can be illustrated with city planning that prioritizes public transportation, walking and cycling to enable sustainable consumption and lifestyles.

Empathic rationality is proactive in terms of the goal of meeting needs through preventing harm. Information and consultation for how to buy, live and recycle ecologically are useful policy options to prevent harm. Concrete examples of preventive policies can be found within law enforcement work when a shift from a reactive to proactive law enforcement is promulgated and with the precautionary principle in environmental policy making. This principle argues that it has to be shown that something does not do any harm before it is allowed.

In empathic rationality, care aims at preventing future harm and satisfying current needs. A key dilemma for the green state is when care demands collide with progress and economic growth. Prevention and precaution may have a constraining effect, in terms of minimizing risk that unintended consequences occur. Furthermore, care also has to do with accepting things as they are and learn to be content with what we have, whereas economic growth often assumes a discontent with the current situation and a seemingly insatiable consumption. Finally, the emphasis on human care in the ethics of care tradition may lead to a conflict. If the choice is between human care values and ecological care values, it is likely that human care values are prioritized due to an anthropocentric bias of the ethics of care tradition.

Empathic rationality does not only include the activities of satisfying need, but also is responsive to whether the actual needs have been met. If initiatives are continuously evaluated on the basis of whether their needs have been met, this may constitute a ground for moving quicker to solutions that actually protect nature also for the future. This works against initiatives that are done without any real possibility of evoking a change.

Translated into the arena of environmentalism this would mean that professionals (and experts) in relation to the subject would have the last say in deliberation. In this sense professionals are understood as represented by general experts on environmental issues. In empathic rationality, the notion of generalists is preferred before experts, just in the same way as plurality or variety is preserved and the experience of interdependence is deliberately broadened to as many people as possible. At the same time stakeholders have a natural position in this plurality of voices that should be complemented with a deeper solidarity with everything around us that may evolve through learning the interdependent condition of our existence.

Conclusion

This chapter took a starting point in the argument of green state scholars that welfare states are better suited to deal with sustainability, environmental and climate challenges. We think this may well be the case, but rather than considering the welfare state potential in relation to its success in managing externalities of production, we suggest the focus should be on the welfare state's relation to care. We propose that since the welfare state is a state that cares, it has a potential for empathic rationality through which it could develop to become a green state. As care is a core feature of welfare states and also of feminist theory we suggested that empathic rationality based on feminist care ethics and related to the three principles – interdependence, context sensitivity and responsiveness – is a fruitful way to think about how policy making can be conducted differently in the green state through empathic rationality. We have demonstrated how empathic rationality rests on care ethics and green political ideas without being a utopian or esoteric concept. It has resonance and relevance for current policy making and is a likely option for the emergent green state. The empathic rationality is both a normative foundation and an underlying principle that can guide priorities and behavior in the green state.

While we argue that empathic rationality is relevant, even crucial for the continued development of the green state, we are not claiming that empathic rationality is the only way forward for governance. Rather, each rationality – the bureaucratic, market, and deliberative – has each one its core concern but also inherent conflict, as shown in the table above. Thus, each rationality has its limitations. In our view, it is likely that the green state will need to rely on all four rationalities in order to be successful in the transition toward sustainability and climate goals. However there needs to be increasing emphasis on the deliberative, and above all, empathic rationality.

Note

1   The literature on environmental citizenship contributes here, also with a view on the role of the individual in the green state that goes beyond the consumer to specific ideas about the role, rights and duties of citizens (Dobson 2006, 2003; Dobson and Bell 2005).

References

Acker, J., 2004 Gender, capitalism and globalization. *Critical Sociology* 30(1): 17–41.

Ball, T., 2006 Democracy. In Dobson, A., and Eckersley, R., (eds) *Political Theory and the Ecological Challenge* 131–47. Cambridge University Press, Cambridge.

Barnes, M., 2012 *Care in Everyday Life: An Ethic of Care in Practice*. Policy Press, Bristol.

Berry, R.J., (ed) 2006 *Environmental Stewardship*. Continuum, London.

Capra, F., 1982 *The Turning Point: Science, Society and the Rising Culture*. Wildwood House, London.

Carter, N., 2007 *The Politics of the Environment*, 2nd edn. Cambridge University Press, Cambridge.

Cheney, J., 1987 Eco-feminism and deep ecology. *Environmental Ethics* 9: 115–45.

Christoff, P., 2005 Out of chaos, a shining star? Toward a typology of green states. In Barry, J., and Eckersley, R., (eds) *The State and the Global Ecological Crisis* 25–51. MIT Press, Cambridge, MA.

Daly, M., and Rake, K., 2003 *Gender and the Welfare State*. Polity Press, Cambridge.

Devall, B., and Sessions, G., 1985 *Deep Ecology*. Peregrine Smith Books, Salt Lake City, UT.

Dhamoon, R., 2011 Considerations on mainstreaming intersectionality. *Political Research Quarterly* 64(1): 230–43.

Dobson, A., 1990 *Green Political Thought*. Unwin Hyman, London.

Dobson, A., 2003 *Citizenship and the Environment*. Oxford University Press, Oxford.

Dobson, A., 2006 Citizenship. In Dobson, A., and Eckersley, R., (eds) *Political Theory and the Ecological Challenge* 216–31. Cambridge University Press, Cambridge.

Dobson, A., and Bell, D., (eds) 2005 *Environmental Citizenship*. MIT Press, Cambridge, MA.

Donovan, J., and Adams, C., (eds) 2007 *The Feminist Care Tradition in Animal Ethics*. Columbia University Press, New York.

Dryzek, J., 2010 *Foundations and Frontiers of Deliberative Governance*. Oxford University Press, Oxford.

Dryzek, J., 2013 *The Politics of the Earth: Environmental Discourses*, 3rd edn. Oxford University Press, Oxford.

Dryzek, J., and Dunleavy, P., 2009 *Theories of the Democratic State*. Palgrave Macmillan, Basingstoke.

Eckersley, R., 2004 *The Green State: Rethinking Democracy and Sovereignty*. MIT Press, Cambridge, MA.

Engster, D., 2009 Rethinking care theory: the practice of caring and the obligation to care. *Hypatia* 20(3): 50–74.

Engster, D., and Stensöta, H.O., 2011 Do family policy regimes matter for children's well-being? *Social Politics* 18(1): 82–124.

Ferguson, K., 1984 *The Feminist Case against Bureaucracy*. Temple University Press, Philadelphia, PA.

Fuchs, D., 2013 Sustainable consumption. In Falkner, R., (ed) *Handbook of Global Climate and Environment Policy* 215–30. John Wiley & Sons, Chichester.

Gaard, G., 2011 Ecofeminism revisited: rejecting essentialism and re-placing species in a material feminist environmentalism. *Feminist Formations* 23(2): 26–53.

Gilligan, C., 1982 *In a Different Voice: Women's Conceptions of the Self and of Morality*. Cambridge University Press, Cambridge.

Goodin, R., 1992 *Green Political Theory*. Polity Press, Cambridge.

Gough, I., and Meadowcroft, J., 2011 Decarbonizing the welfare state. In Dryzek, J.S., Norgaard, R.B., and Schlosberg, D., (eds) *Climate Change and Society* 490–503. Oxford University Press, Oxford.

Hajer, M., 1995 *The Politics of Environmental Discourse: Ecological Modernization and the Policy Process.* Clarendon Press, Oxford.

Hankivsky, O., 2004 *Social Policy and the Ethic of Care.* UBC Press, Vancouver.

Hankivsky, O., 2014 Rethinking care ethics: on the promise and potential of an intersectional analysis. *American Political Science Review* 108(2): 252–64.

Haraway, D., 1987 Situated knowledges. *Feminist Studies* 14(3): 575–99.

Held, V., 2006 *The Ethics of Care: Personal, Political, and Global.* Oxford University Press, Oxford.

Held, V., 2010 Can the ethics of care handle violence? *Ethics and Social Welfare* 4(2): 115–29.

Hernes, H., 1987 *Welfare State and Woman Power: Essays in State Feminism.* Norwegian University Press, Oslo.

Hornborg, A., 1998 Towards an ecological theory of unequal exchange: articulating world system theory and ecological economics. *Ecological Economics* 25(1): 127–36.

Johnsson-Latham, G., 2007 *A Study of Gender Equality as a Prerequisite for Sustainable Development.* Report to the Environment Advisory Council Sweden, 2007: 2. Ministry of the Environment, Stockholm. Retrieved February 16, 2015 from www.atria.nl/epublications/2007/study_on_gender_equality_as_a_prerequisite_for_sustainable_development.pdf.

Kronsell, A., and Bäckstrand, K., 2010 Rationality and forms of governance: a framework for analyzing the legitimacy of new modes of governance. In Bäckstrand, K., Khan, J., Kronsell, A., and Lövbrand, E., (eds) *Environmental Politics and Deliberative Democracy: Examining the Promise of New Modes of Governance* 28–46. Edward Elgar, Cheltenham.

Lewis, J., 1992 Gender and the development of welfare regimes. *Journal of European Social Policy* 3(2): 159–73.

Lövbrand, E., and Khan, J., 2010 The deliberative turn in green political theory. In Bäckstrand, K., Khan, J., Kronsell, A., and Lövbrand, E., (eds) *Environmental Politics and Deliberative Democracy: Examining the Promise of New Modes of Governance* 47–64. Edward Elgar, Cheltenham.

MacGregor, S., 2004 From care to citizenship: calling ecofeminism back to politics. *Ethics and the Environment* 9(1): 56–84.

MacGregor, S., 2006 *Beyond Mothering Earth: Ecological Citizenship and the Politics of Care.* University of British Colombia Press, Vancouver.

Mathews, F., 1991 *The Ecological Self.* Routledge, London.

Meadowcroft, J., 2005 From welfare state to ecostate. In Barry, J., and Eckersley, R., (eds) *The State and the Global Ecological Crisis* 3–23. MIT Press, Cambridge, MA.

Mol, A., Sonnenfeld, D., and Spaargaren, G., (eds) 2009 *The Ecological Modernisation Reader: Environmental Reform in Theory and Practice.* Routledge, London.

Newell, P., 2012 *Globalization and the Environment: Capitalism, Ecology and Power.* Polity Press, Cambridge.

Plumwood, V., 2006 Feminism. In Dobson, A., and Eckersley, R., (eds) *Political Theory and the Ecological Challenge* 51–74. Cambridge University Press, Cambridge.

Pulcini, E., 2009 *Care of the World: Fear, Responsibility and Justice in the Global Age.* Springer, Bologna.

Robinson, F., 2006 Care, gender and global social justice: rethinking 'ethical globalisation.' *Journal of Global Ethics* 2(1): 5–25.

Saward, M., 2006 Representation. In Dobson, A., and Eckersley, R., (eds) *Political Theory and the Ecological Challenge* 183–99. Cambridge University Press, Cambridge.

Sevenhuijsen, S., 1998 *Citizenship and the Ethics of Care: Feminist Considerations on Justice, Morality and Care*. Routledge, London.

Stensöta, H.O., 2004 Den empatiska staten. Jämställdhetens inverkan på daghem och polis 1950–2000 [The Empathetic State: The Impact of Gender Equality on Child Care and Law Enforcement 1950–2000]. PhD thesis, University of Gothenburg, Sweden.

Stensöta, Olofsdotter Helena (2015) Public ethics of care – a general public ethics. *Ethics and Social Welfare*. DOI: 10.1080/17496535.2015.1005551.

Stensöta, H., and Kronsell, A., 2014 Ecological theory meets ethics of care: empathic rationality in the green state. Paper presented at Western Political Science Conference, Seattle, April 16–19.

Thompson, C., 2006 Back to nature? Resurrecting ecofeminism after poststructuralist and third-wave feminisms. *Focus-Isis* 97(3): 505–12.

Tronto, J., 1994 *Moral Boundaries: A Political Argument for an Ethic of Care*. Routledge, New York.

Tronto, J., 2008 Is peacekeeping care work? A feminist reflection on 'the responsibility to protect.' In Whisnant, R., and DesAutels, P., (eds) *Global Feminist Ethics* 179–200. Rowman & Littlefield, Lanham, MD.

Tronto, J., 2013 *Caring Democracy: Markets, Equality, and Justice*. New York University Press, New York.

WCED 1987 Our Common Future. Report of the World Commission on Environment and Development ('the Brundtland Report'). Oxford University Press, Oxford. Retrieved September 2, 2014 from http://conspect.nl/pdf/Our_Common_Future-Brundtland_Report_1987.pdf.

Weale, A., 1992 *The New Politics of Pollution*. Manchester University Press, Manchester.

Weir, A., 2005 The global universal caregiver: imagining women's liberation in the new millennium. *Constellations* 12(3): 308–30.

White J.A., 2000 *Democracy, Justice and the Welfare State: Reconstructing Public Care*. Pennsylvania State University, University Park, PA.

Wiener, J.B., Rogers, M.D., Hammitt, J.K., and Sand, P.H., (eds) 2011 *The Reality of Precaution: Comparing Risk Regulation in the United States and Europe*. Earthscan, London.

Williams, F., 2001 In and beyond New Labour: towards a new political ethics of care. *Critical Social Policy* 21(4): 467–93.

Young, I.M., 2000 *Inclusion and Democracy*. Oxford University Press, Oxford.

14 Conclusion

Karin Bäckstrand and Annica Kronsell

Introduction

The overall conclusion in this book is that the state matters and that the state polity – with its administration, institutions and policy-making processes – matters in environmental governance towards climate and sustainability transitions. This is evident in many chapters that demonstrate how the state is, more or less, deeply implicated in the complex process of achieving climate and sustainability objectives toward low-carbon futures. The book advances the frontier on the green state theory by exploring the emergence of the green state in the context of climate and sustainability transitions. A set of common questions guided the research in the various chapters. How has the green state been conceptualized across fields of political theory, governance and institutional theory? Which states perform well and qualify to be labeled green? Are welfare states or small states in a better position to make the transition to a low-carbon society? And, finally, how can current institutions and governance forms be reformed, or transformed toward societal goals of low-carbon and sustainability transitions? The findings in the chapters collectively contribute with a deeper understanding of the green state, theoretically, empirically and normatively, as well as suggesting new directions for future research. In the following section, the key findings of the various contributions are synthesized and discussed under the following three themes:

1   Theorizing the green state.
2   Green state types and environmental performance.
3   Transforming the state toward climate and sustainability objectives.

Theorizing the green state

In our exposé of the green state scholarship in the introduction, we showed that there are many types and typologies of green states with different labels: from environmental to ecological states, from strong to weak eco-states and from carbon to decarbonized states. In the empirical assessment, there is also a large variation between types of green states, from welfare-oriented to neoliberal green states. Through a review of the green state scholarship we found that three important features determined the status of green states:

- its relationship to the market and to the public sphere;
- the degree of biocentric or ecological values present; and
- the capacity for reflection and deliberation for steering towards climate and sustainability goals.

Typologies and ideal types articulated in political theory, such as Christoff's (2005), have often been employed in comparative political studies to empirically assess degrees of 'greenness' of states. These typologies were used in a similar way by several authors in this book. These typologies seldom translate into real world cases, however, they entice us to think further and deeper on what are the elements that are needed for states to live up to green statehood. This is how the typologies become most useful.

The ecological modernization literature (Mol and Spaargaren 2000; Young 2000) provides an important input to one of the most complex and contentious impetuses for debates on the green state, namely the role of the economy. Can the current economic system be tweaked to climate and sustainability ends, or is a new system of non-growth or de-growth necessary? Seminal work in the green state scholarship (Barry and Eckersley 2005; Eckersley 2004; Meadowcroft 2012) frames this in terms of the priorities of the green state, where ecological values have to be prioritized over economic goals, in contrast to the win–win narrative of ecological modernization which sees ecological and economic values as working in tandem. The literature on green welfare states concerns itself with an additional feature, related to the actual steering capacity of the state, and argues that welfare states have this capacity to reconcile between different interests in society, by remediating social and environmental costs that arise from the externalities of industrial production (Meadowcroft 2005; Gough and Meadowcroft 2011). This capacity is viewed as an important one for the green state, and also the reason why some argue that the welfare state is the most likely candidate to become a green state. An observation is that an important feature for the green polity is its capacity to act. Kronsell and Stensöta (Chapter 13, this volume) suggest that the welfare state has another potential capacity as it is a state that cares, and proposed that the notion of care could be cultivated as a useful normative foundation for the green state. While care in the welfare state has been concerned with assuring that the weak, vulnerable and the young are taken care of, this can be extended to general caring, for the environment, planet and future generations.

Finally, in our review we found that green state scholarship significantly lacked discussions on societal transformation toward low carbon futures. Typologies tend to be static, based on a set of ideal types, and tell us little about how to move from one state type to another. For this reason, we turned to transition theory for inspiration on how states can change to become green, propel climate mitigation or become decarbonized. Transition theory (Grin *et al.* 2011; Markard *et al.* 2012) offers ideas about how the dynamics of change take place between powerful regime actors that tend to support the status quo, and niche actors, which represent change agents (Schot and Geels 2008). Accordingly, transition theory provides tools to study processes of change, but also allows us to look closer at a less unified polity, with different constellations of actors, in networks and alliances, which are differently positioned within the state and resist or spur change (Geels 2014). It suggests that the polity is not a homogenous entity, and it helps us focus on the actors with a change agenda who can mobilize against a powerful regime. Regimes and niches within states may be expressed materially as actors, relations and dependencies and/or as discourses found within different sectors, such as transport and energy (Avelino and Rotmans 2009). The review of the green state scholarship demonstrated this broader set of elements that can be included to enrich future theories of the green state.

The first section of the book advances the frontier of green state theory through a reading of fields such as governance for sustainable development, state theories, and political theory of sovereignty. Lövbrand and Linnér (Chapter 3, this volume) confirm the importance of the state by analyzing a set of articles on non-state climate politics, which bear witness not to a state in retreat, but rather on the rise in new roles. Paradoxically, the persistence of the state has spurred, for example, transnational governance initiatives. In line with Okereke *et al.* (2009), they conclude that governing beyond the state does not entail governing without the state, only that the scope and scale of state activities have been redefined. Lövbrand and Linnér examine state models in the climate governance literature and elaborate on how the responsive pluralist state and the decentering partnering state identified in the analysis resonate with the ideals proposed in the green state literature. Importantly, they note that the limited post-colonial state is the least likely candidate for a green state ideal. They argue that green state theories have been based on the experience of advanced industrialized and welfare states in the northern hemisphere. This particular historical experience of the liberal or social welfare states is less applicable to the post-colonial state. We agree with this insight that is worth taking further in developing green state theory by asking: How can green state theory respond and include the heterogeneous category of developing states that are struggling with legacies of colonialism, authoritarian rule and societal-state struggles?

Erik Hysing (Chapter 2, this volume) also considers the state a pivotal actor, particularly in governance for sustainable development. He argues for a state with political institutions that are stable to promote democracy and the existence of a green public sphere, and thereby aligning itself with democratic welfare states and ideal types of green states. Hysing arrives at his vision of the green state through a careful analysis of the nature of the problem at stake. Since sustainable development is a highly ambitious societal objective but difficult to operationalize, is imprecise and contested, it leaves policy makers with very difficult choices. In order to address the multiple challenges of sustainability, the green state must be reflexive and a learning organization that uses the whole policy toolbox by combining hard steering mechanisms and soft voluntary instruments. Hysing leaves us with the idea that it is only a specific kind of state that can handle the problems of sustainability.

Rickard Andersson (Chapter 4, this volume) worries about the legacy of sovereignty embedded in states and the sovereign state system and the possibility to deal with the transboundary and global problems of climate and sustainability. The principle of state sovereignty concerns the independence of the state and self-determination, but it also places the state in a certain peculiar position in terms of how the state can relate to the current international order. It is a valid concern, as states have shunned from environmental and climate responsibility often exploiting their status and power as sovereign states. The modern state is historically bound to sovereignty, which also conditions state-based politics today and sovereignty is a potential impediment for greening the state and answering to sustainability concerns. The concept of sovereignty in green political theory needs to be re-thought and Andersson offers a re-reading of sovereignty through political theory that comes to terms with the contradictions of sovereignty.

Green state types and environmental performance

This section analyzes key findings related to questions about the environmental performance of states in a comparative perspective: Which states perform well and merit the label green? Are certain types of states, such as welfare states and Nordic states, better equipped to make the transition to a low-carbon society? Contributions in the second and third part of the book compare the environmental performance of 28 European states and small island states in large n-studies as well as conducted single case studies of the US, Sweden and Finland.

From welfare states to green states?

In the scholarly debate on the environmental performance of various states, the Nordic welfare states have in general been viewed as environmental pioneers with comparatively high environmental performance (Andersen and Liefferink 1997; Dryzek *et al.* 2003). In literature on the ecological or green state (Eckersley 2004; Christoff 2005) and governance of sustainable development (Lafferty and Meadowcroft 2000; Lundquist 2004), countries such as the Nordics and in particular Sweden, are argued to most closely resemble the ideal types of the green state. Some of the standard explanations are that Nordic states, partly due to their experience as mature welfare states, are better at managing social and ecological externalities, have a higher degree of democratic deliberation and exhibit deeper forms of ecological modernization. This taps into the academic debate on the parallel genesis of the welfare and the green state (Meadowcroft 2005, 2012) referred to above.

The findings of this book largely confirm that Nordic states merit the label green with a comparatively higher performance. Koch and Fritz (Chapter 5, this volume) test the "synergy hypothesis" proposing that in social-democratic welfare regimes the relationship between environmental and welfare policies is less conflictual than in conservative and liberal regimes. The argument is that social democratic welfare states are better placed to manage the intersection of social and environmental policies compared to liberal market economies. One reason is that the discourse on ecological modernization is widespread in the Nordic countries. They measure whether the green state can be seen as a progression from the welfare state by exploring the relationship between welfare and ecology indicators and, thus, testing whether social democratic welfare states are better equipped for environmental performance (1995 and 2010). Environmental performance indicators, such as renewable energy, carbon emissions and ecological footprint, were employed in the analysis. The two former are related to climate change, while the latter to ecological damage in general. Furthermore, as indicators of 'greenness,' Koch and Fritz include green regulation, such as environmental taxes and green party seats in parliament. They found that the hypothesis that social-democratic welfare states also perform strongly ecologically holds for only two countries: Sweden and, to a lesser degree, Austria. The results showed that while advanced welfare states are leading in establishing 'climate friendliness' in terms of comparatively low CO_2 emissions they fail in achieving ecological sustainability. In other words, the synergy works for climate friendliness (i.e. the degree of renewables and carbon emission reductions), but not for ecological footprint where welfare states have relatively poor performance.

This indicates that the green welfare state is better equipped to tackle climate problems rather than problems related to sustainability. However, according to Koch and Fritz, it has more to do with different states' natural resource endowments (e.g. rivers and lakes that generate hydropower, renewables, etc.) than with low carbon emissions. These findings suggest we should be cautious in celebrating the ecological 'achievements' of countries such as Sweden, since it is hardly an effect of green institutions, but rather related to geographical factors such as territory and resources. Furthermore, some European states with poor socio-economic development indicators, high inequality and low social expenditures are the most sustainable in terms of low ecological footprint. However, these countries also have the least developed forms of environmental regulation. These findings are significant, as they question the assumed links between the welfare and green state. Overall, the analysis demonstrates the importance of distinguishing between environmental regulation and environmental performance and argues for rethinking the role of socio-economic development in the constitution of green states.

There is no natural progression of the green state from existing advanced welfare states. The socio-economic profile of advanced welfare states, such as Sweden, corresponds with comparatively high ecological footprints so that their good ecological performance is largely reduced to relative 'climate friendliness'. Furthermore, it supports the notion that efforts to de-couple advanced levels of socio-economic development and welfare from environmental stress are still largely unsuccessful, despite advanced levels of social and green regulation. This is echoed in studies questioning ecological modernization strategies and the win–

win strategies of 'green growth' and green economy (Jackson 2009; Victor 2008; UNEP 2011).

Sweden – green leader, green state or decarbonized state?

Sweden, as one of the Nordic states, stands out as the most climate-friendly (Friberg 2008; Burck *et al.* 2009), however, with a weaker performance on ecological sustainability in general. Paul Tobin (Chapter 8, this volume) tests Christoff's (2005) classification of Sweden as an 'environmental welfare state' and near-to-be green state against a later context, namely the first term of the Conservative/Liberal alliance government, between 2006 and 2010. He assesses whether the climate politics conducted in this later period confirms Sweden's status or whether this has changed. He does so by studying which prioritizations were made in the headline goals of four sectors: climate emissions, renewables, energy efficiency and transport. Tobin concludes that Sweden continues to be a climate policy pioneer, but not a green state. The reason is that during the first term of the Conservative/Liberal alliance government, many policy decisions were based on the ambition to improve efficiency – such as in the transport sector – rather than to reduce overall emissions. Only reduction of overall emissions reflects principles of strong ecological modernization. He finds elements of strong ecological modernization in the area of hydropower, exemplified with a push for investments in wind energy instead of expanding the use of untapped energy in rivers in the North. This signals the presence of biocentric values, respecting the intrinsic values of nature by preserving the rivers. Yet, these developments clashed with the government's 2009 turn toward nuclear energy, which tacitly weakened the renewables sector and facilitated the continued production of nuclear waste, while low in carbon emissions, highly environmentally damaging in other respects. By using the normative ideal offered by Eckersley and Christoff, Tobin concludes that Sweden has not yet emerged a green state, because of the failure to fully engage in strong ecological modernization.

Hildingsson and Khan (Chapter 9, this volume) develop this theme further and suggest a differentiation between how the state deals with climate and with sustainability challenges. Different conditions apply for the two issue areas and for this purpose they developed the idea of a *decarbonized green state*. Their argument is that it is only a decarbonized green state that can achieve climate objectives, because this is a state committed to, and engaged in, promoting transformative social change beyond short-term climate mitigation. They analyze how low-carbon transitions in Sweden were induced in a set of policy sectors in order to reduce carbon emissions, spur innovation and enter policy paths towards decarbonization. Climate governance arguably provides venues to move towards decarbonization, but when assessing to what extent the present climate governance arrangements in the electricity, heating, industry and transport sectors support decarbonization, they found Sweden to be successful in supporting transitions in the energy sector, while decarbonization had not been institutionalized in the transport and industry sectors. Only the energy sectors (electricity and heating) are on their way to becoming fully decarbonized and resulted in the total greenhouse gas (GHG) emissions in Sweden decreasing 16 percent in 2011 compared to 1990. This is largely because of the conversion from fossil fuels to bioenergy for combustion purposes in heating and industry sectors. Hildingsson and Khan conclude that other sectors have not been successful in decarbonization because they have not engaged in promoting transformative change. Climate policies dominated by the market-based policies and market-liberal norms of cost efficiency are insufficient to incentivize transitions to long-term decarbonization. Accordingly, Sweden can be characterized as an advanced climate mitigating state rather than a decarbonizing green state. Echoing Tobin's conclusion, the climate mitigation strategy has proven effective in sectors where mature technological alternatives have been present, such as in the energy sector, but has so far been less successful in sectors with stronger needs for innovation and changed patterns of behavior (i.e. process industry and transportation).

Both chapters in this volume studying Sweden (Chapters 8 and 9) used ideal models as a way to test the progression of the green state and clearly demonstrated how useful they can be for empirical analysis. In analyzing Sweden's national climate and sustainability policies, both contributions revealed that the green state is also fragmented as its 'green' conduct seems to vary between sectors, and between different types of environmental problems from sustainability to climate change. In attempts by the state to decarbonize, transform and transition toward climate objectives, divisions between political, administrative units and actors emerge across sectoral lines. Energy, transport, industry sectors seem to have their own logics, interests and power bases that impact their potential to accommodate climate objectives. This suggests the relevance of transition theory to better understand dynamics within single green states, on how different regimes are formed, as networks and alliances, in different sectors, and how such constellations turn into powerful incumbent regimes that resist change and are reluctant to take on new ideas and innovation. This in contrast to regimes that are more open to change, and even can become niche actors which are important for a climate transition to take form. Transition theory can help make sense of what appears to be a fragmented green state, and the forces that move it forward or hampers it, in the process toward climate and sustainability transition.

Outliers? American style green state and small island states

What is the optimal polity for the green state: the US federal state, the EU, smaller states like Finland or Sweden and Denmark, or island states? Which is the optimal relation between the central polity and other jurisdictional levels and the population? If we think about size, do we need to re-locate also different issues; for example, is climate change a concern to be located to the international or the local? This ties in to a larger debate about policy-making, federalism and centralization vs. decentralization, which the green state literature takes on as well as some of the contributions of this book.

In the contemporary green state literature the US is often not included, because it is generally viewed as a climate laggard. Bomberg (Chapter 7, this volume) concurs with this view, and agrees with Christoff's (2005) typology, where the US is seen as a prime example of a neoliberal environmental state. Bomberg's definition of the green state is "one capable of developing policies and practices designed to limit harmful emissions and achieve a sustainable future for its citizens". As this book concerns the transition toward green statehood, an interesting question in this context is: How does the United States fare in transforming to a green state? Bomberg demonstrates how barriers preventing the transition to a low carbon and sustainable polity are further entrenched by powerful discursive frames that favor anti-state, anti-climate advocates. Bomberg's analysis of the United States' laggardness in relation to sustainability and climate issues, demonstrates that the institutional and ideological barriers in combination constitute significant obstacles for green statehood to emerge. A fairly complex picture of the US resistance to greening emerges through Bomberg's careful discursive and institutional analysis. She shows the significance of veto players, entrenched adversarialism and fragmentation as institutional barriers in the US policy-making system. Of the ideological barriers the most dominant one is the neoliberal framing evident in congressional voting patterns, which favor markets over state action and make it difficult for governments to take a proactive role and a preference for "more market, less state". Finally, a strong discursive barrier to state action on change is the overall narrative of *climate denialism*, mobilized by climate skeptics. Opinion polls show significant skepticism surrounding the science of climate change. Compared to citizens in most other countries, Americans show much greater doubt about the existence, science and severity of climate change.

State intervention in terms of executive action is more likely to be successful if it is re-framed as economic and technological opportunities rather than climate or carbon reduction initiatives. The Obama administration has an increasing tendency to present climate initiatives (such as renewables) as a technologically savvy and economic opportunity. Other ways would be to relocate state action to sub-federal and local levels. The literature on climate action in US cities and states suggests how climate advocates on the subnational level are creating new initiatives or expanding existing ones. State-led collaborative initiatives to combat climate change, including GHG inventories, mandatory caps and multi-state carbon cap and trade programs, are other examples.

Bomberg's analysis of the US suggests that scholarship on the green state should scrutinize the relationship between the state and the public sphere. This is not merely a matter of setting up institutional mechanisms that can be inclusive and accommodate public mobilization and the green sphere, but also how they are inclusive as Dryzek *et al.* (2003) have argued. The US case shows the difficulty for the state polity to create a more climate-friendly discourse when the public discourse entertains a view of the state as devoid of trust and legitimacy. An important question in this context is: Can the climate agenda be a way to legitimize the state, or does green state theory presuppose a highly legitimate state already?

In rethinking the green state there is a need to also think about the geographic features of the state. Which resources a state possesses seem to matter for climate governance. Several contributions in this book have shown that Sweden's hydropower and forests have provided renewable energy and lowered CO_2 emissions. What about the size of the state, how does it matter? Are smaller states better equipped to deal with the challenges of climate change and the transition to sustainability? Povitkina (Chapter 6, this volume) suggests this is the case. Her chapter advances a number of theoretical arguments for why small island states have a potential to conform to normative ideals of the green state. She proposes that specific characteristics of islands – believed to contribute to advancing democracy on islands – favor transformation to a green state. At the same time, small island states possess limited resources, are remote and isolated and exposed to various natural hazards, with the corollary that small island states face pressing problems of natural resource management. Through a comparative analysis of a sample of 23 island states against an Environmental Performance Index, she asks whether small island states perform better in protecting their environment than continental states and large islands. While small island states on average perform better with respect to most of the environmental indicators included, some indicators show negative and surprising results. Small island states take better care of their scarce resources, such as forests and fresh water, and strongly protect their fisheries, which are vital resources. However, the relatively weak environmental performance in the field of agricultural management is surprising because the assumption was that island states would prioritize protecting their scarce resources on land as well. While the results are mixed and not conclusive in this pioneering study of small island states, it suggest that geographical factors may be taken more seriously into the green state scholarship. Further empirical analysis is needed in order to be able to conclude whether small island states are more likely to develop as green states. However, it underlines the importance of general questions, such as how size, location, access to natural resources and other geographic factors relate to institutional development of green states.

Transforming the state towards climate and sustainability objectives

This section discusses how the current polity – administrations and policy-making – can be reformed toward societal goals of climate and sustainability transitions. In reviewing the normatively oriented field of governance for sustainable development, Hysing (Chapter 2, this volume) argues that we need to reform – not replace – the state, both in terms of its ways of interacting with society (governance) and its political orientation (sustainable development), while ensuring that key values (e.g. democracy) and capacities (regulative and redistributive powers) that are upheld by the state remain in place. The objective of a green state is a normative orientation to sustainable society. The state should take on different roles and responsibilities in terms of policy, polity as well as politics. In all these three areas the governance toward sustainability calls for the reformation of the state. The challenges of sustainable development relate to the complex character and the uncertainty of the problems to be dealt with. For sustainability it may entail the integration of forestry and agricultural policy with finance, and climate issues with energy, transport and housing, and connect areas usually handled separately and in silos (i.e. environmental policy integrating). Furthermore, there is a need to coordinate between levels from the local to the international. Networks are suggested as possible forms to manage this, and can potentially work more effectively under the authority of the state polity, because it is more likely to assure accountability and transparency. Finally, the green state has to deal with the challenge of sustainability governance in the realm of politics, seek acceptance for long-term objectives over short-term ones, for other species and for the rights of future generations to exist, against short-term goals and immediate interests. In the realm of politics, the green state is important in encouraging and guarding a green public sphere. The green state possesses a unique capacity and legitimacy to foster and lead the transition toward a more sustainable society.

A proposal that is more in line with strengthening the role of the polity is advanced by Åsa Knaggård and Håkan Pihl (Chapter 12, this volume) as they ask: Could the green state emerge through constitutional reform? Knaggård and Pihl highlight the topic of green constitutional design, and how the green polity can introduce green values through the constitution. They base their claim on Eckersley's (2004) argument that the state needs to be both pushed and bound to achieve necessary changes, and propose that green constitutional design can be a way to accomplish this. It is important for the green state to commit to long-term objectives. Knaggård and Pihl propose self-binding as a way to fix long-term climate objectives in the polity. They draw lessons from monetary policy and propose that the climate policy field could learn from successful elements of monetary policy such as: the possibility to assure a long-term commitment through long-term binding targets, avoiding interferences by powerful interests through an autonomous authority and securing the voice of those who are not represented in politics, such as future generations or other species. These are important features for the green state that may be advanced through a constitutional design. The major advantage of self-binding institutions, such as those found in monetary policy, is that they secure long-term commitment while they increase credibility and reduce uncertainty. The conclusion is that if climate policy is modeled on monetary policy, an autonomous climate authority led by experts and safe from direct political influence would have the power and authority to set short-term fixed targets that correspond with long-term climate objectives. The instrument to be used would be one that provides a price on all emissions, such as a tax on greenhouse gases, a cap and trade scheme, or a hybrid form, which could replace the wide variety of climate policy instruments used today. However, through their comparison, the dilemma between efficient policy-making and democracy is highlighted, and the risk to climate policy had such an institutional design been adopted. Democratic legitimacy may be eroded and flexibility to adapt to changing conditions would shrink. Monetary politics works within a system and aims to maintain it, while climate policy has an ambition to change the system. This is an important difference between the two policy areas, which leads to the conclusion that while we can learn important lessons from monetary policies on how to use constitutional design in the polity of the green state, it has to be carefully designed to assure that there is room for system change so flexibility and democratic legitimacy can be maintained.

Kronsell and Stensöta (Chapter 13, this volume) align themselves with green state scholars who argue that welfare states are better suited to deal with sustainability, environmental and climate challenges. Rather than considering the welfare state's potential in its success in managing externalities of production, it is because the welfare state is a state that cares, that it has a potential for greening. The focus on the logic and rationality of the policy-making institutions suggest that this dimension of the state also must be reformed in order to accommodate sustainability and climate objectives. A state that cares has the potential to develop empathic rationality for the polity and policy making in the green state. The strength of care is that it is a core human principle experienced by everyone and that care can be extended to non-humans and future generations. Empathic rationality is derived from feminist care ethics in combination with green political ideas, but it is not a utopian or esoteric concept. Empathic rationality is both a normative foundation and an underlying principle that can guide priorities and behavior in the green state, as well as a fruitful way to think about how policy making can be conducted differently in the green state through empathic rationality.

Fritz and Koch (Chapter 5, this volume) conclude that the coexistence of environmental problem pressure and advanced levels of green regulation, which we see in the advanced social democratic welfare states, that are most likely candidates for green states, has hitherto not improved environmental performance. One way to break the deadlock is stronger political capital in terms of green political constituencies and votes, which can initiate the necessary ecological transformation of production and consumption patterns, especially in the most advanced capitalist countries. The empirical evidence for absolute decoupling of economic growth, resource input and, consequently, ecological stress is very weak, which is confirmed in previous studies by Jackson (2009) and Victor (2008) who fundamentally question 'green growth' policy options – the idea that economic growth can be organized is both socially equitable and ecologically sustainable. In fact, if welfare goals are to be combined with ecological sustainability, it is difficult to see how the top priority of economic growth in policy-making can continue. A barrier to reform the state toward green statehood revolves around whether strategies of ecological modernization can promote climate and sustainability transitions. Several contributions of this book question if the relationship between environmental protection and economic growth is compatible. Koch and Fritz's work challenges the ecological modernization thesis (i.e. that there can be a win–win between growth and ecological performance, and that decoupling is possible). Even the social democratic welfare states, as the most likely candidates to conform to ideals of green states, rely first and foremost on the idea that continuous economic growth is possible and desirable. Matthew Cashmore and Jaap G. Rozema (Chapter 11, this volume) observe that this can be manifested in the micropolitical practices of climate governance within the state. There is a general and broad reluctance to address the possible conflict that may be inherent in the relation between environmental protection and economic growth in the public debate. This prevailing norm assumes that we can have the cake and eat it too. Accordingly, we need to adapt to climate change but that can be done without changing much in current practices, expect perhaps to consider how climate risk is related more broadly to other societal issue and concerns and think more in the long term.

Similarly, in Tuula Teäväinen-Litardo's account of the discourse of green growth in Finland (Chapter 10, this volume), we see framings in line with the ideals of ecological modernization or varieties thereof, although the discourse is diversified. The most dominant discourse is about new technological innovation that is less resource intense, more environmentally efficient and backed by strong public commitment to industry and the market, which is perceived as the way forward in Finland. The question that needs to be addressed, not just by ecological modernization scholars, but also by green state scholars, is to what extent technological innovation is necessary in the green state? What type of innovation policy, if any, is suitable to the green state? If systemic changes are needed, how far is systemic change removed from the ideas prevailing in the dominant discourses assuming that economic growth, technological development and environmental protection, climate and sustainability objectives are compatible and can work together to advance the green state?

The four discourses on green growth that Tuula identifies – green growth as an umbrella concept, as an extension of national innovation policy, as resource management, as system level change – all rely heavily on state actors both in terms of who articulates the discourses and who is given agency through them. The four discourses are not equally influential: the most dominant ones reflect business as usual, and the dominant economic interests and actors and ecological modernization. It is an approach where 'technology-and-industry-knows-best', thus empowering these actors rather than social movements or civil society. Hence, the actively inclusive policy model Teräväinen-Litardo refers to, building on Dryzek *et al.* (2003), seems to be a model that actively includes the voices of certain groups only, primarily those who have traditionally been involved in economic, innovation and technology issues. The discourses that articulate more profound transformation of the state and its practices in the economic and technological sectors are also more marginal and perhaps even marginalized.

Final reflections

The rationale for this book was to advance theorizing on the green state as well as bring new empirical insights from greening of states in the Nordic, European and US context. There is both a need for theoretical refinement on what constitutes a green state as well as empirical assessment of the "greenness" of existing states on their path to green statehood, which could be based on comparative or single case studies. Such empirical studies should be able to inform theoretical work when they apply and refine, but also challenge predominant theoretical frameworks and typologies. Further empirical studies can enable the scholarship on green states to expand beyond the Nordic welfare states, to develop ideas on how other types of states can be greened. The state matters because it has authority, capacity and steering mechanisms to enable policies and governance paths to reaching climate and sustainability objectives. The state can offer new imaginaries, possibilities and visions in the transition to a low-carbon, or even fossil free, societal development. The green state can build a more sustainable and decarbonized world through the transformation of the state polity toward global sustainability and planetary protection.

There is not one way to green or transform the state, but it builds on a mix of framing strategies and initiatives, which should reflect individual state characteristic while seeking common global solutions. What are the prospects for overcoming barriers toward green statehood? One route would be to grant the state a stronger interventionist role in promoting transformation toward climate and sustainability goals. An ecological modernization approach, which reframes climate as an economy-boosting, welfare-enhancing, technology-rich and security-enhancing project, is an important step in the construction of a green state. However, these features gain their full potency only if they are embedded in public discourse. Consequently, to transform the public discourse is both a key challenge and the opportunity for the bumpy road toward greening of the state. A version of ecological modernization emphasizing economic opportunities and the role of innovation is promising, and if married with security concerns, may have significance. However, in this version of ecological modernization, the transformation is to take place through the mechanisms of the market and only lightly enabled by the state. Hence, it is not a fundamental transformative process to the green state because it does not involve the non-state actors of the public. If efforts at greening are to become successful there is a need to re-frame the state and citizens' role therein. This underlines the need to develop the green state scholarship to better understand how the conditions of greening the state also depend on frames, narratives and discourses on the role of the state in its various functions, in political but also public and media debates.

We share the view with several authors in the book, and in the green state scholarship at large, that the transformation toward green statehood must come from "below" the state, and involve a change not just in government policy and practice but also in discourse and citizen engagement and deliberation. Engaging citizens is a crucial dimension in the transformation toward the green state, where there is a need for larger visions and imaginaries of state and citizens' role in low carbon and sustainability transition. It will mean ensuring that green and decarbonization initiatives are not concentrated at state level but are re-located to the subnational and local level and citizens themselves. In short, greening needs to come from below. It needs to be re-framed not as a centralized green state endeavor but as a bottom-up and citizen-inspired venture.

References

Andersen, M., and Liefferink, D., 1997 *European Environmental Policy: The Pioneers*. New York: Manchester University Press.

Avelino, F., and Rotmans, J., 2009 Power in transition: an interdisciplinary framework to study power in relation to structural change. *European Journal of Social Theory* 12(4): 543–69.

Barry, J., and Eckersley, R., (eds) 2005 *The State and the Global Ecological Crisis*. MIT Press, Cambridge, MA.

Burck, J., Bals, C., and Ackermann, S., 2009 *The Climate Change Performance Index 2009*. Germanwatch, Bonn/Climate Action Network Europe, Brussels. Retrieved January 22, 2013 from http://germanwatch.org/klima/ccpi09res.pdf.

Christoff, P., 2005 Out of chaos, a shining star? Toward a typology of green states. In Barry, J., and Eckersley, R., (eds) *The State and the Global Ecological Crisis* 25–52. MIT Press, Cambridge, MA.

Dryzek, J., Downies, D., Hunold, C., Schlosberg, D., and Hernes, H., 2003 *Green States and Social Movements. Environmentalism in the United States, United Kingdom, Germany and Norway*. Oxford University Press, Oxford.

Eckersley, R., 2004 *The Green State: Rethinking Democracy and Sovereignty*. MIT Press, Cambridge, MA.

Friberg, L., 2008 Conflict and consensus: the Swedish model of climate politics. In Compston, H., and Bailey, I., (eds) *Turning Down the Heat: The Politics of Climate Policy in Affluent Democracies* 164–82. Palgrave Macmillan, Basingstoke.

Geels, F., 2014 Regime resistance against low-carbon transitions: introducing politics and power into the multi-level perspective. *Theory, Culture and Society* 31(5): 21–40.

Gough, I., and Meadowcroft, J., 2011 Decarbonizing the welfare state. In Dryzek, J., Norgaard, R., and Schlosberg, D., (eds) *The Oxford Handbook on Climate Change and Society* 490–503. Oxford University Press, Oxford.

Grin, J., Rotmans, J., and Schot, J., 2011 *Transitions to Sustainable Development: New Directions in the Study of Long Term Transformative Change*. Routledge, London.

Jackson, T., 2009 *Prosperity without Growth: Economics for a Future Planet*. Earthscan, London.

Lafferty, W., and Meadowcroft, J., 2000 Patterns of governmental engagement. In Lafferty, W., and Meadowcroft, J., (eds) *Implementing Sustainable Development: Strategies and Initiatives in High Consumption Societies* 337–421. Oxford University Press, Oxford.

Lundqvist, L.J., 2004 *Sweden and Ecological Governance: Straddling the Fence*. Manchester University Press, Manchester.

Markard, J., Raven, R., and Truffer, B., 2012 Sustainability transitions: an emerging field of research and its prospects. *Research Policy* 41(6): 955–67.

Meadowcroft, J., 2005 From welfare state to ecostate. In Barry, J., and Eckersley, R., (eds) *The State and the Global Ecological Crisis* 3–23. MIT Press, Cambridge, MA.

Meadowcroft, J., 2012 Greening the state. In Steinberg, P., and VanDeveer, S., (eds) *Comparative Environmental Politics: Theory, Practice and Prospects* 63–87. MIT Press, Cambridge, MA.

Mol, A.P.J., and Spaargaren, G., (eds) 2000 *Ecological Modernisation Around the World: Perspectives and Critical Debates*. Frank Cass, London.

Okereke, C., Bulkeley, H., and Schroeder, H., 2009 Conceptualizing climate governance beyond the international regime. *Global Environmental Politics* 9(1): 58–78.

Schot, J., and Geels, F., 2008 Strategic niche management and sustainable innovation journeys: theory, findings, research agenda, and policy. *Technology Analysis and Strategic Management* 20(5) 537–54.

UNEP 2011 *Towards a Green Economy*. United Nations Environment Programme, Nairobi.

Victor, P.A., 2008 *Managing without Growth: Slower by Design, Not Disaster*. Edward Elgar, Cheltenham.

Young, S., (ed) 2000 *The Emergence of Ecological Modernization: Integrating the Environment and the Economy?* Routledge, New York.

Index